Recent currency crises in Europe and Mexico have provided stark reminders of the importance and, at the same time, the fragility of international financial markets. These experiences have led some commentators to conclude that open international capital markets are incompatible with financial stability. But the pre-1914 gold standard is an obvious challenge to the notion that open capital markets are sources of instability. Between 1879 and 1914 the major currencies were stably linked at fixed rates of exchange, capital controls were absent, and capital flowed in large quantities from core countries to the periphery.

To deepen our understanding of how this system worked, this volume draws together recent research on the gold standard by empirically, theoretically, and historically oriented international economists. Theoretical models are used to guide qualitative discussions of historical experience, while econometric methods are used to help the historical data speak clearly. The result is an overview of the gold standard, a survey of the relevant applied research in international macroeconomics, and a demonstration of how the past can help to inform the present.

Modern perspectives on the gold standard

Modern perspectives on the gold standard

edited by

TAMIM BAYOUMI
International Monetary Fund

BARRY EICHENGREEN
University of California at Berkeley

MARK P. TAYLOR
University of Liverpool

332.422
M689

Published by the Press Syndicate of the University of Cambridge
The Pitt Building, Trumpington Street, Cambridge CB2 1RP
40 West 20th Street, New York, NY 10011-4211, USA
10 Stamford Road, Oakleigh, Melbourne 3166, Australia

First published 1996

Printed in Great Britain at the University Press, Cambridge

A catalogue record for this book is available from the British Library

Library of Congress cataloguing in publication data

Modern perspectives on the gold standard / edited by Tamim Bayoumi,
    Barry Eichengreen, Mark P. Taylor.
        p.   cm.
    Includes index.
    ISBN 0 521 57169 3 (hc)
    1. Gold standard. I. Bayoumi, Tamim A.   II. Eichengreen, Barry
J. III. Taylor, Mark P., 1958–
HG297.M64   1966
332.4'222–dc20   96–6462   CIP

ISBN 0 521 571693 hardback

BS

SE

Contents

Correction

The title of chapter 6 should be given
on page vii and pages 165–88
as "The gold standard and
the international monetary system."

Figures

Tables

Contributors

Tamim Bayoumi is an economist in the Research Department of the International Monetary Fund. He received his doctoral degree from Cambridge University. He has written extensively on issues of international finance, including the history of, and prospects for, the international monetary system.

Michael D. Bordo is Professor of Economics and Director of the Center for Monetary History at Rutgers University. He is the editor of the Cambridge University Press series *Studies in Macroeconomic History*. Other publications include *A Retrospective on the Classical Gold Standard* (with Anna J. Schwartz) and *A Retrospective on the Bretton Woods International Monetary System* (with Barry Eichengreen), *Monetary Regimes in Transition* (with Forrest Capie) and many journal articles in monetary economics and economic history.

Charles W. Calomiris is Associate Professor of finance and co-director of the office for banking research at the University of Illinois, Urbana-Champaign, and a faculty research fellow of the National Bureau of Economic Research. His research areas include banking, corporate finance, financial history, and monetary economics. Professor Calomiris received a BA in economics from Yale University in 1979 and a PhD in economics from Stanford University in 1985.

Forrest Capie is Professor of Economic History in the Department of Banking and Finance at the City University Business School. He has authored or co-authored or edited sixteen books and over a hundred articles on monetary, banking and trade topics. He is Editor of the *Economic History Review*.

Trevor J.O. Dick is Professor of Economics at the University of Lethbridge. He was educated at Carleton University (BA (Honours) 1957) and the University of Washington (MA 1968; PhD 1970) and has held visiting scholar appointments at the University of Chicago, Harvard University, and the University of California at Berkeley. His main fields of research are macroeconomic history and international finance.

Barry Eichengreen is John L. Simpson Professor of Economics and Political Science at the University of California, Berkeley.

John E. Floyd is Professor of Economics at the University of Toronto. He was educated at the University of Saskatchewan (BComm 1958, Honours Economics 1959) and at the University of Chicago (PhD 1964). His specialty is International Monetary Economics.

C. Paul Hallwood is Professor of Economics at the University of Connecticut. He has written many books and papers in the field of international economics, including on international finance, commodity trade policy, the theory of the multinational corporation, and international political economy.

R. Glenn Hubbard is the Russell L. Carson Professor of Economics and Finance at Columbia University, and a Research Assistant of the National Bureau of Economic Research. He received his PhD in Economics from Harvard (1988) and taught at Northwestern; he has also held positions as an Olin Fellow at the NBER, and John M. Olin Visiting Professor at the University of Chicago.

Graciela L. Kaminsky is currently an Economist in the Division of Monetary Affairs at the Board of Governors of the Federal Reserve System, and a Visiting Associate Professor at the Department of Economics, Johns Hopkins University. She received her Ph.D. from MIT and was an Assistant Professor of Economics at the University of California at San Diego before joining the Board of Governors. She has been a Consultant and Visiting Scholar at the IMF and World Bank and has published extensively on issues in open economy macroeconomics.

Michael Klein is Associate Professor of International Economics at the Fletcher School and is a Faculty Research Fellow of the National Bureau of Economic Research. He has been a visiting scholar at the International Monetary Fund, the Board of Governors of the Federal Reserve, and the Boston Federal Reserve Bank. Klein's research focuses on international economic issues such as the efficacy of foreign exchange market intervention, devaluation policy in Latin America, the determinants of foreign direct investment in the United States, and import pricing.

Finn E. Kydland is Professor of Economics at Carnegie Mellon University and Research Associate at the Federal Reserve Banks of Cleveland, Dallas, and St Louis. He has held faculty posts at the Norwegian School of Economics and Business Administration and the University of Texas at Austin. Current research interests include the roles of monetary policy and of inside and outside money for business cycle behavior. His PhD is from Carnegie Mellon University.

Ronald MacDonald is currently Professor of International Finance at the University of Strathclyde, Glasgow. He previously held the Robert Fleming Chair of Finance and Investment at the University of Dundee and has been a Visiting Scholar at the International Monetary Fund. He is the author of over 100 articles and two books in the area of International Money and Finance.

Ian W. Marsh is a lecturer in the Economics department of the University of Strathclyde, where he recently completed his doctorate. He also holds degrees from the University of Sheffield and Birkbeck College, London. In addition to his academic experience, Ian has worked in the Research Department of the International Monetary Fund and as a financial markets economist in the City of London.

Panos Michael is Lecturer in Economics at Liverpool University, having been previously employed by the University of Southampton. His first degree was from the University of Athens. His main research interests are in applied monetary and financial economics and nonlinear time series analysis. He has co-authored a number of papers with D.A. Peel and A.R. Nobay and has publications in *Oxford Economic Papers*, the *Journal of International Money and Finance* and the *International Economic Review*.

Terence C. Mills is Professor of Economics at Loughborough University, having previously held professorial appointments at the City University Business School and the University of Hull. He is the author of *Time Series Techniques for Economists* and *The Econometric Modelling of Financial Time Series* (both published by Cambridge University Press), as well as over eighty articles in journals and books.

A. Robert Nobay was appointed to the Brunner Chair of Economic Science at Liverpool University in 1980. He previously held appointments at the Electricity Council, the National Institute of Economic Research and the University of Southampton. He was also a post-doctoral fellow and held visiting appointments at the Universities of Chicago, UCLA, and Northwestern University. His main research interests are in exchange rate economics, monetary economics, and currency unions. He has co-authored a number of papers with P. Michael and D.A. Peel and has publications in the *Economic Journal*, *Oxford Economic Papers*, the *Journal of International Money and Finance* and the *International Economic Review*.

Lawrence H. Officer is Professor of Economics at the University of Illinois at Chicago. He is the author of over forty scholarly articles and six books, and is the editor of five other books. His most recent publication is *Between the Dollar–Sterling Gold Points* (Cambridge University Press). He received his BA from McGill University and his PhD from Harvard University. In 1975 he served as Consultant at the International Monetary Fund.

David A. Peel is Professor of Economics at the University of Liverpool. He has written on a wide variety of topics in numerous journals. His main research interests are in applied monetary and financial economics, macroeconomics, labour market economics and nonlinear time series analysis. He has recently published a number of articles in the *Manchester School, Economica* and the *Journal of Forecasting*. He has also co-authored a number of papers with P. Michael and A.R. Nobay and has publications in *Oxford Economic Papers*, the *Journal of International Money and Finance* and the *International Economic Review*.

David Pope is a Professor in Economics, Research School of Social Sciences, Australian National University, Canberra. He has written extensively on Australian growth, migration, and capital flows.

Mark P. Taylor is Professor of Economics the University of Liverpool, having previously worked for several years as a Senior Economist at the International Monetary Fund. He has held a Chair in Economics at the City University Business School and has been a Visiting Professor at New York University. He holds an MA degree and a BA from the University of Oxford and a MSc and a PhD from London University. He is the author of numerous books and articles in macroeconomics, finance, international finance, and applied econometrics. His publications include articles in the *Journal of Political Economy*, the *Journal of Economic Literature*, the *Review of Economics and Statistics*, the *Economic Journal, Economica*, the *Journal of Money, Credit and Banking*, and others.

Geoffrey E. Wood is Professor of Economics at the City University London. He is the co-author/co-editor of ten books which deal with the finance of international trade, monetary policy, and bank regulation. Among his professional papers are studies of exchange rate behavior, interest rate determination, monetary unions, tariff policy, and bank regulation. He has also written extensively on the New Zealand economy.

I

Introduction

1 Modern perspectives on the gold standard: introduction

Tamim Bayoumi, Barry Eichengreen and Mark P. Taylor

Economic liberalism is back in style. Around the world governments are opening their economies to trade, privatizing government enterprises, and deregulating markets. These changes have already had profound effects in many areas of the world. Some of the most dramatic changes that have occurred to date are in international capital markets, where transactions between countries in the developed world are now essentially free of government regulation. By contrast, as little as two decades ago the vast majority of industrial countries maintained a wide array of capital controls.

The liberalization of international capital markets has provided benefits to the world economy through improved financial intermediation. However, the new system has not been without costs. Increasing capital mobility is often seen as one of the underlying causes of the break-up of the Bretton Woods fixed exchange rate system in the early 1970s.[1] More recently, abrupt changes in market sentiment have generated capital flows which have disrupted efforts to peg exchange rates between national currencies. Speculative crises forced the members of the Exchange Rate Mechanism (ERM) in Europe to abandon their 2¼ percent currency bands in 1993 in favor of more permissive 15 percent bands, and forced the United Kingdom and Italy to suspend membership in the Mechanism the previous year. Similar market pressures have also forced countries operating unilateral fixed exchange rate banks, such as Finland, Sweden, and Chile, to widen their exchange rate bands or abandon them entirely.

The devaluation of the Mexican peso in December 1994 was accompanied by instability in other emerging markets reminiscent of the problems in the mid-1980s during the debt crisis, when the abrupt interruption of access to international capital markets caused economic disruption throughout the developing world. Some observers have concluded that the growth of foreign exchange transactions, now reputed to exceed $1 trillion per day, has left governments at the mercy of market whims, unable to control their exchange rates or, in the developing world, their access to foreign capital.

The pre-1914 gold standard that prevailed over much of the world is an obvious challenge to the notion that open capital markets are incompatible with stable exchange rates and international economic relations. Between 1879, when the United States rejoined the system after its Civil War, and the outbreak of the Great War in 1914 the currencies of the major industrial countries were convertible by law into fixed quantities of gold, and bilateral exchange rates were fixed to bands of roughly plus or minus one half of 1 percent through arbitrage in private markets.[2] The fixed gold parities and stable bilateral exchange rates they implied were maintained for a period of decades despite the absence of controls on capital flows and the presence of high international capital mobility.[3] Furthermore, this system sustained large net capital flows from the core to the periphery, although not without occasional disruptions similar to those experienced during the debt crisis of the 1980s.[4]

For those concerned with the implications of financial liberalization for economic policy in general and for exchange rate policy in particular, the gold standard therefore continues to be of relevance and interest. This volume draws together recent research on the gold standard by economists motivated by an interest in international financial issues.

As is characteristic of modern applied economics, the contributions assembled here make liberal use of economic theory and econometrics. Theoretical models are used to guide qualitative discussions of historical experience and to structure hypothesis tests. Econometric methods are used to help the historical data speak clearly. The contributors to this volume therefore provide the reader with an overview of the recent economic literature on the gold standard, and a sense of the state of applied research in international macroeconomics.

The contributions build on both the historical literature and recent advances in economic theory and time series econometrics. Chapters 1 and 2 therefore provide introductions to these respective bodies of scholarship. This chapter relates the contributions in this volume to the existing literature, both theoretical and historical, on the gold standard's operation. Chapter 2, by Terence Mills, provides a guide to the time series methods used to analyze historical data.

The textbook explanation for the stability of exchange rates under the gold standard is that national monetary authorities faithfully followed the "rules of the game." They increased money supplies only when acquiring gold reserves and reduced them when reserves were lost, buttressing the credibility of their commitment to the maintenance of gold convertibility and facilitating adjustment through the operation of the price–specie–flow mechanism (Hume, [1752] 1898).[5] In fact, 19th-century specialists (such as Walter Bagehot, 1873) were aware that the conduct of policy was more complex than implied by this simple model, and that central bankers and government officials sometimes adapted policy to accommodate or offset fluctuations in economic activity and intervened to stabilize the domestic financial system rather than validating the effects of international gold flows. Forty years ago, Arthur Bloomfield (1959) hammered the final nail into the coffin of the textbok view by documenting just how much scope existed for discretionary monetary policy under the 19th-century gold standard.

Ironically, Bloomfield's demolition of the simple policy rule explanation for the stability of the gold standard preceded by only a few years theoretical developments in economics pointing to circumstances under which rules are preferable to discretion (Friedman, 1968; Kydland and Prescott, 1977). Contributors to this literature pointed out that when the private sector adapts its behavior to take into account the anticipated actions of policymakers, the benefits of discretionary policy may be neutralized, leaving only costs. In the model of Barro and Gordon (1983), discretionary policy is incapable of affecting output and employment in equilibrium but raises the average rate of inflation above that which would prevail under a policy rule of stable growth of money. Theorists found it tempting to invoke the gold standard as an example of the operation of such a rule, despite the difficulties of squaring the historical evidence with such theoretical formulations.

Subsequent research led to the development of a literature on escape clauses and conditional policy rules that has helped to reconcile theory with evidence. It explored the circumstances under which contingent rules can be feasibly implemented and have superior performance characteristics to simple rules. The theory of escape clauses emphasizes that a monetary "rule" can be violated (by changing a "fixed" rate of exchange, for example) without undermining the authorities' commitment to its maintenance in normal times if such changes are initiated only in response to exceptional shocks that are directly observable or otherwise independently verifiable, and if those shocks are not initiated by the authorities themselves.[6] If these conditions are met, then the costs of maintaining exchange rate stability under normal circumstances will be relatively low. When no exceptional shock justifying a permanent depreciation has been observed, market participants, when they see the exchange rate weakening, will expect the authorities to intervene in its support. Traders will purchase domestic money in anticipation of those measures of support, strengthening the rate without the need for intervention and minimizing the costs of stabilizing the exchange rate. But in the event of an exceptional shock requiring far-reaching adjustment, the authorities will be able to alter the exchange rate or otherwise deviate from the monetary rule without undermining the credibility of their commitment to it in normal times.

In chapter 3, Michael Bordo and Finn Kydland explore whether these models can be usefully applied to the classical gold standard. They argue that it is indeed useful to conceive of the gold standard as a contingent rule. By this interpretation, the commitment of central banks and governments to the maintenance of gold convertibility under all but exceptional circumstances lent credibility to the policy regime and moderated exchange rate fluctuations without preventing the authorities from suspending those rules in the event of extraordinary disturbances. This insight makes it possible to reconcile evidence of discretionary policy with the emphasis in earlier accounts on the gold standard as a monetary rule.

Can this view of the gold standard be tested? The recent literature on exchange rate target zones (Krugman, 1991; Svensson, 1992) provides a battery of relevant techniques. Paul Krugman showed that a credible commitment to the maintenance of a target zone should modify the linear relationship between the exchange rate and fundamentals that otherwise prevails in standard models. The belief that the authorities are committed to intervening once exchange rate fluctuations reach a certain point creates "bias in the band," according to which the exchange rate fluctuates less than fundamentals as the edge of the band is approached. Lars Svensson and others have shown that the model implies a variety of empirical tests of target zones credibility.[7]

An early contribution to the empirical literature by Flood, Rose and Mathieson (1990) implemented one of these tests using gold standard data, looking for evidence of a nonlinear relationship between exchange rates and fundamentals. Its results were weakly supportive of the target zone model. Alberto Giovannini (1993), applying another test of target zone credibility, related movements in gold standard exchange rates to interest rate differentials. If the domestic interest rate, a measure of expected future change in the exchange rate, declines when the currency depreciates relative to its central parity, this indicates that traders expect the exchange rate to recover toward its central parity subsequently, indicating that the authorities' commitment to the regime is credible. For 1880–1913, Giovannini's results suggest that the commitment of the French and German authorities to stabilizing their currencies against the British pound was credible but that the commitment of the US authorities was not. This result is plausible insofar as the Free Silver Movement and the rise of the Populist presidential candidate William Jennings Bryan raised questions about the likely future stance of US international monetary policy in the 1890s (Eichengreen, 1995).

Calomiris (1993) also analyzed interest differentials and exchange rates during this period and found evidence that during some episodes in the 1890s the US government's commitment to the gold standard was weak.[8] But, consistent with the Bordo–Kydland model, Calomiris argues that the market was mainly concerned about a short-term suspension of convertibility, not a long-run switch to a silver standard.

In chapter 5, Paul Hallwood, Ronald MacDonald and Ian Marsh offer a comprehensive investigation of the credibility of the gold standard regime. They find that both the Classical and interwar gold standards were credible in the sense that the exchange rate remained within the range defined by the costs of arbitrage.[9] This conclusion is supported by the more detailed study of the efficiency of the interwar gold standard in chapter 4 by Lawrence Officer. But Hallwood, MacDonald and Marsh show, by applying the techniques to both time periods, that monetary authorities were more willing to subordinate other objectives to stabilizing the price of gold during the Classical period than during the interwar years.[10] This bears on more recent experience with pegged exchange rate systems, suggesting that they may disintegrate as the interwar system ultimately did in September 1931, unless monetary authorities accept the discipline required to maintain the exchange rate peg.

Another hypothesis that may explain how exchange rate stability was reconciled with capital mobility under the gold standard is that the period saw a relatively low incidence of macroeconomic shocks. Adverse shocks to aggregate supply and demand threaten to destabilize exchange rates and heighten the dilemma facing the authorities. A disturbance that both weakens the exchange rate and raises unemployment, for example, confronts the central bank with the choice of whether to raise interest rates to defend the exchange rate or to lower them to encourage the recovery of output and employment. If shocks were small and/or symmetrically distributed across countries (enabling different national officials to respond in similar ways to changes in domestic economic conditions and hence to do so without threatening the currency peg), then the stability of exchange rates under the gold standard is properly attributable to characteristics of the economic environment rather than to the operation of the international monetary system itself.

Keating and Nye (1991), Bayoumi and Eichengreen (1994), and Bordo (1993) have used time series econometrics – specifically, structural vector autoregression (VAR) techniques developed by Blanchard and Quah (1989) – to identify macroeconomic disturbances and compare them across regimes. These methods do not suggest that aggregate supply and demand disturbances were unusually small during the gold standard years;

if anything, the opposite was true. It would appear that a relatively placid environment cannot explain the classical gold standard's successful operation.

For several countries, the standard Blanchard–Quah identification suggests, peculiarly, that aggregate demand schedules sloped upward during the Classical gold standard years. In their contribution to this volume (chapter 6), Bayoumi and Eichengreen modify the estimation strategy to take account of the commodity market arbitrage that connected price levels in different countries under the gold standard. This extension eliminates the anomaly of upward-sloping demand curves and reinforces the picture of significant underlying disturbances.

The factor which largely explains the success of the gold standard, Bayoumi and Eichengreen suggest, was relatively fast adjustment to disturbances by the industrial economies. Short-run aggregate supply curves were steep in price–output space, as if wages and other variable costs of production were fast to adjust to shocks. Even though shocks displaced output from full employment levels, fast adjustment facilitated the restoration of equilibrium, attenuating the conflict between internal and external balance and encouraging the authorities' pursuit of exchange rate stability. Declining macroeconomic flexibility, they also suggest, can explain the move over time by the major industrial countries to greater monetary autonomy and exchange rate flexibility.

Why was macroeconomic adjustment under the gold standard so fast? One possibility is greater flexibility of wages and prices than characterizes more institutionally structured 20th-century economies. This is the view of Calomiris and Hubbard (1989). Calomiris and Hubbard estimated a structural model of the late 19th-century US economy in which prices and interest rates are flexible. They found that that their model fits the time series data for the late 19th-century economy relatively well, consistent with the assumption of relatively high levels of flexibility.

Another potential explanation is the faster adjustment of quantities rather than prices. The pre-World War I period was characterized by considerable international migration at business cycle frequencies (Fenoaltea, 1988; Hatton and Williamson, 1994); this allowed labor supplies to adjust to demand. International capital mobility and the absence of restrictions on financial markets worked in the same direction, as did the international integration of markets for commodities and gold. Whereas the price–specie–flow model posited gradual adjustment in the absence of capital mobility and the presence of sluggish relative price adjustment, Trevor Dick, John Floyd and David Pope, in their chapter 8 on Canada and Australia, and Charles Calomiris and Glenn Hubbard in their chapter 7 on the United States and Great Britain, suggest that internal and external balance were restored rapidly through portfolio adjustments, relative price movements, and rapid adjustment of the trade account. They show that their models are capable of explaining quite well the dynamic behavior of the late 19th-century Canadian, Australian, British, and US economies.

Even in countries where prices were flexible and macroeconomic adjustment was fast, cyclical fluctuations remained. Authors of differing methodological persuasions disagree on how those macroeconomic movements are best explained. In chapter 9, Forrest Capie and Geoffrey Wood describe British aggregate fluctuations in Britain during the gold standard years in terms of monetary impulses and the classic monetary propagation mechanism and argue that the British cycle was relatively moderate and price fluctuations modest because of the Bank of England's pursuit of a stable money supply rule. While it is difficult, as a result, to identify connections between money and the business cycle in Britain, in countries like the United States, where the monetary policy process was more volatile, so was the business cycle, and the links between the two variables are clear.[11]

In contrast to Capie and Wood's monetary framework, Calomiris and Hubbard develop a credit based model of business cycles under the gold standard. Maintaining that prices were too flexible to allow for long-lived business cycle responses to monetary impulses, they argue that cycles occurred because information in 19th-century financial markets was incomplete, allowing shocks to financial markets to disrupt the supply of bank credit and provoke debt deflation.

Though these two sets of authors stake out rather different positions, their perspectives may not be entirely incompatible. During the gold standard years Britain suffered no major financial crises in which the stability of its financial system was threatened; the maturation of a Bank of England conscious of its lender-of-last-resort responsibilities, together with a banking system composed of large banks with countrywide branch networks, limiting the scope for crisis. The United States, in contrast, possessed no central bank, and its financial system was characterized by a large number of geographically restricted unit banks and periodic surges of bank failures (Grossman, 1993). It is not surprising that the incidence of financial crises was greater in the United States or that the implications of credit channels for the business cycle were correspondingly more pronounced.

In Capie and Wood's perspective, the demand for money was the critical economic relationship on which the operation of the gold standard hinged. They find that money demand was stable during the gold standard years, ruling out one potential source of macroeconomic shocks. This stability of the money demand function, they suggest, reflected the stability and predictability of the money supply. Chapter 10 by Mark Taylor and Geoffrey

Wood speaks to this hypothesis. Taylor and Wood test a forward-looking model of money demand in which desired money holdings at each point in time depend not only on the current prices, incomes, and interest rates but, due to adjusting money balances, on their expected future values as well. Their estimates for Britain confirm the existence of a stable, well behaved money demand function and are consistent with its attribution to a stable money supply process.

Although nominal exchange rates were remarkably stable among the core members of the gold standard system, differential movements in domestic prices translated into significant changes in real rates of exchange. While the period was not marked by the day-to-day volatility in real rates characteristic of floating exchange rates today, these real exchange rate movements still require explanation. In chapter 11, Graciela Kaminsky and Michael Klein argue that economic fundamentals provide a relatively good explanation for movements in the real rate of exchange between the US dollar and the pound sterling between 1879 and 1913, a period over which the real rate varied from peak to trough by about 20 percent. They find that disturbances to the supply of commodities were by far the most important determinant of real rate movements, presumably reflecting the impact of transitory harvest fluctuations on the relative price of agricultural goods. Aggregate supply fluctuations continue to be important determinants of the real exchange rate at longer intervals, along with fiscal policy and, in the US case, the risk that the exchange rate might be devalued.

Although nominal exchange rates were generally stable under the gold standard, countries did on occasion suspend convertibility. For example, the United States left at the start of its Civil War and resumed in 1879, while Great Britain suspended convertibility in 1919 and returned in 1925. There is a growing literature on the interaction between credibility, monetary reform, and exchange rate dynamics.[12] One application of this work has been to the United Kingdom's return to gold in April 1925, where these models provide a theoretical basis for the suggestion by Keynes (among others) that the appreciation of sterling against the dollar prior to the return to gold reflected an anticipation by the market of a reinstatement of the gold peg rather than fundamentals.[13] Chapter 12 by Panos Michael, Robert Nobay and David Peel analyzes the empirical behavior of the exchange rate of sterling in the period leading up to resumption using the insights from these models. Contrary to some other recent contributions, they conclude that there is evidence that such anticipations did indeed play a role in the appreciation of sterling prior to resumption.

The findings reported here suggest that a particular conjuncture of historical circumstances supported the operation of the fixed rate gold standard system. Compared to their 20th-century successors, economies were blessed with superior wage and price flexibility, and hence with greater capacity to adjust to shocks. Central banks, while they never followed the simple textbook monetary rules, obeyed contingent rules that allowed for discretionary responses in the event of shocks threatening financial stability. Aside from these circumstances, however, the money supply process was stable and predictable, lending credibility to the commitment to defend the exchange rate and inducing financial capital to flow in stabilizing directions. The demand for money was stabilized, along with prices. Where doubts existed, as in the United States, about the commitment of the authorities to the pursuit of their contingent rule, neither the domestic financial system nor the international gold standard functioned as smoothly.

Might it be possible today to run a system of pegged exchange rates between national currencies on this basis? Barry Eichengreen's concluding chapter 13 casts doubt on this possibility. He argues that the political and economic conditions that lent credibility to 19th-century governments' commitments to gold convertibility are no longer present. As the franchise has been broadened and the connections between monetary policy and economic activity have come to be appreciated more widely, governments have found it more difficult to commit to a monetary rule. The political pressures created by rising unemployment may induce a government wishing to enhance its chances of reelection or reappointment to renege on its exchange rate commitment.[14] Knowing this, currency traders have an incentive to force the issue. In modern democratic societies, Eichengreen concludes, the elimination of exchange controls and resulting high capital mobility are inevitably associated with financial instability.

This is one way to understand the difficulty experienced by industrial countries when they have attempted to stabilize their exchange rates in the twenty-five years since the collapse of the Bretton Woods System. It is notable that in one part of the world with a particularly strong commitment to exchange rate stability, the European Union, an attempt is underway to eliminate fluctuations in intra-European exchange rates by creating a monetary union and establishing a European Central Bank empowered to replace the separate sovereign currencies of EU member states with a single European currency. Eichengreen asks what guidance for the construction of such a system can be gleaned from the history of the Classical gold standard. While gold standard experience suggests that a currency area can encompass countries characterized by very different economic conditions, he cautions that the factors which lent the gold standard this capacity, such as tolerance for international labor mobility and extensive wage and price flexibility, are not present in Europe today.

Thus, the 19th-century world which emerges from these pages is at the same time familiar and alien. It is familiar to the extent that, then as now, supplies of money and credit could play important roles in output and relative price fluctuations. Then as now, money demand could be stable. Then as now, a commitment to the maintenance of fixed exchange rates could provide a useful anchor for policy, but merely adopting a gold standard did not suffice to lend that commitment permanence and credibility.

The contrast with today, to hark back to the opening of this chapter, was the success of a number of advanced industrial countries, mainly in Europe, in maintaining the fixed exchange rates of the gold standard in the absence of capital controls and the presence of extensive international capital mobility. The flexibility of nominal variables, and hence their capacity to respond to shocks, appears to have contributed to this success. This adjustment capacity minimized the persistence of disruptions due to macroeconomic shocks and relieved the authorities of pressure to respond in ways that could have undermined the fixed rate regime. This, along with a unique constellation of domestic political conditions – a limited franchise, limited unionization, limited awareness of the connections between monetary policy and domestic economic conditions – allowed the authoritites to attach priority to their exchange rate target. Perhaps the narrowness of policymakers' objectives is the real difference between the gold standard era and today. If so, the present political and economic environment is less congenial to efforts to peg exchange rates between national currencies.

Notes

1. Garber (1993).
2. Lawrence Officers's chapter 4 in this volume analyzes arbitrage under the interwar gold standard. While Officer focuses on the interwar gold standard of 1925–1931, the mechanics of its operation were essentially the same as in the pre-1913 period, as discussed in chapter 5 by Hallwood, MacDonald and Marsh.
3. Bayoumi (1990). Predictably, Keynes wrote the most lucid description of the period.

   The inhabitant of London could order by telephone, sipping his morning tea in bed, the various products of the whole earth, and in such quantity as he might see fit, and reasonably expect their early delivery upon his doorstep; he could at the same moment and by the same means adventure his wealth in the natural resources and new enterprises of the world, and share, without exertion or even trouble, in their prospective fruits and advantages; or he could decide to couple the security of his fortunes with the good faith of the townspeople of any substantial municipality in any continent that fancy or information might recommend . . . But, most important of all, he regarded this state of affairs as normal, certain, and

permanent, except in the direction of further improvement, and any deviation from it as aberrant, scandalous, and avoidable. (Keynes, 1919, 9–10, quoted in Obstfeld, 1986b)
4. Fishlow (1985).
5. According to the price–specie–flow mechanism, an outflow of reserves accompanied by a contraction of the money supply should place downward pressure on the price level, enhancing the international competitiveness of domestic goods, improving the trade balance, and thereby stemming the reserve outflow. The compatibility of this model with alternative formulations of the adjustment mechanism is discussed in Eichengreen (1985).
6. See Canzoneri (1985) and Obstfeld (1986a). On the theory of escape clauses, see Grossman and van Huyck (1988), De Kock and Grilli (1989), Flood and Isard (1989), Drazen and Masson (1993), Cukierman, Kiguel and Leiderman (1993) and Giovannini (1993).
7. Bertola and Caballero (1992) established the conditions under which bias in the band would remain despite the presence of conditions under which the authorities were prepared to realign their currency zone (in other words, to devalue the currency).
8. This point is also made about the United States in the 1890s in chapter 7 by Charles Calomiris and Glenn Hubbard in this volume.
9. Like Giovannini and Calomiris, however, Hallwood *et al.* find that the credibility of the US dollar in the early 1890s was relatively low.
10. Why this might have been the case is addressed in Barry Eichengreen's chapter 13 in this volume. We return to the issue when discussing his chapter below.
11. A similar conclusion is reached by Friedman and Schwartz (1982).
12. Pioneering contributions include Sargent (1985) and Flood and Garber (1983).
13. For example Miller and Sutherland (1994) and Smith and Smith (1990).
14. A number of recent authors, including Obstfeld (1994) and Isard (1994), have established this point using a policy-optimizing framework.

References

Bagehot, W. (1873). *Lombard Street, A Description of the Money Market*, London: Kegan Paul, Trench
Barro, R. and D. Gordon (1983). "A Positive Theory of Monetary Policy in a Natural Rate Model," *Journal of Political Economy* 91 (August), 589–610
Bayoumi, T. (1990). "Saving–Investment Correlations: Immobile Capital, Government Policy, or Endogenous Behavior?," *IMF Staff Papers* 37 (June), 360–387
Bayoumi, T. and B. Eichengreen (1994). "Economic Performance Under Alternative Exchange Rate Regimes: Some Historical Evidence," in P. Kenen, F. Papadia and F. Saccamoni (eds.), *The International Monetary System*, Cambridge: Cambridge University Press, 257–297
Bertola, G. and R. Caballero (1992). "Targets Zones and Realignments," CEPR, *Discussion Paper* 398

Blanchard, O. and D. Quah (1989). "The Dynamic Effects of Aggregate Demand and Supply Disturbances," *American Economic Review* 79, 655–673

Bloomfield, A. (1959). *Monetary Policy Under the International Gold Standard*, New York: Federal Reserve Bank of New York

Bordo, M. D. (1993). "The Gold Standard, Bretton Woods and Other Monetary Regimes: A Historical Appraisal," *Federal Reserve Bank of St. Louis Review* 72(2), 123–191

Calomiris, C. (1993). "Greenback Resumption and Silver Risk: The Economics and Politics of Monetary Regime Change in the United States, 1862–1900," in M. D. Bordo and F. Capie (eds.), *Monetary Regimes in Transition*, Cambridge: Cambridge University Press, 86–132

Calomiris, C. and R. G. Hubbard (1989). "Price Flexibility, Credit Availability, and Economic Fluctuations: Evidence for the United States 1894–1909," *Quarterly Journal of Economics* 104 (August), 429–452

Canzoneri, M. (1985). "Monetary Policy Games and the Role of Private Information," *American Economic Review* 75, 1056–1070

Cukierman, A., M. Kiguel and L. Leiderman (1993). "Balancing Credibility and Flexibility in the Choice of Exchange Rate Bands," Tel Aviv University, unpublished manuscript

De Kock, G. and V. Grilli (1989). "Endogenous Exchange Rate Regime Switches," NBER, *Working Paper* 3066

Drazen, A. and P. R. Masson (1993). "Credibility of Policies Versus Credibility of Policymakers," NBER, *Working Paper* 4448

Eichengreen, B. (1985). *The Gold Standard in Theory and History*, London: Methuen

   (1995). "The Endogeneity of Exchange Rate Regimes," in P. B. Kenen (ed.), *Understanding Interdependence*, Princeton: Princeton University Press, 3–44

Fenoaltea, S. (1988). "International Resource Flows and Construction Movements in the Atlantic Economy: The Kuznets Cycle in Italy, 1861–1913," *Journal of Economic History* 48, 605–638

Fishlow, A. (1985). "Lessons from the Past: Capital Markets in the 19th Century and the Interwar Period," *International Organization* 39, 383–439

Flood, R. and P. Garber (1983). "Models of Stochastic Process Switching," *Econometrica* 51 (May), 537–551

   (1984). "Gold Monetization and Gold Discipline," *Journal of Political Economy* 92, 90–107

Flood, R. and P. Isard (1989). "Monetary Policy Strategies," *IMF Staff Papers* 36 (September), 612–632

Flood, R., A. Rose and D. Mathieson (1990). "An Empirical Investigation of Exchange Rate Target Zones," NBER, *Working Paper* 3543

Friedman, M. (1968). "The Role of Monetary Policy," *American Economic Review* 58 (March), 1–17

Friedman, M. and A. J. Schwartz (1982). *Monetary Trends in the United States and in the United Kingdom 1870–1970*, Chicago: University of Chicago Press for NBER

Garber, P. (1993). "The Collapse of the Bretton Woods Fixed Exchange Rate System," in M. D. Bordo and B. Eichengreen (eds.), *A Retrospective on the Bretton Woods System: Lessons for International Monetary Reform,* Chicago: University of Chicago Press for NBER, 461–484

Giovannini, A. (1993). "Bretton Woods and its Precursors: Rules versus Discretion in the History of International Monetary Regimes," in M. D. Bordo and B. Eichengreen (eds.), *A Retrospective on the Bretton Woods System: Lessons for International Monetary Reform,* Chicago: University of Chicago Press for NBER, 109–154

Gordon, R. (1982). "Why US Wage and Employment Behavior Differs from that in Britain and Japan," *Economic Journal* 92, 13–44

Grossman, H. and J. van Huyck (1988). "Sovereign Debt as a Contingent Claim: Excusable Default, Repudiation, and Reputation," *American Economic Review* 78, 1088–1097

Grossman, R. (1993). "The Macroeconomic Consequences of Bank Failures Under the National Banking System," *Explorations in Economic History* 30, 294–320

Hatton, T. J. and J. Williamson (1994). "International Migration and World Development: A Historical Perspective," in H. Giersch (ed.), *Economic Aspects of International Migration,* Berlin: Springer Verlag, 3–56

Hume, D. ([1752] 1898). "On the Balance of Trade," in David Hume, *Essays, Moral, Political, and Literary,* vol. 1, London: Longmans Green

Isard, P. (1994). "Realignment Expectations, Forward Rate Bias, and Sterilized Intervention in an Adjustable Peg Exchange Rate Model with Policy Optimization," International Monetary Fund, unpublished manuscript

Keating, J. W. and J. V. Nye (1991). "Permanent and Transitory Shocks in Real Output: Estimates from Nineteenth Century and Postwar Economies," *Working Paper* 160, Department of Economics, Washington University in St. Louis

Krugman, P. (1991). "Target Zones and Exchange Rate Dynamics," *Quarterly Journal of Economics* 56 (August), 669–682

Keynes, J. M. (1919). *The Economic Consequences of the Peace,* London: Macmillan

Kydland, F. and E. Prescott (1977). "Rules Rather than Discretion: The Inconsistency of Optimal Plans," *Journal of Political Economy* 85 (June), 473–492

Miller, M. and A. Sutherland (1994). "Speculative Anticipations of Sterling's Return to Gold: Was Keynes Wrong?," *Economic Journal* 104 (July), 804–812

Obstfeld, M. (1986a). "Rational and Self-Fulfilling Balance-of-Payments Crises," *American Economic Review* 46, 72–81

(1986b). "Capital Mobility in the World Economy: Theory and Measurement," *Carnegie–Rochester Series on Public Policy* 24, 55–104

(1993). "The Adjustment Mechanism," in M. D. Bordo and B. Eichengreen (eds.), *A Retrospective on the Bretton Woods System: Lessons for International Monetary Reform,* Chicago: University of Chicago Press for NBER, 201–268

(1994). "The Logic of Currency Crises," NBER, *Working Paper* 4060

Ozkan, F. G. and A. Sutherland (1993). "A Model of the ERM Crisis," University of York, unpublished manuscript

Sargent, T. J. (1995). *Rational Expectations and Inflation*, New York: Harper & Row

Smith, W. S and R. T. Smith (1990). "Stochastic Process Switching and the Return to Gold, 1925," *Economic Journal* 100 (March), 164–175

Svensson, L. (1992). "An Interpretation of Recent Research on Exchange Rate Target Zones," *Journal of Economic Perspectives* 6, 119–114

2 Unit roots, shocks and VARs and their place in history: an introductory guide

Terence C. Mills

Introduction

In this chapter we develop, within a common framework, the econometric techniques used in many of the subsequent chapters. We begin by analyzing a fundamental problem in much historical empirical work, that of separating an observed time series into trend and cyclical components. This leads naturally on to investigating the underlying stochastic processes that generate economic time series and to discriminating between them, in particular between processes that contain a unit root and those that are generated as stationary fluctuations around a deterministic trend.

We then move to a multivariate setting and introduce the vector autoregression (VAR) framework, within which the concept of Granger causality fits naturally. Various extensions to the VAR framework, known as structural VARs, are used in this volume; these are also discussed. Nonstationarity must also be tackled within a multivariate setting and this enables the concept of cointegration – the presence of common trends within a group of time series – to be introduced into the analysis. These issues are the subject of the penultimate section, before some comments conclude the chapter.

Trends and cycles in macroeconomic time series

Researchers studying the growth and cyclical behavior of industrialized economies are immediately faced with the problem of separating out cyclical fluctuations from the longer-term trend, or secular, movements. The difficulties in doing this are well appreciated by economists and economic historians alike, but the methods of trend and cycle decomposition have often been essentially ad hoc, designed primarily for ease of computation without real regard for the statistical properties of the time series (or set of series) under analysis.

The underlying model in such analyses is typically one in which a time series y_t, observed over the period $t=1, 2,...,T$, is decomposed additively into a trend, μ_t, and a cyclical component, ϵ_t, which are assumed to be statistically independent of each other, i.e.

$$y_t=\mu_t+\epsilon_t, \qquad t=1, 2,...,T,$$
$$E(\mu_t\epsilon_s)=0, \text{ for all } t \text{ and } s. \tag{1}$$

The series y_t is often the logarithm of the series under consideration, while the data are usually observed annually. The extension to, say, quarterly or monthly observations with the incorporation of a third, seasonal, component is, conceptually at least, straightforward.

The trend and cycle components are, of course, unobservable, and hence need to be estimated. The methods of estimation that have traditionally been employed are termed "ad hoc" above because they do not arise from any formal statistical analysis of y_t or its components. Perhaps the simplest model for μ_t that we might consider is the linear time trend

$$\mu_t=\alpha+\beta t \tag{2}$$

which, if y_t is measured in logarithms, assumes constant exponential growth. Estimation of the regression model

$$y_t=\alpha+\beta t+\epsilon_t \tag{3}$$

by ordinary least squares (OLS) then produces asymptotically efficient estimates of α and β, although the variances of these estimates will be biased unless the errors (i.e. the cyclical component, ϵ_t) are both serially uncorrelated and homoskedastic (Fuller, 1976, chapter 9). Given such estimates $\hat{\alpha}$ and $\hat{\beta}$, the trend component is then

$$\hat{\mu}_t=\hat{\alpha}+\hat{\beta}t,$$

and the cyclical component is obtained by residual as

$$\hat{\epsilon}_t=y_t-\hat{\mu}_t.$$

Note that the trend component will only be efficiently estimated in small samples, an important proviso given the limited number of observations often available on historical economic time series, if the cyclical component is, *inter alia*, serially uncorrelated. This is unlikely to be so if cycles are in fact present in the data, in which case generalised least squares (GLS) or an equivalent technique is required for efficient trend estimation.

Although the linear trend model has been used on many occasions, particularly by economists, economic historians have typically rejected the view that trend growth is constant through time, preferring models that allow for variable trend growth rates. Traditionally, piecewise discontinuous linear trends have been used (see Mills, 1992), but recently attention has focused on trend functions that are smooth. Such smoothness can be obtained by considering the class of *segmented* or *breaking trend* models, to use the terminologies of Rappoport and Reichlin (1989) and Perron (1989), respectively, these being a special case of *grafted polynomials*; see, for example, Fuller (1976, chapter 9). A segmented linear trend can be written as

$$y_t = \alpha + \beta t + \sum_{i=1}^{m} \delta_i \varphi_{it} + \epsilon_t, \tag{4}$$

where the functions φ_{it} are given by

$$\varphi_{it} = \begin{cases} t - T_i, & t > T_i \\ 0, & \text{otherwise,} \end{cases}$$

and extensions to higher order trend polynomials are straightforward.

The common feature of the linear trend model and its extensions is that trend growth across cycles is regarded as being *deterministic*, so that *all* fluctuations in y_t must be attributable to the cyclical component. Furthermore, any fluctuation from trend is only temporary: since the cyclical component ϵ_t is estimated by the residual from a regression, it must have zero mean and be *stationary* (for a formal definition of this term, see n. 2 below), so that any shocks to y_t that force it away from its trend path must dissipate through time. The importance of this implication is discussed in more detail later in the chapter. The other potential drawback of these models is that the "break points" $T_1, ..., T_m$ have to be determined *a priori*, so that such choices could be subjectively biased.

Because of these shortcomings, alternative methods of trend estimation based on *moving averages* are sometimes used. Formally, a trend component estimated by a $(2h+1)$-moving average of y_t can be defined as

$$\mu_t = \frac{1}{2h+1} \sum_{j=-h}^{h} y_{t+j}, \qquad t = h+1, ..., T-h-1. \tag{5}$$

An advantage of using a moving average to estimate the trend component, apart from the obvious one of computational simplicity, is that the trend now becomes stochastic and, although "smooth," is influenced by the local behavior of y_t: fluctuations in y are therefore not entirely allocated to the cyclical component. Indeed, a property of moving averages is that a $(2h+1)$-moving average will smooth out a $2h+1$-year cycle from the data. For annual historical macroeconomic series, h is often set at 4, thus smoothing out a 9-year "business" cycle.

One obvious disadvantage of moving averages is that $2h$ trend observations, equally allocated at the beginning and end of the sample period, are necessarily lost and this can cause major difficulties when the number of available observations is limited, as they are for the interwar years, where less then twenty annual observations are available.

A less well known disadvantage of using moving averages of the form (5) is that, although they eliminate a linear trend, which is certainly what is required, they also tend to smooth the detrended series too much: this is particularly so for series that are only weakly autocorrelated after differencing, a feature of many macroeconomic series. The result is the injection of trend into the cyclical component, rather than its elimination, manifesting itself in the form of low order autocorrelation. As a consequence, the cycles obtained by residual from this procedure may be spuriously smooth, thus leading to erroneous conclusions concerning their regularity and stability.[1]

A more sophisticated form of moving average is the filter proposed by Hodrick and Prescott (1980), which has a long tradition as a method of fitting a smooth curve through a set of points, versions of it being used as actuarial graduation formulae. Given the traditional decomposition $y_t = \mu_t + \epsilon_t$, the trend series μ_t is obtained as the solution to the problem of minimizing

$$\sum_{t=1}^{T} \left(y_t - \mu_t \right) + \lambda \sum_{t=1}^{T} \left((\mu_t - \mu_{t-1}) - (\mu_{t+1} - \mu_t) \right)$$

with respect to $\mu_1, \mu_2, ..., \mu_T$. The first order condition for this minimisation problem is

$$y_t = \lambda \left(\mu_{t+2} - 4\mu_{t+1} + (6 + \lambda^{-1})\mu_t - 4\mu_{t-1} + \mu_{t-2} \right).$$

If an infinite series of y values were available, it can be shown (see, for example, King and Rebelo, 1993) that μ_t would be given by the infinite-length moving average

$$\mu_t = \sum_{j=-\infty}^{\infty} \alpha_j y_{t-j}, \qquad \alpha_j = \alpha_{-j}.$$

King and Rebelo (1993) provide expressions for the α_j, which do not take a simple form. Fortunately, Hodrick and Prescott (1980) provide an algorithm which removes the necessity of having to calculate the moving average weights and so allows the trend to be computed when only a finite number of y observations are available. Typically, following Hodrick and Prescott (1980), λ is set at 100 if annual data is used or 1600 for quarterly or monthly data. While this filter has proved to be rather popular in recent years for computing trends, particularly in the real business cycle literature (see, for example, Kydland and Prescott, 1990; Blackburn and Ravn, 1992), it has been criticized on the grounds that the arbitrary setting of λ may

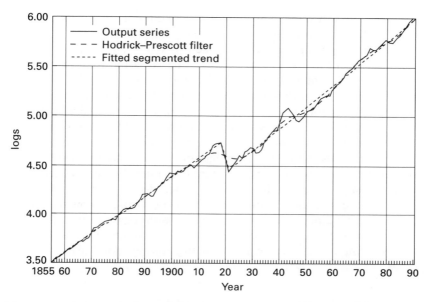

Figure 2.1 UK output, 1855–1990, trend components

create spurious cycles and/or distort the estimates of the components: see, for example, King and Rebelo (1993) and Harvey and Jaeger (1993).

We may illustrate these decomposition techniques by considering the series for annual UK output (measured in logarithms) over the period 1855–1990 shown in figure 2.1. It is apparent from this plot that a linear trend would be inappropriate, but a segmented linear trend, having breaks at 1918 and 1921, is a plausible contender, i.e. if output can be decomposed as $y_t = \mu_t + \epsilon_t$, then the trend function μ_t is

$$\mu_t = \alpha + \beta t + \delta_1 \varphi_{1t} + \delta_2 \varphi_{2t},$$

where $\varphi_{it} = (t - T_i)$ if $t > T_i$ and 0 otherwise; $T_1 = 64$ and $T_2 = 67$ being the break points 1918 and 1921. Fitting this model by GLS (to take account of serial correlation in the cyclical component) yields (see Mills, 1994, for details):

$$y_t = 3.474 + 0.0196t - 0.1109\varphi_{1t} + 0.1136\varphi_{2t} + \epsilon_t.$$

This model has some simple and easily interpretable properties. Trend growth is 1.96 percent per annum up to 1919 and $(1.96 - 11.09 + 11.36)$ percent $= 2.23$ percent from 1922, the level of trend output falling 27.4 percent in the intervening three years. The component ϵ_t can be modeled by a second order autoregressive process whose parameters imply that output exhibits stationary cyclical fluctuations around the trend growth path, the cycles having an average period of 8.1 years.

The fitted segmented trend component is shown superimposed on the output series in figure 2.1. Also superimposed is the trend component obtained by applying the Hodrick–Prescott (H–P) filter (the trend estimated using a 9-year ($h=4$) moving average (9MA) is almost identical to this and is therefore not shown). The trends are almost identical up to 1912, but the H–P filter has difficulty in modeling the post-World War I "crash" and from then on follows the observed output series much more closely than does the segmented trend; of course, with a moving average filter trend growth is no longer constant over time. As a consequence, the cyclical components obtained from the two decompositions, shown in figure 2.2, are substantially different after 1912. We also show the cyclical component obtained from fitting the 9MA: although it is difficult to distinguish between the H–P and 9MA trends, there are periods when the cyclical components diverge, most notably during World War I and the 1930s.

Discriminating between trend stationary and difference stationary processes

From the above discussion, it is clear that both the linear trend and the moving average filter can have important defects when used to decompose an observed series into trend and cyclical components. Moreover, as our output example has shown, these methods can lead to markedly different decompositions into trend and cyclical components. While we would certainly not argue that these techniques are *necessarily* defective, it would obviously be desirable if alternatives existed and methods were available to statistically discriminate between different decompositions. This is particularly so given that the allocation of fluctuations to components, and the determination of whether such fluctuations have permanent or transitory effects, can be heavily dependent upon the decomposition chosen. Recent developments in time series analysis have, however, made available a set of techniques and models that are designed to do just this and which have already begun to be employed with considerable success in a number of areas of macroeconomics and economic history.

By way of introduction, consider again the simple linear trend model of (3):

$$y_t = \alpha + \beta t + \epsilon_t, \tag{6}$$

where the residuals ϵ_t are now explicitly assumed to be *stationary*, but not necessarily serially uncorrelated.[2] Although we have concentrated on this model in the previous section, secular (trend) movement need not be

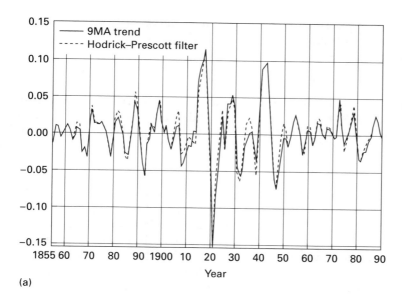

(a)

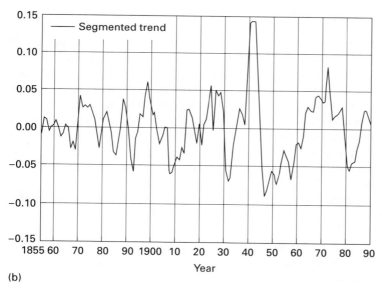

(b)

Figure 2.2 UK output, 1855–1990, cyclical components, alternative estimates

modeled by a deterministic function of time and one alternative, popular-
ised by Box and Jenkins (1976), allows y_t to be the accumulation of changes
that are themselves stationary, so that

$$y_t = y_{t-1} + \beta + e_t, \tag{7}$$

where e_t is a stationary, but again not necessarily serially uncorrelated,
series with mean zero and variance σ_e^2, and where β is the (fixed) mean of
the changes. Accumulating these changes from an initial value, y_0 say, yields

$$y_t = y_0 + \beta t + \sum_{i=1}^{t} e_i, \tag{8}$$

which looks superficially like (6), but has two fundamental differences. The
intercept is no longer a fixed parameter but now depends upon the initial
value y_0, and the error is not stationary, for its variance and covariances all
depend on time. For example, if the e_t do happen to be serially uncorrelated,
so that y_t is a *random walk with drift* (of β), then the error variance is $t\sigma_e^2$,
which obviously increases as t increases. Nelson and Plosser (1982) refer to
models of the class (6) as *trend stationary* (TS) processes and those of class
(8) as *difference stationary* (DS) processes.

The distinction between these two processes has important implications
for the analysis of both economic growth and business cycles. If y_t is of the
TS class then, as was pointed out on p. 19, all variation in the series is attributable to fluctuations in the cyclical component and any shock must only
have a temporary effect as the series always returns to a linear growth path.
If the series is a DS process, however, its trend component must be a nonstationary stochastic process rather than a deterministic function of time,
so that a shock to it will have an enduring effect on the future path of the
series. Hence treating y_t as a TS rather than as a DS process is likely to lead
to an overstatement of the magnitude and duration of the cyclical component and to an understatement of the importance and persistence of the
trend component.[3]

Given that the properties of the two classes of models are so different, it
is essential to be able to correctly distinguish between them. Moreover, the
importance of such discrimination is exacerbated by the consequences of
incorrectly assuming that a series is TS when, in fact, it is a member of the
DS class. Nelson and Kang (1981, 1984) have considered the effects of such
misspecification in some detail and they conclude that it is very easy to
mistake a DS process for a TS process that seems to provide a good fit to
the data, with a high R^2, small residual variance and significant coefficients,
and which generates spuriously long cycles in the detrended data.

Given that modeling a DS process as TS is fraught with potential pitfalls,
what dangers are attached to the converse misspecification? Very few it

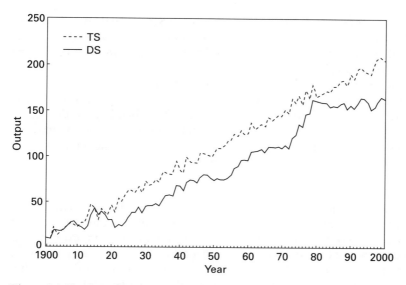

Figure 2.3 Simulated TS and DS series, 1900–2000

would seem, for the OLS estimator of β will still be unbiased and will have approximately a normal (or Student-t) distribution, and although the efficiency of the estimator is reduced, this will not be serious if the induced serial correlation in ϵ_t is simultaneously modeled.

These conclusions are neatly illustrated by the following simulated example. Figure 2.3 plots TS and DS processes generated for $T=100$ by assuming $\beta=2$, $\alpha=y_0=10$, and the sequences ϵ_t and e_t to be both normal and serially uncorrelated with zero mean and variance 25. It is readily apparent from figure 2.3 that the observed TS series is generated from such a process and, indeed, OLS regression of the series on a constant and a time trend yields intercept and slope estimates of 9.46 and 2.001, respectively, and a residual variance estimate of 25.7.

Visual inspection of the DS series might also suggest that it too was generated by a TS process, albeit with a flatter slope. In fact, an OLS regression of the series against time obtains a slope estimate of 1.71, which is accompanied by a t-ratio in excess of 50, and an R^2-statistic of 0.963! Moreover, the residual variance of the regression is 95.1, whereas the true error variance of the random walk by the end of the sample should be $T\sigma_e^2=2500$.

The appropriate estimation method for the DS process is to regress the first differences of the series on a constant: OLS yields an intercept estimate of 1.55 with a standard error of 0.51, and an estimate for σ_e^2 of 25.7.

However, regressing the first difference of the TS generated series on a constant yields an estimate of 1.97, thus illustrating how misspecifying a TS process as a DS process nevertheless still enables an accurate estimate of the slope coefficient β to be obtained.

How can a researcher distinguish whether an observed time series is a member of the TS or DS class of processes? An easily implemented method has been proposed by Nelson and Plosser (1982), building on the earlier work of Dickey and Fuller (1979, 1981) on testing for *unit roots* in univariate time series. In its simplest form, this takes the DS model as the null hypothesis, embodied in the regression.

$$y_t = \alpha + \rho y_{t-1} + \beta t + v_t, \tag{9}$$

where v_t is a residual, as $H_0: \rho = 1$, $\beta = 0$. Under this null, standard t-ratio testing procedures are strongly biased towards finding stationarity around a trend, i.e. they are biased towards rejecting a DS process in favor of a TS process, tending to reject the unit root hypothesis of $\rho = 1$ when it is true in favor of the stationary alternative $\rho < 1$, and tending to reject the hypothesis $\beta = 0$ when it is true in favor of the typical alternative $\beta > 0$.

Assuming that e_t in (7) is serially uncorrelated, the appropriate testing strategy is to use the standard t-ratio $\hat{\tau}_\rho = (\hat{\rho} - 1)/s(\hat{\rho})$, where $s(\hat{\rho})$ is the standard error of the least squares estimator $\hat{\rho}$, to test the null hypothesis $\rho = 1$ against the alternative $\rho < 1$, but to use the critical values given originally in Fuller (1976, 373), and more recently extended by Guilkey and Schmidt (1989) and Mackinnon (1991), rather than the conventional critical values taken from Student-t tables.[4]

The importance of using the correct critical values is seen by comparing, for example, the 0.01 critical values for an infinite sample size: the correct value is $\hat{\tau}_{\rho, 0.01} = -3.96$, while the incorrect value from the t-distribution is -2.58. A joint test of $H_0: \rho = 0$ may be carried out by computing the standard F-ratio, denoted Φ_3, but now comparing the resultant test statistic to the critical values of the statistic given in Dickey and Fuller (1981, 1062).[5] The hypothesis that y_t is a DS process is rejected in favor of the alternative that it is a TS process if the test statistics *exceed* (in absolute value) their critical values.

How powerful are such tests? The limited number of observations available on many historical economic time series, usually only recorded annually, may be thought to be an obvious problem. As discussed in Perron (1988) and Shiller and Perron (1985), however, the power of unit root tests depends much more on the *span* of the data than on the number of observations *per se*. This has the implication that increasing the number of observations does not necessarily lead to tests having higher power if there is also a change in the sampling interval, e.g. if quarterly rather than annual observations are used but the sample period remains unaltered. With historical economic time series, the relevant alternative to a DS process is often a TS process exhibiting *trend reversion* over a period of an order similar to business cycles. Hence a long span of annual data is to be preferred to a shorter span with, say, quarterly observations even if the latter affords a greater number of values.

Nevertheless, any test of a unit root will have low power against stationary alternatives with roots close to unity: see, for example, DeJong *et al.* (1992a, 1992b). Such roots would imply that trend reversion occurs over very long periods of time and theoretical models embodying just this property have been developed by West (1987) and would, for example, be implied by the behavior of the price level during the gold standard (see Mills, 1990b). Again, this highlights the importance of the span of available data rather than merely the number of observations and is a point that has also been made, albeit with a somewhat different emphasis, by Cochrane (1988) in the context of examining the stochastic properties of US output.

In assessing the power of unit root tests, the set of confidence intervals for the largest autoregressive root provided by Stock (1991) are a useful supplement. Stock assumes that the true value of ρ can be modeled as $\rho = 1 + c/T$, where c is a fixed constant, and constructs asymptotic confidence intervals for ρ based on the statistic $\hat{\tau}_\rho$. Since the distribution of this statistic is nonnormal and the dependence on c is not a simple location shift, such confidence intervals cannot be constructed using a simple rule such as "plus or minus 2 standard errors." The intervals are highly nonlinear, exhibiting a sharp "bend" for values of c just above zero (see Stock, 1991, figures 1 and 2): for positive values of $\hat{\tau}_\rho$ the intervals are tight, for large negative values they are wide. Stock provides tables from which confidence intervals for ρ can be calculated given a value of $\hat{\tau}_\rho$ and the sample size T.

Given these power problems associated with tests of the null hypothesis of a unit root (DS process) against the alternative of a TS process, Kwiatkowski *et al.* (1992) consider testing the null hypothesis of trend stationarity against the alternative of a unit root. They propose the following Lagrange Multiplier (LM) statistic

$$\eta = T^{-2} \sum_{t=1}^{T} S_t^2 / s^2,$$

where S_t is the partial sum process of the residuals from (6),

$$S_t = \sum_{i=1}^{t} \epsilon_i, \qquad t = 1, 2, \dots, T,$$

and s^2 is an estimate of the "long-run variance"

$$\sigma^2 = \lim_{T \to \infty} T^{-1} \operatorname{E}(S_T^2).$$

The formula to compute s^2 is to be found in Kwiatkowski *et al.*, who also provide selected critical values for the test statistic η.

Bearing in mind the earlier discussion concerning structural changes and segmented trend models, an alternative argument as to why unit root tests may have low power is that a TS process, embodying as it does the hypothesis of constant trend growth, is not sufficiently well parameterized to capture the infrequent changes in trend growth which Rappoport and Reichlin (1989) and Perron (1989) argue may well be a better characterization of the behavior of macroeconomic time series than are the frequent changes implied by the DS model. The testing procedure outlined above can be extended to consider segmented trend models of the form (4) as an alternative to the DS model of (7). Consider the following extension to (9):

$$y_t = \alpha + \beta t + \sum_{i=1}^{m} \delta_i \varphi_{it} + \rho y_{t-1} + v_t. \tag{10}$$

The null hypothesis of a DS process is now $H_0: \rho = 1$, $\beta = \delta_1 = \ldots = \delta_m = 0$ and can again be tested by computing the $\hat{\tau}_\rho$-statistic. However, the critical values of this statistic will differ from those obtained for the simpler model and Rappoport and Reichlin (1989) present critical values, obtained by Monte Carlo simulation, for a sample size of $T = 100$. These values tend to be appreciably larger than those for the TS alternative: with $m = 1$, $\hat{\tau}_{\rho, 0.05} = -4.23$ for $T_1 = 50$ and -4.08 for $T_1 = 25$, while for $m = 2$ and break points at $T_1 = 25$ and $T_2 = 75$, $\hat{\tau}_{\rho, 0.05} = -4.76$, the usual critical value being -3.45. They also find that the critical values are not biased towards rejecting the DS model if, as would naturally be the case in practice, the break points are selected after viewing the data. Further analysis of segmented trend models is provided by Perron (1989, 1990), where detailed critical values are tabulated for various types of structural change, by Christiano (1992) and Zivot and Andrews (1992), where sequential techniques for determining the break points are examined, and by Campbell and Perron (1991), where a general testing framework is outlined.

The methods developed above are predicated on the assumption that the error sequence e_t is uncorrelated but, from (7), there is no reason why this should be so. However, if the error sequence is correlated, then either the estimation method must be changed (i.e. another regression model must be adopted) or the statistics described above must be modified. Adopting the first approach, Said and Dickey (1984) show that if e_t is a general ARMA(p,q) process with p and q unknown, then the regression model (9) can be amended to

$$y_t = \alpha + \rho y_{t-1} + \beta t + \sum_{j=1}^{l} \gamma_j \nabla y_{t-j} + v_t, \tag{11}$$

where the number of lags, l, of $\nabla y_t = y_t - y_{t-1}$ introduced as regressors increases with the sample size at the controlled rate ($T^{1/3}$). In this case the $\hat{\tau}_\rho$ statistic computed from the estimate of $\hat{\rho}$ has the same limiting distribution, and hence critical values, as the statistic calculated from the regression (11).

A potential difficulty with this approach is that if the moving average component of e_t is important, then the number of extra lags of ∇y_t needed as regressors in the autoregressive correction may be quite large. Since one effective observation is lost for each extra ∇y_t introduced, this approach may have substantially lower power than when the errors are serially uncorrelated if the series under consideration is relatively short, a relevant consideration in many historical applications. Furthermore, as shown by Schwert (1987, 1989), the correction does not work well, in the sense that the empirical distribution of the test statistic is far different from the distribution of $\hat{\tau}_\rho$ reported by Dickey and Fuller (1979), if the moving average parameter is large. Since it is generally believed, and much empirical work supports this view, that moving average terms are present in many macroeconomic time series after first differencing, the above approach may face serious practical difficulties.

Phillips and Perron (1988) adopt the second approach, that of modifying the test statistics, to account for serial correlation and, indeed, certain forms of heteroskedasticity. The exact forms of their modified test statistics are conveniently set out in Perron (1988, table 1) and will not be repeated here. Their disadvantage is that the modifications necessitate corrections to the standard error of $\hat{\rho}$ and hence the modified statistics cannot be taken directly from the output of a standard regression package. Moreover, their performance in the presence of important moving average components can be worse than that of the autoregressive corrections outlined above, and this leads Schwert (1989) to recommend that the Said and Dickey test should be the one to use when errors are serially correlated, perhaps setting the number of lags of ∇y_t at $l = T^{1/4}$, rounded to the nearest integer, so that when $T = 25$, $l = 2$; when $T = 50$, $l = 3$; when $T = 200$, $l = 4$, etc. Nevertheless, it is strongly recommended that extreme care be taken to establish the presence and form of serial correlation *before* tests of unit roots are carried out, since the importance of making correct inferences is essential to the appropriate analysis of trend and cycle.

Let us use these techniques to investigate the question of whether the UK output series shown in figure 2.1 is best represented by a TS or DS process. Estimating (11) with l set at 3 using "Schwert's rule" ($T = 136$) yields $\hat{\rho} = 0.941$

and $\hat{\tau}_\rho = -2.03$, while setting l at 2, a choice based on the significance of the γ coefficients, yields $\hat{\rho} = 0.924$ and $\hat{\tau}_\rho = -2.66$, so that in neither case can the null of a unit root, $\rho = 1$, be rejected, for even the 0.15 critical value of the test statistic's distribution is -3.15. Consistent with this, Stock's (1991) 95 percent confidence interval based on the former value of $\hat{\rho}$ is $0.905 \leq \rho \leq 1.034$, while Kwiatkowski *et al.*'s (1992) LM test is able to reject the TS null in favor of the DS alternative at less than the 0.05 critical level.

Such a clear consensus in favor of the DS process should not surprise us, however, because we have already seen that a segmented trend is more appropriate than a linear trend as an alternative to a DS process. Estimating (10) with breaks at 1918 and 1921 yields $\hat{\rho} = 0.627$ and a test statistic of $\hat{\tau}_\rho = -7.06$. While Rappoport and Reichlin's critical values are not directly applicable here, the size of the statistic is certainly such as to allow rejection of the DS null in favor of the segmented TS alternative. Furthermore, both the Perron and Campbell and Perron approaches also lead to the same conclusion.

An alternative approach to discriminating between DS and TS processes is obtained if we return to one of their fundamental differences: shocks to a DS process are persistent, while shocks to a TS process are transitory. To show this algebraically, suppose that y_t does contain a unit root, but that e_t in (7) is autocorrelated. We may assume that e_t can be written as a linear combination of the present and past values of a series a_t, whose values are independent and identically distributed with common variance σ_a^2: the sequence a_t is known as *white noise*.[6] (7) can then be written as

$$\nabla y_t = \beta + a_t + \sum_{j=1}^{\infty} \psi_j a_{t-j}. \tag{12}$$

From (12), the impact of a shock in period t, a_t, on the change in y in period $t+k$, ∇y_{t+k}, is ψ_k. The impact of the shock on the *level* of y in period $t+k$, y_{t+k}, is therefore $1 + \psi_1 + \ldots + \psi_k$. The ultimate impact of the shock on the level of y is the infinite sum $\Psi = 1 + \psi_1 + \psi_2 + \ldots$, which can be taken as a measure of how persistent shocks to y are. For example, for the random walk model (7), $\Psi = 1$ since $\psi_j = 0$ for all j, but other more general forms of DS models would yield measures of persistence for which $\Psi > 0$. However, suppose we extend the TS process (6) analogously to

$$y_t = \alpha + \beta t + a_t + \sum_{j=1}^{\infty} \phi_j a_{t-j}.$$

This has the representation (12) but with $\psi_1 = \phi_1 - 1$ and $\psi_j = \phi_j - \phi_{j-1}$, for $j \geq 2$. Thus, for a TS process, $\Psi = 0$, and this distinction between the two models forms the basis for Cochrane's (1988) *variance ratio* measure of persistence.

The variance ratio is defined as $V_k = \sigma_k^2/\sigma_1^2$, where

$$\sigma_k^2 = k^{-1}\mathrm{var}(y_t - y_{t-k}).$$

If y_t is a pure random walk, then the variance of its kth differences will grow linearly with k, i.e. $\mathrm{var}(y_t - y_{t-k}) = k\sigma_1^2$, and so $V_k = 1$. On the other hand, if y_t is TS, then $\mathrm{var}(y_t - y_{t-k})$ tends towards a constant as $k \to \infty$, so that $V_k \to 0$, thus mimicking the behavior of Ψ. If fluctuations in y_t are partly permanent and partly temporary, so that the series can be modeled as a combination of random walk and stationary components (see the discussion below), V_k will be positive.

An unbiased estimator of σ_k^2 is given by

$$\hat{\sigma}_k^2 = \frac{T}{k(T-k)(T-k+1)} \sum_{t=k}^{T} \left[y_t - y_{t-k} - \frac{k}{T}(y_T - y_0) \right]^2$$

so that the variance ratio can be estimated as $\hat{V}_k = \hat{\sigma}_k^2/\hat{\sigma}_1^2$.

The importance of the random walk component in y_t can then be assessed by examining the size of $\hat{V}_k$ for various values of k, although it should be recognized that the measure is accompanied by a large standard error and the "window size" k can be difficult to determine.

On some occasions it might be interesting to test whether y_t is generated by a "pure" random walk, i.e. to test the null hypothesis that $V_k = 1$. While there are various tests which may be used, the variance ratio has been found to have useful power properties for relevant alternatives in these circumstances. Lo and MacKinlay (1988, 1989) define the test statistic

$$M(k) = \hat{V}_k - 1$$

and show that the normalized statistic,

$$z(k) = M(k) \left(\frac{2(2k-1)(k-1)}{3Tk} \right)$$

is asymptotically distributed as a standard normal. They also derive a version that is robust to heteroskedasticity. It should be emphasized, however, that this large sample normal approximation only works well when k is small and T is large: for large k the distribution of $z(k)$ is highly skewed and, although the empirical sizes of the test statistic are close to their nominal values, almost all rejections occur in the upper tail of the distribution.

For the UK output series, Mills (1991) reports persistence measures for the pre-1919 period of $V_{10} = 0.47$ and $V_{30} = 0.25$, while for the post-1921 period they are $V_{10} = 1.18$ and $V_{30} = 0.29$. These estimates thus confirm that persistence is low in the former period, but that its extent in the latter period is hard to determine, reflecting the difficulty in choosing k. Moreover, in no case is the $M(k)$ statistic significant: since three of the values lie in the lower tail of the $z(k)$ distribution, this is not surprising.

One question that needs to be considered is the form of the trend component of the general DS process (12). Given the trend cycle decomposition (1), in which μ_t and ϵ_t are independent, Watson (1986) shows that often an admissible unobserved components (UC) model is

$$\mu_t = \mu_{t-1} + \beta + a_t^\mu, \qquad \mathrm{var}(a_t^\mu) = \sigma_{a\mu}^2, \tag{13}$$

and

$$\epsilon_t = a_t^\epsilon + \sum_{j=1}^\infty \psi_{\epsilon j} a_{t-j}^\epsilon, \ \mathrm{var}(a_t^\epsilon) = \sigma_{a\epsilon}^2, \ \mathrm{E}(a_t^\epsilon a_{t-j}^\mu) = 0, \text{ for all } j.$$

Here the trend component follows a random walk with drift, while the cycle is a zero mean stationary stochastic process evolving independently of the trend. The linear trend model is a special case of this UC model and corresponds to the restriction $\sigma_{a\mu}^2 = 0$.

It is not always possible to decompose a process into a random walk trend and an independent stationary cycle, as both Watson (1986) and Nelson and Plosser (1982) point out. For example, the popular ARIMA(1,1,0) process

$$y_t = y_{t-1} + \beta + \theta(y_{t-1} - y_{t-2}) + a_t,$$

for which $\psi_j = \theta^j$, is ruled out. Moreover, the independent component assumption can be replaced by one of *perfect correlation* between components. In this case the trend and cycle are driven by the *same* errors, and this provides the basis for the Beveridge and Nelson (1981) decomposition, although many economists may feel uncomfortable with such an assumption.

Given that an admissible decomposition exists, an optimal estimate of the trend component is then given by a *weighted* moving average of the observed values of y_t,

$$\hat{\mu}_t = \sum_{j=-\infty}^\infty \lambda_j y_{t-j}, \tag{14}$$

where the λ_j weights, which sum to unity, are functions of the variances σ_a^2 and $\sigma_{a\mu}^2$ as well as the ψ_j weights. The moving average introduced earlier as (5) is thus seen to be a special case of (14), obtained by setting λ_j equal to $(2h+1)^{-1}$ for $-h \le j \le h$ and zero elsewhere, and does not correspond to any model of the form (14).[7]

A more general formulation of the UC model (13) is to let the drift parameter β vary through time by also allowing it to be a random walk, i.e.

$$\mu_t = \mu_{t-1} + \beta_t + a_t^\mu, \qquad \mathrm{var}(a_t^\mu) = \sigma_{a\mu}^2, \tag{15}$$

where

$$\beta_t = \beta_{t-1} + a_t^\beta, \qquad \text{var}(a_t^\beta) = \sigma_{a\beta}^2, \tag{16}$$

and a_t^μ and a_t^β are independent white noise processes. With such a setup it is usual to specify the form of the cyclical component explicitly. Clark (1987) and Crafts, Leybourne and Mills (1989, 1990), for example, use the AR(2) process

$$\epsilon_t = \theta_1 \epsilon_{t-1} + \theta_2 \epsilon_{t-2} + a_t^\epsilon, \tag{17}$$

while Harvey (1985, 1990) and Capie and Mills (1992) prefer a sinusoidal process that explicitly exhibits cyclical behavior. Such an UC model was fitted to our UK output series. Plots of the estimated trend and cycle are not shown as they are almost identical to the H–P filter components shown in figures 2.1 and 2.2. More interestingly, the estimate of $\sigma_{a\mu}^2$ is zero, while that of $\sigma_{a\beta}^2$ is significantly positive, so that all movement in the trend component comes through shifts in the growth rate. This implies that there are no "once-and-for-all" shifts in trend, in stark contrast to the segmented trend model, which allows no shifts in trend except at the break points 1918 and 1921!

Granger causality and vector autoregressions

The discussion so far has concentrated on analyzing individual time series. When two or more series are to be modeled jointly, we typically want to analyze the causal links existing between them. Suppose we consider the relationship between two time series, y_t and x_t. It is well known that the presence of a high (contemporaneous) correlation between them does not constitute evidence of any relationship between the underlying variables, y and x. Moreover, an assumption such as "x causes y" cannot be established on the basis of data alone: indeed, such an assumption is often taken for granted on the basis of economic theory.

Given the limitations imposed by nonexperimental data, some researchers have thus taken the view that fitting a regression model is primarily an exercise in measurement. That a relationship exists is not actually questioned: what is important is the measured effect of one variable on another. While this approach has underlain a good deal of econometric modeling in the past, it does seems to place an inordinate amount of faith in prior knowledge from economic theory and it certainly implies that untestable assumptions are brought into the model.

The wish to examine the assumptions underlying an econometric model estimated from nonexperimental time series data has led to a particular concept of causality being developed. It must be stressed, however, that this notion of causality is purely statistical and does not correspond to any acceptable definition of cause and effect in the philosophical sense. Instead, this idea of causality, formalized by Granger (1969), refers to the more limited concept of *predictability*. Two basic rules are taken to apply. The first is that the future cannot predict the past. The second is that it is assumed that it is only meaningful to discuss causality for a group of *stochastic* variables. The variable x is then said to *Granger-cause* y if taking account of past values of x enables better predictions to be made for y, all other things being equal: formal definitions of Granger causality may be found in, for example, Granger (1969) and Pierce and Haugh (1977).

There are various ways in which tests of Granger causality may be carried out. Perhaps the most straightforward is the *direct test*. Consider the regression of y_t on lagged values of itself and lagged values of x_t:

$$y_t = \gamma_0 + \sum_{i=1}^{m} \gamma_i y_{t-i} + \sum_{i=1}^{n} \delta_i x_{t-i} + v_t. \tag{18}$$

The hypothesis that x Granger-causes y can then be examined by testing the joint significance of the lagged values of x in (18): if $H_0 : \delta_1 = \delta_2 = ... = \delta_n = 0$ can be rejected, then x Granger-causes y. The hypothesis can be tested by conventional procedures such as an F-test or a likelihood ratio test, the only problem being to choose the lag lengths m and n so as to ensure that the residual v_t is white noise and that all relevant lags of x_t are included in the regression.

Tests of the hypothesis that y Granger-causes x can be carried out simply by transposing x_t and y_t in (18), but there is no reason to preclude the possibility that y Granger-causes x *and* x Granger-causes y, i.e. that there is *feedback* between x and y. This is most easily analyzed using a *vector autoregression* (VAR) of the two variables. A VAR of order p, denoted VAR(p), in x and y can be written as

$$x_t = \theta_{10} + \sum_{i=1}^{p} \theta_{11i} x_{t-i} + \sum_{i=1}^{p} \theta_{12i} y_{t-i} + v_{1t}$$

$$y_t = \theta_{20} + \sum_{i=1}^{p} \theta_{21i} x_{t-i} + \sum_{i=1}^{p} \theta_{22i} y_{t-i} + v_{2t}. \tag{19}$$

The hypothesis that y does not Granger-cause x is thus H_0: $\theta_{121} = \theta_{122} = ... = \theta_{12p} = 0$, while x does not Granger-cause y is encapsulated in $H_0 : \theta_{211} = \theta_{212} = ... = \theta_{21p} = 0$. If both hypotheses are rejected then there is feedback between the variables.

The VAR framework also allows *spurious causality* resulting from the omission of, say, a third variable z to be investigated. To examine the consequences of causality between x and y being dependent upon z, lags of z are simply introduced into the VAR equations (19), while patterns of causality within the trivariate system (x,y,z) can be investigated using a VAR of dimension 3: for a development of causality testing in VARs, see Mills (1990a, chapter 14).

It is important to note that no contemporaneous values of y and x are included as regressors in the VAR equations (19). If they were, then the two equations making up the VAR would be statistically indistinguishable from each other and there would be an identification problem, a manifestation of the assertion that "correlation does not imply causation." But, of course, contemporaneous relationships between economic variables are a typical occurrence and a model that cannot allow for them would be of little use to economists. Contemporaneous correlations enter the VAR through a nonzero covariance between the errors v_{1t} and v_{2t}. These errors are assumed to be zero mean white noise processes, with variances σ_1^2 and σ_2^2, which are independent of each other except contemporaneously, so that $E(v_{1s}v_{2t})=\sigma_{12}$ for $s=t$ and zero for $s\neq t$.

Estimation of VARs is straightforward: OLS applied to each equation in isolation will yield consistent and efficient estimates of the VAR coefficients, while the estimated variances and covariances of the residuals will provide estimates of the corresponding moments of the innovations. Of course, the order of the VAR, p, must first be determined: this can either be set *a priori*, or chosen by some statistical criterion (see, for example, Mills, 1990a, chapter 14 for discussion).

To provide further analysis of VARs, it is convenient to use a matrix formulation, although we set $p=1$ and ignore constant terms for simplicity. Thus suppose we have a VAR of dimension m in the variables $x_1,x_2,...,x_m$, gathered together in the vector x. The VAR can then be written

$$\begin{pmatrix} x_{1t} \\ x_{2t} \\ \vdots \\ x_{mt} \end{pmatrix} = \begin{pmatrix} \theta_{11} & \theta_{12} & \cdots & \theta_{1m} \\ \theta_{21} & \theta_{22} & \cdots & \theta_{2m} \\ \vdots & \vdots & & \vdots \\ \theta_{m1} & \theta_{m2} & \cdots & \theta_{mm} \end{pmatrix} \begin{pmatrix} x_{1t-1} \\ x_{2t-1} \\ \vdots \\ x_{mt-1} \end{pmatrix} + \begin{pmatrix} v_{1t} \\ v_{2t} \\ \vdots \\ v_{mt} \end{pmatrix}$$

or

$$x_t = \theta x_{t-1} + v_t. \tag{20}$$

The error vector $v_t' = (v_{1t},v_{2t},...,v_{mt})$ has zero mean and covariance matrix

$$E(v_t v_s') = \begin{cases} \Sigma \text{ (positive definite)}, & t=s \\ 0 & t\neq s. \end{cases}$$

An important equivalent way of writing (20) is as the *moving average representation* (MAR)

$$x_t = v_t + \sum_{i=1}^{\infty} \Psi_i v_{t-i}, \qquad (21)$$

where the elements of the Ψ_i matrices are functions of the θ coefficients. The MAR enables the dynamic relationships between the x variables to be examined in greater detail, because the Ψ_i matrices can be interpreted as the dynamic multipliers of the system since they represent the model's response to a unit shock in each of the variables. The response of x_i to a unit shock in x_j (i.e. to v_{jt} taking the value unity) is given by the sequence, known as the *impulse response function*,

$$\psi_{ij1}, \ \psi_{ij2}, \ \psi_{ij3}, \dots,$$

where ψ_{ijk} is the ijth element of the matrix Ψ_k. There is, however, a complication caused by the fact that the components of v_t can be contemporaneously correlated. If these correlations are high, simulation of a shock to x_j, while all other components of x are held constant, could be misleading, as there is no way of separating out the response of x_i to x_j from its response to other shocks that are correlated with the shock to x_j.

A popular method of overcoming this complication is to transform the MAR into *recursive* form. We do this by defining the lower triangular matrix S such that $SS' = \Sigma$, using which we can define the *orthogonalized innovations* $n_t = S^{-1} v_t$, which have the property that $E(n_t n_t') = I_m$, i.e. that they are contemporaneously uncorrelated. The MAR can then be renormalized as

$$x_t = \Psi_0^* n_t + \sum_{i=1}^{\infty} \Psi_i^* n_{t-i},$$

where $\Psi_i^* = \Psi_i S^{-1}$, so that $\Psi_0^* = S^{-1}$ is lower triangular. The impulse response function of x_i to a unit shock in x_j is then given by the sequence Ψ_{ij0}^*, Ψ_{ij1}^*, Ψ_{ij2}^*, ... The uncorrelatedness of the n_ts allows the error variance of the H step-ahead forecast of x_i to be decomposed into components accounted for by these shocks, or innovations as they are sometimes called: hence the phrase coined by Sims (1981) for this technique, that of *innovation accounting*. In particular, the components of this error variance accounted for by shocks to x_j is given by

$$\sum_{h=0}^{H} \Psi_{ijh}^{*2}.$$

For large H, this *variance decomposition* allows the isolation of those relative contributions to variability that are, intuitively, 'persistent.' Further details of this technique are provided by Sims (1980, 1982) but, as these references point out, there is an important disadvantage to the technique.

The choice of S matrix is not unique, so that a different ordering of the x variables will change S, thus altering the Ψ^*_{ijk} coefficients and hence the impulse response functions and variance decompositions. The extent of these changes will depend upon the size of the contemporaneous correlations between the shocks. This noninvariance property has generated much detailed analysis and criticism of the variance decomposition methodology, focusing on the inability of VARs to be regarded as "structural" in the traditional econometric sense, so that shocks cannot be uniquely identified with a particular variable unless prior identifying assumptions are made, without which the computed impulse response functions and variance decompositions would be invalid.

To make this point more concrete, let us assume that there is a *structural* model linking the variables in x of the form

$$A_0 x_t = A_1 x_{t-1} + B e_t; \tag{22}$$

e_t is a vector of *structural disturbances*, assumed to have zero cross-correlation: hence $E(e_t e'_t) = D$, a diagonal matrix. The diagonal elements of A_0 and B are normalized to unity: this associates each structural equation with a natural left-hand side variable and with a particular structural disturbance. Contemporaneous interactions are captured by nonzero off-diagonal elements in these matrices; A_0 capturing interactions between the variables, B modeling the direct effects of disturbances on variables other than those appearing on the left-hand side of the structural equations.

Premultiplying both sides of (22) by A_0^{-1} gives the reduced form

$$x_t = A_0^{-1} A_1 x_{t-1} + A_0^{-1} B e_t \tag{23}$$

which is the VAR (20) on defining $\theta = A_0^{-1} A_1$ and $A_0 v_t = B e_t$. This latter expression makes it clear that the reduced form, VAR, errors v_t are linear combinations of the structural disturbances e_t – hence the need for identifying restrictions. The triangular orthogonalization discussed above follows from the fact that $A_0 \Sigma A'_0 = BDB'$ and hence $S^{-1} = B^{-1} A_0$. The assumption that S^{-1} is lower triangular is then satisfied if B is diagonal and A_0 is lower triangular.

Numerous authors have argued that these assumptions have no particular economic rationale, that they are *atheoretical*, using the term of Cooley and Leroy (1985; see also Leamer, 1985). This has led to the development of other sets of identifying restrictions that are based more explicitly on macroeconomic considerations. Bernanke (1986), Blanchard and Watson (1986) and Blanchard (1989), for example, impose sets of restrictions on the A_0 and B matrices which are consistent with a particular (Keynesian) macroeconomic perspective. Since these two matrices relate the reduced form shocks and structural disturbances through the relationship

$A_0 v_t = B e_t$, these restrictions in effect constrain the short-run impact of shocks to the x variables.

Blanchard and Quah (1989) and Shapiro and Watson (1988), on the other hand, exploit a different set of restrictions which constrain the long-run effects of shocks to x and thus impose restrictions across A_0, A_1 and B. The Blanchard–Quah restrictions can be obtained in the following way. Note that (23) can be "solved" as

$$x_t = \sum_{i=0}^{\infty} \Phi_i e_{t-i},$$

where

$$\Phi_i = (A_0^{-1} B)(A_0^{-1} A_1)^i.$$

Since the variables making up x_t are assumed to be stationary, we suppose that x_1, say, is the first difference of a variable, Y, that contains a single unit root. A shock to x_1, for example, will have no long-run effect on $x_1 = \nabla Y_t$, but will have a long-run effect on Y that is given by $\sum_{i=0}^{\infty} \Phi_{11i}$. For such a shock to have no long-run effect on Y, as required by Blanchard and Quah, we must have that $\sum_{i=0}^{\infty} \Phi_{11i} = 0$ which, from the definition of Φ_i, places restrictions on the structural matrices A_0, A_1 and B.

It is also possible to use combinations of short- and long-run restrictions and, as long as the restrictions are not overidentifying, a two-step estimation approach can be used. This estimates the unconstrained reduced form (VAR) in the first stage and then recovers the A_0 and B matrices using the estimated reduced form errors and the set of identifying restrictions. The structural disturbances can then be obtained from $A_0 v_t = B e_t$.

The above discussion has made explicit that this analysis of VARs and their associated techniques assumes that all the variables appearing in the x vector are stationary, possible after an initial transformation such as first differencing. When some or all of the variables are nonstationary then matters become somewhat more complicated, particularly when drawing inferences from estimated models: for example, Granger causality tests typically have nonstandard distributions. The analysis of nonstationary multivariate models is the topic to which we now turn.

Nonstationarity, differencing and cointegration

As intimated above, when building multivariate models involving nonstationary variables, care must be taken to ensure that any inferences drawn from the models are valid. As an example of this, consider the well known problem in econometrics of "nonsense" or "spurious" regressions. Granger and Newbold (1974) have examined the likely empirical consequences of such regressions, focusing attention on the standard textbook warning about the presence of serially correlated errors invalidating conventional procedures of inference. In particular, they were concerned with the specification of regression equations in terms of the *levels* of economic times series which, as has been shown above, are typically nonstationary, often appearing to be near random walks. Such regression equations, argue Granger and Newbold, frequently have high R^2-statistics yet also typically display highly autocorrelated residuals, indicated by very low Durbin–Watson (DW)-statistics. They contend that, in such situations, the usual significance tests performed on the regression coefficients can be very misleading, and they provide Monte Carlo simulation evidence to show that conventional significance tests are seriously biased towards rejection of the null hypothesis of no relationship, and hence towards acceptance of a spurious relationship, even when the series are generated as statistically independent random walks.

These findings led Granger and Newbold (1974) to suggest that, in the joint circumstances of a high R^2 and a low DW-statistic (a useful rule of thumb being $R^2 > DW$), regressions should be run on the first differences of the variables, and these essentially empirical conclusions have since been placed on a firm analytical foundation by Phillips (1986) and Phillips and Durlauf (1986).

Nevertheless, even given the strong implication from these studies that regression analysis using the levels of economic time series can only be undertaken with great care, many economists feel unhappy about analyzing regressions fitted to first differences, which is the obvious "time series analyst" solution to the nonstationarity problem. Phrases like "throwing the baby out with the bath water" and, less prosaically, "valuable long-run information being lost" are often heard. These worries center around the existence of long-run, steady state equilibria, a concept to which (primarily static) economic theory devotes considerable attention.

To develop this argument, consider a simple dynamic model of the form

$$y_t = \alpha + \beta x_t + \gamma x_{t-1} + \delta y_{t-1} + u_t, \tag{24}$$

where all variables are measured in logarithms. In steady state equilibrium, in which $y_t = y_{t-1} = y_e$, $x_t = x_{t-1} = x_e$ and $u_e = 0$, we have the solution

$$y_e = \alpha_1 + \beta_1 x_e,$$

where $\alpha_1 = \alpha/(1-\delta)$ and $\beta_1 = (\beta + \gamma)/(1-\delta)$. If, on the other hand, the differenced model

$$\nabla y_t = \beta \nabla x_t + \gamma \nabla x_{t-1} + \delta \nabla y_{t-1} + v_t \tag{25}$$

is considered, all differences are zero in the steady state and so no solution is obtainable: we can say nothing about the long-run relationship between

y_t and x_t. Moreover, in a constant growth equilibrium, where $\nabla y = \nabla x = g$, the levels model (24) has the solution

$$y_e = \alpha_2 + \beta_1 x_e,$$

where $\alpha_2 = (\alpha - g(\gamma + \delta))/(1 - \delta)$; this, of course, reducing to the steady state equilibrium solution when $g = 0$. The differenced model (25) again has no such solution in terms of y_e and x_e.

Of course, models relating series generated by DS, or *integrated*, processes may indeed not provide any information about long-run relationships; such relationships may simply not exist. But it is obviously important to allow for their possibility when building models between economic time series, which just using differenced variables will fail to do.

There is, in fact, a linkage between these two, seemingly diametrically opposed, views of the model building process. This is the concept of *cointegration*, which offers a connection between relationships between integrated processes and the concept of (steady state) equilibrium. This was originally introduced by Granger (1981) and a formal development is contained in Engle and Granger (1987); useful elementary discussion of the concept may be found in Granger (1986) and the implications it has for econometric modeling are discussed in Hendry (1986) and reviewed in, for example, Dolado, Jenkinson and Sosvilla-Rivero (1990), Dickey, Jansen and Thornton (1991) and Banerjee and Hendry (1992).

Some useful notation is needed to develop the concept of cointegration. A time series that requires differencing d times for it to be stationary is said to be an *integrated process of order d*, denoted $I(d)$. Thus a series that is already stationary is $I(0)$, while if a series is $I(1)$ its first difference is stationary. These two processes are sufficient for our purposes, although a completely general analysis in terms of vector $I(d)$ processes is available in Engle and Granger (1987).

An $I(1)$ series will be rather smooth, with dominant long swings, when compared to an $I(0)$ series. Because the variance of an $I(1)$ series goes to infinity, while an $I(0)$ series has finite variance, the sum of an $I(0)$ and an $I(1)$ series will be $I(1)$. Moreover, if x_t and y_t are both $I(1)$, then it is *generally* true that the linear combination

$$z_t = y_t - \beta x_t \tag{26}$$

will also be $I(1)$. However, it is possible for z_t to be $I(0)$ and, when this occurs, a special constraint operates on the long-run components of x_t and y_t. Since x_t and y_t are both $I(1)$, they will be dominated by "long-wave" components, but z_t, being $I(0)$, will not be: y_t and βx_t must therefore have long-run components that virtually cancel out to produce z_t. In such circumstances, x_t and y_t are said to be cointegrated, with β being called the cointegrating parameter; equivalently, they can be said to contain a *common trend* (Stock and Watson, 1988).

To relate this idea to the concept of long-run equilibrium, suppose that such an equilibrium is defined by the relationship

$$y_t = \beta x_t$$

or

$$y_t - \beta x_t = 0.$$

Thus z_t given by (26) measures the extent to which the system (x_t, y_t) is out of equilibrium, and can therefore be termed the "equilibrium error." Hence if x_t and y_t are both $I(1)$, then the equilibrium error will be $I(0)$ and z_t will rarely drift far from zero, if it has zero mean, and will often cross the zero line. In other words, equilibrium will occasionally occur, whereas if x_t and y_t are not cointegrated, so that z_t is $I(1)$, the equilibrium error can wander widely and zero-crossings would be rare, suggesting that under such circumstances the concept of equilibrium has no practical implications.

It is this feature of cointegration that links it with the spurious regression analysis discussed earlier. A regression on the differences of time series provides no information about the long-run equilibrium relationship, which can only be provided by a regression estimated on the levels of the data. But, if the series are integrated, standard statistical inference on levels regression breaks down completely, except in one special case: when the series are cointegrated![8] Thus, only if integrated series are cointegrated can inference be carried out on models estimated in levels, and only if they are cointegrated is there a meaningful equilibrium relationship between them. If the series are not cointegrated, then there is no equilibrium relationship existing between them and analysis *should* therefore be undertaken on their differences.

The importance of being able to test whether a pair, or in general a vector, of integrated time series are cointegrated is thus clear. Furthermore, given that such series are cointegrated, estimation of the cointegrating parameter (in general, the cointegrating vector) is then an essential second step. In fact, such testing and estimation are intimately related.

As a prerequisite it must first be determined whether x_t and y_t are $I(1)$ processes: this can be done by using the unit root tests introduced earlier. Given that both series are $I(1)$ processes, a convenient method of testing whether they are cointegrated is to estimate the "cointegrating regression"

$$y_t = \alpha + \beta x + u_t \qquad (27)$$

and then test if the residual $\hat{u}_t$ appears to be $I(0)$ or not. Although a number of tests have been proposed, perhaps the simplest is to perform a unit root test on the residuals, i.e to estimate the regression

$$\hat{u}_t = \rho\hat{u}_{t-1} + \sum_{j=1}^{l}\gamma_j\nabla\hat{u}_{t-j} + e_t$$

and compute the usual $\hat{\tau}_\rho$ statistic to test the hypothesis that $\rho=1$, i.e. to test the null hypothesis that y and x are *not* cointegrated: rejection of this null is evidence that they *are* cointegrated. The use of residuals in this test invalidates the Fuller (1976) critical values, but Mackinnon (1991) provides the appropriate tables, extended to situations when there are more than two variables being considered.

When x_t and y_t are cointegrated, the OLS estimate $\hat{\beta}$ of the slope coefficient in (27) should provide, in large samples, an excellent estimate of the true cointegration parameter, even though the error u_t will typically be highly serially correlated. The reasoning for this is as follows. If x_t and y_t are cointegrated, then u_t will be $I(0)$ and will have a finite variance. All omitted dynamics in (27) can be reparameterized purely in terms of ∇y_{t-i}, ∇x_{t-j} and $(y_{t-k}-\hat{\beta}x_{t-k})$, all of which are $I(0)$ under cointegration and therefore can be subsumed within u_t. Thus β can be *consistently* estimated despite the complete omission of all dynamics. Furthermore, it is also the case that OLS estimates of β are highly efficient, with $\hat{\beta}$ converging rapidly to β at a rate that is much faster than that of standard econometric estimators (Stock, 1987). Of course, the conventional least squares formula for estimating the variance of $\hat{\beta}$ remains invalid due to the serial correlation in u_t.

How, though, does the existence of cointegration between y_t and x_t enable equilibrium relationships to be modeled while at the same time avoiding difficult problems of statistical inference? It does so through Granger's Representation Theorem (Engle and Granger, 1987). This shows that if y_t and x_t are both $I(1)$ and cointegrated, then there exists an *error correction representation*, a simple form of which is

$$\nabla y_t = \omega_0 + \omega_1\nabla x_t - \gamma(y_{t-1} - \beta x_{t-1}) + \epsilon_t. \tag{28}$$

All terms in (28) are $I(0)$, so that no inferential difficulties arise. When $\nabla y_t = \nabla x_t = 0$ the "no change" steady state equilibrium of

$$y_t = \beta x_t + \omega_0/\gamma$$

is reproduced, while the steady state growth path, obtained when $\nabla y_t = \nabla x_t = g$, takes the form

$$y_t = \beta x_t + (\omega_0 - g(1 - \omega_1))/\gamma.$$

Models of this simple form have been shown to be capable of being generated by a variety of economic mechanisms based upon minimizing adjustment costs in a partial manner: for a survey, see Alogoskoufis and Smith (1991).

The implications of cointegrated variables can also be analyzed within the VAR framework discussed on pp. 34–35. An alternative way of writing the VAR(p) model

$$x_t = \sum_{i=1}^{p} \theta_i x_{t-i} + v_t$$

is as

$$\nabla x_t = \sum_{i=1}^{p-1} C_i \nabla x_{t-i} + C_p x_{t-p} + v_t, \qquad (29)$$

where $\nabla x_t = x_t - x_{t-1}$ and

$$C_i = -I + \sum_{j=1}^{i} \theta_j \qquad j=1,...,p.$$

Suppose that each of the m components of x_t is $I(1)$. There can then be $r < m$ *cointegrating vectors*, in which case there exists an $r \times m$ matrix B', of rank r, such that $B'x_t$ is stationary. Granger's Representation Theorem then asserts that

$$C_p = -I + \theta_1 + ... + \theta_p = \gamma B',$$

where γ is an $m \times r$ matrix of coefficients of rank r. The VAR (29) then becomes

$$\nabla x_t = \sum_{i=1}^{p-1} C_i \nabla x_{t-i} + \gamma B' x_{t-p} + v_t, \qquad (30)$$

which is the vector generalization of the error correction model (28) and hence may be referred to as a VECM. If there is no cointegration between the variables, $r=0$, $\gamma=0$ and (30) is simply a VAR in the first differences ∇x_t. This representation forms the basis for Johansen's (1988) multivariate test of cointegration, in which the maximum number of cointegrating vectors, $\hat{r}$, is determined and the associated matrix of cointegrating vectors, $\hat{B}$, is estimated.[9]

With the matrix of cointegrating vectors, B, estimated, so that $B'x_t$ can be calculated, estimation of the system (30) is a straightforward application of least squares, leading to maximum likelihood estimates of the C_i and Σ (Johansen, 1988). Other representations of cointegrated systems are possible, however, and these can lead to other modeling strategies. Phillips and Loretan (1991) provide a detailed discussion of these alternatives, focusing amongst other things on their small sample performance. They find that a single equation technique, related to the error correction representation, and which is asymptotically equivalent to Johansen's system maximum likelihood estimator, has excellent small sample properties. Suppose we partition x_t as (y_t, x_{1t}), and that the single cointegrating relationship is $y_t = \beta' x_{1t} + u_t$, where u_t is a stationary error term. The cointegrating vector β and the short-run dynamics of the relationship can be jointly estimated from the equation.

$$y_t = \beta' x_{1t} + \delta_0 + \sum_{i=1}^{k} \delta_{1i}(y_{t-i} - \beta' x_{1,t-i}) + \sum_{i=-K_1}^{K_2} \delta_{2i} \nabla x_{1,t-i} + v_t. \tag{31}$$

Note that future values of ∇x_1 are included as regressors – this accounts for feedback from y to x_1 and produces an asymptotically efficient estimator of β, which has to be estimated by *nonlinear* least squares, given the way that this vector appears in (31). Because such an estimation technique can have computational disadvantages, Phillips and Loretan suggest that a two-stage modeling procedure may be preferable. This is to estimate β by a system method such as maximum likelihood, and then to use this estimate in the construction of an error correction-type model for each of the dependent variables, such as

$$(y_t - \hat{\beta}' x_{1t}) = \delta_0 + \sum_{i=1}^{k} \delta_{1i}(y_{t-i} - \hat{\beta}' x_{1,t-i}) + \sum_{i=0}^{K} \delta_{2i} \nabla x_{1,t-i} + v_t, \tag{32}$$

no leads of ∇x_1 being required as the first stage estimation of β takes account of any feedback.

Finally, we note that "structural" VARs can also be specified within a cointegration framework. For example, King, Plosser, Stock and Watson (1991) and Cochrane (1994) discuss how Blanchard–Quah-type restrictions involving permanent and transitory innovations can be incorporated within the VECM (31).

Conclusions

As this chapter has shown, recent advances in time series econometrics has altered beyond recognition how macroeconomists tackle important empirical questions, particularly of the type considered in this volume. Many of the subsequent chapters use unit root and cointegration tests as a matter of course in their analysis (see Dick, Floyd and Pope, chapter 8 and Taylor and Wood, chapter 10), while others utilize some of the more specific techniques discussed. For example, Hallwood, MacDonald and Marsh (chapter 5) use the variance ratio test to examine mean reversion in exchange rates during the gold standard.

Several chapters utilize structural VARs: for example, both Calomiris and Hubbard (chapter 7) and Kaminsky and Klein (chapter 11) employ structural VARs identified using the framework of Bernanke (1986) and Blanchard (1989), although while the former employ differenced data in their formulation of an international business cycle model, the latter concentrate on modeling the levels of the real exchange rate and related variables, thus implicitly assuming that their series do not contain unit roots. Bayoumi and Eichengreen, on the other hand (chapter 6), identify their macroeconomic model by way of Blanchard–Quah (1989) long-run restrictions.

It is clear from these chapters that such econometric techniques have enhanced the research reported here and enabled important questions to be analyzed and, in some cases, to be resolved satisfactorily.

Notes

1. This result is proved in Pierce (1978), albeit in the context of seasonal adjustment. It is also natural to ask for what model of the observed series y will a moving average provide an optimal trend estimate. This question has been considered by Tiao and Hillmer (1978), unfortunately only in the limited case when the cyclical component is assumed to be serially uncorrelated. However, in this case the models for y would appear to be autoregressive processes of order $h-1$ in the first differences, thus again pointing towards the procedure being suboptimal for the typical series having only weakly autocorrelated first differences.
2. A series is said to be stationary (or, to be more precise, *weakly* stationary) if its mean and variance are constant through time and its autocovariances (the covariance between ϵ_t and ϵ_{t-k} for values of k) depend only on the time lag k and not on time itself: for further discussion, see, for example, Mills (1990a, chapter 5).
3. A related distinction between the two processes is in their forecasting properties. The forecast errors from a TS process are bounded no matter how far into the future forecasts are made because ϵ_t has finite variance. Moreover, while autocorrelation in ϵ_t can be exploited in making short-term (cyclical) forecasts, over long horizons the only relevant information about a future y is its mean, $\alpha+\beta t$, so that neither current nor past events will alter long-term expectations. Contrast this with forecasts made from a DS process. Here the forecast error variance will increase without bound, since it is an increasing function of time, while long-term forecasts will always be influenced by historical events through the accumulation of the shocks e_t. The actual form of the trend component of a DS process will be discussed later in the chapter.

   Furthermore, as West (1987) points out, if y is DS then, since all shocks are permanent, the concept of a stationary natural rate of growth will have little meaning, for a shock will, on average, never be offset by a return to some constant trend growth rate.
4. Note that the test can also be carried out by using the conventional t-statistic for testing whether the coefficient of y_{t-1} is zero in the regression of (y_t-y_{t-1}) on a constant, t and y_{t-1}.

5. Both $\hat{\tau}_\rho$ and Φ_3 are invariant with respect to y_0 and α, but they are not invariant with respect to β, the trend parameter, even asymptotically. In practice this is not a problem in the type of situations typically of interest to economic historians, since one usually wishes to test for a series with a unit root and a drift *against* the hypothesis that the series is stationary around a linear trend. The hypothesis of a unit root with a trend is usually excluded *a priori* since, if y is in logarithms, it implies an ever-increasing (or decreasing) rate of change. If the null hypothesis is that of a unit root without a drift and the alternative is simply that of a stationary series, as might be the case with interest or exchange rates, then a different set of regressions and test statistics must be used. Both these and more general testing procedures are discussed in, for example, Dolado, Jenkinson and Sosvilla-Rivero (1990).
6. This representation, known as the Wold decomposition, is a perfectly general one and is the foundation of time series analysis (see, for example, Mills, 1990a, chapter 5).
7. The formula for generating the λ_j weights may be found in, for example, Watson (1986). Note that, in general, (14) is an *infinite* two-sided moving average. In practice, with only a finite sample of observations $Y^T = \{y_0, y_1, ..., y_T\}$ available, unknown values $y_{-1}, y_{-2}, ...$ and $y_{T+1}, y_{T+2}, ...$ may be replaced by their forecasts constructed from Y^T and the model for y_t.
8. The formal development of these arguments may be found in Stock (1987), Phillips and Durlauf (1986) and Sims, Stock and Watson (1990). Mills (1990a, chapter 13) provides a textbook discussion of these matters.
9. A number of other tests for cointegration have been proposed: the common trends test of Stock and Watson (1988), the related approach of Fountis and Dickey (1989), the spectral regression technique of Phillips and Ouliaris (1988) and the error correction formulation of Kremers, Ericsson and Dolado (1992). Similarly, there are alternative ways of estimating the cointegrating vector: for example, Engle and Yoo's (1991) "three-step" estimator, Phillips and Hansen's (1990) and Park's (1992) two-step frequency-zero seemingly unrelated regression estimators, and Saikkonen's (1991) and Stock and Watson's (1993) "dynamic OLS and GLS" estimators.

References

Alogoskoufis, G. and R. Smith (1991). "On Error Correction Models: Specification, Interpretation, Estimation," *Journal of Economic Surveys* 5, 97–128

Banerjee, A. and D. F. Hendry (1992). "Testing Integration and Cointegration: An Overview," *Oxford Bulletin of Economics and Statistics* 54, 225–255

Bernanke, B. S. (1986). "Alternative Explanations of the Money–Income Correlation," *Carnegie–Rochester Series on Public Policy* 25 (Autumn), 49–100

Beveridge, S. and C. R. Nelson (1981). "A New Approach to Decomposition of Economic Time Series into Permanent and Transitory Components with Particular Attention to Measurement of the 'Business Cycle'," *Journal of Monetary Economics* 7, 151–174

Blackburn, K. and M. Ravn (1992). "Business Cycles in the UK: Facts and Fictions," *Economica* 59, 383–401

Blanchard, O. J. (1989). "A Traditional Interpretation of Macroeconomic Fluctuations," *American Economic Review* 79, 1146–1164

Blanchard, O. J. and D. Quah (1989). "The Dynamic Effects of Aggregate Demand and Supply Disturbances," *American Economic Review* 79, 655–673

Blanchard, O. J. and M. W. Watson (1986). "Are Business Cycles All Alike?," in R. Gordon (ed.), *The American Business Cycle: Continuity and Change*, Chicago: NBER and University of Chicago Press, 123–156

Box, G. E. P. and G. M. Jenkins (1976). *Time Series Analysis: Forecasting and Control*, rev. ed., San Francisco: Holden–Day

Campbell, J. Y. and P. Perron (1991). "Pitfalls and Opportunities: What Macroeconomists Should Know About Unit Roots," in O. Blanchard and S. Fischer (eds.), *NBER Macroeconomics Annual 1991*, Cambridge, MA: MIT Press, 141–201

Capie, F. H. and T. C. Mills (1992). "Money and Business Cycles in the United States: A Reexamination of Friedman and Schwartz," *Explorations in Economic History* 29, 251–273

Christiano, L. (1992). "Searching for Breaks in GNP," *Journal of Business and Economic Statistics* 10, 237–250

Clark, P. K. (1987). "The Cyclical Component of US Activity," *Quarterly Journal of Economics* 103, 797–814

Cochrane, J. H. (1988). "How Big is the Random Walk in GNP?," *Journal of Political Economy* 96, 893–920

(1994). "Permanent and Transitory Components of GNP and Stock Prices," *Quarterly Journal of Economics* 109, 241–265

Cooley, T. F. and S. F. Leroy (1985). "Atheoretical Macroeconometrics: A Critique," *Journal of Monetary Economics* 16, 283–308

Crafts, N. F. R., S. J. Leybourne and T. C. Mills (1989). "Trends and Cycles in British Industrial Production, 1700–1913," *Journal of the Royal Statistical Society, Series A* 152, 43–60

(1990). "Measurement of Trend Growth in European Industrial Output Before 1914: Methodological Issues and New Estimates," *Explorations in Economic History* 27, 442–467

DeJong, D. N., J. C. Nankervis, N. E. Savin and C. H. Whiteman (1992a). "The Power Problems of Unit Root Tests in Time Series with Autoregressive Errors," *Journal of Econometrics* 53, 323–343

(1992b). "Integration Versus Trend Stationarity in Time Series," *Econometrica* 60, 423–433

Dickey, D. A. and W. A. Fuller (1979). "Distribution of the Estimators for Autoregressive Time Series with a Unit Root," *Journal of the American Statistical Association* 74, 427–431

(1981). "Likelihood Ratio Tests for Autoregressive Time Series with a Unit Root," *Econometrica* 49, 1057–1072

Dickey, D. A., J. W. Jansen and D. L. Thornton (1991). "A Primer on Cointegration with an Application to Money and Income," *Federal Reserve Bank of St. Louis Review* (2), 58–78

Dolado, J. J., T. Jenkinson and S. Sosvilla-Rivero (1990). "Cointegration and Unit Roots," *Journal of Economic Surveys* 4, 249–273

Engle, R. F. and C. W. J. Granger (1987). "Co-Integration and Error Correction: Representation, Estimation and Testing," *Econometrica* 55, 251–276

Engle R. F. and B. S. Yoo (1987). "Forecasting and Testing in Co-Integrated Systems," *Journal of Econometrics* 35, 143–159

(1991). "Cointegrated Economic Time Series: An Overview with New Results," in R. F. Engle and C. W. J. Granger (eds.), *Long-Run Economic Relationships*, Oxford: Oxford University Press, 237–265

Fountis, N. G. and D. A. Dickey (1989). "Testing for a Unit Root Nonstationarity in Multivariate Autoregressive Time Series," *Annals of Statistics* 17, 419–428

Fuller, W. A. (1976). *Introduction to Statistical Time Series*, New York: John Wiley

Granger, C. W. J. (1969). "Investigating Causal Relations by Econometric Models and Cross-Spectral Methods," *Econometrica* 37, 424–438

(1981). "Some Properties of Time Series Data and Their Use in Econometric Model Specification," *Journal of Econometrics* 16, 121–130

(1986). "Developments in the Study of Cointegrated Economic Variables," *Oxford Bulletin of Economics and Statistics* 48, 213–228

Granger, C. W. J. and P. Newbold (1974). "Spurious Regressions in Econometrics," *Journal of Econometrics* 2, 111–120

Guilkey, D. K. and P. Schmidt (1989). "Extended Tabulations for Dickey–Fuller Tests," *Economics Letters* 31, 355–357

Harvey, A. C. (1985). "Trends and Cycles in Macroeconomic Time Series," *Journal of Business and Economic Statistics* 3, 216–227

(1990). *Forecasting, Structural Time Series Models, and the Kalman Filter*, Cambridge: Cambridge University Press

Harvey, A. C. and A. Jaeger (1993). "Detrending, Stylized Facts and the Business Cycle," *Journal of Applied Econometrics* 8, 231–247

Hendry, D. F. (1986). "Econometric Modelling with Cointegrated Variables: An Overview," *Oxford Bulletin of Economics and Statistics* 48, 201–212

Hodrick, R. E. and E. C. Prescott (1980). "Postwar US Business Cycles: An Empirical Investigation," *Discussion Paper* 451, Carnegie–Mellon University

Johansen, S. (1988). "Statistical Analysis of Cointegration Vectors," *Journal of Economic Dynamics and Control* 12, 231–254

King, R. G., C. I. Plosser, J. H. Stock and M. W. Watson (1991). "Stochastic Trends and Economic Fluctuations," *American Economic Review* 81, 819–840

King, R. G. and S. T. Rebelo (1993). "Low Frequency Filtering and Real Business Cycles," *Journal of Economic Dynamics and Control* 17, 207–232

Kremers, J. J. M., N. R. Ericsson and J. J. Dolado (1992). "The Power of Cointegration Tests," *Oxford Bulletin of Economics and Statistics* 54, 325–348

Kwiatkowski, D., P. C. B. Phillips, P. Schmidt and Y. Shin (1992). "Testing the Null Hypothesis of Stationarity Against the Alternative of a Unit Root," *Journal of Econometrics* 54, 159–178

Kydland, F. E. and E. C. Prescott (1990). "Business Cycles: Real Facts and a Monetary Myth," *Federal Reserve Bank of Minneapolis, Quarterly Review* (Spring), 3–18

Leamer, E. E. (1985). "Vector Autoregressions for Causal Inference?," *Carnegie–Rochester Conference Series on Public Policy* 22, 255–304

Lo, A. W. and A. C. MacKinlay (1988). "Stock Prices do not Follow Random Walks: Evidence from a Simple Specification Test," *Review of Financial Studies* 1, 41–66

(1989). "The Size and Power of the Variance Ratio Test in Finite Samples: A Monte Carlo Investigation," *Journal of Econometrics* 40, 203–208

Mackinnon, J. G. (1991). "Critical Values for Cointegration Tests," in R. F. Engle and C. W. J. Granger (eds.), *Long-Run Economic Relationships*, Oxford: Oxford University Press, 267–287

Mills, T. C. (1990a). *Time Series Techniques for Economists*, Cambridge: Cambridge University Press

(1990b). "A Note on the Gibson Paradox Under the Gold Standard," *Explorations in Economic History* 27, 277–286

(1991). "Are Fluctuations in UK Output Permanent or Transitory?," *Manchester School* 59, 1–11

(1992). "An Economic Historian's Introduction to Modern Time Series Techniques in Econometrics," in S. N. Broadberry and N. F. R. Crafts (ed.), *Britain in the International Economy, 1870–1939*, Cambridge: Cambridge University Press, 28–46

(1994). "Segmented Trends and the Stochastic Properties of UK Output," *Applied Economics Letters* 1, 132–133

Nelson, C. R. and H. Kang (1981). "Spurious Periodicity in Inappropriately Detrended Time Series," *Econometrica* 49, 741–751

(1984). "Pitfalls in the Use of Time as an Explanatory Variable in Regression," *Journal of Business and Economic Statistics* 2, 73–82

Nelson, C. R. and C. I. Plosser (1982). "Trends and Random Walks in Macroeconomic Time Series: Some Evidence and Implications," *Journal of Monetary Economics* 10, 139–162

Park, J. Y. (1992). "Canonical Cointegrating Regressions," *Econometrica* 60, 119–144

Perron, P. (1988). "Trends and Random Walks in Macroeconomic Time Series: Further Evidence from a New Approach," *Journal of Economic Dynamics and Control* 12, 297–332

(1989). "The Great Crash, the Oil Price Shock and the Unit Root Hypothesis," *Econometrica* 57, 1361–1401

(1990). "Testing for a Unit Root in a Time Series With a Changing Mean," *Journal of Business and Economic Statistics* 8, 153–162

Phillips, P. C. B. (1986). "Understanding Spurious Regressions in Econometrics," *Journal of Econometrics* 33, 311–340

Phillips, P. C. B. and S. N. Durlauf (1986). "Multiple Time Series with Integrated Processes," *Review of Economic Studies* 53, 473–495

Phillips, P. C. B. and B. E. Hansen (1990). "Statistical Inference in Instrumental Variables Regression with $I(1)$ Processes," *Review of Economic Studies* 57, 99–125

Phillips, P. C. B. and M. Loretan (1991). "Estimating Long-run Economic Equilibria," *Review of Economic Studies* 58, 407–436

Phillips, P. C. B. and S. Ouliaris (1988). "Testing for Cointegration Using Principal Components Methods," *Journal of Economic Dynamics and Control* 12, 205–230

Phillips, P. C. B. and P. Perron (1988). "Testing for a Unit Root in Time Series Regression," *Biometrika* 75, 335–346

Pierce, D. A. (1978). "Seasonal Adjustment when both Deterministic and Stochastic Seasonality are Present," in A. Zellner (ed.), *Seasonal Analysis of Economic Time Series*, Washington, DC: US Department of Commerce, Bureau of the Census, 365–397

Pierce, D. A. and L. D. Haugh (1977). "Causality in Temporal Systems: Characterizations and a Survey," *Journal of Econometrics* 5, 265–293

Rappoport, P. and L. Reichlin (1989). "Segmented Trends and Non-stationary Time Series," *Economic Journal* 99 (Supplement), 168–177

Said, S. E. and D. A. Dickey (1984). "Testing for Unit Roots in Autoregressive Moving-Average Models with Unknown Order," *Biometrika* 71, 599–607

Saikkonen, P. (1991). "Asymptotically Efficient Estimation of Cointegrating Regressions," *Econometric Theory* 7, 1–21

Schwert, G. W. (1987). "Effects of Model Specification on Tests for Unit Roots in Macroeconomic Data," *Journal of Monetary Economics* 20, 73–103

(1989). "Tests for Unit Roots: A Monte Carlo Investigation," *Journal of Business and Economic Statistics* 7, 147–160

Shapiro, M. and M. W. Watson (1988). "Sources of Business Cycle Fluctuations," in S. Fischer (ed.), *NBER Macroeconomics Annual 1988*, Cambridge, MA: MIT Press, 111–156

Shiller, R. J. and P. Perron (1985). "Testing the Random Walk Hypothesis: Power Versus Frequency of Observation," *Economics Letters* 18, 381–386

Sims, C. A. (1980). "Macroeconomics and Reality," *Econometrica* 48, 1–48

(1981). "An Autoregressive Index Model for the US 1948–1975," in J. Kmenta and J. B. Ramsey (ed.), *Large-Scale Macroeconometric Models*, Amsterdam: North-Holland, 283–327

(1982). "Policy Analysis with Econometric Models," *Brookings Papers on Economic Activity* 1, 107–164

Sims, C. A., J. H. Stock and M. W. Watson (1990). "Inference in Linear Time Series Models with Unit Roots," *Econometrica* 58, 113–144

Stock, J. H. (1987). "Asymptotic Properties of Least Squares Estimators of Cointegrating Vectors," *Econometrica* 55, 1035–1056

(1991). "Confidence Intervals for the Largest Autoregressive Root in US Macroeconomic Time Series," *Journal of Monetary Economics* 28, 435–459

Stock, J. H. and M. W. Watson (1988). "Testing for Common Trends," *Journal of the American Statistical Association* 83, 1097–1107

(1993). "A Simple Estimator of Cointegrating Vectors in Higher Order Integrated Systems," *Econometrica* 61, 783–820

Tiao, G. C. and S. C. Hillmer (1978). "Some Consideration of Decomposition of a Time Series," *Biometrika* 65, 497–502

Watson, M. W. (1986). "Univariate Detrending Methods with Stochastic Trends," *Journal of Monetary Economics* 18, 49–75

West, K. D. (1987). "On the Interpretation of Near Random Walk Behavior in GNP," *American Economic Review* 78, 202–209

Zivot, E. and D. W. K. Andrews (1992). "Further Evidence on the Great Crash, the Oil Price Shock, and the Unit Root Hypothesis," *Journal of Business and Economic Statistics* 10, 251–270

II

Operation of the gold standard

3   The gold standard as a commitment mechanism

Michael D. Bordo and Finn E. Kydland

Introduction

The gold standard has been a subject of perennial interest to both economists and economic historians. Attention has focused on three aspects of the gold standard's performance: as an international exchange rate arrangement; as a provider of macroeconomic stability; and as a constraint on government policy actions.

The balance of payments adjustment mechanism, or the links between the money supplies, price levels, and real outputs of different countries under fixed exchange rates, has long been studied as the key aspect of the international exchange rate arrangement of the gold standard.[1] The durability of fixed exchange rates, the absence of exchange market crises, and the smooth adjustment to the massive transfers of capital in the decades before 1914 have been features stressed in monetary reform proposals ever since.

The gold standard has often been viewed as ensuring long-run, though not necessarily short-run, price stability via the operation of the Classical commodity theory of money. Recent comparisons between the classical gold standard and subsequent managed fiduciary monetary regimes suggest, however, that the record is mixed with respect both to price level and real output performance.[2]

Finally, the gold standard has also been viewed as a form of constraint over monetary policy actions – as a form of monetary rule. The Currency School in England in the early 19th century made the case for the Bank of England's fiduciary note issue to vary automatically with the level of the Bank's gold reserve ("the currency principle"). Following such a rule was viewed as preferable (for providing price level stability) to allowing the note issue to be altered at the discretion of the well meaning and possibly well informed directors of the Bank (the position taken by the opposing Banking School).[3]

In this chapter, we focus on the third aspect of the gold standard's performance – on the gold standard as a rule. However, our meaning of the concept of a "rule" differs radically from what used to be the traditional one. In our view, a rule can be regarded as a way of binding policy actions over time. This view of policy rules, in contrast to the earlier tradition that stressed both impersonality and automaticity, stems from the recent literature on the time inconsistency of optimal government policy. Suppose the government calculates today an optimal plan, according to its objectives, for current and future policy choices. Now suppose that, some time in the future, the remainder of the plan is re-evaluated by calculating the optimal plan from then on. Assuming the objectives have not changed, is this plan simply the continuation of the original one? The answer generally is "no." This is what it means for government policy to be time inconsistent. Discretion, in this context, means setting policy sequentially, which then could lead to policies and outcomes that are very different from the optimal plan. The literature on time inconsistency has demonstrated that, in almost all intertemporal policy situations, the government would benefit from having access to a commitment mechanism preventing it from changing planned future policy. In this chapter, we use that literature as a framework for understanding the historical operation of the gold standard.

For the period from 1880 to 1914, the gold standard is often viewed as a monolithic regime where all countries religiously followed the dictates of the rule of a fixed price of gold. Before 1880, most countries were on a form of specie standard: either bimetallism or silver or gold monometallism. As we point out below, however, from our perspective the bimetallic standards that many countries followed were a variant of the gold standard rule. This is contrasted to the period since 1914, when central banks and governments to a great extent have geared their policies to satisfy more immediate objectives without considering intertemporal consequences in terms of lack of commitment to a long-run rule governing policy. In this chapter, we show that the rule followed by a number of key countries – England, the United States, and France – before 1914 was consistent with such a commitment. The experiences of these major countries suggest that the gold standard was intended as a contingent rule. By that, we mean that the authorities could temporarily abandon the fixed price of gold during an emergency (such as a war) on the understanding that convertibility at the original price would be restored when the emergency passed.

The next section presents a framework for discussing the benefits of being able to commit to future government policy. Moreover, it interprets the institutions of the gold standard era in light of this framework. We then survey the historical record on the adherence to the gold standard rule by three core countries: England, the United States, and France, and by a country that is generally believed not to have adhered to the rule: Italy. The final section attempts to draw some lessons from history.

The gold standard as a contingent rule

The value of commitment

A long-standing question in public finance is how to finance varying quantities of government expenditures in such a way as to minimize deadweight loss to society. In the last decade, this question, which dates back to the pioneering work by Ramsey (1927), has shifted more and more from static to dynamic environments. We shall argue that the intertemporal framework presented in this literature is the appropriate one for evaluating the operation of the gold standard.

The focus of this literature initially centered around the incentives (in the absence of a commitment mechanism to prevent the government from changing its policy rule in the future) for excessive taxation of capital income. Clearly, however, similar arguments can be made with respect to the taxation of (or default on) government debt. We discuss the source of time inconsistency of optimal policy in both contexts. We start with the former because capital income, at least in this century, probably would be a main source of emergency financing, for example during a war, for a government without the credibility to issue much debt. Then, we introduce government debt policy, which we contend is the major reason why the gold standard was adhered to in some countries for long periods of time.

Consider the following prototype model of optimal taxation.[4] The economy is inhabited by a large number of consumers who, for simplicity, are treated as identical. Each consumer maximizes infinite-horizon discounted utility,

$$E\Sigma_{t=0}^{\infty}\beta^t u(c_t,n_t,g_t,\sigma_t),$$

where c_t is consumption, n_t is hours of work, g_t is *per capita* government purchases, and β is the subjective discount factor. The parameter σ_t is stochastic and may indicate, for instance, how the value of defense expenditures varies over time depending on the political situation. There is little loss of generality, however, in simply assuming that the g_t process itself is exogenous. Thus, the typical consumer is assumed to maximize

$$E\sum_{t=0}^{\infty}\beta^t u(c_t,n_t,g_t) \tag{1}$$

subject to

$$k_{t+1}+c_t\leq k_t+(1-\theta_t)r_t k_t+(1-\tau_t)w_t n_t$$

and nonnegativity constraints. Here, w_t is the real wage rate, and θ_t and τ_t are the tax rates for capital and labor income, respectively. One can think of k_t as including various forms of capital, with r_t being the rental income from owning the capital stock. With little modification, one could also include human capital, which in practice can be taxed more heavily, for example, by increasing the progressivity of the income tax schedule.

In this economy, consumers choose sequences of c_t, n_t, and k_{t+1}, while the government decides on sequences θ_t and τ_t. Interpreting aggregate quantities as measured in *per capita* terms, a formulation of the optimal taxation problem is: choose a sequence

$$\pi_0 = \{\theta_t, \tau_t\}_{t=0}^\infty$$

so as to maximize the typical consumer's utility function (1) subject to the government budget constraint

$$g_t \leq \theta_t r_t k_t + \tau_t w_t n_t$$

and the constraints implied by equilibrium aggregate behavior of the atomistic private agents. Their decisions can be written as sequences

$$x_0(\pi_0) = \{c_t(c_t(\pi_0), \quad n_t(\pi_0), \quad k_{t+1}(\pi_0)\}_{t=0}^\infty;$$

in other words, the equilibrium aggregate private decisions at any time t depend on the entire sequence of government policy. The solution, π_0^*, to this optimal taxation problem, together with the associated equilibrium, $x_0(\pi_0^*)$, is sometimes called a Ramsey allocation.

The heart of the time consistency issue is as follows. Suppose π_0^* is the plan that solves the optimal taxation problem as of time zero. Imagine now that the analogous problem is contemplated as of time $s>0$. The optimal taxation problem then has a solution π_s^*, which generally is different from the part of π_0^* that specifies the plan for periods $t=s,s+1,...$ In other words, the original plan, π_0^*, is inconsistent with the passage of time. The reason is that π_0^* takes into account the effects of government policy planned for dates on or after period s on private behavior at dates before s. At time s, however, when π_s^* is computed, private behavior at earlier dates, of course, can no longer be affected.

This prototype model highlights two points. One is that the source of time inconsistency is not that the objective function of the government has a different form than the individuals' utility functions. Secondly, time inconsistency arises in spite of an unchanging objective function over time. Instead, the key factor is that decisions are made sequentially over time in environments in which future government policy affects current private behavior.

In the optimal plan, when an increase in g_t occurs, the effects on labor input of raising τ_t are weighed against the effects on savings behavior from changing θ_t. Once the capital stock is in place, however, the optimal plan from then on, taking history up to that point as given, is to tax that capital more heavily, as it will be supplied inelastically, and to reduce future capital taxation. Of course, such an action by the government is likely to create the belief among the public that a similar change of plans will take place again some time in the future, government announcements to the contrary notwithstanding.

This framework assumes that the government balances its budget in every period. If the changes in government expenditures at times are large, for example during wars, the required changes in tax rates would severely reduce the incentives for economic activity just when the need for such activity is the greatest. Borrowing from the public gives the government the flexibility to smooth tax rates over time. The benefits of tax smoothing, not only during wars, but also under normal circumstances, are discussed in Barro (1979) and in Kydland and Prescott (1980b).

Introducing debt affects neither consumers' objectives nor those of the government. The key difference is in the budget constraints. To illustrate, we use notation that follows closely that of Chari and Kehoe (1989), who build upon the characterization of Ramsey policies with debt in Lucas and Stokey (1983). Consider the government budget constraint,

$$g_t + (1 - \delta_t) q_t \cdot b_t \leq a_t + q_t \cdot b_{t+1}.$$

Here, a_t stands for tax revenue (the sum of revenue from capital and labor taxation and other sources, such as customs duties), δ_t is the rate of default on the government debt (usually because of inflation), and b_t is government debt of different maturities, treated as discount bonds, with prices q_t. We think of high-powered money (for example, greenbacks during the Civil War) as a form of debt and include it in b. Let $_s b_t$ be the amount of debt maturing in period s that is outstanding at the beginning of period t, and let $_s q_t$ be its corresponding price. Define the notation

$$q_t \cdot b_t = \Sigma_{s=t+1}^{\infty} {}_s q_t {}_s b_t.$$

In practice, the quantities $_s b_t$ will usually equal zero if s is large enough. In the case of a one-period bond, for example, the price $_{t+1} q_t$ of new debt issue is determined by

$$_{t+1} q_t = (1 - \delta_{t-1})/(1 + r_t),$$

where r_t is the interest rate between periods t and $t+1$, and δ_{t-1} is the default rate expected to prevail in period $t+1$.

The time consistency problem is that in the absence of a commitment mechanism, the government in period $t+1$ would like to default to a greater extent than the original plan specifies. Such default reduces the need for distortionary taxes, but also affects expectations of future defaults and therefore the price q at which the public is willing to hold government debt. In Prescott (1977), for example, the government can finance a given stream of expenditures either through taxes on labor income (abstracting from capital) or by selling debt. For that model, Prescott finds that if the government has no commitment mechanism for future actions, the government will always default on outstanding debt to avoid levying distorting taxes. As a consequence, the equilibrium implies that government debt is zero and that the government always runs a balanced budget. This policy and the implied allocation are, of course, inferior to the Ramsey allocation for that model.

Some more recent papers investigate circumstances under which Ramsey policies are sustainable in the sense of being an equilibrium arising endogenously within the environment considered. Chari and Kehoe (1989, 1990) have studied this issue for situations in which time consistency problems can arise either because of capital taxation or because of the presence of government debt. An expository introduction is in Chari (1988). The typical finding is that a Ramsey allocation will not occur in equilibrium when the horizon is finite. When the horizon is infinite, on the other hand, the Ramsey allocation may be one among a large, usually infinite, number of equilibriums. The conditions that have been used to achieve this result restrict the applicability severely. What supports Ramsey policies as equilibriums in those cases is the belief by consumers that as long as the government has chosen Ramsey policies in the past, it will continue to do so.[5]

To overcome the shortcomings associated with the lack of an endogenous commitment mechanism, society may attempt to design such mechanisms, for example in the form of laws that are hard to change. Such is the case with patent protection. The law may ensure sufficient incentives for inventive activity by allowing firms the exclusive use of new inventions for a period of time without fear that the government will remove the patent right and allow the price of the product to be driven toward the competitive price. Our thesis is that, although the gold standard is easier to change than, for example, the patent law, this institutional arrangement has the potential for working as an explicit, transparent, well understood rule.

In an uncertain world, the Ramsey plan generally would be a contingent plan or rule. Strictly speaking, in a realistic environment the Ramsey plan would include many contingencies, some of which may make little difference to society's welfare. In the patent case, one can imagine that an optimal arrangement occasionally, under special circumstances, would permit nonexclusive use. Drawbacks of including many contingencies, however, are lack of transparency and possible uncertainty among the public regarding the will to obey the original plan. Thus, a practical rule may include only the contingency that is considered most important. In this sense, the rule does not quite reach the maximum of the social welfare function, but the sacrifice is small. By discretion, then, we mean any purposeful deviation, under whatever guise, from such a rule. The excuse for such a deviation could be a "bad outcome," in the language of Grossman and van Huyck (1988), that is not included as a contingency in the original plan. Deviations are tempting because of their immediate benefits (perhaps accompanied by promises not to repeat the breach of the rule). Because of the effect on future beliefs, however, these benefits are outweighed by the long-run implications of having given up on the original, nearly optimal, rule.

The gold standard

The essence of the gold standard rule is that each country would define the price of gold in terms of its currency and keep the price fixed. This involves defining a gold coin as a fixed weight of gold called, for example, one dollar. The dollar in 1792 was defined as 24.75 grains of gold with 480 grains to the ounce, equivalent to $19.39 per ounce. The monetary authority was then committed to keep the mint price of gold fixed through the purchase and sale of gold in unlimited amounts. The monetary authority was willing to convert into coin gold bullion brought to it by the public, to charge a certain fee for the service – called brassage – and also to sell coins freely to the public in any amount and allow the public to convert them into bullion or export them.[6]

This rule applies to a pure gold coin standard. In fact, the standard that prevailed in the 19th century was a mixed standard containing both fiduciary money and gold coins. Under the mixed standard, the gold standard rule required that fiduciary money (issued either by private banks or by the government) be freely convertible into gold at the fixed price.

Most countries, until the third quarter of the 19th century, maintained bimetallic systems using both gold and silver at a fixed ratio. Defining the weight of both gold and silver coins, freely buying and selling them, and maintaining the ratio fixed can be viewed as a variant of the basic gold standard rule, since it is a fixed value of the unit of account that is the essence of the rule.[7]

A variant of the gold standard rule that we believe is particularly pertinent applies to the case of a war. Assume for the moment that a country finds the gold standard rule to have good operating characteristics if the gold standard is maintained under all circumstances except for a war. Let z_t equal one if the country is on the gold standard at time t and zero otherwise. Let h_i represent the start of war i and e_i its end. A reasonable rule could be to choose $z_t=0$ if $t\epsilon[h_i, e_i+d]$ for all i and $z_t=1$ otherwise; in other words, it is understood that in order to finance the war, the gold standard will be suspended for the duration of the war plus a delay period d, which is the same in every war. Such a policy, if implemented as planned, is consistent with a gold standard rule. It is clear that when people foresee a war in the near future, this rule will result in different prices q_t for the issue of new debt than under the unconditional $z_t = 1$ rule. These effects would be regarded as negative, although they presumably would be outweighed by the benefits of being better able to finance the war.

This description is consistent with the results of Lucas and Stokey (1983), in which financing of wars is a contingency rule that is optimal in one of their environments. In their example, where the occurrence and duration of the war are uncertain, the optimal plan is for the debt not to be serviced during a war. Under this policy, people realize when they purchase the debt that effectively it will be defaulted on in the event that the war continues. Under the rule, the sovereign maintains the standard – keeps fixed the price of its currency in terms of gold – except in the event of a major war, in which circumstances it can suspend specie payments and issue paper money to finance its expenditures, and it can sell debt issues in terms of the nominal value of its currency on the understanding that the debt will eventually be paid off in gold. The rule is contingent in the sense that the public understands that the suspension will last only for the duration of the wartime emergency plus some period of adjustment; it assumes that, afterward, the government will follow the deflationary policies necessary to resume payments.

In this situation, an example of discretion is, after war i has ended, to decide at time $e_i + d$ to delay further the resumption of the gold standard, perhaps as a result of the perceived current situation in terms of the fraction of the war that has been paid for and the undesirable effects of alternative means of financing, such as by raising taxes. This change is all the more tempting if the public had accepted the debt at a reasonably high price q in the expectation that the gold standard would be resumed as scheduled. If the government breaks the rule by effectively choosing a high default rate δ in the future, it is obvious that, should there be another war within memory of the previous one, then people's behavior would be quite different from that in the previous war, even if the situation is otherwise similar and the government claims to subscribe to the same fixed delay rule.

Finally, a second contingency aspect of the rule could arise during financial crises. Temporary restrictions on convertibility of bank liabilities could be used to reduce the extent of a banking panic.

Commitment mechanisms

How was the gold standard rule enforced? One possible explanation focuses on reputational considerations within each country. Long-run adherence to the rule was based on the historical evolution of the gold standard itself. Gold was accepted as money because of its intrinsic value and desirable properties such as durability, storability, divisibility, portability, and uniformity. Paper claims, developed to economize on the scarce resources tied up in commodity money, became acceptable only because they were convertible into gold.[8]

In turn, the reputation of the gold standard would constrain the monetary authorities from breaching convertibility, except under well understood contingencies. Thus, when an emergency occurred, the abandonment of the standard would be viewed by all to be a temporary event since, from their experience, only gold or gold-backed claims truly served as money.

An alternative commitment mechanism was to guarantee gold convertibility in the constitution. This was the case in Sweden before 1914, where laws pertaining to the gold standard could be changed only by two identical parliamentary decisions with an election in between (Jonung, 1984, 368).

With respect to outright suspension of convertibility, it is difficult to distinguish between a suspension as part of the operation of a contingent rule as mentioned above, or as evidence of a change in regime. As we discuss below, statements by the monetary authorities, debates in Parliament, frequency of suspension, and changes in expectations as reflected in people's decisions all can be used to distinguish between the two.

Technical adjustments, or opportunity for discretion?

There are some aspects of the operation of a gold standard that are not so clear-cut. In designing its details (for example, the gold/silver ratio under bimetallism – a variant of the gold standard), it can be difficult to anticipate exactly what the optimal ratio is. New knowledge may be gained over time that would have been helpful when the standard was designed. When the new information is revealed, a potentially difficult question is what happens if the government goes ahead and makes the technical adjustment in the standard. If most people accept the claim that new information is the reason for the change, then the associated private behavior should be approximately the same as if this had been the standard from the very beginning. On the other hand, the greater the suspicion among the public that the change is partly a form of discretion, for which the government certainly has a strong incentive, the greater will be the change in private behavior reflecting the adjustment in the public's beliefs about likely future discretionary actions by the government. The same argument can be made regarding the choice of a different price when the gold standard is resumed after a temporary abandonment.[9]

An international rule

The gold standard rule also has an international dimension. Under the rule, there would be no restriction on the nationality of individuals who presented bullion to the mint to be coined, or who exported coin or bullion to foreign countries. Moreover, because every country following the rule fixed the price of its currency in gold, this created a system of fixed exchange rates linking all countries on the same standard. The international aspect of the gold standard may have been particularly important to the countries that were relatively less developed and therefore depended on access to international debt markets. The thesis of this chapter, however, is that the essence of the gold standard rule was as a domestic commitment mechanism. To the extent that the commitment was honored in relation to other countries, this served to strengthen the credibility of the domestic commitment.[10]

An aspect of the international gold standard given considerable attention in the literature is the operation of the "rules of the game." According to the traditional story, central banks or the monetary authorities were supposed to use their monetary policy to speed up the adjustment mechanism to a change in external balance. To the extent that the "rules" were followed, this presumably would strengthen the commitment to convertibility.

The enforcement of the international gold standard seems to have taken a particular form that was conducive to making it credible. A key factor may have been the role of England – the leading financial and commercial center of the gold standard era. The financial institutions of London provided the world with a well defined and universally accepted means, based on gold, of executing bilateral trades and obtaining credit. As we shall argue later, the gold standard provided England with the necessary benefits to enforce it and for many other countries to follow England's lead. Exchange in both goods and capital was facilitated if countries adhered to a standard based on a rule anchored by the same commitment mechanism. This arrangement may also have contributed to making the commitment mechanism a transparent one, a condition that we think is important for its likely success.

History of the gold standard as a rule

In this section, we discuss the history of the gold standard, viewed first as a domestic rule binding the monetary authorities. In this context, we survey in some detail the operation of the gold standard as a contingent rule in four countries: England and the United States – two key nations under the standard; and France and Italy – the former a "core" country of the

Classical gold standard, the latter an important peripheral country.[11] We also summarize briefly the gold standard experience of other countries. Then, we survey the record of the gold standard as an international rule governing the interrelationships between nations.

Our survey extends primarily from the early 19th century to 1933, with the main focus on the Classical period ending in 1914. Although the United States continued to maintain gold backing for the dollar until 1971 and although the Bretton Woods system from 1945 to 1971 was based in part on gold, we view the period after World War II as far enough removed from the gold standard rule to be omitted from this survey.[12]

The gold standard as a domestic rule

England, 1717–1931

England can be viewed as the most important country to follow the gold standard rule. The gold standard in England, as in other Western European countries, evolved from the use of a commodity as money. Standardization of coins of specific weight evolved by the early 18th century from a rudimentary bimetallic specie standard where coins frequently circulated by weight, not tale (face value).[13] England adopted a *de facto* gold standard in 1717, after having been on a *de facto* silver standard at least back to the 13th century. Over the 500-year period on silver, the price of silver and the bimetallic ratio were rarely changed – the principal exception being the Great Debasement of the 16th century. According to Glassman and Redish (1988), this episode represented an attempt to gain seigniorage – to follow discretionary policy – rather than a technical adjustment in the coinage.[14]

The early standard was plagued by the problems of deterioration in quality and counterfeiting. This was especially serious for small-denomination silver coins and may explain periodic recoinage and occasional debasement in the early modern era (Glassman and Redish, 1988). The emergence of the standard in its modern guise reflects the development of milling and other techniques of producing high-quality coin. The gold standard emerged in England *de facto* by the unintended overvaluation of gold at the mint from 1717 by the Master of the Mint, Sir Isaac Newton. It became *de jure* in 1816.[15]

The gold standard prevailed, with the price of gold fixed at £3.85 per ounce, from 1717 to 1931, with two major departures: 1797–1821 and 1914–1925. The first departure, referred to as the "Suspension Period" or the "Paper Pound" during the Napoleonic wars, is generally viewed as an example of the operation of a contingent rule (Barro, 1987). The suspension of payments on February 26, 1797, whereby the Bank of England received permission from the government not to have to redeem its notes in terms of gold, followed a run on the country banks and the depletion of the Bank of England's gold reserve with the threat of a French invasion.[16] Figure 3.1 portrays monthly movements in the price of the pound in terms of the Hamburg Schillingen Banco, the only exchange rate series continuously available over the entire period. (The par of exchange before suspension was approximately 35.)[17]

The suspension was universally viewed as a temporary event, initially expected to last for a period of months.[18] As the French wars dragged on, however, and the Bank of England freely discounted government securities to finance military expenditures, the pound depreciated on the foreign exchange market. Consequently, the Bank repeatedly requested an extension of the suspension. Concern about the depreciation of the paper pound led to the *Bullion Report* of 1810, which attributed the depreciation to the Bank of England's note issue.

The *Bullion Report* recommended that immediate steps be taken to resume payments in two years from the date of the report at the presuspension parity.[19] The debate that ensued in Parliament and in the press revolved around the themes of the extent, if any, of depreciation, and responsibility for the depreciation – the Bank of England blaming it on external real factors.[20] There was little discussion of the possibility of not resuming payments or of resuming at a depreciated level of the pound in the ensuing ten years.

Despite the government's opposition to resumption during wartime conditions, there exists considerable evidence that the government wished to confirm its commitment to a return to the gold standard once hostilities ceased (Bordo and White, 1991).[21] Several attempts were made to pick a date for resumption (1816, 1818), but as each occasion approached, the Bank requested a postponement on the grounds that the exchanges were unfavorable. It is important to note that this occurred after the wartime emergency ended in 1815.[22] Finally, Parliament agreed on July 2, 1819 (Peel's Act) on resumption in stages from February 1, 1820, to full redemption on demand on May 1, 1823,[23] and it was agreed that the government would retire its outstanding securities held by the Bank and the Bank would reduce its note issue to achieve the aim. During the year preceding resumption, considerable opposition to the plan emerged in Parliament by interests (especially agriculture and the Birmingham industrial area) hurt by deflation. They advocated return to parity at a depreciated pound. This opposition was not sufficient, however, to prevent resumption from being achieved (Feavearyear, 1963, 224–225; Fetter, 1965, 73–76; Laidler, 1987).

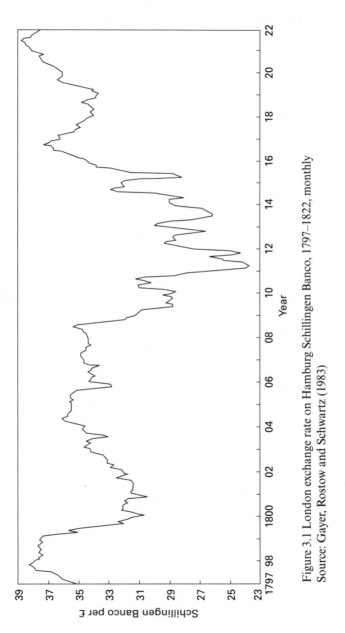

Figure 3.1 London exchange rate on Hamburg Schillingen Banco, 1797–1822, monthly
Source: Gayer, Rostow and Schwartz (1983)

We interpret the repeated requests for postponement, especially after the end of hostilities in 1815, as the use of discretionary policy.[24] Moreover, each postponement gave a negative signal to the public of the government's intention of ever resuming. Nevertheless, the fact that resumption was achieved suggests that observing the rule was paramount.

Evidence for the credibility of the commitment to the gold standard in the Napoleonic War is provided in Bordo and White (1991). There it is shown that although the British government pursued a policy of tax smoothing (setting tax rates over time so as to minimize deadweight losses), it did not follow a policy of revenue smoothing (smoothing revenue from both taxes and seigniorage). These results suggest that, although specie payments were suspended, the commitment to resume prevented the government from acting as it would have done under a pure fiat regime.

The Bank Charter Act 1844 and the separation of the Bank of England, into the Issue department to regulate the currency and the Banking department to follow sound commercial banking principles, further demonstrated England's commitment to the gold standard rule. The Issue department, by varying directly its fiduciary issue (over and above a statutory limit of £14 million) with the level of gold reserves ("the currency principle"), was designed to make the long-run maintenance of the (mixed) gold standard more credible.[25]

A second contingency aspect of the rule developed with experience of financial crises. Restrictions on convertibility of bank liabilities for gold were used to reduce the extent of a banking panic. The Bank was authorized to expand its unbacked note issue in the face of a depletion of its reserves without suspending convertibility of its notes into gold.

From 1821 to 1914, the gold standard rule was continuously honored. However, on three occasions – the crises of 1847, 1857, and 1866 – the second contingent aspect of the rule came into play. The policy was successful in alleviating the pressure, and the Bank retired the excess issue shortly thereafter.[26]

The Overend Gurney crisis of 1866 was the last real financial crisis (that is, banking panic) in British financial history (Schwartz, 1986). After that point, the Bank of England learned to follow Bagehot's rule – in the face of both an external and an internal drain "to lend freely but at a penalty rate." Although Bagehot intended the Bank to use its discretion (in the traditional sense) to avert a financial crisis, it can be argued that the successful performance of the Bank as lender of last resort actually served to strengthen the credibility of the Bank's commitment to the gold standard rule, because a key threat to the maintenance of convertibility was removed. Evidence of the credibility of England's commitment to the gold standard

Table 3.1 *The financing of wartime expenditures in the French wars and World War I*

	French wars 1793–1815 (Great Britain)	World War I 1914–1918 (United Kingdom)[a]
Percentage of total wartime expenditures financed by:		
Taxes[1]	58.0	31.8
Bonds[2]	40.5	64.4
High-powered money[3]	1.5	3.8

Note:
[a] Wartime expenditures are calculated as total government expenditures *less* 1903–1913 annual average of total government expenditures.
Source:
1. 1793–1815: O'Brien (1967, table 4); 1914–1918: Mitchell and Deane (1962, 392–395, 396–398).
2. 1793–1815: O'Brien (1967, table 4); 1914–1918: Mitchell and Deane (1962, 392–395, 396–398).
3. 1793–1815: Mitchell and Deane (1962, 441–443); 1914–1918: Capie and Webber (1985, table 1(1), 52–59).

rule is provided by private short-term capital inflows during the incipient crises of 1890 and 1907 (Eichengreen, 1992).

The 1914–1925 episode was similar in many respects to the earlier suspension period, although the extent of the inflation and the depreciation of the pound were considerably greater. Indeed, it appears that the successful resumption of 1821 may have been a factor enabling the British to finance an even larger share of the World War I expenditures by debt finance and the issue of fiat money (see table 3.1).[27]

Figure 3.2 shows monthly movements in the dollar/sterling exchange rate from 1914 to 1925. Note that from the beginning of hostilities in August 1914 until March 1919, the country was still formally on the gold standard, but the monetary authorities prevented conversion and pegged the pound close to the old parity (Crabbe, 1989).

After hostilities ended, the official view in the *Cunliffe Report* (1918) and other documents was for an immediate resumption at the old parity of $4.867. Consequently, the Bank of England began following a deflationary policy in early 1920. The exchange rate was close to parity by December 1922, but resumption was delayed because of unfavorable events on the continent (the Germans' refusal to pay reparations and the Belgian–French

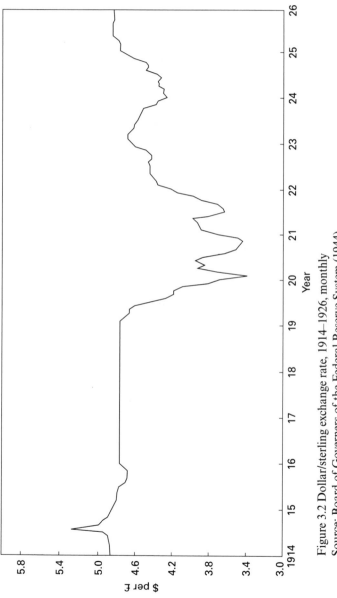

Figure 3.2 Dollar/sterling exchange rate, 1914–1926, monthly
Source: Board of Governers of the Federal Reserve System (1944)

occupation of the Ruhr in 1923). By the end of 1924, the pound was again close to parity and resumption was announced by Winston Churchill in the Budget Speech of April 28, 1925.

Though the official view from 1920 to 1925 was in favor of resumption, and a key argument made was the maintenance of credibility by returning to gold at the old par,[28] vociferous opposition to it was voiced by J. M. Keynes ([1925] 1972) and other academics, by labor (not the official Labour Party), and by industry groups. Most of the opposition, however, with the principal exception of Keynes, was opposed not to resumption at the old parity *per se* but to the deflationary policies used to attain it.[29] The successful resumption in 1925 and the painful deflation that accompanied it can be viewed as evidence of the British commitment to the gold standard rule.[30]

The United States, 1792–1933

The US Constitution (Section 8) gave Congress power over the currency – "to coin money and regulate the value thereof." The Coinage Act 1792 defined US coinage as both gold and silver. Thus, the original monetary standard was a bimetallic standard. One dollar was defined as 371.25 grains of silver or 24.75 grains of gold. This yields a bimetallic ratio of the value of gold to silver of 15:1. Soon after instituting the 15:1 ratio, the market ratio increased to 15½:1. Consequently, silver became overvalued at the mint, gold became undervalued, and, via the operation of Gresham's Law, the United States after a few years was on a *de facto* silver standard.

The situation was altered by a new Coinage Act in 1834 and another in 1837, which changed the bimetallic ratio to 16:1, presumably in an attempt to restore bimetallism. As it turned out, gold became overvalued at the mint, silver became undervalued, and the United States switched to a *de facto* gold standard. If we interpret periodic adjustment of the bimetallic mint ratio to the market ratio as an example of a contingent rule, and if the public expects such adjustments, then the question arises whether the switch from 15:1 to 16:1 rather than to 15½:1 was a mistake or a deliberate use of discretionary policy. Indeed, O'Leary (1937) viewed this episode as a deliberate attempt by the Jacksonians to discredit the Second Bank of the United States. The resultant flood of gold coins would obviate the necessity for its notes. The 1834 Act was also passed at the urging of the gold producing states of South Carolina, North Carolina, and Georgia (Friedman, 1990a).

Figure 3.3 shows the dollar/pound exchange rate on an annual basis from 1792 to 1925. The market exchange rate is defined in terms of gold, so that during the period when the United States was on a bimetallic standard it varied, reflecting changes in the market bimetallic ratio, changes in the official ratio, and other forces in the market for foreign exchange.[31] As can be seen in figure 3.3, the exchange rate in the bimetallic era before the Civil War was much less stable than during the pure gold standard period, from 1879 to 1913.

The fixed price of \$20.67 per ounce prevailed from 1837 to 1933 with one significant departure – the greenback episode in 1862–1879. Figure 3.4 plots the greenback price of gold over that period. It can be viewed in conjunction with the exchange rate in figure 3.3

The greenback episode, at least at the outset, can be interpreted as the operation of a contingent rule. The federal government originally intended to finance its expenditures through borrowing and taxation, but within a year resorted to the issue of paper notes. Under the Legal Tender Acts, these notes were issued on the presumption that they would be convertible, but the date and provisions for convertibility were not specified.

Shortly after the war, the government made its intentions clear to resume payments at the prewar parity in the Contraction Act of April 12, 1866, which provided for the limited withdrawal of US notes. Declining prices from 1866 to 1868 led to a public outcry and to repeal of the Act in February 1868. Over the next seven years a fierce debate raged between the hard money forces – advocates of rapid resumption – and the soft money forces, some of whom were opposed to restoring the gold standard, others who wanted to restore it at a devalued parity, and yet others who just wanted to prevent any undue deflation and allow the economy to grow up to its money supply (Unger, 1964; Sharkey, 1959). Alternating victories by the conflicting forces were manifest in legislation, alternately contracting and expanding the issue of greenbacks (the Public Credit Act 1869 contracting it, the reissue of \$26 million of retired greenbacks in 1873 expanding it) and, in Supreme Court decisions, initially declaring the Legal Tender Acts unconstitutional (*Hepburn* v. *Griswold*, February 1870), and then reversing the decision (*Knox* v. *Lee*, May 1871). Finally, the decision to resume payments on January 1, 1879, was made in the Resumption Act 1875, which the lame-duck Republican Congress passed by a majority of one. Despite the announcement of resumption, however, and of steps taken by the Treasury to accumulate a gold reserve and to retire greenbacks, the bitter election of 1876 was fought between Cooper (the greenback candidate, who was opposed to resumption), Tilden (a soft money Democrat), and Hayes (a hard-money Republican). Hayes won by one electoral vote. Yet, had Tilden won, according to one authority, resumption would not have been prevented; only the date may have been changed (Unger, 1964, 310–311).

Though the ferocity of the reversals in policy suggest to us that many features of the post-Civil War period can be interpreted as incorporating

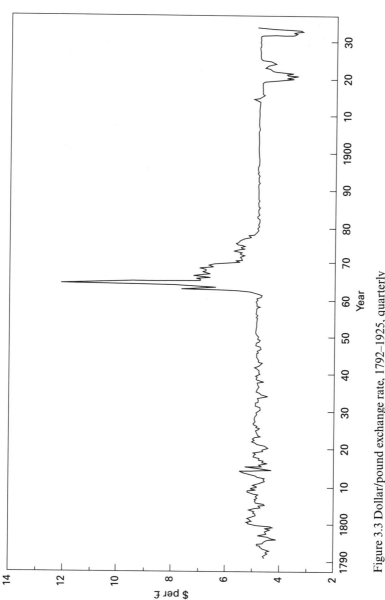

Figure 3.3 Dollar/pound exchange rate, 1792–1925, quarterly
Source: Friedman and Schwartz (1982); Officer (1983, 1985)

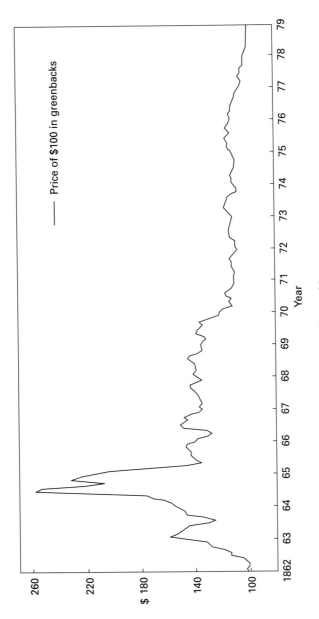

Figure 3.4 Price of gold in greenbacks, 1862–1879, monthly
Sources: Mitchell (1908); Friedman and Schwartz (1963)

elements of a discretionary regime, other evidence argues in favor of the contingent gold standard rule. As Calomiris (1988) points out, credibility in the restoration of the gold standard rule was probably established in 1869 by the actual redemption of bond principal in gold by the Act of March 18, 1869, guaranteeing payment in gold, and the Supreme Court decision in *Venzie Bank* v. *Fenno*, which supported the constitutionality of gold clauses (Calomiris, 1988, 208fn).[32]

Moreover, both Roll (1972) and Calomiris (1988) present evidence of expected appreciation of the greenback based on a negative interest differential between bonds that were paid in greenbacks and those paid in gold. Calomiris (see table 3.2) calculates the appreciation forecast error on a semi-annual basis from January 1869 to December 1878, defined as the difference between his calculation of expected appreciation and actual appreciation. The errors are close to zero for most of the periods, with two exceptions: January–June 1869, when the error is 1.53, and January–June 1876, when it is −1.49. The former positive exchange rate surprise reflects the credibility of the government's commitment to the redemption of bond principal in gold; the latter negative surprise reflects the temporary threat to resumption by the election of 1876.

In the ensuing seventeen years, though the United States was back on a gold basis, the battle between hard and soft money forces continued over the issue of free coinage of silver. Silver advocates can be classified into several groups. There were those who believed that, had silver not been demonetized by the "Crime of '73" (the Coinage Act of February 1873), then bimetallism at 16:1 would have yielded less deflation than actually occurred from 1873 to 1896, as relatively more abundant silver was substituted for increasingly scarce gold. Such a position is consistent with maintenance of a rule. Other silver advocates (such as the Populist party), however, viewed the issue of silver certificates as a potential engine of inflation to stimulate the economy, as well as to reverse the redistribution of income from debtors to creditors. In this sense, the pressure in favor of discretion did not disappear.

The free-silver forces succeeded in passing two pieces of legislation that increased the outstanding stock of silver coins: the Bland–Allison Act 1878 and the Sherman Silver Purchase Act 1890. The latter increased the stock of high-powered money sufficiently to threaten convertibility into gold (Friedman and Schwartz, 1963). As Grilli (1989, figure 3) shows, however, the probability of a speculative attack on the gold dollar at the height of the agitation over silver in 1893 (before the repeal of the Sherman Silver Purchase Act) was not much greater than 6 percent.[33]

A second departure from the gold standard, an embargo during World War I (1917–1919) on gold exports, did not affect internal convertibility of

Table 3.2 *Expected and actual appreciation of the greenback dollar,*
1869–1878

		Average differential between gold and greenbacks' yield[a]	Expected appreciation (current differential *less* differential for July–December 1878)	Average actual rate of greenbacks' appreciation to 1881[b]	Appreciation forecast error ((2)–(3))	
			(1)	(2)	(3)	(4)
January–June	1869		1.33	3.53	2.00	1.53
July–December	1869		0.49	2.69	1.85	0.84
January–June	1870		−0.52	1.68	0.93	0.75
July–December	1870		−0.42	1.78	0.93	0.85
January–June	1871		−1.01	1.19	1.09	0.10
July–December	1871		−0.95	1.25	1.10	0.15
January–June	1872		−0.02	2.18	1.26	0.92
July–December	1872		0.01	2.21	1.40	0.81
January–June	1873		−0.09	2.11	1.90	0.21
July–December	1873		−0.26	1.94	1.39	0.55
January–June	1874		−0.65	1.55	1.60	−0.05
July–December	1874		−0.45	1.75	1.50	0.25
January–June	1875		0.07	2.27	2.36	−0.09
July–December	1875		0.09	2.29	2.30	−0.01
January–June	1876		−1.19	1.01	2.50	−1.49
July–December	1876		−1.07	1.13	1.76	−0.63
January–June	1877		−1.22	0.98	1.36	−0.38
July–December	1877		−1.21	0.99	0.84	0.15
January–June	1878		−1.32	0.88	0.40	0.48
July–December	1878		−2.20	0.00	0.10	−0.10

Notes:

[a] $\frac{1}{6}\sum_{j=1}^{6}[i_{ap}(j)-i_{gr}(j)]=d.$

[b] The average of monthly exchange rate closings for the period was used to
measure current gold price of greenbacks. The 6s of 1881 were redeemable June 1,
1881.

Source: Calomiris (1988, table 5).

gold. Hence, we believe it should be viewed as merely a temporary adjustment in the standard.[34]

Financial crises characterized by banking panics were frequent in US
monetary history until the establishment of the Federal Reserve System.

Before 1914, pressure on the banking system's reserves was often relieved by a restriction on convertibility of bank notes and deposits into high-powered money. The restrictions in 1837–1838, 1839, and 1857 did involve suspensions of convertibility into gold. It could be argued, however, that such temporary departures were viewed as a contingent aspect of the rule. The restrictions of 1873, 1893, and 1907–1908 did not involve suspension of convertibility into gold and hence cannot be viewed as breaking the gold standard rule.

Franklin Roosevelt's decision to devalue the dollar in 1933 (in order to raise the price level) represents a clear departure from the gold standard rule and a clear case of discretion. Though the price of gold was again fixed, at $35 per ounce, gold ownership by US residents was prohibited, and the standard that reemerged has been described as "a discretionary fiduciary standard" with gold just a commodity whose price was fixed by an official support program (Friedman and Schwartz, 1963).

France

France followed a bimetallic standard from the Middle Ages until 1878. From the 13th to the 15th century, the rule was honored in the breach more than the observance, with frequent debasements, devaluations, and revaluations. This reflects internal political instability, frequent wars, and the lack of an adequate tax base (Bordo, 1986). By the 16th century, France had developed a stable bimetallic system, although the ancient regime was punctuated by several devaluations and revaluations (Murphy, 1987), and the infamous system of John Law – a paper-money-induced inflation – from 1716 to 1720 (Bordo, 1987a).

The French revolution spawned the assignat hyperinflation from 1789 to 1795 – the aftermath of which led to the establishment of official bimetallism with the fixing of the ratio of silver to gold at 15½:1 in 1803, a rule that was successful for 75 years (Bordo and White, 1991). Until the late 1840s, abundant supplies of silver threatened to displace gold, but with gold discoveries in California and Australia the process was reversed until the 1860s, when major silver discoveries again threatened the bimetallic standard. In 1865, France formed the Latin Monetary Union with Belgium, Switzerland, and Italy (later joined by the Papal States, Greece, and Romania). By agreeing to mint silver coins of the same fineness, these countries expanded the size of the bimetallic currency area. The Latin Monetary Union continued the free coinage of silver until, swamped by massive supplies of new silver from discoveries in the Americas and by the abandonment of the silver standard in Germany and other European countries emulating the gold standard example of Britain, the leading commercial power (Friedman, 1990b), it limited silver coinage in 1874 and fully demonetized silver in 1878 (Bordo, 1987b).

France followed the gold standard rule (albeit in its bimetallic form until 1878) until World War I. Figure 3.5 shows the pound/franc exchange rate from 1821 to 1938. As can be seen, the rate was very stable until 1914, rarely departing more than one percentage in gold points from the parity of 25.22 francs to the pound. France, like the other two countries in this period, suspended specie convertibility in times of national emergency. On two occasions, the Bank of France announced *Cours Forcé* – the first from March 15, 1848 to August 6, 1850, following the February 1848 revolution, and the second during and after the Franco–Prussian war from August 12, 1870 to January 1, 1878. It is interesting to note that during these periods, the exchange rate varied close to parity. On both occasions, the Bank of France limited its note issue, acting as if it were constrained by the gold standard rule (Lacroix and Dupieux, 1973).

Like other belligerents in World War I, France switched to fiat-money issue to finance the war, intending to resume payments after hostilities ended. Unlike the British case, the aftermath of the war was a period of rapid inflation and depreciation of the franc. The forces of discretion carried the day even with the ultimate return of the franc to gold convertibility at a vastly depreciated level in 1928.[35] France stayed on the gold standard until 1936.

Italy

In contrast to England, France and the United States, Italy departed from the gold standard rule more than it followed it. The newly unified Italian state adopted a gold standard in 1865 but abandoned it in May 1866 and did not return to convertibility until March 1883. According to Fratianni and Spinelli (1984), inconvertibility was a consequence of both financing the war against Austria in 1866 and conducting the government's subsequent liberal fiscal policy. According to Fratianni and Spinelli, "Politicians had no difficulties in throwing off the straitjacket of the gold standard when it stood in the way of large budget deficits" (419). A return to sound fiscal policy permitted restoration of gold payments from 1883 to February 1894, after which the Italian currency remained inconvertible until December 1927, when gold convertibility was resumed at a depreciated value of the lira.[36] During the pre-World War I period, however, the monetary authorities acted as if they were on the gold standard. The exchange rate with France returned close to parity in 1903 and remained there until the outbreak of war. Money growth was low, and the budget was often in surplus (Tonniolo, 1990, 188). This episode suggests that commitment to the gold standard rule was of considerable importance to the Italian monetary authorities.

Evidence for the credibility of the commitment to the gold standard can

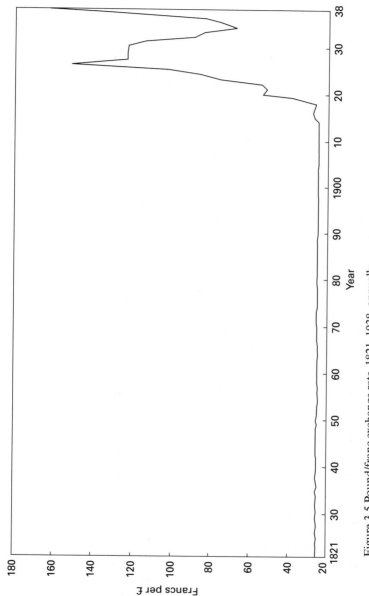

Figure 3.5 Pound/franc exchange rate, 1821–1938, annually
Sources: Gayer, Rostow and Schwartz (1953); British Parliamentary Papers (1888); St. Marc (1983)

be seen in the risk premium on Italian government long-term securities relative to their French counterparts over the period 1866 to 1912, shown in figure 3.6.[37] In the first period of inconvertibility (1866–1883), the risk premium averaged more than 2 percent per year; in the gold standard period (1884–1894), it average close to zero; and in the second inconvertibility period (1894–1912), it declined from 2 percent in the first half of the period to 0.5 percent after 1902.

A number of other countries followed the gold standard rule until 1914 as strictly as the three core countries just discussed.[38] These include Germany (the fourth "core" country), the Scandinavian countries, and the British Dominions. The latter two sets of countries, like England, returned to gold at the original parity in the mid-1920s. A number of countries that were not formally on the gold standard acted as if they were, by maintaining price levels as stable as the gold standard countries. These include Spain and the Austro–Hungarian empire before 1892. Finally, a number of countries, most notably Argentina, followed the example of Italy by alternately following and then abandoning gold convertibility during the period of falling prices, 1880–1900, and of rising prices, 1900–1913 (Ford, 1962).[39]

Some evidence for the credibility of the gold standard rule

We have described the gold standard experience of four important countries: three "core" countries (England, the United States, and France) that followed the gold standard rule, and Italy, a country that, though officially on the gold standard, suspended convertibility more than half the time. One way to summarize this experience is to present evidence on the persistence of inflation.

Barsky (1987) presents evidence for the United Kingdom and the United States that inflation under the gold standard was very nearly a white noise process. This is compared to the post-World War II period, when the inflation rate exhibited considerable persistence. Evidence for the absence of inflation persistence does not prove that countries followed the gold standard rule. It is, however, not inconsistent with the suggestion that market agents expect that the monetary authorities will not continuously follow an inflationary policy – an expectation that is also consistent with belief in following a convertibility rule.

To develop this further, following Barsky's approach, we examine in table 3.3 the autocorrelations of inflation using annual wholesale price indices for the four countries for different periods covering the entire gold standard experience. The results in table 3.3 confirm those of Barsky: inflation in all four countries was very nearly white noise, as seen in the low autocorrelations. These results hold for different subperiods when the countries concerned followed the bimetallic variant of the rule and for subperiods when

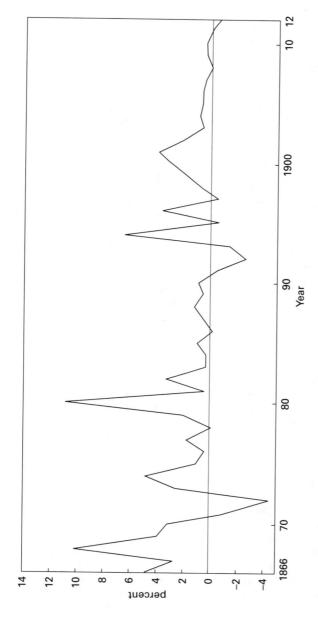

Figure 3.6 Risk premium, lira/franc exchange rate, 1866–1912, Italian government bond yield *minus* French 3 percent *rentes*
Source: Fratianni and Spinelli (1984)

Table 3.3 *Autocorrelations of inflation (wholesale prices, annual data)*

Sample period	Regime	Ljung–Box Q-test 5% critical value (standard error)	Lags	Autocorrelations			
United Kingdom							
1730–	de facto	$Q(18)=16.79$	1–4	−0.02	−0.59	−0.13	−0.32
1796	Gold	$C(18)=28.87$	5–8	0.11	−0.05	0.02	0.09
		(0.12)	9–12	0.04	−0.04	0.12	0.02
1797–	Paper	$Q(12)=15.21$	1–4	0.26	−0.37	−0.41	0.11
1821	pound	$C(12)=21.03$	5–8	0.37	−0.03	−0.12	0.03
		(0.20)	9–12	0.12	−0.10	−0.19	0.08
1822–	Gold	$Q(24)=25.50$	1–4	0.04	−0.01	−0.14	−0.22
1913	standard	$C(24)=36.42$	5–8	−0.20	0.01	0.13	0.14
		(0.10)	9–12	0.17	0.04	−0.07	−0.10
1914–	Paper and	$Q(6)=3.71$	1–3	0.32	0.09	0.03	
1931	gold exchange	$C(6)=14.07$ (0.24)	4–6	−0.05	−0.10	−0.29	
1730–	Mixed	$Q(24)=44.50$	1–4	0.12	−0.15	−0.24	−0.15
1913		$C(24)=36.42$	5–8	0.10	0.08	0.04	0.09
		(0.07)	9–12	0.07	−0.05	−0.02	0.02
1730–	Mixed	$Q(24)=35.69$	1–4	0.20	−0.05	−0.11	−0.10
1931		$C(24)=36.42$	5–8	0.05	−0.05	0.00	0.10
		(0.07)	9–12	0.09	−0.02	−0.07	−0.03
United States							
1793–	Bimetallic	$Q(24)=34.69$	1–4	0.16	−0.10	−0.13	0.12
1861		$C(24)=36.42$	5–8	−0.04	−0.20	−0.34	0.13
		(0.24)	9–12	0.14	0.09	0.05	−0.15
1862–	Greenback	$Q(6)=5.53$	1–3	0.51	0.17	−0.07	
1878		$C(6)=14.07$ (0.24)	4–6	−0.04	−0.05	−0.17	
1879–	Gold	$Q(12)=3.75$	1–4	0.05	0.18	0.04	−0.16
1913	standard	$C(12)=21.03$	5–8	0.01	−0.07	0.16	−0.02
		(0.17)	9–12	0.02	0.09	0.02	−0.06
1914–	Gold	$Q(6)=3.76$	1–3	0.23	0.05	0.02	
1933	exchange	$C(6)=14.07$ (0.22)	4–6	−0.33	−0.15	0.02	
1793–	Mixed	$Q(24)=55.97$	1–4	0.26	−0.01	−0.12	−0.02
1913		$C(24)=36.42$	5–8	−0.06	−0.23	−0.17	0.13
		(0.09)	9–12	0.18	0.15	−0.07	−0.08
1793–	Mixed	$Q(24)=50.12$	1–4	0.25	0.01	0.07	−0.11
1933		$C(24)=36.42$	5–8	−0.08	−0.15	−0.10	0.11
		(0.09)	9–12	0.13	0.18	−0.03	−0.11

Table 3.3 (*cont.*)

Sample period	Regime	Ljung–Box Q-test 5% critical value (standard error)	Lags	Autocorrelations			
France							
1803–1869	Bimetallic	$Q(18)=10.98$ $C(18)=28.87$ (0.12)	1–4 5–8 9–12	0.11 0.06 −0.03	0.04 −0.12 −0.01	−0.04 0.11 −0.19	−0.09 −0.02 −0.10
1870–1878	Suspension	$Q(3)=1.34$ $C(3)=7.82$ (0.33)	1–3	0.18	−0.26	−0.22	
1879–1913	Gold standard	$Q(12)=9.49$ $C(12)=21.03$ (0.17)	1–4 5–8 9–12	0.35 −0.06 0.00	0.01 −0.04 0.20	−0.07 0.21 0.20	−0.11 0.09 0.15
1914–1938	Paper and gold exchange	$Q(8)=4.68$ $C(8)=15.51$ (0.20)	1–4 5–8	0.27 −0.15	0.18 −0.07	0.14 −0.10	−0.14 0.08
1803–1913	Specie	$Q(24)=17.28$ $C(24)=36.42$ (0.10)	1–4 5–8 9–12	0.15 0.05 −0.00	0.02 −0.11 0.03	−0.05 0.12 −0.14	−0.07 −0.00 −0.07
1803–1938	Mixed	$Q(24)=33.25$ $C(24)=36.42$ (0.09)	1–4 5–8 9–12	0.29 −0.03 0.08	0.16 −0.02 0.06	0.11 −0.01 0.02	−0.07 0.11 −0.04
Italy							
1861–1913	Mixed	$Q(18)=16.38$ $C(18)=28.87$ (0.14)	1–4 5–8 9–12	0.06 0.21 0.02	−0.26 0.09 −0.12	−0.17 −0.13 0.03	0.01 −0.06 0.19

Sources:
United Kingdom: Mitchell and Deane (1962).
United States: Jastram (1977).
France: Mitchell (1975).
Italy: Mitchell (1975).

they departed from convertibility following the contingent aspect of the rule. As did Klein (1975) and Barsky (1987), we observe negative serial correlation at a number of lags in all the subperiods.[40] This is consistent with the commodity money adjustment mechanism of the gold standard discussed by Rockoff (1984) and Barsky and Summers (1988). The Q-statistics, which test the joint hypothesis that the first n autocorrelations are all zero for specified n, do not reject the white noise hypothesis for any of the subperiods. Over the entire period 1730–1938 for the United Kingdom and the entire periods 1793–1913 and 1793–1933 for the United States, however, the hypothesis is rejected at the 5 percent significance level. These periods represent conglomerates of different regimes that had different mean rates of inflation. Aggregation then may induce serial correlation.

We also tested for a unit root in the inflation series using the Dickey–Fuller test. In only one episode – the United States, 1862–1878 – could one be detected at the 10 percent significance level.

In sum, we interpret this evidence as consistent with agents' beliefs in the credibility of the commitment to the gold standard convertibility rule. Because the power of the tests is admittedly low, however, this evidence is only suggestive.

The gold standard as an international rule

The classical gold standard emerged as a true international standard by 1880 following the switch by the majority of countries from bimetallism, silver monometallism, and paper to gold as the basis of their currencies.[41] As an international standard, the key rule was maintenance of gold convertibility at the established par. Maintenance of a fixed price of gold by its adherents in turn ensured fixed exchange rates. Recent evidence suggests that, indeed, exchange rates throughout the 1880–1914 period were characterized by a high degree of fixity in the principal countries. Although exchange rates frequently deviated from par, violations of the gold points were rare (Officer, 1986), as were devaluations (Eichengreen, 1985).[42]

The international gold standard was a successful example of a fixed exchange rate system, although gold convertibility is not required to operate a fixed exchange rate system successfully (as is evident from the case of the European Monetary System (EMS) in the late 1980s, see Giavazzi and Giovannini, 1989). The gold standard rule was primarily a domestic rule with an important international dimension. This dimension in turn may have served to make the domestic gold standard rule more credible in a number of significant ways. In addition to the reputation of the domestic gold standard and constitutional provisions as discussed on p. 63, adherence to the international gold standard rule may have been enforced by other mechanisms. These include improved access to international capital markets, the operation of the "rules of the game," and the hegemonic power of England.

Many countries viewed maintenance of gold convertibility as important in obtaining access at favorable terms to the international capital markets of the "core" countries, especially England and France. It was believed that creditors would view gold convertibility as a signal of sound government finance and the future ability to service debt. This was the case both for developing countries wishing to have access to long-term capital, such as Austria–Hungary (Yeager, 1984) and Latin America (Fishlow, 1989), and for countries wishing to finance war expenditures, such as Japan, which financed the Russo–Japanese war of 1905–1906 with foreign loans seven years after joining the gold standard (Hayashi, 1989). Once on the gold standard, such countries feared the consequences of departure.[43] The fact that England, the most successful country of the 19th century, as well as other "progressive" countries were on the gold standard was probably a powerful argument for joining (Gallarotti, 1991; Friedman, 1990b).

The operation of the "rules of the game," whereby the monetary authorities were supposed to alter the discount rate to speed up the adjustment to a change in external balance, may also have been an important part of the commitment mechanism to the international gold standard rule. Thus, for example, when a country was running a balance of payments deficit and there was a gold outflow, the monetary authority, observing a decline in its gold reserves, was supposed to raise its discount rate in order to reduce domestic credit. The resultant drop in the money supply would reduce the price level. The adjustment process would be aided by higher short-term domestic interest rates attracting capital from abroad. To the extent the "rules" would be followed and adjustment facilitated, this would strengthen the commitment to convertibility, as conditions conducive to abandonment would be lessened.

There exists considerable evidence on the operation of the "rules of the game." Bloomfield (1959), in a classic study, showed that, with the principal exception of England, the rules were frequently violated in the sense that discount rates were not always changed in the required direction (or by sufficient amounts) and in the sense that changes in domestic credit were often negatively correlated with changes in gold reserves.[44] In addition, a number of countries used gold devices – practices to prevent gold from leaving.[45] According to Goodfriend (1988), central banks operating under the gold standard did so to achieve "interest rate smoothing" through the use of gold stockpiling. Such practices, in our approach, could be viewed as a form of discretion, because following them could lead the public to believe that ultimately convertibility would be abandoned.

For the major countries, however, at least before 1914, such policies were not used extensively enough to threaten the convertibility into gold – evidence for commitment to the rule (Schwartz, 1984). Moreover, as McKinnon (1993) argues, to the extent that monetary authorities followed Bagehot's rule and prevented a financial crisis while seemingly violating the "rules of the game," the commitment to the gold standard in the long run may have been strengthened.

An additional enforcement mechanism for the international gold standard rule may have been the hegemonic power of England, the most important gold standard country (Eichengreen, 1989). A persistent theme in the literature on the international gold standard is that the Classical gold standard of 1880–1914 was a British-managed standard (Bordo, 1984). Because London was the center for the world's principal gold, commodities, and capital markets, because of the extensive outstanding sterling-denominated assets, and because many countries used sterling as an international reserve currency (as a substitute for gold), it is argued that the Bank of England, by manipulating its bank rate, could attract whatever gold it needed and, furthermore, that other central banks would adjust their discount rates accordingly. Thus, the Bank of England could exert powerful influences on the money supplies and price levels of other gold standard countries.

The evidence suggests that the Bank did have some influence on other European central banks (Lindert, 1969). Eichengreen (1987) views the Bank of England as engaged in a leadership role in a Stackelberg strategic game with other central banks as followers. The other central banks accepted a passive role because of the benefits to them of using sterling as a reserve asset. According to this interpretation, the gold standard rule may have been enforced by the Bank of England.[46] Thus, the monetary authorities of many countries may have been constrained from following independent discretionary policies that would have threatened the adherence to the gold standard rule.[47]

The benefits to England as leader of the gold standard – from seigniorage earned on foreign-held sterling balances, from returns to activities generated by its central position in the gold standard, and from access to international capital markets in wartime – were substantial enough to make the costs of not following the rule extremely high.

The lessons from history

The history of the gold standard suggests that the gold convertibility rule was followed continuously by only a few key countries – the best example being England from 1821 to 1914. Most major countries, however, did follow the rule during the heyday of the Classical gold standard, 1880–1914. Peripheral countries and several fairly important nations – Italy and Argentina – alternately followed and then departed from the rule, but even they were constrained in a looser sense.

The gold standard rule also proved to be successful as a commitment mechanism for England, the United States, and France in preventing default on debt and ensuring that paper-money issues were not permanent.

It may have been successful as a commitment device because it had the virtues of being simple and transparent.

We have suggested a number of reasons why the gold standard rule was so successful as a commitment mechanism before 1914. First, as a contingent rule it permitted nations to have access to revenue in times of wartime emergency. The commitment to return to gold parity after the war would enable the authorities to issue debt and to collect seigniorage at more favorable terms than otherwise.[48]

Second, in England and possibly in other countries, gold emerged early on as a way of certifying contracts. This certifying characteristic of gold carried forward to the relationship between the private and public sectors. Abandoning gold convertibility was viewed as a serious breach of contract. The gold standard emerged in the stable political environment of England after the 17th century, where the rule of law sanctified private contracts.[49] Only a few countries had comparable stability. Countries fraught with more unstable internal politics found it more difficult to refrain from running budget deficits, ultimately financed by paper-money issue (for example, Italy and Argentina), although the benefits of convertibility placed some constraints on their behavior.[50]

The gold standard was also successful as an international rule: by pegging their currencies to gold, countries became part of a fixed exchange rate system. The international aspect of the gold standard may have reinforced the domestic commitment mechanism because of the perceived advantages of more favorable access to international capital markets, by the operation of the "rules of the game," and by the importance of England as a hegemonic power.

The advantages accruing to England as the center of the gold standard world – the use of sterling as a reserve asset and the location in London of the world's key asset and commodity markets – made the costs of not following the gold standard rule (except in wartime emergency) extremely high. Furthermore, because England was the most important country in the gold standard era and access to the London capital market was considered to be of great benefit to developing countries, it is likely that many countries adhered to the gold standard that otherwise would not have, given the high resource costs of maintaining gold reserves. Also, because of the Bank of England's leadership role, other central banks may have been prevented from using discretionary policies, threatening adherence to the rule.

A comparison of the pre-1914 period with the subsequent period is of great interest. The gold exchange standard, which prevailed for only a few years from the mid-1920s to the Great Depression, was an attempt to restore the essential features of the Classical gold standard while allowing a greater role for domestic stabilization policy. It also attempted to economize on gold reserves by restricting its use to central banks and by encouraging the use of foreign exchange as a substitute. As is well known, the gold exchange standard suffered from a number of fatal flaws (Kindleberger, 1973; Eichengreen, 1992; Temin, 1989). These include the use of two reserve currencies, the absence of leadership by a hegemonic power, the failure of cooperation between the key members, and the unwillingness of its two strongest members, the United States and France, to follow the "rules of the game," instead exerting deflationary pressure on the rest of the world by persistent sterilization of balance of payment surpluses. The gold exchange standard collapsed, but according to Friedman and Schwartz (1963), Temin (1989), and Eichengreen (1992b), not before transmitting deflation and depression across the world.

While the gold standard rule was widely upheld before 1914, it has not been since, although to a lesser extent both the short-lived gold exchange standard and the Bretton Woods system incorporated a number of its features. Today, one could characterize most nations as following a discretionary standard, although rhetoric over the importance of rules abounds. This may seem surprising, since the benefits of having a commitment mechanism seem more relevant today than 100 years ago. On the other hand, there may have been the perception that government debt was, and is, less important as an emergency source of funds than it was in the gold standard era. For example, the stocks of physical and human capital have risen substantially. The time inconsistency literature has taught us that the incomes therefrom have broadened the scope for policymakers to use discretionary policy. For example, marginal tax rates for people with above-average human capital rose dramatically during World War II. In the absence of a commitment mechanism, these rates were not returned to prewar levels.

The gold standard rule was simple, transparent, and, for close to a century, successful. Even though it was characterized by some defects from the perspective of macroeconomic performance, a better commitment mechanism has not been adopted. Despite its appeal, many of the conditions that made the gold standard so successful vanished in 1914, and the importance that nations attach to immediate objectives casts doubt on its eventual restoration.

Notes

For helpful comments and suggestions on earlier drafts of this chapter we would like to thank Charles Calomiris, Barry Eichengreen, Marvin Goodfriend, Lars Jonung, Leslie Presnell, Hugh Rockoff, Anna Schwartz, Guido Tabellini, Warren Weber, and participants at seminars at

Carnegie–Mellon University, the Federal Reserve Bank of Richmond, Columbia University, Queens University, Carleton University, the NBER Macroeconomic History Conference (June 1989), and the NBER Summer Institute (1991). For valuable research assistance we thank Mary Ann Pastuch and Bernard Eschweiler.

1. For surveys of this literature, see Bordo (1984) and Eichengreen (1985, 1992a).
2. See Bordo (1981), Cooper (1982), and Meltzer and Robinson (1989).
3. For a discussion of the Currency Banking School debate, see Viner (1937), Fetter (1965), and Schwartz (1987).
4. The following framework is essentially identical to that in Kydland and Prescott (1980a). Also in the main example of Kydland and Prescott (1977) time inconsistency is the result of the effects of tax policy on the incentives for capital accumulation.
5. The idea that reputation may support optimal policy has been studied in a different context by Barro and Gordon (1983).
6. Strictly speaking, the government need define a gold coin only in terms of the unit of account. Private mints could then supply the demand for coin. Indeed, this was the case shortly after the California gold discoveries (Bancroft, 1890, 165). In most countries, however, the mint was under government authority.
7. Viewed, however, as a rule in the traditional sense – as an automatic mechanism to ensure price stability – bimetallism may have had greater scope for automaticity than the gold standard because of the additional cushion of a switch from one metal to the other. See Friedman (1990b). Garber (1986) regards bimetallism as a gold standard with an option.
8. Goodfriend (1989) describes how the evolution of contractual arrangements in the financial system in 18th- and 19th-century England had to overcome the problem of fraud. Private markets developed an elaborate system of monitoring financial arrangements, but ultimately convertibility into gold lay behind them.
9. An additional source of discretion was government policies to regulate gold production, such as taxation, the enforcement and relaxation of environmental regulations, and subsidies to encourage gold production in periods of depression. For examples of the use of such policies, see Rockoff (1984, 632–639).
10. The role of spillover effects on reputation through multiple relationships is discussed in Cole and Kehoe (1991).
11. We do not include Germany, the fourth "core" country of the Classical gold standard, in the survey because its history as a unified nation on the gold standard – from 1871 to 1914 – did not include a period of contingent suspension of payments (McGouldrick, 1984).
12. See Bordo (1993). McKinnon (1993), however, views the Bretton Woods system as a dollar standard with a set of rules that incorporated many of the features of the classical gold standard.
13. Even under the pre-1914 gold standard, however, weight mattered for sovereigns. Bankers had tiny scales for weighing sovereigns, which might be credited at less than 20 shillings. Loss on light gold was clearly a consideration for

George Rae, himself a leading banker at the time (*The Country Banker*, 1885, Letter XIX). (Our thanks to Leslie Presnell for bringing this to our attention.)

14. By contrast to England, monetary authorities in medieval France and Burgundy would often change arbitrarily the face value of silver coins to raise revenue – a discretionary breach of the rule, a policy that would succeed until the public caught on, raising prices in proportion to the change in unit of account.

15. One interpretation of England's early abandonment of bimetallism is the continuous difficulties encountered in providing a fractional silver coinage (Redish, 1990). Alternatively, Lord Liverpool's decision to adopt gold may have been strongly influenced by Ricardo's ([1819] 1952) belief that technical change in silver mining would lead to a massive increase in its supply. See Friedman (1990b).

16. Though the Bank of England was a private institution until 1946, we treat its policies as not independent of the wishes of the government. The government had two powerful checks over the Bank: periodic renewal of its charter, and its role as the government's banker. For a contrary view, see Gallarotti (1991).

17. In interpreting this exchange rate, adjustments must be made to allow for the Hamburg currency being on silver and sterling being effectively on gold, as well as the interest charge implicit in the prices of bills of exchange used to derive the series. As Ricardo pointed out, when these factors are taken into account, the Hamburg exchange rate understated the depreciation of the Bank of England note in terms of gold (Fetter, 1965, 28).

18. The Order in Council of February 26, suspending the specie convertibility of Bank of England notes, recommended resumption by June 24, 1797.

19. The report's exact words were:

> Your Committee would suggest, that the restriction on cash payments cannot safely be removed at an earlier period than two years from the present time; but your Committee is of the opinion, that early provision ought to be made by parliament for terminating, by the end of the period, the operation of the several statutes which have imposed and continued that restriction. (*Report from the Select Committee on the High Price of Bullion; Bullion Report* [1810] 1978, cclxi)

It went on to stress that, even if peace came in less than two years, two years should be allowed for resumption because of the increase likely, both in mercantile activity on the coming of peace, and in demands on the Bank for discount. But, "even if the war should be prolonged, cash payments should be resumed by the end of that period [of two years from the date of the Report]."

20. The "Bullionist debate" pitted the Bullionists, who blamed the depreciation of the pound on the excessive issue of Bank of England notes, against the anti-Bullionists, who attributed the depreciation to extraordinary wartime foreign remittances and other real factors. See Laidler (1987) and Viner (1937).

21. The government's failure to confront the *Bullion Report*'s criticism directly can be understood in this light. The government felt unable to argue that continued suspension was justified by wartime fiscal needs because it was concerned

that this position would weaken both internal and external confidence in the paper pound. Instead, the government took the much maligned position of both disputing the facts of depreciation and presenting a list of nonmonetary causes (O'Brien, 1967, chapter 6).

22. According to Neal (1991), the Bank was opposed to resumption after hostilities ceased because it feared the loss of its gold reserves as capital was repatriated to the continent.

23. Initially, resumption would be at £4. 15s. 0d. on gold bars. The price would then be reduced in stages and the terms extended finally to include coin at mint par of £3. 17s. 10½d. (Clapham, 1944, 71).

24. Although one could argue that the war did not really end until reparations were paid and the Allies ended their occupation of France in 1818. See White (1991).

25. The Bank Charter Act was criticized on two grounds: (1) the currency principle ignored the role of deposits as an increasingly important component of the money stock; and (2) the Banking department, in operating on a sound commercial banking basis, could not act responsibly as a central bank. The latter criticism was at the heart of the traditional case for "discretion." This criticism culminated in the 1860s with the formulation by Walter Bagehot, the influential editor of *The Economist*, of the "responsibility doctrine" and the establishment of guidelines for a central bank under a gold standard (Bordo, 1984, 45–46).

26. On all three occasions, the Treasury issued a letter allowing the Bank to expand its fiduciary issue, but only in 1857 did it actually do so. On the other two occasions, the announcement alone was sufficient to allay the panic (Clapham, 1944, vol. II, 208–209).

27. The contribution of high-powered money to the finance of wartime expenditure is a lower bound estimate of the contribution of money to wartime finance, since in both episodes the banking system participated in the operation.

28. According to Moggridge (1969), the key reason cited was the maintenance of London's prominent position in international finance.

29. See Pollard (1970, editor's Introduction), and especially Brown (1929), Sayers (1960), and Hume (1963).

30. Smith and Smith (1990) view resumption in 1925 as an example of a stochastic process switch. Their numerical estimates suggest that, contrary to some contemporary views, the appreciation of sterling prior to April 1925 appears to have been due to fundamentals, such as restrictive monetary policy, rather than to the expectation of a change in regime.

31. See Officer (1983, 1985) for a valuable discussion on measuring both the par of exchange and the market exchange rate.

32. According to Calomiris (1988), following Mitchell (1903) and Roll (1972), the pace and timing of resumption depended solely on fiscal news – legislation and policy announcements affecting the government's budget. Rolnick and Wallace (1984) also view interpretation of this episode as dependent only on overall government fiscal expectations.

33. Garber and Grilli (1986) present estimates of silver risk in the yields of dollar-denominated assets in this period. Also see Garber (1986) for estimates of the value of the silver option on bimetallic bonds.
34. The United States, unlike the British example comparing World War I to the French wars, did not finance a larger fraction of its expenditures in World War I by debt and fiat money issue than in the Civil War. The fractions are:

	Civil War 1861–1865	World War I 1917–1918
	Percentage of wartime expenditure financed by:	Percentage of wartime expenditure financed by:
Taxes[1]	21	25
Bonds[2]	61	61
High-powered money[3]	18	14

Sources: 1.–3. 1861–1865: Friedman (1952).
                1.–3. 1917–1918: Walton and Rockoff (1989, 443).

35. According to Eichengreen (1992b), following Alesina and Drazen (1991), the rapid inflation in the early 1920s and the *de facto* stabilization of the franc at an undervalued rate in 1926 reflected a compromise outcome from a war of attrition between debtors and creditors. By contrast, Britain's return to the old parity represented a victory by the creditor class.
36. This did not occur until after wartime inflation was in large part reversed by Mussolini's contractionary policies. See Kindleberger (1984, 383).
37. Following Fratianni and Spinelli (1984), we calculate the country risk premium as

$$D_t = \ell n(1 + i_{I,t}) - \ell n(1 + i_{F,t}) - \ell n E_{t+1}^t + \ell n E_t,$$

where $i_{I,t}$ is the yield on Italian bonds at time t; $i_{F,t}$ is the yield on French bonds, E_{t+1}^t is the lira/franc exchange rate for $t+1$ expected at t, and E_t is the exchange rate at t. Their calculation holds constant transactions costs and assumes perfect foresight in the exchange market, that is, $\ell n E_{t+1}^t = \ell n E_{t+1}$. We also calculated the risk premium using an alternative measure of the expected change in the exchange rate, $\ell n E_t - \ell n E_{t-1}$, and the picture was virtually the same.
38. See Bordo and Kydland (1990) for a more detailed discussion.
39. Other Latin American countries also had experiences of alternating adherence to gold convertibility. See Fishlow (1987).
40. Klein (1975) also presents evidence for mean reversion of the price level under the gold standard.
41. See Eichengreen (1985, 5) for a chronology of countries adopting gold.
42. Giovannini (1993) views the facts that both exchange rates and short-term interest rates varied within the limits set by the gold points in the 1899–1909 period as consistent with market agents' expectations of a credible commitment by the four "core" countries to the gold standard rule in the sense of this chapter.

43. See Eichengreen (1992a, 60) and Fishlow (1987, 1989).
44. According to Giovannini (1986), however, the Bank of England did not follow the "rules," while the Reichsbank did.
45. Alternatively, the gold devices could be interpreted as an effort to strain every nerve to *avoid* abandoning convertibility.
46. According to Eichengreen (1992a), the Bank of England's ability to ensure convertibility was aided by cooperation with other central banks. In addition, as mentioned above, belief based on past performance that England attached highest priority to convertibility encouraged stabilizing private capital movements in times of threat to convertibility, such as in 1890 and 1907.
47. According to Giovannini's (1989) regressions, the French and German central banks adapted their domestic policies to external conditions, whereas the British did not. This can be interpreted as evidence for British management.
48. Grossman's (1990) interpretation of the historical record, though emphasizing different factors, accepts this view. Thus, according to him, the ratio of government debt to GNP increased during major wartime episodes in Britain and the United States from the mid-18th century until after World War I, reflecting intertemporal substitution. Such borrowing represented a temporary effort to shift resources from the future to the present. Following each war, the ratio of debt to income would then be reduced by contractionary fiscal policy accompanied by deflationary monetary policies that maintained the real rate of return on outstanding bonds. According to Grossman, such a policy was an investment in the credibility capital of the sovereign borrower – a reputation for responsible repayment of the principal and for preservation of the real value of interest payments that enhanced the probability of being able to borrow heavily again at favorable rates in the event of a future war.
49. According to North and Weingast (1989), this process was complete by the Glorious Revolution of 1688. After that date, capital markets developed in an environment free of the risk of sovereign appropriation of capital.
50. An alternative and complementary explanation to that offered in this chapter relates to political economy considerations and the distribution of income. The configuration of political interest groups in the 19th century was favorable to the hard money, pro-gold standard rule position. This may have been related to the more limited development of democracy and less-than-universal suffrage. Thus, a comparison of the debates over resumption in England from 1797 to 1821 and in the United States from 1865 to 1878 suggests that the more limited suffrage in England in the early period served as a brake on the soft money forces favoring permanent depreciation. In the United States, the soft money forces favoring redistribution of income to debtors and other groups (such as Midwestern manufacturers) almost carried the day.

References

Alesina, A. and A. Drazen (1991). "Why Are Stabilizations Delayed?," *American Economic Review* 81(8), 1170–1188

Bancroft, H. H. (1890). *History of California*, VII, San Francisco: The History Company

Barro, R. J. (1979). "On the Determination of the Public Debt," *Journal of Political Economy* 87, 940–971

(1987). "Government Spending, Interest Rates, Prices, and Budget Deficits in the United Kingdom, 1701–1918," *Journal of Monetary Economics* 20, 221–248

Barro, R. J. and D. B. Gordon (1983). "Rules, Discretion and Reputation in a Model of Monetary Policy," *Journal of Monetary Economics* 12, 101–121

Barsky, R. B. (1987). "The Fisher Hypothesis and the Forecastability and Persistence of Inflation," *Journal of Monetary Economics* 19(1) (January), 3–24

Barsky, R. B. and L. H. Summers (1988). "Gibson's Paradox and the Gold Standard," *Journal of Political Economy* 96(3) (June), 528–550

Bloomfield, A. (1959). *Monetary Policy Under the International Gold Standard, 1880–1914*, New York: Federal Reserve Bank of New York

Board of Governors of the Federal Reserve System (1994). *Banking and Monetary Statistics*, New York

Bordo, M. D. (1981). "The Classical Gold Standard: Some Lessons for Today," *Federal Reserve Bank of St. Louis Review* 64(5) (May), 2–17

(1984). "The Gold Standard: The Traditional Approach," in M. D. Bordo and A. J. Schwartz (eds.), *A Retrospective on the Classical Gold Standard, 1821–1931*, Chicago: University of Chicago Press for NBER, 23–199

(1986). "Money, Deflation and Seigniorage: A Review Essay," *Journal of Monetary Economics* 18(3), 337–346

(1987a). "John Law," in P. Newman, M. Milgate and J. Eatwell (eds.), *The New Palgrave Dictionary of Economics*, London: Macmillan

(1987b). "Bimetallism," in R. Newman, M. Milgate and J. Eatwell (eds.), *The New Palgrave Dictionary of Economics*, London: Macmillan

(1993). "The Bretton Woods International Monetary System: An Historical Overview," in M. D. Bordo and B. Eichengreen (eds.), *A Restrospective on the Bretton Woods System: Lessons for International Monetary Reform*, Chicago: University of Chicago Press for NBER

Bordo, M. D. and F. E. Kydland (1990). "The Gold Standard as a Rule," NBER, *Working Paper* 3367 (May)

Bordo, M. D. and E. N. White (1991). "A Tale of Two Currencies: British and French Finance During the Napoleonic Wars," *Journal of Economic History* (June), 303–316

(1993). "British and French Finance During the Napoleonic Wars," in M. D. Bordo and F. Capie (eds.), *Monetary Regimes in Transition*, Cambridge: Cambridge University Press

British Parliamentary Papers (1888). "Second and Final Reports From the Royal Commission on the Recent Changes in the Relative Values of Precious Metals with Minutes of Evidence, Appendices, and Index," Shannon, Ireland: Irish University Press

Brown, W. A. (1929). *England and the New Gold Standard, 1919–1926*, New Haven: Yale University Press

Bullion Report ([1810] 1978) *Report from the Select Committee on the High Price of Bullion*, New York: Arno Press

Calomiris, C. W. (1988). "Price and Exchange Rate Determination During the Greenback Suspension," *Oxford Economic Papers* (December)

Capie, F. and A. Webber (1985). *A Monetary History of the United Kingdom, 1870–1982*, vol. 1, *Data, Sources, Methods*, London: George Allen & Unwin

Chari, V. V. (1988). "Time Consistency and Optimal Policy Design," *Quarterly Review*, Federal Reserve Bank of Minneapolis (Fall)

Chari, V. V. and P. J. Kehoe (1989). "Sustainable Plans and Debt," Federal Reserve Bank of Minneapolis, *Staff Report* 125

(1990). "Sustainable Plans," *Journal of Political Economy* 98, 783–802

Clapham, J. (1944). *The Bank of England: A History*, vols. I and II, Cambridge: Cambridge University Press

Cole, H. L. and P. J. Kehoe (1991). "Reputation With Mulitple Relationships: Reviving Reputation Models of Debt," Federal Reserve Bank of Minneapolis, *Staff Report* 137

Cooper, R. (1982). "The Gold Standard: Historical Facts and Future Prospects," *Brookings Papers on Economic Activity* 1, 1–45

Crabbe, L. (1989). "The International Gold Standard and Monetary Policy in the United States from the First World War to the New Deal," Board of Governors of the Federal Reserve System, mimeo

Cukierman, A. (1988). "Rapid Inflation – Deliberate Policy or Miscalculation?," *Carnegie–Rochester Conference Series on Public Policy* 29, 11–76

Cunliffe Report (1918). *First Interim Report of the Committee on Currency and Foreign Exchanges After the War*, Cmnd. 9182, reprint, New York: Arno Press

Eichengreen, B. (1985). "Editor's Introduction," in B. Eichengreen, *The Gold Standard in Theory and History*, London: Methuen

(1987). "Conducting the International Orchestra: Bank of England Leadership Under the Classical Gold Standard," *Journal of International Money and Finance* 6, 5–29

(1989). "Hegemonic Stability Theories of the International Monetary Systems," in R. Bryant (ed.), *Can Nations Agree: Aspects of International Cooperation?*, Washington: Brookings Institution

(1992a). "The Gold Standard Since Alec Ford," in S. M. Broadberry and N. F. R. Crafts (eds.), *Britain in the International Economy, 1870–1939*, Cambridge: Cambridge University Press

(1992b). *Golden Fetters: The Gold Standard and the Great Depression, 1919–1939*, New York: Oxford University Press

Feavearyear, A. (1963). *The Pound Sterling*, Oxford: Clarendon Press

Fetter, F. (1965). *Development of British Monetary Orthodoxy, 1797–1875*, Cambridge, MA: Harvard University Press

Fischer, S. (1980). "Dynamic Inconsistency. Cooperation, and the Benevolent Dissembling Government," *Journal of Economic Dynamics and Control* 2, 93–108

Fishlow, A. (1987). "Market Forces or Group Interests: Inconvertible Currency in Pre-1914 Latin America," University of California at Berkeley, mimeo
  (1989). "Conditionality and Willingness to Pay: Some Parallels from the 1890s," in B. Eichengreen and P. Lindert (eds.), *The International Debt Crisis in Historical Perspective*, Cambridge, MA: MIT Press
Ford, A. G. (1962). *The Gold Standard, 1880–1914: Britain and Argentina*, Oxford: Clarendon Press
Fratianni, M. and F. Spinelli (1984). "Italy in the Gold Standard Period, 1861–1914," in M. D. Bordo and A. J. Schwartz (eds.), *A Retrospective on the Classical Gold Standard, 1821–1931*, Chicago: University of Chicago Press for NBER
Friedman, M. (1952). "Price, Income and Monetary Changes in Three Wartime Periods," *American Economic Review* (May), 612–625
  (1990a). "The Crime of 1873," *Journal of Political Economy* 98 (December), 1159–1194
  (1990b). "Bimetallism Revisited," *Journal of Economic Perspectives* 4(4), 85–104
Friedman, M. and A. J. Schwartz (1963). *A Monetary History of the United States, 1867–1960*, Princeton: Princeton University Press for NBER
  (1982). *Monetary Trends in the United States and in the United Kingdom 1870–1970*, Chicago: University of Chicago Press for NBER
Gallarotti, G. M. (1991). "Centralized versus Decentralized International Monetary Systems: The Lessons of the Classical Gold Standard," in J. Dorn (ed.), *Alternatives to Government Fiat Money*, Dordrecht: Kluwer
Garber, P. (1986). "Nominal Contracts in a Bimetallic Standard," *American Economic Review* 76, 1012–1030
Garber, P. and V. Grilli (1986). "The Belmont–Morgan Syndicate as an Optimal Investmnt Banking Contract," *European Economic Review* 30, 641–677
Gayer, A. D., W. W. Rostow and A. J. Schwartz (1953). *The Growth and Fluctuations of the British Economy, 1790–1850*, Oxford: Clarendon Press
Giavazzi, F. and A. Giovannini (1989). *Limiting Exchange Rate Flexibility*, Cambridge, MA: MIT Press
Giovannini, A. (1986). "'Rules of the Game' during the International Gold Standard: England and Germany," *Journal of International Money and Finance* 5, 467–483
  (1989). "How Do Fixed Exchange-Rate Regimes Work: The Evidence From the Gold Standard, Bretton Woods and the EMS," in M. Miller, B. Eichengreen and R. Portes (eds.), *Blueprints for Exchange Rate Management*, London: CEPR, 13–46
  (1993). "Bretton Woods and its Precursors: Rules versus Discretion in the History of International Monetary Regimes," in M. D. Bordo and B. Eichengreen (eds.), *A Retrospective on the Bretton Woods System: Lessons for International Monetary Reform*, Chicago: University of Chicago Press for NBER, 109–154
Glassman, D. and Redish, A. (1988). "Currency Depreciation in Early Modern England and France," *Explorations in Economic History* 25

Goodfriend, M. (1988). "Central Banking Under the Gold Standard," *Carnegie–Rochester Conference Series on Public Policy* 19, 85–124

(1989). "Money, Credit, Banking and Payments System Policy," in D. B. Humphrey (ed.), *The US Payments System: Efficiency, Risk, and the Role of the Federal Reserve*, Boston: Kluwer Academic

Grilli, V. (1989). "Managing Exchange Rate Crises: Evidence from the 1890s," NBER, *Working Paper* 3068 (August)

Grossman, H. (1990). "The Political Economy of War Debts and Inflation," in W. S. Haraf and P. Cagan (eds.), *Monetary Policy for a Changing Financial Environment*, Washington, DC: American Enterprise Institute

Grossman, H. I. and J. B. Huyck (1988). "Sovereign Debt as a Contingent Claim: Excusable Default, Repudiation, and Reputation," *American Economic Review* 78, 1088–1097

Hayashi, F. (1989). "Japan's Saving Rate: New Data and Reflections," NBER, *Working Paper* 3205

Hume, L. J. (1963). "The Gold Standard and Deflation: Issues and Attitudes in the Nineteen Twenties," *Economica* 30, 225–242

Jastram, R. (1977). *The Golden Constant: The English and American Experience, 1560–1976*, New York: John Wiley

Jonung, L. (1984). "Swedish Experience Under the Classical Gold Standard, 1873–1914," in M. D. Bordo and A. J. Schwartz (eds.), *A Retrospective on the Classical Gold Standard, 1821–1931*, Chicago: University of Chicago Press for NBER

Keynes, J. M. ([1913] 1971). *Indian Currency and Finance, The Collected Writings of John Maynard Keynes*, vol. I, reprinted in London: Macmillan and New York: Cambridge University Press for the Royal Economic Society

([1925] 1972). "The Economic Consequences of Mr. Churchill," in *The Collected Writings of John Maynard Keynes*, vol. IX, *Essays in Persuasion*, London: Macmillan

Kindleberger, C. P. (1973). *The World in Depression, 1929–1939*, Berkeley, CA: University of California Press

(1984). *A Financial History of Western Europe*, London: George Allen & Unwin

Klein, B. (1975). "Our New Monetary Standard: Measurement and Effects of Price Uncertainty, 1880–1973," *Economic Inquiry* 13, 461–484

Kydland, F. E. and E. C. Prescott (1977). "Rules Rather than Discretion: The Inconsistency of Optimal Plans," *Journal of Political Economy* 85 (June), 473–492

(1980a). "Dynamic Optimal Taxation, Rational Expectations and Optimal Control," *Journal of Economic Dynamics and Control* 2, 79–91

(1980b). "A Competitive Theory of Fluctuations and the Feasibility and Desirability of Stabilization Policy," in S. Fischer (ed.), *Rational Expectations and Economic Policy*, Chicago: University of Chicago Press for the NBER

Lacroix, A. and P. Dupieux (1973). *Le Napoleon ou les drames de la monnaie française depuis deux mille ans*, Paris: Les Presses de L'Imprimerie, Tardy-Quevey-Auvergne

Laidler, D. E. W. (1987). "The Bullionist Controversy," in P. Newman, M. Milgate and J. Eatwell (eds.), *New Palgrave Dictionary of Economics*, London: Macmillan

Lindert, P. (1969). *Key Currencies and Gold, 1900–1913, Princeton Studies in International Finance* 24, Princeton: Princeton University Press

Lucas, R. E. Jr. and N. L. Stokey (1983). "Optimal Fiscal and Monetary Policy in an Economy Without Capital," *Journal of Monetary Economics* 12, 55–93

McCullum, B. (1989). *Monetary Economics: Theory and Policy*, New York: St. Martin's Press

McGouldrick, R. (1984). "Operations of the German Central Bank and the Rules of the Game, 1879–1913," in M. D. Bordo and A. J. Schwartz (eds.), *A Retrospective on the Classical Gold Standard, 1821–1931*, Chicago: University of Chicago Press for NBER

McKinnon, R. (1993). "Alternative International Monetary Systems: The Rules of the Game Reconsidered," *Journal of Economic Literature* 31, 1–44

Meltzer, A. H. and S. Robinson (1989). "Stability Under the Gold Standard in Practice," in M. D. Bordo (ed.), *Money, History and International Finance: Essays in Honor of Anna J. Schwartz*. Chicago: University of Chicago Press

Mitchell, B. R. (1975). *European Historical Statistics, 1750–1970*, London: Macmillan

Mitchell, B. R. and P. Deane (1962). *Abstract of British Historical Statistics*, Cambridge: Cambridge University Press

Mitchell, W. C. (1903). *A History of the Greenbacks*, Chicago: University of Chicago Press

(1908). *Gold, Prices and Wages Under the Greenbacks Standard*, Berkeley, CA: University of California Press

Moggridge, D. (1969). *The Return to Gold, 1925: The Formulations of Economic Policy and Its Critics*, London: Cambridge University Press

Murphy, A. (1987). *Richard Cantillon: Entrepreneur and Economist*, Oxford: Clarendon Press

Neal, L. (1991). "A Tale of Two Revolutions: The Effects of Capital Flows 1789–1815," *Bulletin of Economic Research* 43(1) (January), 57–92

North, D. and B. Weingast (1989). "Constitution and Commitment: Evolution of Institutions Governing Public Choice," *Journal of Economic History*, 69(4) (December), 803–837

O'Brien, P. (1967). "Government Revenue 1793–1815: A Study in Fiscal and Financial Policy in the Wars Against France," Oxford University, unpublished D. Phil. thesis

O'Leary, P. M. (1937). "The Coinage Legislation of 1834," *Journal of Political Economy* 45, 80–94

Officer, L. (1983). "Dollar–Sterling Mint Parity and Exchange Rates, 1791–1834," *Journal of Economic History*, 43(3) (September), 579–616

(1985). "Integration in the American Foreign Exchange Market, 1791–1900,' *Journal of Economic History*, 45(3) (September), 557–586

(1986). "The Efficiency of the Dollar–Sterling Gold Standard, 1890–1908," *Journal of Political Economy* 94 (October), 1038–1073

Pollard, S. (ed.) (1970). *The Gold Standard and Employment Policies Between the Wars*, London: Methuen

Prescott, E. (1977). "Should Control Theory Be Used for Economic Stabilization?," *Carnegie–Rochester Conference Series on Public Policy* 7, 13–38

Presnell, L. S. (1956). *Country Banking in the Industrial Revolution*, Oxford: Clarendon Press

(1982). "The Sterling System and Financial Crises Before 1914," in C. P. Kindleberger and J. P. Laffargue (eds.), *Financial Crises: Theory, History and Policy*, New York: Cambridge University Press

Rae, G. (1885). *The Country Banker*, London

Ramsey, F. (1927). "A Contribution to the Theory of Taxation," *Economic Journal* 37, 47–61

Redish, A. (1990). "The Evolution of the Gold Standard in England," *Journal of Economic History* (December), 789–806

Ricardo, D. ([1819] 1952). "Minutes of Evidence Taken Before the Secret Committee on the Expediency of the Bank Resuming Cash Payments," (March 4, 1819), reprinted in P. Sraffa (ed.), *The Works and Correspondence of David Ricardo*, vol. 5, *Speeches, Evidence*, Cambridge: Cambridge University Press

Rockoff, H. (1984). "Some Evidence on the Real Price of Gold, its Cost of Production, and Commodity Prices," in M. D. Bordo and A. J. Schwartz (eds.), *A Retrospective on the Classical Gold Standard, 1821–1931*, Chicago: University of Chicago Press for NBER

Roll, R. (1972). "Interest Rates and Price Expectations During the Civil War," *Journal of Economic History* 32

Rolnick, A. J. and N. Wallace (1984). "Suspension and the Financing of the Civil War: A Critique of Newcomb and Mitchell," Federal Reserve Bank of Minneapolis, *Working Paper* 265

St. Marc, M. (1983). *Histoire monétaire de la France, 1800–1980*, Paris: Presses Universitaires de France

Sayers, R. S. (1960). "The Return to Gold, 1925," in L. S. Presnell (ed.), *Studies in the Industrial Revolution*, London

Schwartz, A. J. (1984). "Introduction," in M. D. Bordo and A. J. Schwartz (eds.), *A Retrospective on the Classical Gold Standard, 1821–1931*, Chicago: University of Chicago Press for NBER

(1986). "Real and Pseudo Financial Crises," in F. Capie and G. E. Wood (eds.), *Financial Crises and the World Banking System*, London: Macmillan

(1987). "Banking School, Currency School, Free Banking School," in P. Newman, M. Milgate and J. Eatwell (eds.), *New Palgrave Dictionary of Economics*, London: Macmillan

Sharkey, R. D. (1959). *Money, Class, and Party*, Baltimore: Johns Hopkins University Press

Smith, W. S. and R. T. Smith (1990). "Stochastic Process Switching and the Return to Gold 1925," *Economic Journal* 100 (March), 164–175

Temin, P. (1989). *Lessons from the Great Depression*, Cambridge, MA: MIT Press

Tonniolo, G. (1990). *An Economic History of Liberal Italy: 1850–1918*, New York: Routledge

Unger, I. (1964). *The Greenback Era: A Social and Political History of American Finance, 1865–1879*, Princeton: Princeton University Press

Viner, J. (1937). *Studies in the Theory of International Trade*, Chicago: University of Chicago Press

Walton, G. and H. Rockoff (1989). *History of the American Economy*, 6th edn., New York: Harcourt, Brace & Jovanovich

White, E. (1991). "French Reparations after the Napoleonic Wars," Rutgers University (July), mimeo

Yeager, L. (1976). *International Monetary Relations*, 2nd edn., New York: Harper & Row

(1984). "The Image of the Gold Standard," in M. D. Bordo and A. J. Schwartz (eds.), *A Retrospective on the Classical Gold Standard, 1821–1931*, Chicago: University of Chicago Press

4 Market efficiency and regime efficiency under the 1925–1931 dollar/sterling gold standard

Lawrence H. Officer

The gold standard is typically analyzed as a fixed exchange rate regime. While the existence of a gold-point spread is recognized (if only implicitly), the location of the exchange rate is deemed irrelevant as long as the rate remains within the spread. The common procedure, then, is simply to represent the exchange rate by the mint parity, a practice justified by long-term automatic adjustment processes that eliminate balance of payments disequilibria that can exist only at (or beyond) a gold point. In particular, the interwar dollar/sterling gold standard is universally viewed as involving a pound substantially overvalued at the mint parity but with corrective processes stymied by altered circumstances and policies compared to the prewar period, eventually leading to the demise of the gold standard. So the existing studies of the stability of the interwar gold standard are long-term in nature, making no reference to the gold-point spread or the movement of the exchange rate within it.[1]

In this chapter a different focus is adopted. The functioning of a gold standard in general – with the dollar/sterling interwar experience as the case study – is analyzed from the standpoint of short-run efficiency in which the precise location of the exchange rate plays the central role. Two concepts of "efficiency" are utilized: *market efficiency*, involving the behavior of private parties in response to the profit opportunities afforded by the gold standard, and *regime efficiency*, pertaining to the probability of maintenance of the gold standard with the existing mint parity.

As a criterion, market efficiency has the usual definition from the asset market literature: a situation in which private market participants (arbitrageurs and speculators) cannot earn a predictable or persistent economic profit on the basis of publicly available information. A theory of gold standard market efficiency is offered in the first section, data for testing the theory presented in the next, and empirical results discussed in the third. Innovations are (i) joint consideration of uncovered interest arbitrage, covered interest arbitrage, and forward

101

speculation, and (ii) careful attention to transactions cost, risk premium, and taxation.

The criterion of regime efficiency, a new concept, is that private participants and central banks behave in such a way that the probability of maintenance of the gold standard is, ideally, maximized, or at least enhanced. The implications of fulfilled market efficiency for regime efficiency are drawn in the fourth section, and the influence of market forces and policy variables on regime efficiency explored in the fifth and sixth. In the final section the net regime efficiency of the interwar gold standard is computed and compared to that of the classical gold standard.[2]

Market efficiency: theory

Tests of exchange market efficiency have two dimensions. First, they can involve (1a) pure arbitrage, (1b) pure speculation, or (1c) a combination of arbitrage and speculation. Second, they can incorporate (2) a gold-point spread, (3) an exchange rate norm value, usually mint parity but here the mid-point of the gold-point spread, or (4) neither. The spread and norm value are characteristics of a gold standard (and other fixed rate) and not of a floating rate; so testing that excludes both are *prima facie* excluded.

The activities considered, with their properties, are gold-point arbitrage (1a, 2), uncovered interest arbitrage (1c, 2, 3), covered interest arbitrage (1a, 4), forward speculation (1b, 2, 3), and covered interest arbitrage combined with forward speculation (1c, 2, 3). Covered interest arbitrage by itself is included because it is intertwined with uncovered interest arbitrage and forward speculation.

All these forms of arbitrage and speculation involve operations in the foreign exchange market. After World War I, the cable became "by far" the dominant exchange market instrument, at least in the interbank market, replacing the venerable bill of exchange (Einzig, 1970, 238). Therefore the exchange market transactions that are described pertain to cable.

Operations in favor of the pound

Gold-import arbitrage
Operations in favor of the pound involve an immediate purchase of pounds (either spot or forward, depending on the operation), thus increasing the exchange value of the pound (in one or the other market). Let RS denote the spot exchange rate and GM the US gold-import point, both expressed in dollars per pound. For $RS < GM$, there is a positive profit from the gold-import form of gold-point arbitrage (GPA). Spot pounds are

purchased, pushing up RS to GM, where arbitrage profit is eliminated. Therefore efficient gold-import arbitrage involves the spot exchange rate being no lower than the gold-import point: $GM \leq RS$.

Arbitrage profit is of the nature of a capital gain, and in 1925–1931 the dominant gold-point arbitrageurs were the large New York banks. During this period the United States treated capital gains and losses as ordinary income for corporate tax purposes, while the United Kingdom did not tax capital gains (Blakey and Blakey, 1940, 588; Spaulding, 1927, 127). Therefore after-tax profit under GPA is the product of $(1 - t_{US})$ and pretax profit, where t_{US} is the US *ad valorem* (one-hundredth the percentage) corporate tax rate. The value of GM (and, later, of GX, the gold-export point) and the existence of GPA profit is independent of taxation; only, the amount of profit is reduced proportionately.[3]

Uncovered interest arbitrage

As a form of exchange rate speculation, uncovered interest arbitrage (UIA) can be either stabilizing or destabilizing. The UIA of interest involves stabilizing speculation and emanates from absolute confidence of the arbitrageurs that, over their horizon (say, N months), the existing gold standard will be maintained and efficient gold-import arbitrage will govern; so the expected spot exchange rate is no lower than the gold-import point: $RS^* \geq GM$, where RS^* is the spot rate expected to prevail N months in the future. The principal interest arbitrageurs (covered or uncovered) were the large New York banks for arbitrage in favor of the pound, the large London banks for arbitrage in favor of the dollar (Einzig, 1937, 172). The arbitrageur purchases pounds at the current spot rate (RS), planning to reverse her transaction after N months, that is, to sell pounds at the expected spot rate (RS^*). In the interim the funds are invested in the London rather than the New York money market.

The interwar arbitrageur operated under double taxation of international investment income. The United States taxed the entirety of the New York bank's arbitrage income, while the United Kingdom taxed the investment income earned in London. However, the United States permitted in effect an *ad valorem* tax credit on foreign taxes up to the US tax rate, with any excess foreign taxes deductible from taxable income.

Unlike the United States, which had simple corporate taxation, the United Kingdom had an integrated system of personal and corporate taxation. Corporations paid the standard income tax rate, but were allowed to deduct the tax paid on dividends distributed. Foreign corporations, such as the New York bank, though subject to tax on their UK source income, were also allowed to make this deduction.[4] Letting t_{UK}^n denote the UK *ad valorem* income tax rate, and p the taxed firm's (in this case, the New York bank's) dividend-payout ratio (ratio of dividends to gross profit), the effective UK tax rate (t_{UK}) is the nominal tax rate (t_{UK}^n) reduced by the ratio of undistributed to gross profit $(1-p)$: $t_{UK}=(1-p)\cdot t_{UK}^n$, where $0\le p\le 1$.

Allowing for the taxation environment, the interwar arbitrageur thought in terms of a strict separation of exchange rate and interest gains, albeit its mathematical impossibility (Officer, 1993, 102–103). Exchange rate gain is a capital gain (if positive) or a capital loss (if negative), treated as ordinary income under US corporate taxation. Therefore expected after-tax exchange rate gain is $E_L^{uia}=[(RS^*-RS)/RS]\cdot(1-t_{US})$. However, net interest return depends on the relationship of t_{US} to t_{UK}, the US and UK effective tax rates. Let I_{UK} denote the London and I_{US} the New York interest rate, each expressed (as is inherently the exchange rate gain) in *ad valorem* terms per N-month period. For $t_{US}<t_{UK}$ (case a), the interest return is $I_{La}=I_{UK}\cdot[1-t_{UK}+t_{US}\cdot(t_{UK}-t_{US})]-I_{US}\cdot(1-t_{US})$, while for $t_{US}>t_{UK}$ (case b) the return is $I_{Lb}=(I_{UK}-I_{US})\cdot(1-t_{US})$. The subscript "$L$" is used for operations in favor of the pound, because *lower* exchange rate bounds are determined by market efficiency.

There are two components of cost. First is transactions cost, TC, expressed in *ad valorem* terms as a proportion of the amount invested. It is assumed that the entirety of TC is deductible from taxable income, although in reality only the monetary costs of exchange market and money market transactions have this property.[5] It is also assumed that the deduction is taken totally on taxable income for the home country (the United States, for operations in favor of the pound) and none for the foreign country.

The second cost component is a risk premium for exchange rate risk. A reasonable specification of this risk premium is that it is proportional to the maximum *ad valorem* exchange rate loss. In the present case, the risk premium is $R_L^{uia}=r\cdot(RS-GM)/RS$, where $0\le r\le 1$ and r may be called the risk premium parameter. A zero value of r involves risk neutrality, while a value of unity implies extreme risk aversion: arbitrageurs require full compensation for their maximum possible exchange rate loss, given their absolute confidence that the future spot exchange rate will not be below the gold-import point: $RS^*\ge GM$. Risk premium is a deduction from economic but not accounting (taxable) profit.

Expected economic profit (on an *ad valorem* basis per N-month period) is the exchange rate gain *plus* the interest return *minus* transactions cost *minus* risk premium: $\pi_{Lx}^{uia}=E_L^{uia}+I_{Lx}-TC\cdot(1-t_{US})-R_L^{uia}$, for $x=a, b$. Solving $\pi_{Lx}^{uia}=0$ for RS yields

$$RS_{Lx}^{uia}=[RS^*\cdot(1-t_{US})+r\cdot GM]/[(1-t_{US})\cdot(1+TC)-I_{Lx}+r],$$

for $x=a,b$. If and only if the exchange rate falls below this critical value, $RS<RS_{Lx}^{uia}$, does UIA in favor of the pound yield a positive profit.

Covered interest arbitrage

The New York bank can cover the exchange rate risk by selling pounds N months forward, resulting in covered interest arbitrage (CIA). Then the risk premium parameter, r, is zero and the expected spot rate, RS^*, is replaced by the N-month forward rate, RF. After-tax exchange rate gain is now $E_L^{cia} = [(RF-RS)/RS]\cdot(1-t_{US})$. Economic profit is exchange rate gain *plus* interest return *minus* transactions cost:
$\pi_{Lx}^{cia} = E_L^{cia} + I_{Lx} - TC\cdot(1-t_{US})$, for $x=a, b$. Solving $\pi_{Lx}^{cia}=0$ for RS yields

$$RS_{La}^{cia} = [RF\cdot(1-t_{US})]/[(1+TC)\cdot(1-t_{US})-I_{La}]$$
$$RS_{Lb}^{cia} = RF/[(1+TC)-(I_{UK}-I_{US})].$$

In case b, the taxation element behaves the same way as for GPA. The UK tax is irrelevant and the US tax rate affects profit proportionately via the factor $(1-t_{US})$; RS_{Lb}^{cia} is the same as if $t_{UK}=t_{US}=0$. Again, if and only if the exchange rate falls below the critical value, $RS<RS_{Lx}^{cia}$, does CIA in favor of the pound involve a positive profit.

Forward speculation

The type of forward speculation (FS) of interest, as the type of UIA, is stabilizing, and so likewise involves, with full confidence, the expected spot rate no lower than the gold-import point: $RS^*\geq GM$. The forward speculator purchases forward pounds at RF, planning to sell them spot in N months at RS^*. For FS compared to UIA, RF replaces RS and $I_{UK}=I_{US}=0$. Expected after-tax exchange rate gain is
$E_L^{fs} = [(RS^*-RF)/RF]\cdot(1-t_{US})$ and risk premium is $R_L^{fs} = r\cdot(RF-GM)/RF$. Expected economic profit is the exchange rate gain *minus* transactions cost *minus* risk premium: $\pi_L^{fs} = E_L^{fs} - TC\cdot(1-t_{US}) - R_L^{fs}$ which, equated to zero, generates $RF_L^{fs} = [RS^*\cdot(1-t_{US})+r\cdot GM]/[(1+TC)\cdot(1-t_{US})+r]$. With no interest investment, t_{UK} does not enter the formula for RF_L^{fs}. If and only if the forward rate is below this critical value, $RF<RF_L^{fs}$, does FS in favor of the pound produce a positive profit.

Operations in favor of the dollar

Gold-export arbitrage

Operations in favor of the dollar entail an immediate sale of pounds (either spot or forward, depending on the operation), thereby reducing the exchange value of the pound (in one or the other market). Letting GX denote the US gold-export point (expressed in dollars per pound), for $RS>GX$ there is a positive profit from the gold-export form of gold-point arbitrage (GPA).

Either spot or forward pounds are sold, depending on whether the arbitrageur bears the exchange risk or covers it. Correspondingly, RS decreases to GX or the short-term forward rate decreases, the latter increasing the cost of forward cover and pushing GX up to RS. Either way, the arbitrage profit is eliminated (Officer, 1993, 100). Therefore efficient gold-export arbitrage involves the spot exchange rate no higher than the gold-export point: $RS \leq GX$. The comments on taxation apply here as well.

Uncovered interest arbitrage

Underlying uncovered interest arbitrage (UIA) in favor of the dollar is full confidence that efficient gold-export arbitrage will exist in the next N months, so the expected spot rate is no higher than the gold-export point: $RS^* \leq GX$. The interest arbitrageur (typically, a large London bank) sells pounds at RS, planning to purchase pounds at RS^* in N months. In the meantime the funds are invested in the New York rather than the London money market. For uncovered arbitrage, with capital gains excepted from taxable income under UK law, expected exchange rate gain is untaxed at $E_U^{uia}=(RS-RS^*)/RS$. As for UIA in favor of the pound, interest income abroad (now in New York) was taxed in both countries. However, UK tax law did not permit a tax credit for taxes paid abroad; rather, such taxes were deductible from taxable income. Therefore interest return is the negative of $I_U=I_{UK}\cdot(1-t_{UK})-I_{US}\cdot[1-t_{US}-t_{UK}\cdot(1-t_{US})]$. Symmetrical to UIA in favor of the pound, risk premium is $R_U^{uia}=r\cdot(GX-RS)/RS$. Expected economic profit is exchange rate gain *plus* interest return *minus* transactions cost *minus* risk premium: $\pi_U^{uia}=E_U^{uia}-I_U-TC\cdot(1-t_{UK})-R_U^{uia}$. Solving $\pi_U^{uia}=0$ yields

$$RS_U^{uia}=[RS^*+r\cdot GX]/[1-I_U-TC\cdot(1-t_{UK})+r].$$

UIA generates a positive profit if and only if the exchange rate exceeds this critical value: $RS>RS_U^{uia}$. The subscript "U" is used for operations in favor of the dollar, because *upper* exchange rate bounds are determined by market efficiency.

Covered interest arbitrage

Under covered interest arbitrage (CIA), the London bank buys N-month forward pounds at RF. Exchange rate gain is $E_U^{cia}=(RS-RF)/RS$ and economic profit, exchange rate gain *plus* interest return *minus* transactions cost, becomes $\pi_U^{cia}=E_U^{cia}-I_U-TC\cdot(1-t_{UK})$. Setting $\pi_U^{cia}=0$ yields

$$RS_U^{cia}=RF/[1-I_U-TC\cdot(1-t_{UK})].$$

CIA results in a positive profit if and only if the exchange rate exceeds this critical value: $RS>RS_U^{cia}$.

Forward speculation

The forward speculator of interest, like the uncovered interest arbitrageur has, with complete confidence, the expected exchange rate no higher than the gold-export point: $RS^* \leq GX$. The speculator sells forward pounds at RF, planning to buy pounds spot at RS^* in N months. Expected exchange rate gain, again untaxed, is $E_U^{fs} = (RF - RS^*)/RF$ and risk premium is $R_U^{fs} r \cdot (GX - RF)/RF$. Expected economic profit is exchange rate gain *minus* transactions cost *minus* risk premium: $\pi_U^{fs} = E_U^{fs} - TC \cdot (1 - t_{UK}) - R_U^{fs}$ which, equated to zero, yields

$$RF_U^{fs} = [RS^* + r \cdot GX]/[1 - TC \cdot (1 - t_{UK}) + r].$$

A positive profit is generated if and only if the forward rate exceeds the critical value: $RF > RF_U^{fs}$.

Efficiency bands

If the exchange rate is below the lower critical value for uncovered interest arbitrage (UIA) or covered interest arbitrage (CIA), $RS < RS_{Lx}^{uia}(RS_{Lx}^{cia})$ for $x=a,b$, then there is a positive profit, $\pi_{Lx}^{uia}(\pi_{Lx}^{uia}) > 0$, and efficient UIA (CIA) would bid up RS, as pounds are purchased to take advantage of profit opportunity, reducing the exchange rate gain, $E_L^{cia}(E_L^{cia})$, and increasing the risk premium, R_L^{uia} (no analogue under CIA). The process continues until profit is zero, $\pi_{Lx}^{uia}(\pi_{Lx}^{cia}) = 0$, and the exchange rate ceases to be below the lower critical value, $RS \geq RS_{Lx}^{uia}(RS_{Lx}^{cia})$. If the exchange rate is above the upper critical value, $RS > RS_U^{uia}(RS_U^{cia})$, a similar mechanism wipes out profit opportunity and makes the exchange rate no greater than that value, $RS \leq RS_U^{uia}(RS_U^{cia})$. Therefore $[RS_{Lx}^{uia}, RS_U^{uia}]$, meaning the set of all RS such that $RS_{Lx}^{uia} \leq RS \leq RS_U^{uia}$, is the UIA efficiency band, and RS_{Lx}^{uia} (RS_U^{uia}) may be termed the lower (upper) UIA efficiency point or limit.[6] Similarly, $[RS_{Lx}^{cia}, RS_U^{cia}]$ is the CIA efficiency band.[7] Quite analogously, the efficiency band under gold-point arbitrage (GPA) is $[GM, GX]$, commonly called the gold-point spread.

A parallel argument to that for uncovered interest arbitrage (UIA) shows that $[RF_L^{fs}, RF_U^{fs}]$ is the forward speculation (FS) efficiency band; but this band pertains to RF rather than RS.[8] To obtain a corresponding band for RS, FS may be combined with CIA. For operations in favor of the pound (dollar), the interest arbitrageur sells (buys) forward pounds while the forward speculator buys (sells) these pounds. The result is a roundabout reduction to UIA, and may be called the joint operation of FS with CIA, or indirect UIA. The lower (upper) efficiency point, RS_{Lx}^{j} (RS_U^{j}) is obtained by substituting RF_L^{fs} (RF_U^{fs}) into RS_{Lx}^{cia} (RS_U^{cia}), and the "FS with CIA" (also called "joint" or "indirect UIA") efficiency band is $[RS_{Lx}^{j}, RS_U^{j}]$ for $x=a, b$. The efficiency limits are:

$$RS_{La}^j = \{(1-t_{US})\cdot[RS^*\cdot(1-t_{US})+r\cdot GM]\}/\{[(1+TC)\cdot(1-t_{US})+r]\cdot[(1+TC)\cdot(1-t_{US})-I_{La}]\}$$

$$RS_{Lb}^j = \{RS^*\cdot(1-t_{US})+r\cdot GM\}/\{[(1+TC)\cdot(1-t_{US})+r]\cdot[1-(I_{UK}-I_{US})+TC]\}$$

$$RS_U^j = \{RS^*+r\cdot GX\}/\{[1-TC\cdot(1-t_{UK})+r]\cdot[1-TC\cdot(1-t_{UK})-I_U]\}.$$

The derivation of the "FS with CIA" efficiency limits requires the assumption that the horizon (N) and transactions cost (TC) are the same for the forward speculators and the interest arbitrageurs.[9] If the resulting efficiency bands are to be compared with corresponding UIA bands, it must also be assumed that TC has the same value for UIA and CIA.[10] More pertinent, it would be absurd for an economic agent to pursue UIA indirectly and thereby add unnecessarily to transactions cost. Rather, the joint "FS with CIA" operation may be viewed as undertaken by different agents, resulting in the joint efficiency limits. It may be noted that the corresponding direct and indirect UIA efficiency limits – RS_{La}^{uia} versus RS_{La}^j, RS_{Lb}^{uia} versus RS_{Lb}^j, and RS_U^{uia} versus RS_U^j – are not identical, with more complex formulas for the indirect limits. Contrary to intuition, setting $TC=0$ would not make the corresponding limits equal.

Market efficiency: parameters and data

A perfectly efficient operation involves the pertinent exchange rate always within the efficiency band of that operation. Perfectly efficient gold-point arbitrage (GPA) requires absolute confidence in the maintenance of the gold standard over the time needed for the operation to be completed. In turn, perfectly efficient uncovered interest arbitrage (UIA) and forward speculation (FS) (and in fact the applicability of the UIA, FS model developed above) require full confidence in perfectly efficient GPA over the agent's horizon. Covered interest arbitrage (CIA) has no such condition for its efficiency, because that operation behaves the same way under a gold standard as under a flexible exchange rate system.

For perfect efficiency, (i) perfect knowledge of the relevant parameters in the efficiency band (or, equivalently, in the associated profit formulas) and (ii) instantaneous adjustment are also needed. In this chapter, monthly data are used, so efficiency is tested in a less-than-perfect sense. "Efficient" market behavior can involve intra-month profit opportunities that average out for the month.

To test for GPA efficiency – the current spot exchange rate between the gold points, $GM \leq RS \leq GX$ – monthly values are needed for the spot exchange rate (RS) and gold points (GX and GM) over May 1925–August 1931.[11] These data are described and listed in Officer (1993, 105–107,

119–124). About 95 percent of the GPA operation was completed in eight days; so it is not unreasonable to relate contemporaneous monthly values of RS and GX, GM.

To test for the confidence in future GPA efficiency that underlies UIA and FS – the expected spot exchange rate between the gold points, $GM \leq RS^* \leq GX$ – the value of N (recalling that RS^* is N months ahead) must be discerned and data on RS^* obtained. A horizon of three months ($N=3$) is assumed, because a shorter horizon can allow a small adverse exchange rate movement to wipe out the interest gain of UIA – a factor apparently taken into account by interest arbitrageurs in 1925–1931 (Einzig, 1937, 244).

The value of the expected spot rate (RS^*) is unknown. Two alternative representations are considered: (i) the three-month forward rate (RF), the conventional proxy for the expected spot rate and the time series for which is described in Officer (1993, 105, 119), (ii) the mid-point (RM) of the gold-point spread, obtained as $RM=(GX+GM)/2$. The justification for RM is as follows. In 1925–1931 the banks' subjective probability distribution of the exchange rate was apparently nearly uniform within the gold-point spread (with zero probability assigned to the exchange rate outside the spread). If the banks engage in repeated transactions, the appropriate RS^* is the mean value of their subjective probability distribution, and in this case the mean value is RM.[12] Another justification is that representation of RS^* by RM enhances the analysis of regime efficiency (see below).

The interest arbitrage (UIA and CIA) efficiency bands involve interest rates in London and New York (I_{UK} and I_{US}). The dominant money market instruments were bankers' bills and treasury bills in London, bankers' bills and stock exchange time loans in New York. Therefore I_{UK} (I_{US}) is the average of the three-month rates on bankers' acceptances and treasury bills (stock exchange time loans), converted from percent per annum to *ad valorem* per three-month period.[13]

The risk premium parameter, r, enters the UIA and FS efficiency limits. There is evidence that in 1925–1931 the interest arbitrageurs operated on an r of unity (Officer, 1993, 107–108), a value projected to the forward speculators. Transactions cost of 0.5 percent per annum, implying *ad valorem* TC of 0.00125 per three-month period, is well established for interest arbitrage in the interwar period (Officer, 1993, 108, 112) and is assigned also to forward speculation.

Values of taxation parameters over time, needed for the testing of interest arbitrage and forward speculation, are presented in table 4.1. The US corporate tax rate, $100 \cdot t_{US}$, obtained from Blakey and Blakey (1940, 524) is shown in column (5). The UK nominal tax rate, $100 \cdot t_{UK}^n$, from Mitchell

Table 4.1 *Corporate tax rates, May 1925–June 1931, percent*

Period	Critical Dividend payout ratio (p_c) (1)	UK for dividend payout ratio of			US (5)
		0 (2)	$p_c/2$ (3)	$(1+p_c)/2$ (4)	
May 1925–Dec. 1925	0.3500	20.00	16.50	6.50	13.00
Jan. 1926–Dec. 1927	0.3250	20.00	16.75	6.75	13.50
Jan. 1928–Dec. 1928	0.4000	20.00	16.00	6.00	12.00
Jan. 1929–Dec. 1929	0.4500	20.00	15.50	5.50	11.00
Jan. 1930–Mar. 1930	0.4000	20.00	16.00	6.00	12.00
Apr. 1930	0.4565	22.08	17.04	6.00	12.00
May 1930–Mar. 1931	0.4667	22.50	17.25	6.00	12.00
Apr. 1931	0.5118	24.58	18.29	6.00	12.00
May 1931–Jun. 1931	0.5200	25.00	18.50	6.00	12.00

(1988, 645), is in column (2). The lower efficiency limits for UIA and CIA each have two alternative formulas, depending on whether case a ($t_{US}<t_{UK}$) or case b ($t_{US}>t_{UK}$) is applicable. Recalling that $t_{UK}=(1-p)\cdot t_{UK}^n$, for $p<(>)$ p_c, case a (b) applies, where $p_c=1-t_{US}/t_{UK}$. The value of the dividend/payout ratio (p) is unknown; but three alternative values of p centered around p_c and bounded by [0, 1] are 0, $p_c/2$, and $(1+p_c)/2$. Corresponding values of t_{UK} are t_{UK}^n, $(1-p_c/2)\cdot t_{UK}^n$, and $(1-p_c)\cdot t_{UK}^n/2$; and their values over time are shown in columns (2), (3), and (4) of table 4.1.

Market efficiency: results

Gold-point arbitrage (GPA) was uniformly efficient, the exchange rate within the gold-point spread ($GM\leq RS\leq GX$), for all 76 months of May 1925–August 1931 (Officer, 1993, 109). Confidence in future GPA efficiency, mandated for stabilizing uncovered interest arbitrage (UIA) and forward speculation (FS), is justified by the expected spot rate within the spread: fulfillment of $GM\leq RS^*\leq GX$. For the expected rate at the spread mid-point ($RS^*=RM$), this relationship holds by definition. However, for the expected rate equal to the forward rate ($RS^*=RF$), the relationship is violated in July and August 1931, the last two months of the gold standard, when $RF<GM$. As the US gold-import point is the UK gold-export point, lack of confidence in Britain's adherence to the gold standard is indicated, and these months are deleted from the sample.

For RS^* proxied by RF, there are no violations of UIA or FS efficiency, and so this representation is dropped from further consideration as uninteresting. For RS^* proxied by RM, there are 15–20 months (the number varying with the value of p) for which $RS < RS_{Lx}^{uia}$, one month for which $RS < RS_{Lx}^{cia}$, and 29 months for which $RF < RF_L^{fs}$. The only upper-limit violations of efficiency pertain to CIA, with 4–5 months (the number dependent on p) for which $RS > RS_U^{cia}$. With a total of 74 months for which the model is applicable, the number of market inefficiencies is not small. Even more serious than the existence and number of inefficiencies is their persistence – with a three-month, four-month, and two six-month periods of consecutive violations of RS_{Lx}^{uia} and a two-, three-, four-, five-, and thirteen-month successive violation of RF_L^{fs}.

However, the magnitude of the violations is less striking than their number and persistence. Table 4.2 lists the violations and presents two measures of magnitude: (i) unexploited profit on a percentage per annum basis (obtained as $400 \cdot \pi_{Lx}^{uia}$ for the UIA lower-limit violations, and similarly for the other violations); and (ii) the distance of RS (RF, for FS) from the violated efficiency point as a percentage of the full distance of the nearer gold point (GM for a lower limit violation, GX for an upper-limit violation) from the efficiency point. For the UIA violations, for example, (ii) is $100 \cdot [(RS_{Lx}^{uia} - RS)(RS_{Lx}^{uia} - GM)]$. For uncovered and covered interest arbitrage (UIA and CIA), results are shown for three alternative values of p (one of which is the range, $[p_c, 1]$, for which case b applies, for the lower-point violations).

Given efficient GPA, the distance measure is bounded by [0, 100] percent. In contrast, the upper bound of profit is not so intuitive. Let a "serious" inefficiency be defined as the distance exceeding 50 percent. Then there are only five instances of serious inefficiencies: two for UIA, three for FS. Four of these are in 1925, the first year of the gold standard.

What could explain the totality of inefficiencies and their concentration on the lower efficiency limits? One explanation is that there were periodic episodes of lack of confidence in Britain's ability or willingness to maintain the gold standard, that is, a temporary positive probability that the pound would be devalued. In effect, the risk premium (r) would exceed unity. A sufficiently high risk premium can make profit (π_{Lx}^{uia} or π_L^{fs}) zero, thus wiping out the UIA and FS inefficiencies, but the model as such becomes invalid.[14] Because the episodic loss of confidence was asymmetrical, regarding UK rather than US maintenance of the gold standard, the concentration of inefficiencies on the lower efficiency points can also be explained in this way.[15]

An alternative explanation, for UIA and CIA inefficiencies, is institutional limits imposed by banks on the volume of their international interest arbitrage, emanating from a desire to have sufficient liquid funds

Table 4.2 *Violations of market efficiency, May 1925–June 1931*

Month	Profit (percent p.a.) (1)			Distance to gold point[a] (percent) (2)		
Lower efficiency point violated[b]						
Uncovered interest arbitrage (for p: 0, $p_c/2$, $[p_c, 1]$)						
1925: May	0.46,	0.59,	0.73	21,	25,	29
Sept.	0.46,	0.57,	0.68	39,	44,	48
Oct.	0.89,	1.00,	1.11	79,	81,	82
Nov.	0.53,	0.65,	0.76	43,	48,	53
Dec.	0.58,	0.73,	0.87	29,	34,	38
1926: Oct.	0.36,	0.50,	0.63	21,	27,	31
Nov.	0.72,	0.85,	0.98	40,	44,	47
Dec.	0.16,	0.29,	0.42	9,	15,	21
1927: Jan.	—,	—,	0.10	—,	—,	6
Feb.	0.36,	0.48,	0.60	23,	28,	33
Mar.	0.23,	0.35,	0.47	14,	20,	26
Jun.	—,	0.10,	0.22	—,	6,	12
Jul.	0.22,	0.34,	0.46	14,	20,	26
Aug.	—,	—,	0.07	—,	—,	4
1930: Nov.	—,	0.03,	0.13	—,	3,	12
Dec.	—,	0.08,	0.19	—,	7,	15
1931: Jan.	0.45,	0.56,	0.66	40,	45,	49
Feb.	0.28,	0.39,	0.51	18,	24,	29
Mar.	0.26,	0.38,	0.50	17,	23,	29
Apr.	0.01	0.15,	0.29	1,	9,	17
Covered interest arbitrage (for p: 0, $p_c/2$, $[p_c, 1]$)						
1925 Dec.	—,	0.02,	0.19	—,	3,	20
Forward speculation						
1925: May	1.25			75		
Jun.	0.46			27		
Jul.	0.18			10		
Sep.	1.01			59		
Oct.	0.75			43		
Nov.	0.72			42		
Dec.	0.15			9		
1926: May	0.49			29		
Sep.	0.26			15		
Oct	0.55			31		
Nov.	0.68			39		
Dec.	0.20			11		
1927: Jan.	0.07			4		

Table 4.2 (*cont.*)

Month	Profit (percent p.a.) (1)	Distance to gold point[a] (percent) (2)
Feb.	0.48	29
Mar.	0.51	33
Apr.	0.20	13
May	0.09	5
Jun.	0.28	18
Jul.	0.53	35
Aug.	0.38	25
Sep.	0.06	4
1929: Aug.	0.01	1
Sep.	0.15	10
1930: Dec.	0.17	16
1931: Jan.	0.50	48
Feb.	0.75	72
Mar.	0.50	48
Apr.	0.19	18
Jun.	0.01	1

Upper efficiency point violated[b]

Covered interest arbitrage (for p: 0, $p_c/2$, $(1+p_c)/2$)

Month						
1928: Jun.	0,	0,	0[c]	0,	0,	0[d]
1929: Apr.	0.21,	0.24,	0.31	5,	6,	8
May	0.12,	0.15,	0.22	3,	4,	5
1930: Mar.	0.05,	0.06,	0.07	2,	2,	3
Apr.	—,	—,	0[c]	—,	—,	0[d]

Notes:

[a] Distance of exchange rate from violated speculation point as percentage of distance of nearer gold point from speculation point.

[b] A dash indicates no violation for the specified dividend/payout ratio (p).

[c] Less than 0.005 percent.

[d] Less than 0.5 percent.

to satisfy regular customers (Einzig, 1937, 171–172, 180–181). The concentration of inefficiencies at the lower limit could be due to a relatively greater concern of New York banks for their domestic customers, in light of the city's recent rise as an international financial center. The stigma attached to forward speculation at the time (Einzig, 1937, 143–145) may similarly explain the FS inefficiencies, although not their concentration at the lower point.

Regime efficiency under market efficiency

Notwithstanding the inefficiencies discerned empirically above, in this section universal market efficiency is assumed and the implications for regime efficiency are explored. It must be emphasized that the regime efficiency considered in this chapter is short-run in nature, encompassing only the horizon of the interest arbitrageurs and forward speculators. It is certainly true that long-run regime efficiency of the dollar/sterling gold standard was low – because of Britain's overvalued currency relative not just to the dollar but also to the undervalued currencies of Britain's trading competitors (France and Belgium), Britain's downwardly rigid wages, unfavorable shifts in comparative advantage, capital account weakness, and the precariousness of short-term foreign funds in London. However, these unstable elements may not have been noticed by arbitrageurs and speculators, or the connection to confidence in Britain's adherence to the gold standard not made, or the elements may have been viewed by these economic agents as not applicable to their, short-run, horizon. As Williams (1963, p. 524) comments: "When confidence [in sterling] did finally break (15/16 July [1931]) it came as a surprise."

Consider first the importance of efficient gold-point arbitrage (GPA) for regime efficiency. Maintenance of the gold standard is enhanced by the absence of gold-point violations, because such violations contain the danger of turning the stabilizing speculation of uncovered interest arbitrage (UIA) and forward speculation (FS) into destabilizing speculation. Gold-point violations can directly destroy the subjective probability distribution that underlies stabilizing UIA and FS (in particular, that there is a zero probability of RS violating a gold point within the agent's horizon). They also involve gold flows, implying a reserves decline for one of the countries, the continuance of which can lead to a general loss of confidence in that country's ability to maintain the gold standard, whence destabilizing speculation.[16] Clearly, the market efficiency of GPA that existed in May 1925 – June 1931 was a strong positive force for regime efficiency.

This argument suggests the desirability of a given exchange rate change having a minimum probability of leading to a gold-point violation. The implication is that the distance of the exchange rate (RS) from a gold point should be maximized; equivalently, the distance of the rate (RS) from the spread mid-point (RM) should be minimized. The ideal value of RS, therefore, from the standpoint of short-run regime efficiency, is RM. To the extent that the direct UIA, indirect UIA, or covered interest arbitrage (CIA) efficiency bands are within the GPA efficiency band (gold-point spread), under market efficiency they enhance regime efficiency by

Table 4.3 *Asymmetries in efficiency bands, May 1925–June 1931*

Dividend/ payout ratio (p) (1)	Number of observations			
	Beyond gold point		Beyond spread mid-point[a]	
	Lower[b] (2)	Upper[c] (3)	Lower[d] (4)	Upper[e] (5)
Uncovered interest arbitrage				
0	11	0	0	0
$p_c/2$	7	0	0	0
$(1+p_c)/2$	3[f]	0	0[f]	0
Covered interest arbitrage				
0	28	0	0	57
$p_c/2$	22	0	0	55
$(1+p_c)/2$	20[f]	0	2[f]	51
Forward speculation with covered interest arbitrage				
0	35	0	0	12
$p_c/2$	31	0	0	12
$(1+p_c)/2$	28[f]	44	0[f]	0

Notes:
[a] Spread mid-point outside efficiency band.
[b] Lower limit of efficiency band below gold-import point.
[c] Upper limit of efficiency band above gold-export point.
[d] Lower limit of efficiency band above spread mid-point.
[e] Upper limit of efficiency band below spread mid-point.
[f] For lower limit, $p_c \leq p \leq 1$.

reducing the maximum distance of RS from RM (half the width of the gold-point spread under efficient GPA) in at least one direction.

Table 4.3 shows the number of months for which an efficiency limit falls outside a gold point (for example, for $p=0$, there are 11 occurrences of $RS_{La}^{uia} < GM$). Let RS_L denote a given lower efficiency limit for a given operation and RS_U the corresponding upper-efficiency limit. Column (2) of table 4.3 lists the number of months (out of 74) for which $RS_L < GM$ and column (3) the number of observations for which $RS_U > GX$. Define $RSM_L = \max(RS_L, GM)$ and $RSM_U = \min(RS_U, GX)$. Then $(RSM_U - RSM_L)$ may be called the "band-width relative to the band mid-point," and the impact of market efficiency on the range of RS beyond that of efficient GPA is measured by $BW1 = 100 \cdot (RSM_U - RSM_L)/(GX - GM)$, where the percentage improvement in market efficiency is $100 - BW1$.

Table 4.4 *Band-width delimited by market efficiency, May 1925–June 1931*

Dividend/payout ratio (p) (1)	Band mid-point[a] (2)	Spread mid-point[b] (3)
	Mean band-width relative to	
	(percentage of gold-point spread)	
Uncovered interest arbitrage		
0	69.72 (3.47)	37.28
$p_c/2$	68.71 (3.24)	36.58
$(1+p_c)/2$	68.15^c(2.13)	35.52^c
Covered interest arbitrage		
0	31.74 (25.26)	44.74
$p_c/2$	30.23 (23.84)	44.81
$(1+p_c)/2$	29.76^c (22.78)	44.36^c
Forward speculation with covered interest arbitrage		
0	58.46 (32.75)	47.74
$p_c/2$	56.08 (38.08)	48.34
$(1+p_c)/2$	83.55^c (10.28)	50.36^c

Notes:
[a] Coefficient of variation in parentheses.
[b] Mean plus two standard deviations.
[c] For lower limit of band, $p_c \leq p \leq 1$.

What is the theoretically expected value of *BW1*? For simplicity, assume that transactions cost, tax rates, and interest returns are all zero: $TC = t_{UK} = t_{US} = I_{UK} - I_{US} = 0$. Then $RS_{La}^{uia} = RS_{Lb}^{uia} = RS_{La}^j = RS_{Lb}^j = (RM + GM)/2$ and $RS_U^{uia} = RS_U^j = (RM + GX)/2$, while $RS_{La}^{cia} = RS_{Lb}^{cia} = RS_U^{cia} = RF$. Both the direct and indirect UIA efficiency bands are half the width of the gold-point spread ($GX - GM$), symmetrical about RM; so $BW1 = 50$ percent. Table 4.4 (column (2)) shows mean($BW1$) (over the 74 observations) for UIA, CIA, and "FS with CIA" (indirect UIA) under the various alternative values of the dividend/payout ratio (p).

The empirical impact of market efficiency on regime efficiency is less than the 50 percent improvement suggested by the above analysis. Direct UIA efficiency reduces the range of *RS*, on average, by about 30 percent relative to the gold-point spread. Indirect UIA efficiency can reduce it by even more – over 40 percent on average for case a – but the variation of this reduction is much greater than that for direct UIA. The coefficient of variation of *BW1* (standard deviation as a percentage of mean) is shown in parentheses. It should be noted that the mean band-width is defined as a percentage of the width of the gold-point spread, which itself is variable: the coefficient of variation of $(GX-GM)$ is 13.16 percent.

To demonstrate definitively that direct UIA is more conducive to regime efficiency than is indirect UIA, consider the "band-width relative to the spread mid-point" (as a percentage of the width of the gold-point spread): $BW2=100\cdot(|RSM_U-RM|+|RM-RSM_L|)/2\cdot(GX-GM)$. The percentage increase in regime efficiency from pure efficient GPA (RS at GX or GM), for which $BW2=50$, is $50-BW2$. This measure is motivated by the asymmetry of the empirical efficiency bands relative to RM. In fact, there are instances in which $RS_L>RM$ or $RS_U<RM$ (see columns (4) and (5) of table 4.3), so that the efficiency band is entirely on one side of RM. $BW2$ is the average distance of the efficiency band points from RM (with the end points not permitted to exceed the gold points), as a percentage of the width of the gold-point spread. For direct and indirect UIA, the theoretically expected value of $BW2$, under the above simplifying assumptions, is 25 percent.

In light of the variability of the efficiency bands, table 4.4 (column (3)) exhibits the value of the mean *plus* two standard deviations of $BW2$. Efficient direct UIA has the greatest impact, with a 13–14 percent improvement in regime efficiency from pure efficient GPA on average *plus* allowing for two standard deviations from the mean – an excellent performance relative to the 25 percent theoretical improvement in regime efficiency. Efficient indirect UIA (joint "FS with CIA") has the least effect, with efficient CIA in the middle.

Regime efficiency: market forces

With RM, by definition the mid-point of the gold-point spread, the ideal value of RS for regime efficiency, it is doubly natural to define the pound "weak" as the spot exchange rate below the spread mid-point ($RS<RM$) and "strong" as the rate above the spread mid-point ($RS>RM$). When the pound is weak (strong), one wants uncovered and covered interest arbitrage (UIA and CIA) to operate in favor of the pound (dollar), thereby moving RS closer to RM. Should the operation take place in the opposite direction, the effect is to move RS further from RM, perverse for regime efficiency. Therefore, for $RS<(>)$ RM, it is desirable that profit exceed zero: π_{Lx}^{uia}, $\pi_{Lx}^{cia}>0(\pi_U^{uia}, \pi_U^{cia}>0)$. In terms of market (as distinct from policy) variables, the corresponding necessary condition is (i) a positive exchange rate gain: $RM-RS>(<)0$ for UIA, $RF-RS>(<)0$ for CIA, and/or (ii) a positive interest return: the interest rate differential $I_{UK}-I_{US}>(<)0$ for both UIA and CIA. In percentage terms, the market (pretax) exchange rate gain term is $100\cdot(RM-RS)/RS$ for UIA, $100\cdot(RF-RS)/RS$ for CIA, and the market

Table 4.5 *Influences on regime efficiency, May 1925–June 1931*

Variable	Percentage of observations conducive to efficiency		Mean of variable		Correlation Coeff.[c]
	Pound weak[a]	Pound strong[b]	Pound weak[a]	Pound strong[b]	
Spread mid-point *minus* spot rate (percent)	100	100	0.30	−0.16	−0.98
Forward rate *minus* spot rate (percent)	38	100	−0.02	−0.11	−0.54
Spread mid-point *minus* forward rate (percent)	98	60	0.32	−0.05	−0.80
London *minus* New York interest rate (percent per annum)					
Market rates	53	30	−0.20	0.05	0.24
Central bank rates	83	0	0.64	0.66	0.13
Exchange market intervention (*EMINT*) ($ million)	55	90	0.78	−3.92	−0.18

Notes:
[a] Spot rate below mid-point of gold-point spread (strength of pound below 50 percent), 64 observations. Positive value of variable is conducive to efficiency.
[b] Spot rate above mid-point of gold-point spread (strength of pound above 50 percent), 10 observations. Negative value of variable is conducive to efficiency.
[c] With strength of pound, 74 observations. A negative sign is conducive to efficiency.

interest return term in percent per annum is $400 \cdot (I_{UK} - I_{US})$. Interestingly, subcondition (i) is automatically fulfilled for UIA.

Further if one were to choose among UIA, CIA, and joint "FS with CIA" (indirect UIA) as alternative operations for the support of regime efficiency, on the assumption of perfect market efficiency the argument of the previous section is that UIA should be selected. Consider first UIA versus CIA. For $RS < RM$, it is desired that $\pi_{Lx}^{uia} - \pi_{Lx}^{cia} = (1 - t_{US}) \cdot (RM - RF) - (RS - GM) > 0$, a necessary condition for which is $RM - RF > 0$. Similarly, for $RS > RM$, one wants $\pi_{U}^{uia} - \pi_{U}^{cia} = (RF - RM) - (GX - RS) > 0$, with the necessary condition $RM - RF < 0$. In percent, the conditional term is $100 \cdot (RM - RF)/RM$. By a similar argument, for

$RS<(>)$ RM, it is desired that $\pi_{Lx}^{uia}-\pi_L^{fs}>0(\pi_U^{uia}-\pi_U^{fs}>0)$, with the necessary condition $RF-RS>(<)0$ and/or $I_{UK}-I_{US}>(<)0$, which is consistent with conditions previously delineated.

In sum, the fulfillment of any of four market conditions (inequality in the "correct" direction) is conducive to regime efficiency. Furthermore, the non-fulfillment of a condition (inequality in the "incorrect" direction) is unfavorable to regime efficiency. Table 4.5 summarizes the influence of the critical market variables on regime efficiency. There are 64 observations for which the pound is weak ($RS<RM$) and 10 for which the pound is strong ($RS>RM$). As a continuous measure of the strength of the pound, take the deviation of the exchange rate from the gold-import point (which is the UK gold-export point) as a percentage of the width of the gold-point spread: $STRP=100\cdot(RS-GM)/(GX-GM)$ which, under gold-point arbitrage (GPA) efficiency, is zero for RS at the pound's lowest value (GM) and 100 at its highest value (GX). So a "weak" ("strong") pound is defined as $RS<(>)$ RM or $STRP<(>)50$. $STRP$ has a mean value of 22.92 for $RS<RM$ and 65.41 for $RS>RM$.

When the pound is weak, a positive (negative) value of a market variable enhances (detracts from) regime efficiency. The opposite is true for a strong pound. Table 4.5 shows, for the months under which the pound is weak and strong alternatively, the percentage of observations for which efficiency is enhanced by the market variable and the mean value of the variable. As a continuous measure of the impact of a market variable on regime efficiency, the correlation of the variable with $STRP$ is presented: a negative (positive) correlation enhances (diminishes) efficiency.

The $(RM-RS)/RS$ and $(RM-RF)/RM$ variables are most conducive to regime efficiency, especially when the pound is weak. Of course, the former variable can only enhance regime efficiency. When the pound is weak, this variable provides a pretax exchange rate gain of 0.30 percent for UIA. In contrast, the market interest rate differential ($I_{UK}-I_{US}$) is arguably more unfavorable than favorable for regime efficiency. When the pound is weak, this variable is positive barely more often than negative and its mean value is actually negative; furthermore, its correlation with $STRP$ is perverse.

Regime efficiency: policy variables

Of course, market variables are themselves influenced by policy variables, and policy variables can also have a direct influence on regime efficiency. In this chapter only short-run regime efficiency is studied; so basic policies such as the mint value of a country's currency and sterilization of reserves flows are not considered. Two short-term policies of interest are discount rate policy and exchange market intervention.

Discount rate policy

Why were market interest rates not favorable for regime efficiency? Underlying the market rates in London and New York were Bank Rate (the Bank of England's discount rate) and the Federal Reserve Bank of New York discount rate, respectively. Monthly series of these central bank rates are constructed as averages of daily observations.[17] The Bank Rate/Federal Reserve Bank of New York discount rate differential, denoted as $I_{BR}-I_{DR}$, comparable to the market rate differential $(I_{UK}-I_{US})$, is positive for 83 percent of the months (53 out of 64) when the pound is weak (and, perversely, for all ten months when the pound is strong). Also, for $RS<RM$, the mean value of $(I_{BR}-I_{DR})$ is over three-fifths of a percentage point per annum – ostensibly quite conducive to regime efficiency.

However, the average magnitude of the market rate differential, $I_{UK}-I_{US}$, is minus one-fifth of a percentage point per annum under a weak pound, a full four-fifths of a percentage point per annum below the central bank rate differential. Also, the correlation of $(I_{BR}-I_{DR})$ with *STRP* is, like that of $(I_{UK}-I_{US})$, positive (albeit low), which acts against regime efficiency. Therefore, although $I_{BR}-I_{DR}$ often operated in the right direction, (i) its magnitude was, on balance, too low to affect $I_{UK}-I_{US}$ sufficiently to enhance regime efficiency, and (ii) it was not calibrated to the weakness of the pound.

The explanation is that each central bank had its discount rate as a single instrument with which to achieve several policy goals. The Federal Reserve had three targets for its discount rate, emanating, respectively, from the desires "to help the hapless British" (external balance, or the strength of the pound), "to combat speculation in the New York stock market," and of "not depressing the economy" (internal balance) (Temin, 1989, 20–23). There were two policy objectives for Bank Rate: internal and external balance (Cairncross and Eichengreen, 1983, 38–39).

For $I_{BR}-I_{DR}$ strongly conducive to regime efficiency, international cooperation was of paramount importance. This meant the subordination of other targets to external balance, specifically, the strength of the pound. The Federal Reserve was generally unwilling to do this, notwithstanding statements to the contrary.[18] In contrast, the Bank of England often, though not always, kept Bank Rate higher than internal considerations would dictate, for the sake of external balance.[19] However, with minimal Federal Reserve cooperation and a reluctance on the part of the Bank to abdicate Bank Rate policy to the London/New York market interest rate differential ($I_{UK}-I_{US}$ in the present chapter), $I_{BR}-I_{DR}$ was of insufficient magnitude and flexibility to improve regime efficiency markedly.[20]

So discount rate policy was of little help to regime efficiency. While it often involved a higher Bank Rate than the Federal Reserve discount rate (generally desirable for efficiency, given the pound's chronic weakness), the differential was insufficient in magnitude to widen the market rate differential substantially and indeed even to make it on average in favor of London under a weak pound.

Exchange market intervention

Both the Bank of England and the Federal Reserve banks intervened in the foreign exchange market. Their joint net purchase (sale) of pounds for dollars acted to increase (decrease) RS. This joint exchange market intervention variable, denoted as $EMINT$ and measured in million dollars, is the subject of the last row entry in table 4.5.[21] For $RS<(>)RM$, regime efficiency dictates that intervention be in favor of the pound (dollar), that is, $EMINT>(<)0$.

Regime efficiency benefitted minimally from this policy variable. True, $EMINT$ is negatively correlated with $STRP$, but the correlation is low. Also, $EMINT$ is positive only in a slight majority of months when the pound is weak. Finally, and devastatingly, the average value of $EMINT$ under a weak pound is a paltry \$0.78 million – insufficient to affect the value of RS measurably.

Why was exchange market intervention in favor of the pound so little when regime efficiency often warranted a lot? Five reasons may be suggested. First, the Bank itself discouraged too much intervention by the Federal Reserve, because of the fear that financing would delay adjustment (Clarke, 1967, 43–44). Second, after 1927, with the decline in central bank cooperation (see n. 20), the Federal Reserve attitude toward sterling support hardened and the feeling grew that such support should be limited (Moggridge, 1972, 192–193). Third, the amounts of foreign bills held by the Federal Reserve banks traditionally were "very small in proportion to the size of the markets which they were supposed to influence" (Hardy, 1932, 101, 116).

Fourth, there was an ongoing technical dispute between the Bank and the Federal Reserve over the medium of Fed intervention to support the pound (Beckhart, 1932, 458; Clarke, 1967, 161–162, 175). The Fed wanted its sterling in the form of bills, implying direct market intervention, whereas the Bank preferred support via Fed dollar deposits at the Bank, thus giving the Bank itself the wherewithal to intervene in the market. This dispute at times adversely affected the timing, if not the amount, of market intervention. Fifth, there was the problem of the Fed desire to liquidate acquired foreign bill holdings quickly (Beckhart, 1932, 158; Clarke, 1967, 162, 176). Often the effect on regime efficiency was perverse.

Regime efficiency: net outcome

The efficiency bands of the various operations – gold-point arbitrage, uncovered interest arbitrage, covered interest arbitrage, joint "forward speculation with covered interest arbitrage" (GPA, UIA, CIA, joint "FS with CIA") – the extent to which the operations are efficient (within the respective bands), and the influences of the various market and policy variables all combine to generate a certain level of regime efficiency. In a given month one can measure the amount of regime inefficiency (in percent) as the deviation of the exchange rate (RS) from the spread mid-point (RM) as a percentage of mint parity: $ED = 100 \cdot (|RS - RM|/4.8665635)$. This is the experienced (observed) deviation of the exchange rate from the spread mid-point. With RM the ideal value of RS from the standpoint of regime efficiency (see above), ED involves a linear loss function expressed in percent of parity. The lower bound of ED is zero, for RS at RM, where there is perfect regime efficiency. Under perfect GPA, the upper bound is, for RS at GM or GX, half the gold-point spread as a percentage of mint parity.

Mean(ED) summarizes regime inefficiency for the entire gold standard episode. Its value for the 74-month observation period of 1925–1931 is 0.28 percent, which appears low and therefore suggestive of high regime efficiency. However, to judge properly the magnitude of ED, some basis of comparison is needed. One such basis is experienced ED for the classical dollar/sterling gold standard. Mean(ED) for the 204 months of 1890–1906 is computed in Officer (1989, 34).

As table 4.6 shows, mean(ED) for 1925–1931 is actually lower than for 1890–1906. If ED is the appropriate measure, then there was greater regime efficiency in 1925–1931 than in 1890–1906 – perhaps a surprising result in view of the long-run regime inefficiency of the interwar gold standard and the conventional wisdom that the prewar dollar/sterling gold standard was the epitome of stability. However, long-run does not necessarily translate into short-run regime inefficiency (see above); also, for part of the 1890–1906 period there was a significant subjective and objective probability of abandonment of the gold standard, though by the United States rather than by Britain (see Officer, 1989, 24–25)

Nevertheless, ED provides a biased measure of regime efficiency because there is likely to be a positive correlation between ED and the width of the gold-point spread. Define the amount of hypothetical regime inefficiency as the mean deviation of RS from RM under perfect GPA and a uniform distribution of RS within the gold-point spread: $HD = 100 \cdot [(GX - RM)/2]/4.8665635$. This measure is positively correlated with the width of the gold-point spread, and mean(HD) is shown in table 4.6 for the two gold standard episodes. Because the gold-point spread

Table 4.6 *Exchange rate deviation from spread mid-point, 1890–1906 and 1925–1931*

Measure	1890–1906	1925–1931
Mean ED^a	0.29	0.28
Mean HD^a	0.33	0.27
Efficiency ratio[b]	0.87	1.03

Notes:
[a] Percentage of parity.
[b] Ratio of experienced to hypothetical variation.

was narrower in 1925–1931, its *HD* is lower than that for 1890–1906.

Then an unbiased measure of the amount of regime efficiency is the "efficiency ratio," ER=mean (ED)/mean (HD). The reason for the unbiasedness is that *HD* is the regime efficiency under the "neutral" hypothetical situation of the exchange rate taking on all values within the spread with equal probability, given efficient GPA (any value outside the spread having zero probability). For $RS=RM$ for all observations, $ER=0$ and there is maximum regime efficiency. For *RS* at *GX* or *GM* for all observations, $ER=2$ and there is minimum regime efficiency under efficient GPA. If *RS* is uniformly distributed within the gold-point spread, the expected value of *ER* is unity. It is logical to categorize a gold standard experience as "regime efficient" (inefficient) according as $ER<(>)1$. By this criterion, the 1925–1931 dollar/sterling gold standard was slightly inefficient and the 1890–1806 episode somewhat efficient.[22]

The important conclusion is that the regime efficiency of the 1925–1931 dollar/sterling gold standard was far greater than the conventional wisdom concedes. Until confidence in the system collapsed in July 1931, GPA exhibited complete market efficiency (on a monthly unit of observation). Further, from May 1925 through June 1931, speculators and arbitrageurs in the foreign exchange and money markets behaved as if any lack of confidence that they had in the gold standard and in efficient GPA was episodic rather than systemic. The outcome was a value of the exchange rate that, on average, was about as close to the spread mid-point (the "bliss point for regime efficiency") as that associated with a uniform distribution of the exchange rate within the spread.

Appendix: data on exchange market intervention

Bank-Fed joint exchange market intervention variable (*EMINT*): This is constructed as $\Delta FRHP - \Delta BHD$, where *FRHP* (*BHD*) is end-month Federal

Table A4.1 *Exchange market intervention in favor of pound, May 1925–June 1931 (million dollars)*

Month	1925	1926	1927	1928	1929	1930	1931
Jan.		−4.77	−0.14	−4.98	19.47	14.01	0.14
Feb.		−19.69	−0.15	−9.42	0.01	4.87	−26.76
Mar.		0.34	0.14	0.66	−4.82	4.87	−43.83
Apr.		0.08	−0.70	−0.55	0	4.88	14.61
May	0	−0.01	0.05	−0.73	−14.60	−4.86	4.87
Jun.	0	0.44	11.10	−0.16	−9.73	−19.46	0
Jul.	0	−0.61	0.91	14.60	−9.72	−29.20	
Aug.	0	0.01	−4.99	14.60	30.75	0.01	
Sep.	0	5.33	−15.19	14.60	−5.12	4.87	
Oct.	−0.36	0.12	−15.95	25.08	5.71	15.64	
Nov.	−0.27	0.10	−10.85	43.81	−12.44	10.00	
Dec.	0.27	0.47	−0.33	9.73	−0.36	4.40	

Reserve (Bank of England) holdings of pounds (dollars), with corrections to $\Delta FRHP$ or ΔBHD to exclude direct central bank transactions, to the extent such transactions are identifiable. Federal Reserve purchases of sterling bills from the Bank obtained by increasing Bank deposits at a Reserve Bank are not so excluded, but net out to zero because of the joint nature of the *EMINT* variable.

Federal Reserve holdings of pounds (*FRHP*): The basic series is "bills payable in foreign currencies," found in *Annual Report of the Federal Reserve Board* (1925–1931). There are no data prior to September 30, 1925; it is assumed that bill holdings are unchanged from April 30 to September 30 – a reasonable assumption because until mid-1926 month-to-month changes are very small. For June 1931, $\Delta FRHP$ is assumed zero, because the data are contaminated by international credit agreements, which account for the bulk of the holdings. For all months, the series in principle is inclusive of non-sterling bills; however, there is good evidence that virtually all bills (until June 1931) are sterling, with the exception of an operation in Hungarian pengos in July–August 1929 (Beckhart, 1932, 457–460; Hardy, 1932, 101–103). To correct for that operation, $1 million are subtracted from $\Delta FRHP$ in July and added to it in August.

Bank holding of dollars (*BHD*): The basic data are dollar holdings of the Bank of England (Sayers, 1976, 349–355). From information in Moggridge (1972, 135, 181–188) and *Federal Reserve Bulletin* (September 1929, 124), known or estimated direct central bank transactions are excluded. The resulting series is converted to dollars by multiplication by 4.86656. *EMINT* is listed in table A4.1.

Notes

This chapter is based on material in Officer, *Between the Dollar–Sterling Gold Points* (Cambridge University Press, 1996, forthcoming).

1. The most comprehensive such study is Eichengreen (1992).
2. Complementary to this study is Hallwood, MacDonald and Marsh's chapter 5 in this volume. These authors utilize "target zone theory," which is concerned with the value of the exchange rate within a "target zone" set by monetary authorities but is extended to the mainly market determined gold-point spread of a gold standard. The conclusion of Hallwood, MacDonald and Marsh regarding the "stability" of the interwar dollar/sterling gold standard is similar to the finding here regarding its "regime efficiency."

   The target zone model has the advantage of amenability to the sophisticated testing procedures of modern time series analysis. However, the model has two limitations not shared in the present study. First, the model is much more concerned with the behavior of the exchange rate inside the band than outside it, whereas the measures of regime efficiency presented here exhibit no discontinuity at a gold point.

   Second, the model imposes a rigorous framework so that the only manifestation of an exchange rate regime that is of interest is the credibility, and therefore viability, of the target zone. Other issues, such as the efficiency of arbitrage and speculation activities, are not explored. Indeed, the efficiency of interest arbitrage (parity conditions) is assumed rather than tested. In contrast, the present approach involves the testing of both market efficiency and regime efficiency.
3. For an institutional description of GPA under the interwar dollar/sterling gold standard, but abstracting from taxation, see Officer (1993, 99–101).
4. For institutional information on taxation in 1925–1931, see Spaulding (1927), Herndon (1932), Blakey and Blakey (1940), and Richman (1963).
5. Also included in TC are normal profit and a risk premium reflecting the "political" risks of foreign investment.
6. Two alternative models of UIA efficiency under an absolutely credible gold standard are found in the literature. Morgenstern (1959, 166–168, 302–303) and Giovannini (1993, 130–134) both abstract from exchange rate gain and transactions cost. Giovannini also assumes in effect that $r=0$. While Morgenstern recognizes this risk element, his modeling is imprecise, lacking reference to the nature of the arbitrageur's risk aversion. Giovannini goes beyond Morgenstern in recognizing the concept of an efficiency band, but he derives an interest rate rather than exchange rate band. Neither author incorporates taxation, a defect of virtually all studies of interest arbitrage irrespective of period (with Levi, 1977, and Kupferman and Levi, 1978, the conspicuous exceptions), and only Morgenstern applies the model to the interwar experience. A model similar to that of Giovannini is in Svensson (1991).
7. Neither Morgenstern nor Giovannini relates his model of UIA efficiency to CIA or FS. To the best of my knowledge, only Clarke (1967), who ignores

transactions cost and taxation, studies CIA efficiency during the interwar gold standard.

8. I am not aware of any other study of FS efficiency under a credible gold standard.

9. That N is the same is unlikely, because the primary forward speculators were decidedly not the large London and New York banks and therefore not the same agents as the dominant interest arbitrageurs (Einzig, 1937, 144). The assumption of a common TC is heroic, because FS saved the cost of money market transactions.

10. The transactions cost of CIA might include a risk premium to compensate for exchange rate risk not fully covered in a forward contract – the risk of exchange rate loss due to premature repatriation. So TC for CIA in reality might be slightly greater than for UIA. However, the interest arbitrageur, in making the decision whether to cover exchange risk in the forward market, does not change his horizon. So UIA and CIA inherently have the same N.

11. The United States was on the gold standard between March 18, 1922 and March 3, 1933, and the United Kingdom between April 28, 1925, and September 19, 1931. The latter, inner, period thus delineates the dollar–sterling gold standard.

12. For further discussion of RF and RM as alternative representations of RS^*, see Officer (1993, 113–114).

13. For further detail and data sources, see Officer (1993, 108–109).

14. For a detailed explanation of the UIA inefficiencies from June 1927 onward along these lines, see Officer (1993, 115).

15. Also, the relatively small number of CIA inefficiencies could be due to the fact that, unlike UIA and FS, CIA could be carried on under the gold standard without extra risk compared to a flexible exchange rate system.

16. It is true that the adjustment mechanism of a gold standard is itself dependent on gold flows and their nonsterilization by the monetary authorities. However, this consideration is long-run in nature, in contrast to the short-run focus of this chapter. It is also true that GPA can return the exchange rate rapidly to the gold-point spread; but predence demands that reliance on such arbitrage be a last resort.

17. The source data are Sayers (1976, appendixes, 347) and Board of Governors of the Federal Reserve System (1943, 440–441).

18. As Friedman and Schwartz (1963, 269) write:

> foreign considerations were seldom important in determining the [Federal Reserve] policies followed but were cited as additional justification for policies adopted primarily on domestic grounds whenever foreign and domestic considerations happened to coincide.

19. The traditional view of economic historians is that Bank Rate was geared overwhelmingly, if not exclusively, to maintenance of the gold standard, to the neglect of the domestic economy. Temin (1989, 31) notes: "Interest rates were kept high to attract short-term capital and to stabilize the pound." Cairncross and Eichengreen (1983, 38) comment: "Maintenance of a high Bank rate . . . was relied upon to attract capital inflows whenever the exchange rate weak-

ened." However, an econometric study of the goals of Bank Rate policy finds "a sensitivity to domestic conditions when formulating Bank Rate policy" (Eichengreen, Watson and Grossman, 1985, 741).

20. Such central bank cooperation as there was broke down in 1928. This is the story told by Clarke (1967) and generally accepted by economic historians (see Eichengreen, 1984, 66). Eichengreen presents a model of central bank interaction in the interwar gold standard incorporating discount rates as the policy instrument, but ignores the existence of a gold-point spread. He shows that cooperation can lead to improved internal balance for both countries. Elsewhere, Eichengreen, Watson and Grossman (1985, 739) demonstrate econometrically that Bank Rate was not sensitive to the London/New York market interest rate differential.

21. This variable has not been examined systematically in other studies of the dollar/sterling interwar gold standard, perhaps because of the difficulty of disentangling direct central bank transactions from exchange market intervention. The method of constructing *EMINT* is described, and the variable listed, in the appendix.

22. In Officer (1993, 118) the *ER* ratio for 1925–1931 is mistakenly halved – my error. The analysis that follows there is too strong.

References

Beckhart, B. H. (1932). *The New York Money Market*, vol. 3, *Uses of Funds*, New York, Columbia University Press

Blakey, R. G. and G. C. Blakey (1940). *The Federal Income Tax*, London: Longmans, Green & Co.

Board of Governors of the Federal Reserve System (1943). *Banking and Monetary Statistics 1914–1941*, Washington, DC

Cairncross, A. and B. Eichengreen (1983). *Sterling in Decline*, Oxford: Basil Blackwell

Clarke, S. V. O. (1967). *Central Bank Cooperation 1924–31*, New York: Federal Reserve Bank of New York

Eichengreen, B. (1984). "Central Bank Cooperation under the Interwar Gold Standard," *Explorations in Economic History* 21 (January), 64–87

(1992). *Golden Fetters: The Gold Standard and the Great Depression, 1919–1939*, New York: Oxford University Press

Eichengreen, B., M. W. Watson, and R. S. Grossman (1985). "Bank Rate Policy Under the Interwar Gold Standard: A Dynamic Probit Analysis," *Economic Journal* 95 (September), 725–745

Einzig, P. (1937). *The Theory of Forward Exchange*, London: Macmillan

(1970). *The History of Foreign Exchange*, 2nd edn., London: Macmillan

Friedman, M., and A. J. Schwartz (1963). *A Monetary History of the United States 1867–1960*, Princeton: Princeton University Press for NBER

Giovannini, A. (1993). "Bretton Woods and Its Precursors: Rules versus Discretion in the History of International Monetary Regimes," in M. D. Bordo and B.

Eichengreen (eds.), *A Retrospective on the Bretton Woods System: Lessons for International Monetary Reform*, Chicago: University of Chicago Press for NBER, 109–147

Hardy, C. O. (1932). *Credit Policies of the Federal Reserve System*, Washington, DC: Brookings Institution

Herndon, J. Goodwin, Jr. (1932). *The Development of International Reciprocity for the Prevention of Double Income Taxation*, Ph.D. thesis, University of Pennsylvania

Kupferman, M., and M. D. Levi (1978). "Taxation and the International Money Market Investment Decision," *Financial Analysts Journal* 34 (July–August), 61–64

Levi, M. D. (1977). "Taxation and 'Abnormal' International Capital Flows," *Journal of Political Economy* 85 (June), 635–646

Mitchell, B. R. (1988). *British Historical Statistics*, Cambridge: Cambridge University Press

Moggridge, D. E. (1972). *British Monetary Policy 1924–1931: The Norman Conquest of $4.86*, Cambridge: Cambridge University Press

Morgenstern, O. (1959). *International Financial Transactions and Business Cycles*, Princeton: Princeton University Press for NBER

Officer, L. H. (1989). "The Remarkable Efficiency of the Dollar–Sterling Gold Standard, 1890–1906," *Journal of Economic History* 49 (March), 1–41

   (1993). "Gold-Point Arbitrage and Uncovered Interest Arbitrage under the 1925–1931 Dollar–Sterling Gold Standard," *Explorations in Economic History* 30 (January), 98–127

Richman, P. B. (1963). *Taxation of Foreign Investment Income: An Economic Analysis*, Baltimore: Johns Hopkins University Press

Sayers, R. S. (1976). *The Bank of England 1891–1944*, Cambridge: Cambridge University Press

Spaulding, H. B. (1927). *The Income Tax in Great Britain and the United States*, London: P. S. King & Son

Svensson, L. E. O. (1991). "The Simplest Test of Target Zone Credibility," *IMF Staff Papers* 38 (September), 655–665

Temin, P. (1989). *Lessons from the Great Depression*, Cambridge, MA: MIT Press

Williams, D. (1963). "London and the 1931 Financial Crisis," *Economic History Review* 15 (April), 513–528

5   Credibility and fundamentals: were the Classical and interwar gold standards well-behaved target zones?

C. Paul Hallwood, Ronald MacDonald and Ian W. Marsh

Introduction

This chapter investigates the question of whether the international gold standard constituted a credible target zone. The question is not a narrow one, for the answer has a bearing on whether adherence to the gold standard was sufficient to render monetary policy time consistent. That is, did the markets believe that the authorities were truly committed to the international standard, or were the policies adopted seen as threatening the link with gold? Since the Classical gold standard lasted from c. 1873 until 1914 and, according to economic historians, operated more or less according to the "rules of the game," it would not be so surprising to find that during this long period the authorities did create a credible reputation for responsible monetary and interest rate policies. It may be somewhat more surprising if it was to be found that the troubled and short-lived reconstituted interwar gold standard of 1925 to 1931 was similarly credible. This is one of the key issues which we investigate in this chapter.

The literature on the theory of freely floating exchange rates – which typically uses the asset approach – is normally formulated using a linear relationship between an exchange rate and its fundamental determinants, say, the quantity of money and its velocity of circulation (see, for example, the well known works of Dornbusch, 1976; Frenkel, 1976; Mussa, 1976). These models are usually based on the assumption that purchasing power parity holds, at least in the long run. However, by contrast, a feature of "fixed" exchange rate systems is that an exchange rate is usually allowed to float between upper and lower intervention points, but is not allowed to move outside of this narrow intervention range, or what a recent burgeoning literature calls a "target zone." Two examples of this type of target zone are the European Monetary System (EMS) (1979–), and the Bretton Woods System (c. 1959–1971) where members of either system committed themselves actively to intervene in the foreign exchange market if the market exchange rate threatened to deviate outside the target zone.

The gold standard is an interesting member of the class of target zone exchange rate systems. However, a significant difference between the managed exchange rate systems mentioned above and either version of the gold standard is that, while in the former the width of the target zone was defined by international convention, under the gold standard the limits of the target zone were defined in the market, being governed by the cost of international gold arbitrage. In fact, if empirical research on the EMS as a target zone is compared with our empirical findings set out below, it seems that both the Classical and interwar gold standards were the more credible target zones – as judged by exchange rate behavior. Bordo and Kydland (1992) raise a related point, specifically, that the Classical gold standard was time consistent. That is, in practice, adherence by the monetary authorities to the "rules of the game" effectively constrained monetary policy and constituted a credible commitment not to inflate prices. Relatedly, the implications (if not the theory) of time inconsistency of Britain not returning to the gold standard were well understood at the time by Sir Otto Niemeyer, a Treasury advisor, who wrote in 1924 that if it was seen that the UK had lost its nerve over a return to the gold standard

the immediate consequence would be considerable withdrawal of balances and investment (both foreign and British) from London; a heavy drop in Exchange; and to counteract that tendency, a substantial increase in Bank rate. (Quoted in Moggridge, 1969, 47)

As we have indicated, the key issue we intend to investigate in this chapter is the credibility of the Classical and interwar versions of the international gold standards. In general terms, we intend to illuminate this issue by examining the behavior of market exchange rates in these two periods both in a time series context and, additionally, in relation to their fundamental determinants within the target zone. We proceed as follows. The next section outlines the operation of the gold standard within the framework of the target zone literature. The following section presents the theory of target zones, and the fourth and fifth sections the results of our empirical work. We close with a brief summary of our conclusions.

The gold standard as a target zone

The US mint price of gold was set by the Mint Act 1873 at $18.8047 per ounce of gold 9/10 fine and the mint price of gold in Britain had been set ever since 1717 at £3. 17s. 10½d. per ounce of gold 11/12 fine. Officer (1986) adjusts these prices for the quality differences and calculates the mint parity exchange rate as $4.8665 dollars per pound. If the underlying mint prices were fixed and arbitrageurs' transactions costs were zero, the market exchange rate would also be this rate. Naturally, however, transaction costs were positive and resulted in the determination of gold export and import points (see Spiller and Wood, 1988).

Contemporaneous estimates of gold import and export points, made by *The Economist*, put the US gold export and import points at, respectively, $4.890 and $4.827. A later estimate by Morgenstern (1959) is not very different from this. Nor are the still later estimates made by Clark (1984), Officer (1986) and Spiller and Wood (1988). In these three latter cases the gold points are taken to vary with transaction costs – in the approximate range according to Officer (1986) of 0.47–0.78 percent of mint par prices. Transaction costs were a function of a number of variables including interest cost (which fluctuated with short-term money rates); the time taken to cross the Atlantic and, sometimes, in waiting to be paid by the authorities while they melted foreign gold; freight and insurance costs; abrasion of coin (which reduced coin weight below face value); any premium that the authorities might set above the mint price; normal profit and arbitrageurs' risk premiums.

In Officer's (1986) study and that of Spiller and Wood (1988) the relatively high level and variability of transaction costs are both used to explain apparent frequent gold-point violations "discovered" by Morgenstern (1959) and Clark (1984). This is an important matter because frequent violations of the gold points would question the efficiency of the gold standard as a target zone. As it is, this most recent research on gold-point violations supports the views of contemporaries and economic historians that arbitrage was in fact effective in constraining exchange rates between the gold points. Thus Spiller and Wood (1988) conclude that "the gold standard seems to have been a relatively efficient system to provide bounds to exchange rate movements" (p. 89).

The finding that dollar/sterling gold points were rarely breached during the period of the Classical gold standard is complemented by Officer's first meticulous study of dollar/sterling gold-point arbitrage during the interwar period (Officer, 1993). He explains how gold arbitrage by New York and London banks acted to keep the dollar/sterling exchange rate within the gold points. He also introduces the concept of "speculation points" which define the range of exchange rate movements given efficient uncovered arbitrage. Further, he shows that the dollar/sterling exchange rate remained within the gold points over the entire period while the United Kingdom was on the gold standard, April 1925–September 1931. This, and the fact that forward rates also remained within the range, can be used to buttress the notion that the gold points defined credible bounds for exchange rate movements.[1] Officer's (1993) discussion of speculation points utilizes the assumption that speculators' *expected* exchange rate was at the middle of the gold-point range.[2] While this may be somewhat arbitrary, as we shall see, it is not very different from the results obtained from Krugman's (1988) target zone model, which exploits the idea that the expected exchange rate will revert towards the center of the target zone. In addition to Officer's finding that the gold points set credible bounds to exchange rate movements he also shows that rates fluctuated sufficiently within the center of the zone as to be usually consistent with his calculated speculation points. The implication of this is that the credible target zone induces stabilizing uncovered interest arbitrage which further boosts the stability of exchange rates. Had the target zone, as defined by gold points, not been credible then, as expected exchange rates moved outside the zone, speculators would have acted to push actual exchange rates outside the zone – but this did not happen.

Target zones: some theory

The literature on target zones concerns the relationship between an exchange rate and its fundamental determinants. The seminal contribution was made by Krugman (1988), and extended by Miller and Weller (1991). Their theory is briefly outlined in this section. The argument assumes that the market believes that the target zone is credible. Credibility requires that the authorities purposely or automatically adapt monetary policy to defend the zone. As a simplification, it is further assumed that the target zone is defended only when the exchange rate reaches the upper or lower edges of the zone (so-called intra-marginal intervention is ruled out). The exchange rate is determined as

$$s_t = m_t + v_t + \alpha E_t[ds_t]/dt \tag{1}$$

where, in natural logarithms, s_t is the domestic currency price of foreign exchange, m_t is the money supply (which is an exogenous policy variable), α is the semi-elasticity of the demand for money, and v_t is a general purpose term that includes anything else impacting on the demand or supply for money (e.g. changes in real income). Most simply v_t is taken to be the "cumulative value of velocity" (Miller and Weller, 1991). Shocks to velocity are random with mean zero, and normally distributed such that the cumulative value of v follows a continuous time random walk. The sum of m_t and v_t is usually referred to as the composite fundamental term, f_t. The final term, $E_t[ds_t]/dt$, is the *instantaneous* rationally expected rate of change of the exchange rate. Absolute purchasing power parity ($s_t = p_t - p_t^*$) and uncovered interest rate parity ($i_t = i_t^* + E_t[ds_t]/dt$) are assumed to hold continuously. Moreover, as the country is small, p_t^* and i_t^* are parametrically given.

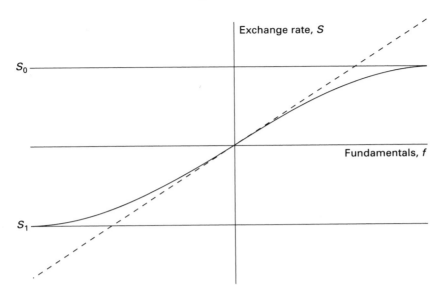

Figure 5.1 Exchange rate in a target zone

Figure 5.1 shows how the exchange rate is expected to behave in response to shocks to v_t. If the exchange rate was permitted to float freely, then from (1) we see that it would be expected to move along the dashed 45° ray line (because the exchange rate is homogeneous of degree one with respect to both the fundamentals entering f_t). However, there is a target zone with S_0 and S_1 as the maximum permitted depreciation and appreciation (under a gold standard, respectively, the gold export and import points). According to the theory of target zones the "S"-shaped curve defines the relationship between the exchange rate and its fundamental determinants.

To see how the exchange rate behaves inside the band suppose that there is a positive random shock to v_t. In this case f_t increases and to balance the domestic money market i_t falls. However, given uncovered interest parity (UIP) a fall in i_t is only possible if $E_t[ds_t]/dt$ is negative – the exchange rate is expected to appreciate. From (1) we see that a negative value of $E_t[ds_t]/dt$ will attenuate the movement of s_t; that is s_t moves by less than it would have done had $E_t[ds_t]/dt$ not become negative. This is called the *honeymoon effect* and represents a free benefit from the announcement of a credible target zone. The generation of the expected appreciation of s_t may be illustrated by considering the situation whereby s has already reached the upper edge of the band. A further random increase in v_t will be offset by a gold outflow induced reduction in m_t. Therefore s_t cannot rise because f_t has an upper limit; but it might fall because the next random shock to v_t

could be negative in which case f_t and s_t fall. Thus on balance, s_t must be expected to fall. It is this expected appreciation, given that UIP holds at all times, that allows i_t to fall below i_t^*. Moreover, the argument holds for any value of s between its upper and central limit.

The target zone model discussed above may be regarded as the base line model. A rather more sophisticated version, due to Bertola and Svensson (1993), pushes the model further. In particular, Bertola and Svensson note that Krugman's basic formulation ignores potential realignments of the fixed parity; such realignments have been fairly frequent in the Exchange Rate Mechanism (ERM) experience with quasi-fixed rates and although they did not occur during the gold standard this does not preclude the possibility that agents held expectations of nonzero realignments.

If market participants, at least in part, anticipate such realignments the target zone cannot be perfectly credible, as is assumed in the basic target zone model. The Bertola and Svensson variant notes first of all that the exchange rate is by definition equal to the sum of the central parity rate, c_t, and what they call the exchange rate within the band, $x_t \equiv s_t - c_t$:

$$s_t \equiv x_t + c_t. \tag{2}$$

Using this expression the expected change in the exchange rate may, in turn, be defined as:

$$E_t[ds_t]/dt \equiv E_t[dx_t]/dt + E_t[dc_t]/dt, \tag{3}$$

where $E_t[dx_t]/dt$ is the expected rate of currency depreciation within the band and $E_t[dc_t]/dt$ is the expected rate of realignment. On using this definition of $E_t[ds_t]/dt$ in (1) and on subtracting c_t from the resulting expression we obtain an equation describing the exchange rate within the band as

$$x_t = h_t + \alpha E_t[dx_t]/dt, \tag{4}$$

where h_t is the new composite fundamental and is equal to $f_t - c_t + \alpha_2 E_t[dc_t]/dt$. (4) has two immediate implications for any empirical test of the target zone model. First, even if UIP holds continuously, this extended target zone model suggests that one cannot say *a priori* what the relationship between the exchange rate and the interest rate differential will be like. This is because UIP holds for the total expected change in the exchange rate which from (3) is equal to two elements. As in our discussion of the Krugman model, one would expect there to be a negative association between the expected rate of currency depreciation within the band and the exchange rate, but one cannot say anything about the relationship between the expected rate of realignment and the exchange rate. Since the latter component of (3) is time varying, it could easily swamp the former component, resulting in a positive or negative relationship between the exchange rate and the interest differential. A second implication of (4) for an empirical test is that one should include the expected rate of realignment in one's measure of the composite fundamentals term.

An implication of (3) is that the expected rate of realignment can be backed out of the total expected change in the exchange rate given by the interest rate differential:

$$E_t[dc_t]/dt \equiv E_t[ds_t]/dt - E_t[dx_t]/dt. \tag{5}$$

All that is needed is a measure of the expected change in the exchange rate within the band which, as we show in the following section, can be estimated via a simple linear regression.

Implications of the target zone model and empirical evidence

The first prediction of the theory of target zones is that, in terms of the basic model, there should be a negative relationship between the expected total change in the exchange rate (given by the interest differential) and the level of the exchange rate. If, however, the target zone is not perfectly credible one cannot make any *a priori* prediction about the relationship. However, the existence of a positive relationship would be *prima facie* evidence of the existence of less than full credibility. Second, there should be a nonlinear relationship between the exchange rate and fundamentals, where following our discussion of potential realignments, care must be taken in the definition of the fundamentals.

For the gold standard period the tests of these two predictions have been conducted by Flood, Rose and Mathieson (1991). With respect to the interest differential exchange rate relationship, using scatterplot analysis, they find some evidence of a negative association for the Classical gold standard period, whilst for the interwar gold standard they report six out of the nine currencies having a negative relationship (the three with a positive relationship are Germany, Italy, and the Netherlands). Furthermore, for both the Classical gold standard and interwar periods the relationship between the exchange rate and fundamentals "seems to be decidedly more non-linear . . . than for the EMS." Indeed, for the Classical gold standard period the scatterplots seem to suggest an S-shaped relationship. Given that our data bases are very similar to those used by Flood, Rose and Mathieson, we do not intend repeating their tests here.

The other testable implications of the target zone model relate to the assumptions underpinning it. By far the most important assumption is that the zone is indeed credible. Svensson (1992) summarizes the results of testing this assumption by arguing that they clearly indicate that perfect credibility is rejected for most modern exchange rate target zones and sample periods. Given that a detailed examination of this assumption has not been conducted for both gold standard experiences we make it the focal point of this chapter. We outline our methods and apply them to the Classical gold standard in the following subsection. We then contrast the findings with those pertaining to the interwar experience.

Credibility of the Classical gold standard

Unfortunately, data limitations restrict the number of currencies which can be analyzed in the target zone framework, and for the Classical gold standard we are forced to focus on the pound/dollar and pound/French franc exchange rates. Two data sets are available, one monthly and the other annual. The annual data include a limited range of fundamental variables (which will be used later) and are available for the full Classical gold standard period from the 1870s to the start of World War I (exact dates depend upon the countries examined). The shorter monthly series on exchange and interest rates span January 1889–December 1907. Further details and sources are given in the data appendix (p. 156).

Svensson's simplest test

Based on the decomposition of the total expected change in the exchange rate into the expected depreciation within the band and the expected rate of realignment, (5), Svensson (1991) proposes what he calls the "simplest test" of credibility. The total expected change in the exchange rate (the interest differential) is simply adjusted for the maximum and minimum possible mean reversion within the band (where such movement is limited here by the gold points) to give a "100 percent" confidence interval for the expected devaluation.

We have placed quotes around 100 percent since the gold points are themselves only estimates. Several authors, both contemporary and modern, have tried to estimate the gold points, each arriving at different values. Most have been forced to provide an average estimate of the gold points for a subperiod of the Classical gold standard, though acknowledging that the component costs of arbitrage were certainly not constant through time (an exception is Spiller and Wood, 1988).

Abstracting from this diversity of estimates, let x_t^u and x_t^l denote "the" upper and lower limits of an exchange rate's deviation from the central parity. The maximum possible changes in the exchange rate within the band are then given by the following weak inequality

$$(x_t^l - x_t)/dt \leq E_t[dx_t]/dt \leq (x_t^u - x_t)/dt. \qquad (6)$$

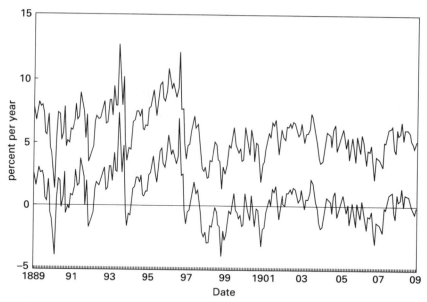

Figure 5.2 Expected realignment rate, dollar/sterling, 1889–1909, 100 percent confidence interval

Assuming that the interest differential measures the total expected change in the exchange rate, the following weak inequality expresses Svensson's "100 percent" confidence interval

$$(i_t - i_t^*) - (x_t^u - x_t)/dt \leq E_t[dc_t]/dt \leq (i_t - i_t^*) - (x_t^l - x_t)/dt. \qquad (7)$$

Adding the maximum possible changes in the exchange rate within the band (using *The Economist*'s relatively wide estimates of the gold points) to the short-term interest rate differential between the United Kingdom and United States (US commercial paper rate *minus* UK open market discount rate) gives the "100 percent" confidence interval for the expected rate of realignment plotted in figure 5.2. For most of the 1890s this interval lay above zero, indicating an expected devaluation of the dollar. After 1897 the confidence interval appears to shift down and spans zero more often than not. Narrower estimates of the gold points would of course provide more examples of expected devaluation over the whole sample period.

Stationarity of the exchange rate within the band

The simple credibility test assumes no knowledge of the time series behavior of the exchange rate within the band. However, according to the target zone theory, the expected change in the exchange rate within the band should be mean reverting – when the exchange rate is near to the top of the band it should be expected to fall back towards the middle. It should be noted that the gold standard target zones were not symmetric about the gold parity rates due to the asymmetries in the costs of gold arbitrage (typically foreign interest rates were above London rates). The exchange rate would therefore be expected to revert towards the middle of the band rather than the parity rate.

A relatively straightforward way of testing for mean reversion would be to use a standard unit root testing methodology. However, it is now widely accepted that such tests are not very powerful in detecting whether a series is stationary or not, particularly when the series contains a root which lies close to the unit circle. An alternative way of testing for unit roots is provided by the variance ratio test, recently popularized in the economics literature by Cochrane (1988) and summarized in chapter 2 in this volume. The variance ratio test is, we believe, especially useful in the present context because it can indicate three types of potential behavior in a time series: whether a series contains a unit root and is therefore nonstationary; whether the series is nonstationary and, additionally, exhibits what we refer to as superpersistence (that is, it has a root greater than unity); or, third, whether the series is mean reverting and therefore stationary. For the last two outcomes the variance ratio test may be regarded as particularly useful since it gives a very straightforward interpretation of how rapidly a series reverts back to, or diverges from, its mean value.

In table 5.1 we present our estimates of V, $z_1(k)$ and $z_2(k)$ for the change in the exchange rate over the Classical gold standard period. The table should be read in the following way. The figures not in parentheses give the estimated variance ratios. The first figure in parentheses immediately below this number is the estimated value of $z_1(k)$ and the second figure in parentheses is the estimated value of $z_2(k)$. The statistics are calculated for a range of k between 2 and 12. Note that both currencies are strongly mean reverting. Thus, at the one percent significance level the estimated value of $z_2(k)$ for the United Kingdom is significantly below unity from lag 2 onwards whilst it is significantly below unity from lag 3 onwards for France.

Bertola and Svensson's test of credibility

Having established that exchange rates are stationary the question remains of how to estimate the mean reversion expected by market participants. Usefully, Bertola and Svensson (1993) suggest that the expected future change in the exchange rate within the band may be approximated by the current exchange rate; both Svensson (1993) and Rose and Svensson (1991) demonstrate empirical support for this proposition using data for currencies participating in the ERM. Conditional on no realignment, the

Table 5.1 *Variance ratio tests of Classical gold standard exchange rates*

	US/UK	FR/UK
2	0.813[a]	0.858
	(2.81)[1b]	(2.14)[2]
	(2.42)[1c]	(1.70)[3]
3	0.633	0.719
	(3.71)[1]	(2.84)[2]
	(4.72)[1]	(3.38)[1]
4	0.545	0.635
	(3.67)[1]	(2.94)[1]
	(4.85)[1]	(3.65)[1]
6	0.447	0.441
	(3.36)[1]	(3.40)[1]
	(5.34)[1]	(5.13)[1]
8	0.338	0.379
	(3.78)[1]	(3.17)[1]
	(6.05)[1]	(5.41)[1]
12	0.195	0.258
	(3.22)[1]	(2.97)[1]
	(6.87)[1]	(6.08)[1]

Notes:
[a] The first figure in each cell gives the ratio of variances.
[b] The first figure in parentheses directly below this gives the estimated value of $z_1(k)$ statistic.
[c] The second figure in parentheses gives the estimated value of $z_2(k)$.
A [1,2] and [3] denote, respectively, significance at the 1, 5 and 10 percent levels.

m-period change in the exchange rate within the band may be estimated from

$$x_{t+m} - x_t = \alpha_0 + \alpha_1 x_t + \varphi_t. \tag{8}$$

That is, the single determinant of the expected change within the band is the current deviation of the exchange rate from the center of the band.[3] In principle, the relationship should be nonlinear, but Bertola and Svensson argue that a linear relationship ought to be acceptable for typical parameter values. In fact many studies of modern target zones use the linear

Table 5.2 *Expected change in exchange rate within the band, Classical period*

	US/UK	FR/UK
Constant	−0.000611	−0.000673
	(2.29)[a]	(3.35)
x	−0.616857	−0.632450
	(7.90)	(9.30)
R^2	0.313	0.325
"DF-test"[b]	4.905	8.301

Notes:
[a] Figures in parentheses are t-statistics computed with GMM standard errors.
[b] The "DF-tests" are t-tests of the hypothesis that $\alpha_1 = 1$.

approximation and find that it produces more sensible estimates than other more complicated methods (see Lindberg *et al.*, 1993; Rose and Svensson, 1991).[4]

As we have noted, the gold points were not necessarily symmetric about the gold parity level. The center of the band therefore changes with the costs of arbitrage and, if the gold points are unknown, is itself unknown. To remove the possible problems with the gold-point estimates we measure the deviation in the exchange rate from the gold parity level. Since a constant is included in the regression this does not constrain the parity level to be the point to which exchange rates revert, but it does force this point to be constant. As the majority of reliable estimates of the gold points are themselves constant we do not feel that any other approach would be profitable.

Our estimates of (8) for the Classical gold standard are presented in table 5.2. Notice that all of the t-ratios on the α_1 coefficients are, in absolute terms, above the critical values of Dickey and Fuller, again confirming that the exchange rate series are stationary.

Bertola and Svensson then show the 95 percent confidence interval for the resulting estimates of expected mean reversion can be subtracted from the interest differential to provide a 95 percent confidence interval for the expected realignment rate. This will be independent of any estimated gold points and should therefore allow an independent check on the credibility of the gold standard. Furthermore, since we are also able to apply this technique to the franc/pound rate this gives us a wider perspective on the operation of the gold standard system during its Classical incarnation.[5]

These are plotted using our monthly and annual data sets in figures

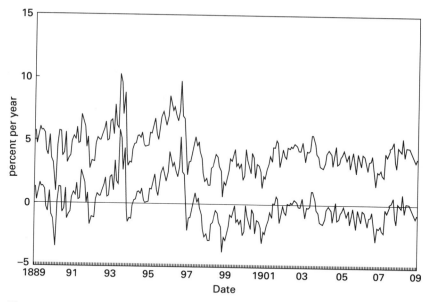

Figure 5.3 Expected realignment rate, dollar/sterling, 95 percent confidence interval, 1889–1909

5.3–5.6.[6] The first point to note is that the sterling/dollar intervals are little different to the 100 percent versions presented above. If anything the 95 percent interval is slightly wider with fewer instances of the range lying above zero. This would seem to indicate that even the widest gold-point estimates are too narrow. Nevertheless, instances of positive devaluation expectations of the dollar are still common and it would appear that one of the key rates of the Classical gold standard was less than perfectly credible.

The expected rate of realignment can be interpreted as the expected devaluation size multiplied by the frequency of realignment. Suppose that, conditional on there being a devaluation, the devaluation will be 5 percent. An expected rate of realignment of 2.5 percent (roughly the average level for the sterling/dollar rate through the less credible early part of the Classical gold standard) implies that the expected frequency of realignment is 0.5 per annum. That is, the market expects a 5 percent devaluation within the year to happen with a 50 percent probability. Equivalently, the expected time to a 5 percent devaluation of the pound is two years. Thus, though the average expected rate of realignment is small it is consistent with substantial devaluation expectations. Of course, for those later periods where the confidence interval spans zero we cannot reject the hypothesis that the expected probability of a 5 percent devaluation is zero.

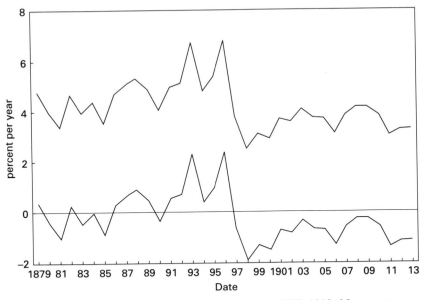

Figure 5.4 Expected realignment rate, dollar/sterling, 1879–1913, 95 percent confidence interval

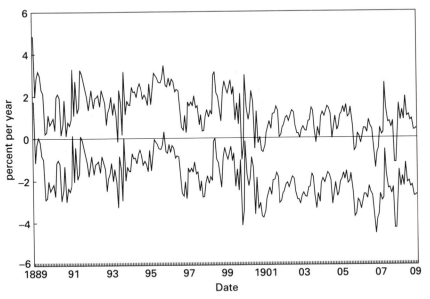

Figure 5.5 Expected realignment rate, franc/sterling, 1889–1909, 95 percent confidence interval

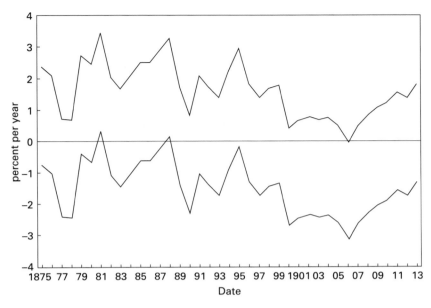

Figure 5.6 Expected realignment rate, franc/sterling, 1875–1913, 95 percent confidence interval

It is reassuring to note that the occurrences of large devaluation expectations coincide with notable periods of tension. Officer (1989) highlights the "eight-year period from 1890 to 1897 [where] there was . . . an acute lack of confidence in the ability of the United States to remain on the gold standard" (1989, 24). The cause of this tension was almost certainly the pro-bimetallist Sherman Silver Purchase Act 1890. Over the 35 months following the passing of the Act, beginning December 1890 and ending with the repeal of the silver clause in November 1893, there were 29 months with significant dollar realignment expectations. The dramatic rise in the confidence of the sterling/dollar link following the repeal proved very temporary, however, mainly because silver still rode high on the political agenda. The persistent devaluation expectations were finally ended by the November 1896 defeat of the pro-silver Presidential candidate, William Jennings Bryan. Figure 5.3 shows that dollar realignment expectations disappeared almost immediately after the election.[7]

By contrast the sterling/franc exchange rate band appears to have been very credible (figure 5.5). Using the annual data, in only one instance was the expected rate of realignment significantly different from zero (and then only very marginally). Using the monthly data a few more periods of less than perfect credibility are revealed, but they were not persistent and were small in magnitude.

Credibility of the interwar gold standard

For the interwar period a greater availability of reliable data should in principle allow us to cover a wider range of currencies. The major data constraint we face is related to the assumption that UIP holds. Interest data of comparable maturity and quality are not readily available for many countries for these years. Fortunately, Einzig (1937) lists weekly spot exchange rates and three-month forward premia against sterling for the dollar, French franc, German mark, Dutch florin, Swiss franc and Belgian Belga. Using triangular arbitrage, these were all converted to dollar bilateral exchange rates.[8] Note that our base country has changed as we move from Classical to interwar standards. In the former, the United Kingdom plays the central role, while the United States assumes this position after World War I. Assuming covered interest parity (CIP) we take the forward premium as our measure of the interest differential. Since monthly series on several fundamental variables are available for this period we sample the data using the observation relating to the last Saturday of each month to produce a monthly data base.[9] Since the pound/dollar exchange rate was still dominant in the interwar period we constrain our analysis to the interval April 1925 to September 1931, during which the sterling/dollar gold link was maintained.

Mean reversion of the exchange rate

Using the same methods as for the Classical period, the degree of mean reversion of the exchange rate can be assessed for the interwar experiment. The Bertola and Svensson simple regression technique reveals very significant mean reversion of a similar magnitude to that experienced during the Classical gold standard. The results for a range of exchange rates are given in table 5.3. The potentially more powerful variance ratio tests give similar results, although the statistical significance is somewhat weaker than for the Classical period. In particular, the ratios for the sterling/dollar rate fall below unity after lag 4 but never significantly so. The ratios for the French franc exchange rate are practically always less than one but only marginally significant at long lags. However, we ascribe these problems to the short data span rather than any lack of mean reversion in the exchange rate since, as we shall see in the following section, the key sterling/dollar spot rate never left the confines of the Officer (1993) gold points. The evidence of mean reversion is much more clear-cut for Belgium, the Netherlands and Switzerland. The full set of variance ratio results are reported in table 5.4.[10]

Table 5.3 *Expected change in exchange rate within the band, interwar period*

	UK/US	FR/US	GE/US	NE/US	SW/US	BE/US
Const. ($\times 10^{-3}$)	0.854	−0.550	0.478	0.430	−0.380	−1.612
	(1.86)[a]	(1.05)	(0.10)	(0.94)	(0.64)	(2.71)
x	−0.622	−0.669	−0.518	−0.737	−0.605	−0.701
	(3.53)	(3.74)	(3.63)	(4.76)	(3.72)	(4.99)
R^2	0.310	0.335	0.248	0.362	0.253	0.352
Std error ($\times 10^{-2}$)	0.197	0.257	0.252	0.281	0.335	0.230

Note:
[a] Figures in parentheses are *t*-statistics computed with GMM standard errors.

Devaluation expectations

Though widely interpreted as less credible than the Classical incarnation, there was never a violation of the gold points by the key sterling/dollar exchange rate during the interwar gold standard. Figure 5.7 shows the spot exchange rate fluctuating widely but always within the Officer (1993) gold points. Notice how the latter also fluctuated, typically narrowing as time passed. We stress, however, that this is not a sufficient condition for there to have been no expectations of realignment.

Based on the Officer (1993) gold points, a "100 percent" confidence interval for the expected rate of realignment of the pound/dollar exchange rate can be estimated. This is plotted in Figure 5.8. Most of the time we are unable to reject the hypothesis that there were no expectations of realignment as the interval spans zero. At the end of the period, however, there was a substantial deterioration in confidence in the currency link and devaluation expectations rose significantly above zero in the final two months.

Similarly, a 95 percent confidence interval can be constructed using the results from the mean reversion equation (reported as figure 5.9). Once more a similar picture is revealed, and though the 95 percent band is narrower than that derived from the simple method, the more relevant lower bound is practically identical. The sterling/dollar exchange rate was almost fully credible during the interwar gold standard but the expected rate of realignment became significantly positive in the last few months of the regime, indicating correctly that the pound was expected to devalue. Nevertheless, the expected devaluation indicated by both methods is small when compared to estimates made of ERM devaluation expectations. Svensson (1993) plots similar 95 percent confidence intervals for the ERM exchange rates against the German mark (figures

Table 5.4 *Variance ratio tests of interwar gold standard rates*

	UK/US	FR/US	GE/US	NE/US	SW/US	BE/US
2	1.062	1.005	0.896	1.263	0.994	0.920
	(0.54)	(0.03)	(0.85)	(2.26)	(0.05)	(0.61)
	(0.63)	(0.03)	(0.80)	(2.66)	(0.06)	(0.84)
3	1.059	0.918	0.793	1.160	0.918	0.822
	(0.34)	(0.40)	(1.13)	(0.92)	(0.45)	(0.91)
	(0.60)	(0.58)	(1.58)	(1.62)	(0.72)	(1.88)
4	1.037	0.875	0.733	0.907	0.833	0.684
	(0.17)	(0.48)	(1.17)	(0.43)	(0.73)	(1.26)
	(0.31)	(0.71)	$(1.74)^3$	(0.78)	(1.13)	$(2.52)^2$
5	0.966	0.812	0.739	0.676	0.706	0.588
	(0.13)	(0.63)	(0.94)	(1.26)	(1.06)	(1.43)
	(0.28)	(1.08)	$(1.70)^3$	(2.73)	$(1.99)^2$	$(3.29)^1$
6	0.908	0.756	0.791	0.585	0.591	0.529
	(0.32)	(0.73)	(0.66)	(1.44)	(1.29)	(1.41)
	(0.67)	(1.26)	(1.26)	(3.09)	$(2.44)^2$	$(3.16)^1$
7	0.866	0.733	0.767	0.586	0.472	0.504
	(0.42)	(0.71)	(0.70)	(1.24)	(1.58)	(1.31)
	(0.97)	(1.38)	(1.41)	(3.08)	$(3,16)^1$	$(3.33)^1$
8	0.816	0.738	0.807	0.633	0.418	0.537
	(0.52)	(0.64)	(0.51)	(1.04)	(1.54)	(1.14)
	(1.24)	(1.25)	(1.11)	$(2.54)^1$	$(3.24)^1$	$(2.84)^1$
9	0.787	0.718	0.833	0.653	0.391	0.547
	(0.56)	(0.63)	(0.41)	(0.92)	(1.49)	(1.01)
	(1.43)	(1.35)	(0.96)	$(2.40)^1$	$(3.39)^1$	$(2.78)^1$
10	0.765	0.678	0.815	0.619	0.365	0.556
	(0.58)	(0.64)	(0.41)	(0.93)	(1.42)	(0.99)
	(1.51)	(1.47)	(1.02)	$(2.51)^1$	$(3.37)^1$	$(2.57)^1$
11	0.762	0.619	0.773	0.559	0.337	0.553
	(0.53)	(0.76)	(0.51)	(0.99)	(1.48)	(0.89)
	(1.53)	$(1.74)^3$	(1.24)	$(2.91)^1$	$(3.52)^1$	$(2.59)^1$
12	0.728	0.570	0.698	0.528	0.288	0.479
	(0.61)	(0.75)	(0.60)	(1.06)	(1.42)	(1.04)
	(1.68)	$(1.89)^2$	(1.60)	$(2.99)^1$	$(3.63)^1$	$(2.88)^1$

Notes:
See table 5.1 for definitions.

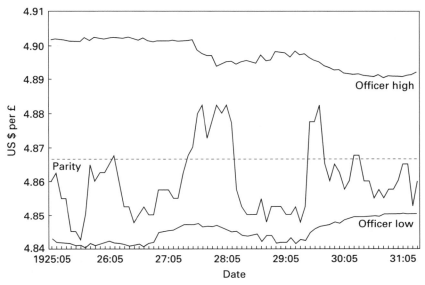

Figure 5.7 Spot rate and gold points, sterling/dollar, 1925–1931

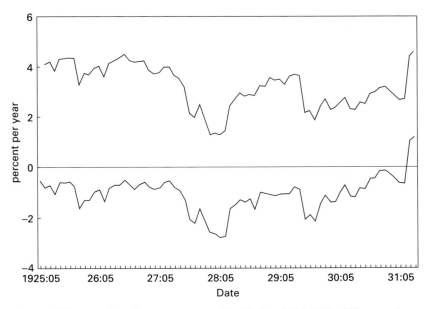

Figure 5.8 Expected realignment rate, sterling/dollar, 1925–1931, 100 percent confidence interval

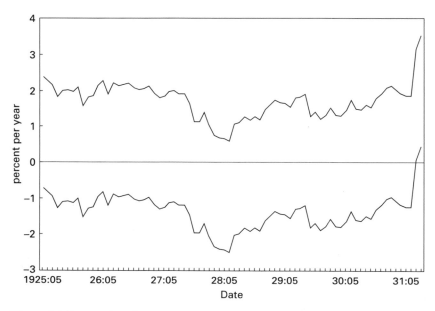

Figure 5.9 Expected realignment rate, sterling/dollar, 1925–1931, 95 percent confidence interval

8a–8f, 786). In the run-up to realignments devaluation expectations usually exceed 10 percent per annum and often exceed 20 percent per annum. This compares with a maximum of around 4 percent for the pound/dollar rate during the interwar period.

The 95 percent confidence interval for the expected rate of realignment of the French franc/dollar rate is plotted in figure 5.10.[11] As in the Classical period the franc link with the central currency (this time the US dollar) appears to have been robust. Realignment expectations were nonzero for the first three months of the regime but once the markets had settled down confidence in the link rose. Reflecting the perceived under-valuation of the franc the mean realignment expectation was negative, indicating that an upward revaluation of the franc was deemed most likely by investors.

Confidence in the mark/dollar link was more volatile (figure 5.11). There were four periods when the confidence interval did not span zero, each instance reflecting expectations of a mark devaluation. A sustained crisis of confidence in mid-1926 (five consecutive months of devaluation expecta-tions) was overcome, but the mean predicted rate of realignment was posi-tive throughout the period. Though realignment expectations were marginally significant, warning bells were not exactly sounding at the end

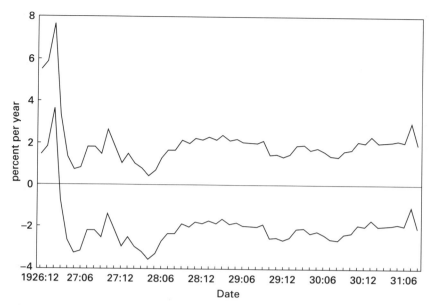

Figure 5.10 Expected realignment rate, franc/dollar, 1926–1931, 95 percent confidence interval

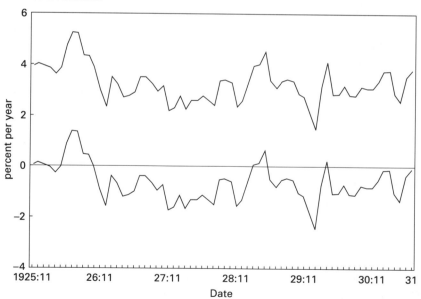

Figure 5.11 Expected realignment rate, mark/dollar, 1925–1931, 95 percent confidence interval

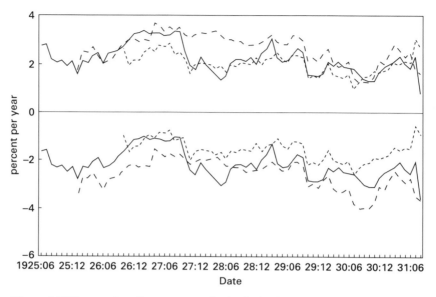

Figure 5.12 Expected realignment rate, florin, Swiss franc and belga/dollar, 1925–1931, 95 percent confidence interval

of the regime, reflecting the sudden onset of the banking crisis that eventually forced the German currency to break with gold and precipitated the end of the interwar gold standard. This is most probably due to the use of foreign exchange controls by Germany.

Figure 5.12 plots realignment expectations for the Dutch, Swiss and Belgian currencies. Without exception expectations were insignificantly different from zero for all currencies and indeed these three currencies plus the French franc maintained their gold links for many more years. The graph clearly shows common trends in confidence for these closely related currencies.

Fundamental determinants of credibility

Once time series of realignment expectations have been estimated the logical step is to relate these measures of credibility to other parameters which influence exchange rates. Several researchers have examined the determinants of the credibility of modern target zones (see Caramazza, 1993; Chen and Giovannini, 1994). However, determinants of devaluation expectations during the gold standards have not, until now, been examined. Data limitations for the Classical gold standard period mean that we can only consider a few possible determinants of realignment expectations, namely money supplies, income levels, and inflation rates. Nevertheless,

Table 5.5 *Fundamental determinants of realignment expectations, classical period*

	US/UK	FR/UK
$m-m^*(-1)^{a,e}$	0.000053	−0.001034
	$(0.01)^b$	(0.11)
$y-y^*(-1)^c$	−0.009735	0.039011
	(0.36)	(1.92)
$\pi-\pi^*(-1)^d$	−0.018076	−0.069565
	(0.28)	(1.33)
$E[dc]/dt(-1)$	0.445554	0.458618
	(2.55)	(2.98)
R^2	0.293	0.487
Std error	0.0089	0.0066
F-test^f	0.344 (0.79)^g	2.065 (0.12)
No. observations	34	38

Notes:
[a] m denotes the money supply.
[b] The figures in parentheses under the coefficient estimates are t-statistics.
[c] y denotes income.
[d] π denotes inflation.
[e] All independent variables are lagged by one period, and a * denotes a foreign (UK) variable.
[f] F-tests are tests that the fundamental determinants excluding the lagged dependent variable are insignificant.
[g] The figures in parentheses after the F-test statistics are the marginal significance level.

these are key variables in most modern theories of the exchange rate and should shed some light on whether the state of the economy and the policies of governments influenced the credibility of the system. We regress the realignment expectations series on a constant and the lagged (log) differences in each variable between the home country and the United Kingdom. The results are reported in table 5.5.

While the equations have reasonably good explanatory power, especially when judged by the criterion for a satisfactory exchange rate equation given by Mussa (1979), only one of the variables is significantly different from zero (the difference between income levels in the UK/France relationship). Furthermore, F-tests indicate that the three fundamental terms are jointly insignificant in both equations. This indicates that the paths of these key fundamental variables were not sufficiently out of line with each other to suggest to market participants that the gold link was under threat. We can therefore find no evidence to contradict the hypothesis that governments played according to the "rules of the game" under the Classical gold standard. The fact of course remains that credibility was not perfect for the dollar/sterling link for the early part of the period. Further investigation of the importance of the dramatic changes in US reserve gold holdings which occurred in the early 1890s would appear to be of particular relevance.[12]

For the interwar period where data are more readily available, we can include several variables which may be important in explaining the credibility of the regime. In particular, we estimate regressions of the following form

$$E_t[dc_t]/dt = \beta_0 + \beta_1[r - r^*]_{t-1} + \beta_2[\pi - \pi^*]_{t-1} + \beta_3[m - m^*]_{t-1}$$

$$+ \beta_4[bp - bp^*]_{t-1} + \beta_5[y - y^*]_{t-1} + \beta_6[q]_{t-1} + \beta_7 E_{t-1}[dc_{t-1}]/dc + \epsilon_t \quad (9)$$

where r denotes reserves, π the inflation rate, m the money supply, bp the balance of payments ratio (exports/imports), y income (proxied by industrial production), and q the real exchange rate. All variables are in logarithms, and an asterisk denotes a foreign (US) variable. Our results are reported in table 5.6 for the three currencies for which nonzero devaluation expectations were found.

The regressions of (9) exhibit a good explanatory power for all exchange rates. Additionally, all of the equations contain a high proportion of significant explanatory variables; are they correctly signed, though? In the United Kingdom, notice that the change in reserves is significantly negative suggesting, as theory would predict, that an increase in domestic foreign exchange reserves results in a decrease in the expected rate of realignment. The money supply term, which is usually interpreted as a government financing term, is also strongly significant, with the expected positive sign. The significantly negative effect of relative UK industrial production indicates that an increase in UK industrial production relative to that in the United States reduces the expected rate of devaluation because it increases the demand for money relative to the supply. Notice that of the other "nonmonetary" variables one enters with an incorrect sign (the balance of payments) and one with the correct sign (the real exchange rate) and that both are strongly significant.

The sign pattern of the variables is more mixed in the French and German equation. For example, although the French inflation term is very significant it is wrongly signed, suggesting that an increase in French inflation led to a decrease in the expected rate of devaluation. Of the other

Table 5.6 *Fundamental determinants of realignment expectations, interwar period*

	UK/US	FR/US	GE/US
$r-r*(-1)^{a,h}$	−0.009374	0.004114	0.006242
	$(2.11)^b$	(1.13)	(0.97)
$\pi-\pi*(-1)^c$	−0.075969	−0.156256	−0.061398
	(0.43)	(3.22)	(0.27)
$m-m*(-1)^d$	0.043533	0.008630	−0.017777
	(2.63)	(0.70)	(1.40)
$bp-bp*(-1)^e$	0.004023	−0.002192	0.003465
	(2.59)	(0.43)	(1.11)
$y-y*(-1)^f$	−0.004411	−0.010759	−0.016547
	(2.74)	(1.70)	(1.85)
$q(-1)^g$	0.069823	0.698732	0.021525
	(0.46)	(2.44)	(0.06)
$E[dc]/dt(-1)$	0.694615	0.411907	0.411707
	(7.75)	(5.05)	(3.69)
R^2	0.800	0.614	0.556
Std error	0.0024	0.0040	0.0052
χ^2-test^i	11.569 (0.07)^j	33.836 (0.00)	15.865 (0.01)
No. observations	74	53	64

Notes:
[a] r denotes reserves.
[b] Figures in parentheses under the coefficient estimates are t-statistics computed with GMM standard errors.
[c] π denotes inflation.
[d] m denotes money supply (M1 for UK, M2 for France, money base for Germany and matching series for the United States).
[e] bp denotes the balance of payments (exports/imports).
[f] y denotes income.
[g] q denotes the real exchange rate.
[h] All independent variables are lagged by one period, and a * denotes a foreign (US) variable.
[i] χ^2-tests are tests that the fundamental determinants excluding the lagged dependent variable are insignificant.
[j] The figures in parentheses after the test statistics are the marginal significance level. Seasonal dummies are included in the estimated equations.

marginally significant variables, the French industrial production and real exchange rate terms appear with the correct sign. Significance levels are low in the German equation, with only the industrial production spread being correctly signed and significant.

However, perhaps the sign differences in the interwar period should not be overemphasized. It is important to remember that the equation under consideration here is a reduced form and the different sign patterns across countries could simply reflect different policy reaction functions. What is important and worth emphasizing, however, is the (joint and individual) significance of the explanatory variables for the interwar equations. This contrasts quite sharply with the picture for the Classical period and indicates that governments may have been pursuing goals in addition to the maintenance of gold parity. Thus the evolution of the fundamental variables was felt by the markets to have an impact on the credibility of the governments' links to gold. These findings may be thought to confirm those of Eichengreen, Watson and Grossman (1985), who argue that the Bank of England's policy towards Bank Rate, a critical monetary variable, was driven by other than simply following the "rules of the game" which simply stated linked changes in interest rates to changes in international reserves. For example, they show that Bank Rate policy also reacted to domestic business conditions, with the Bank of England being reluctant to raise Bank Rate when business conditions were weak.

Nevertheless, realignment expectations were only very rarely significant for all exchange rates, and with the exception of the last few months of the dollar/sterling link and the immediate aftermath of the entry of the French franc, were of small magnitude. However, this is not necessarily a contradiction. The entirety of our results indicate that while the Bank of England (and other central banks) may have deviated somewhat from the strict "rules of the game," it did not do so enough so as to threaten the credibility of its commitment to the gold standard, at least until the final few months.

Summary of conclusions

We now summarize our conclusions regarding the credibility of the two gold standard experiences. For the Classical gold standard period we found that the key dollar/sterling rate was not fully credible, particularly at the start of the period and in the 1890s. In contrast, however, the franc/sterling rate appears to be reasonably credible throughout. Interestingly, we could find no significant association between fundamentals and the expected rate of realignment. Rather, political influences, particularly the Populist Movement of the late 1880s and the Free Silver Movement of the 1890s, appear to have been the source of the dollar's weakness.

Although *a priori* we would have expected the interwar experience to be
much less credible than the Classical period, our results suggest a remarkable degree of stability for this period. For example, the sterling/dollar standard lasted around six years within a band of approximately plus or minus
0.6 percent. This compares very favorably with the much more liberal plus
or minus 2.25 percent ERM, in which the longest period between realignments for the central franc/mark rate was for the period January 1987–June
1993. Our tests suggest that fundamentals were an important determinant
of credibility in the interwar period. We interpret this as suggesting that
governments were more willing to take account of economic conditions
besides the exchange rate in conducting policy during this period, but that
this was not sufficient to completely undermine the credibility of the
system. One interesting result from our interwar data base was the finding
that for both Germany and the United Kingdom, devaluation expectations
rose sharply towards the end of these countries' time on the gold standard.
Given that there was little warning of devaluation from these countries'
interest rates (a finding which parallels Rose's, 1993, study of sterling's
ERM crisis) this suggests the possibility of a speculative attack (in
Germany's case because of the banking crisis) rather than problems with
fundamentals.

We also think that our finding of no substantial differences between
the credibility of the interwar and (latter part of the) Classical gold standards should be of interest to economic historians. Indeed, it will come
as a surprise to some specialists in this area who have pointed to certain
supposed fundamental weaknesses associated with the later period: for
example, that Britain re-entered the gold standard in 1925 with an overvalued exchange rate and that as both France and, to a lesser extent, the
United States acted as "sinks" for monetary gold, world monetary gold
became grossly maldistributed. However, this is not to say that we think
that the interwar gold standard was necessarily as efficient an international monetary mechanism as was the Classical standard, primarily
because the interwar gold standard had to be supported from time to
time by international cooperation. That is, Britain's key role during the
interwar period was shored up through the United States and France
making loans to the Bank of England and, in the early years at least,
the Federal Reserve trimming its discount rate to accommodate the
Bank of England. However, our findings can be used to support the
propositions that for several years international actions such as these
probably did help to underpin the credibility of the system. Future
research could usefully develop explanations of why the interwar gold
standard was so credible despite the apparent flaws in the international
financial regime.

Appendix: data sources and description

Classical gold standard

Annual data

All series are annual averages. Exact calculation methods are given in cited source.

Exchange rates

Sterling/dollar rates from Friedman and Schwartz (1982).
Sterling/franc rates from Mitchell (1993).

Bill rates

US: Prime 60–90 day commercial paper from Homer (1977).
UK: Open market rate of discount from Homer (1977).
France: Open market rate of discount from Homer (1977).

Money supplies

US: Money stock from Friedman and Schwartz (1982).
UK: Money stock from Friedman and Schwartz (1982).
France: Bank notes in circulation from Mitchell (1993).

Income levels

US: Real national income from Friedman and Schwartz (1982).
UK: Real national income from Friedman and Schwartz (1982).
France: Real GDP from Mitchell (1993).

Price series

US: Implicit price deflator from Friedman and Schwartz (1982).
UK: Implicit price deflator from Friedman and Schwartz (1982).
France: Implicit price deflator from Mitchell (1993).

Monthly data

Exchange rates

National Monetary Commission (1910).

Bill rates

National Monetary Commission (1910).

Interwar gold standard

Exchange rates

All countries: Spot and 3-month forward data from Einzig (1937, appendix 1).

Reserves

All countries: Gold reserves from various issues of the League of Nations, *Monthly Bulletin of Statistics*.

Money supplies

US: Money base, M1 and M2 from Friedman and Schwartz (1970).
UK: Money base and M1 from Capie and Webber (1985).
France: M2 from Patat and Luffall (1990).
Germany: Money base (liabilities of Reichsbank) from Federal Reserve Board (1943).

Industrial production indices

US: Industrial production from Federal Reserve Board (1943).
All other countries: Industrial production from various issues of the League of Nations, *Monthly Bulletin of Statistics*. UK data is interpolated from quarterly data.

Balance of payments

All countries: Imports and exports series from various issues of the League of Nations, *Monthly Bulletin of Statistics*.

Price series

All countries: Price levels from Federal Reserve Board (1943).

Notes

The authors are grateful to Tam Bayoumi, Michael Bordo, Barry Eichengreen and an anonymous referee for their helpful comments on an earlier draft of this chapter. MacDonald and Marsh are grateful to the ESRC's Global Economic Institutions Programme for research support (Grant no. L1 2025014).

1. In his contribution to this volume (chapter 4), Officer introduces the concept of "regime efficiency," and applies it to the interwar sterling/dollar gold link.
2. Officer justifies this bold assumption by arguing that speculators had no reason to favor one point estimate over another while the exchange rate was within the gold points. This implies that their probability distributions of expected exchange rates was rectangular with mean in the center of the range.
3. In their empirical implementation of (8), for ERM currencies, Rose and Svensson (1991) include levels of other ERM exchange rates, since the latter may be relevant in a multilateral exchange rate target zone model. Given the wide range of country-specific sample periods, and also the fact that the gold standard experiences do not seem to resemble a multilateral target zone system so much as a group of bilateral relationships, we do not include other gold standard currencies in our estimated relationships.
4. Since the dependent variable consists of overlapping observations Newey and West (1987) generalized method of moments (GMM) standard errors are reported. These allow for both serial correlation and heteroskedasticity.
5. We could not find any reliable estimates of the gold points for French franc exchange rate and so were unable to produce "100 percent" confidence intervals. This also applies to the interwar period examined later.
6. To obtain the confidence intervals based on annual data the mean reversion parameters estimated with the monthly data are combined with the annual exchange and interest rate data.
7. The significant devaluation expectations of the late 1880s are less easily attributed to a single cause. The Bland–Allison Act 1878 reinstated silver as legal tender and may have led the markets to question America's commitment to the monometallic gold standard. However, it has also been suggested that the rise of the Populist Movement may have been sufficiently threatening to the banking community to affect the currency's credibility.

   We note that our results are also compatible with those of Giovannini (1993) who, using a similar data base, found periods of expected dollar devaluation in the 1890s.
8. We should point out that our choice of currencies, dictated by data availability, is likely to be favorable to the gold standard. Belgium, France, the Netherlands and Switzerland all became members of the gold bloc after 1931.
9. The foreign exchange market was typically open on Saturdays during this period. For days when the market was closed the nearest business day is used instead.
10. One interesting extension of our mean reversion tests would be to implement them using recursive methods. In theory, this could shed light on potential variations in mean reversion in the two gold standard periods. Data considerations, however, mean that only the Classical period would be a suitable candidate for such work.

11. We have been unable to locate any gold-point estimates for exchange rates other than for sterling/dollar. This precludes the reporting of 100 percent confidence intervals.
12. See Officer (1993) for a discussion of events in this period.

References

Bertola, G. and L. E. O. Svensson (1993). "Stochastic Devaluation Risk and the Empirical Fit of Target-zone Models," *Review of Economic Studies* 60, 689–712

Bordo, M. and F. Kydland (1992). "The Gold Standard as a Rule," Federal Reserve Bank of Cleveland, *Working Paper* 9205

Capie, F. and A. Webber (1985). *A Monetary History of the United Kingdom, 1870–1982*, vol. 1, *Data, Sources, Methods*, London: Allen & Unwin

Caramazza, F. (1993). "French–German Interest Rate Differentials and Time-varying Realignment Risk," *IMF Staff Papers*, 40, 567–583

Chen, Z. and A. Giovannini (1994). "The Determinants of Realignment Expectations Under the EMS: Some Empirical Regularities," LSE Financial Markets Group, *Discussion Paper* 184

Clark, T. A. (1984). "Violations of the Gold Points, 1890–1908," *Journal of Political Economy* 92, 791–823

Cochrane, J. (1988). "How Big is the Random Walk in GNP?," *Journal of Political Economy* 96, 893–920

Dornbusch, R. (1976). "Expectations and Exchange Rate Dynamics," *Journal of Political Economy* 84, 1116–1176

Eichengreen, B., M. W. Watson and R. S. Grossman (1985). "Bank Rate Policy Under the Interwar Gold Standard – A Dynamic Probit Model," *Economic Journal* 95, 725–745

Einzig, P. (1937). *The Theory of Forward Exchange*, London: Macmillan

Federal Reserve Board (1943). *Banking and Monetary Statistics, 1914–1941*, Washington DC

Flood, R. P., A. K. Rose and D. J. Mathieson (1991). "An Empirical Exploration of Exchange Rate Target-zones," *Carnegie–Rochester Series on Public Policy* 35, 7–66

Frenkel, J. A. (1976). "A Monetary Approach to the Exchange Rate," *Scandinavian Journal of Economics* 2, 200–221

Friedman, M. and A. J. Schwartz (1970). *Monetary Statistics of the United States Estimates, Sources and Methods*, New York: Columbia University Press for NBER

(1982). *Monetary Trends in the United States and in the United Kingdom 1870–1970*, Chicago: University of Chicago Press for NBER

Giovannini, A. (1993). "Bretton Woods and its Precursors: Rules versus Discretion in the History of International Monetary Regimes," in M. D. Bordo and B. Eichengreen (eds.), *A Retrospective on the Bretton Woods System: Lessons for International Monetary Reform*, Chicago: University of Chicago Press for NBER, 109–154

Homer, S. (1977). *A History of Interest Rates*, New Brunswick: Rutgers University Press

Krugman, P. R. (1988). "Target Zones and Exchange Rate Dynamics," NBER, *Working Paper* 2481

Lindberg, H., P. Soderlind and L. E. O. Svensson (1993). "Devaluation Expectations: The Swedish krona 1985–92," *Economic Journal* 103, 1170–1179

Miller, M. and P. Weller (1991). "Currency Bands, Target Zones, and Price Flexibility," *IMF Staff Papers* 38, 184–215

Mitchell, B. R. (1993). *European Historical Statistics, 1750–1970*, London: Macmillan

Moggridge, D. E. (1969). *British Monetary Policy 1924–1931*, Cambridge: Cambridge University Press

Morgenstern O. (1959). *International Financial Transactions and Business Cycles*, Princeton: Princeton University Press for NBER

Mussa, M. (1976). "The Exchange Rate, the Balance of Payments and Money and Fiscal Policy under a Regime of Controlled Floating," *Scandinavian Journal of Economics* 2, 229–248

  (1979). "Empirical Regularities in the Behavior of Exchange Rates and Theories of the Foreign Exchange Market," in *Policies for Employment, Prices and Exchange Rates, Carnegie–Rochester Conference Series on Public Policy* 11, 9–57

National Monetary Commission (1910). *Statistics for the United States, 1867–1809* (compiled by A. P. Andrew), Washington DC: Document 570, 61st Congress, second session, Government Printing Office

Newey, W. and K. West (1987). "A Simple Positive-Definite Heteroskedasticity and Autocorrelation Consistent Covariance Matrix," *Econometrica* 55, 703–708

Officer, L. H. (1986). "The Efficiency of the Dollar–Sterling Gold Standard, 1890–1908," *Journal of Political Economy* 94 (October), 1038–1073

  (1989). "The Remarkable Efficiency of the Dollar–Sterling Gold Standard, 1890–1906," *Journal of Economic History* 49, 1–41

  (1993). "Gold-point Arbitrage and Uncovered Interest Arbitrage under the 1925–1931 Dollar–Sterling Gold Standard," *Explorations in Economic History* 30 (January), 98–127

Patat, J.-P. and M. Luffall (1990). *A Monetary History of France in the Twentieth Century*, New York: St. Martin's Press

Rose, A. N. (1993). "Sterling's ERM Credibility: Did the dog bark in the night?," *Economics Letters* 41, 419–427

Rose, A. K. and L. E. O. Svensson (1991). "Expected and Predicted Realignments: The FF/DM Exchange Rate during the EMS," Federal Reserve Board of Governors, *International Finance Discussion Paper* 395

Spiller, P. T. and R. O. Wood (1988). "Arbitrage During the Dollar–Sterling Gold Standard, 1899–1908: An Econometric Approach," *Journal of Political Economy* 96, 882–892

Svensson, L. E. O. (1991). "The Simplest Test of Target Zone Credibility," *IMF Staff Papers* 38 (September), 655–665

(1992). "An Interpretation of Recent Research on Exchange Rate Target Zones," *Journal of Economic Perspectives* 6, 119–144

(1993). "Assessing Target Zone Credibility: Mean Reversion and Devaluation Expectations in the ERM, 1979–1992," *European Economic Review* 37, 763–802

III

Adjustment mechanisms

6   The stability of the gold standard and the evolution of the international monetary fund system

Tamim Bayoumi and Barry Eichengreen

Introduction

Despite the attention lavished on it by generations of scholars, the question of why the pre-1914 gold standard operated so smoothly for so long remains stubbornly unresolved. Under the gold standard, the exchange rates of the major industrial countries were firmly pegged within narrow bands ("the gold points") in an environment free of significant restrictions on international flows of financial capital. This is precisely the sort of international monetary arrangement that recent experience suggests should be fragile, precarious and difficult to maintain. The breakdown of the Bretton Woods System following the liberalization of international capital markets in the 1960s and the collapse of the narrow-band European Monetary System (EMS) on the heels of the removal of Europe's residual capital controls in the 1980s illustrate the point. How the pre-1914 gold standard managed to avoid the same fate constitutes an analytical mystery and an important policy question.

The literature on this subject can be separated into two strands concerned with the policy regime and with the structure of markets, respectively. The former focuses on the stabilizing nature of the policy rules followed by central banks and governments during the gold standard years. Eichengreen (1992), for example, focuses on credibility and cooperation as the dual pillars of the policy regime. At the core of the system – in Britain, France and Germany – there was no doubt, barring the most exceptional circumstances, that whatever steps were needed would be taken to defend the central bank's gold reserves and the exchange rate peg.[1] Lending credibility to this policy was the fact that the connections between policy and employment remained imperfectly understood. So long as there was no properly articulated theory of the relationship between policy and the economy, observers could reasonably disagree about whether the level of interest rates was aggravating unemployment; their disagreement neutralized pressures that might have been applied to modify policy. Public spending ratios were low, budgets balanced. Governments

generally abided by a balanced budget objective, which could be regarded, in effect, as representing the required fiscal constraint on national policies. (Goodhart, 1992)

Those who suffered most from unemployment were in no position to make their objections felt. The right to vote was generally limited to men of property. Labor parties representing working men were in their formative years. The working man at risk of unemployment when the central bank raised interest rates had little opportunity to voice his objections, much less to expel from office the government and central bankers responsible for the policy.

For all these reasons a negative disturbance to a country's balance of payments did not weaken the exchange rate to the point where painfully large interest rate increases had to be undertaken; instead, any weakness was quickly offset by capital inflows prompted by the expectation that the authorities would do what was required to stabilize it. This fact limited the distress caused by those necessary steps.

The other stabilizing element of the policy regime was international cooperation among central banks and governments. Cooperation was episodic, but it occurred precisely when the system's anchor currencies came under attack. Central banks discounted bills on behalf of the affected country or lent gold to its monetary authority. The most famous such instance was the 1890 Baring Crisis, when the Bank of England was faced with the insolvency of a major British bank, Baring Brothers, which had extended bad loans to the Government of Argentina. The Bank of England borrowed £3 million in gold from the Bank of France and obtained a pledge of £1.5 million in gold coin from Russia. With their help, the exchange rate crisis was surmounted.[2]

Bordo and Kydland (chapter 3 in this volume) attribute the credibility of policymakers' commitment to defend their gold standard parities to the contingent nature of the policy rule. In this view, the monetary authorities adhered faithfully to the fixed price of gold except during major disturbances. In the event of a serious disturbance such as a war, however, specie payments could be suspended in order to facilitate the issue of paper money and debt. This relieved the authorities of the need to assume an insupportable – and hence incredible – commitment to defend their fixed parities. But because there was no question about the temporary, emergency nature of the suspension, it did not undermine confidence in the authorities' commitment to maintain the gold parity in normal times. This contingent rule thus supported a time consistent and credible monetary regime.

Using a similar approach, Eichengreen (1995) explains the viability of temporary suspensions in terms of models of exchange rate escape clauses, in which it is argued that exceptional circumstances can be invoked to justify a temporary suspension of the exchange rate peg without undermining the credibility of the authorities' commitment to defend it in normal times only if those exceptional circumstances are independently verifiable and clearly not of the authorities' own making.[3] Given the nature of the policy regime described above, these preconditions were better satisfied under the pre-1914 gold standard than subsequently. Over time, the conduct of policy became increasingly politicized and the viability of the escape clause declined. Temporary suspensions threatened to raise questions about the dedication of governments to the defense of their gold standard parities and to erode the credibility of a commitment to their maintenance. Invocation of the escape clause became rare, and the gold standard increasingly came to resemble a fixed exchange rate system.

Questions nonetheless remain about whether the policy regime can explain the stability of the gold standard system.[4] Some authors have looked instead to the nature of the underlying economic environment, and to the structure of commodity and factor markets in particular. The maintenance of the gold standard could be attributable simply to a favorable environment (relatively small and infrequent macroeconomic disturbances) or to the flexibility of markets (relatively fast adjustment of prices and quantities to those disturbances which occurred). This strand of literature has been lent new impetus by recent developments in time series econometrics. A number of investigators (Keating and Nye, 1991; Bayoumi and Eichengreen, 1994a; Bordo, 1993) have applied a technique developed by Blanchard and Quah (1989) to extract aggregate supply and aggregate demand disturbances and speeds of adjustment to shocks from time series on output and prices. These studies generally find that shocks were *not* smaller and less prevalent under the gold standard than subsequently but that the adjustment of prices and quantities was faster, as if market flexibility allowed disturbances to be more easily accommodated at low cost during the gold standard years.

The framework employed in these studies is the familiar aggregate supply–aggregate demand model of figure 6.1.[5] It predicts that an aggregate demand disturbance like that depicted in panel (b) will raise output temporarily but prices permanently, while an aggregate supply disturbance like that in panel (c) will raise output and reduce prices in both the short and long run. The empiricial methodology, as described in the appendix (p. 182), does not impose these price responses. While the price level generally responds as predicted when the model is estimated with data for the Bretton Woods System and the post-Bretton Woods float, the same is not true for the gold

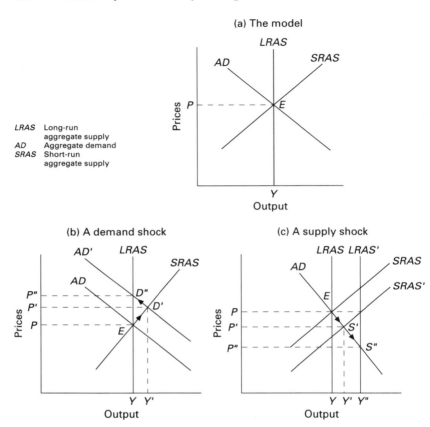

Figure 6.1 The aggregate demand and supply model
(a) The model   (b) A demand shock   (c) A supply shock

standard years. Rather, investigators find a tendency for prices to rise in response to permanent shocks, as if aggregate demand curves sloped upwards. This raises obvious questions about the applicability of the aggregate supply–aggregate demand framework to gold standard experience.

In addition, Neumann (1993) has questioned whether the slopes of the aggregate supply and aggregate demand schedules associated with the variances of the estimated disturbances shift with changes in the exchange rate regime as predicted by the model. Fixed exchange rates like those of the gold standard should be associated with a relatively flat aggregate demand schedule, since domestic prices cannot diverge radically from prices in the rest of the world and the money supply should adjust endogenously to shocks. However, Neumann's numerical calculations, based on Bordo's econometric estimates, imply that aggregate demand curves were steeper under Breton Woods than under floating and only slightly flatter in the gold standard years.

With this debate as background, we reassess the evidence on the incidence of macroeconomic disturbances and the speed of adjustment under the pre-1914 gold standard. Our innovation is to introduce linkages between domestic and foreign prices, further opening up the aggregate supply–aggregate demand framework to transactions with the rest of the world. This extension proves sufficient to resolve several of the paradoxes described above. We still find that shocks were no smaller or less frequent under the gold standard than in the postwar period, but that the adjustment of prices and quantities was faster. Now, however, we find that on average demand curves slope downwards over the short and intermediate runs before international arbitrage restores prices to the levels that prevailed prior to the shock. The exceptions are countries like Australia, for which gold discoveries were a major source of disturbances and one with unique implications for the association between supply shocks and the price level (see chapter 8 in this volume).

Finally, we analyze shifts across international monetary regimes in the slopes of the aggregate demand and aggregate supply schedules. We find that these slopes did in fact shift over time in directions consistent with the predictions of standard models. Aggregate demand curves were flatter under the quasi-fixed exchange rates of the gold standard than the pegged but adjustable rates of Bretton Woods and flatter under Bretton Woods than during the post-Bretton Woods float. Even the interwar period, which encompassed a succession of different exchange rate regimes, is consistent with this taxonomy. Moreover, short-run aggregate supply curves were steeper under earlier international monetary regimes than later ones, consistent with the notion that nominal inertia increased over time. We show that the steady increase in the slope of the short-run aggregate supply curve provided an incentive for policymakers to adopt monetary regimes featuring progressively greater exchange rate flexibility. This analysis thus provides a unified explanation for the historical evolution of the international monetary system.

An analysis of the pre-1914 gold standard

We gathered data for seven countries for which it was possible to obtain consistent estimates of national income in both real and nominal terms for the 1880–1913 gold standard period: the United States, Great Britain, Germany, Italy, Sweden, Australia, and Denmark.[6] Growth and inflation were calculated as the first difference of the logarithm of real GDP and the implicit GDP deflator, respectively. In each case, we included two lagged

Table 6.1 *Standard deviations of disturbances during the gold standard, 1880–1913, selected periods*[a]

	1880–1913	1880–1890	1881–1901	1902–1913
Demand				
Aggregate SD^b	0.019	0.026	0.019	0.010
SD^{*c}	0.019	0.021	0.021	0.015
United States	0.032	0.041	0.033	0.018
Great Britain	0.016	0.019	0.019	0.010
Germany	0.027	0.030	0.030	0.020
Italy	0.032	0.032	0.032	0.031
Australia	0.043	0.046	0.043	0.041
Sweden	0.029	0.038	0.026	0.024
Denmark	0.019	0.022	0.043	0.013
Supply				
Aggregate SD	0.014	0.009	0.014	0.017
SD^*	0.022	0.021	0.026	0.019
United States	0.027	0.024	0.030	0.030
Great Britain	0.024	0.018	0.029	0.024
Germany	0.028	0.033	0.030	0.024
Italy	0.033	0.033	0.037	0.026
Australia	0.047	0.032	0.062	0.044
Sweden	0.033	0.025	0.035	0.031
Denmark	0.029	0.032	0.026	0.030

Notes:
[a] Estimates are from VARs.
[b] SD denotes the standard deviation of our international aggregate, constructed by estimating VARs on individual country data and aggregating the results using GDP weights.
[c] SD^* denotes the GDP-weighted standard deviation of the individual country series around this aggregate.
Source: See text discussion.

values in our bivariate structural vector autoregressions (VARs) so as to preserve the symmetry of specification across countries. The Schwartz–Bayes Information Criterion generally indicated an optimal lag length of one or two. Chow tests provided little evidence of significant structural shifts across subperiods within the gold standard years.

Table 6.1 summarizes the variability of the estimated aggregate supply and aggregate demand shocks from these structural VARs for different countries and periods.[7] We construct the international aggregate by first estimating the VARs on individual country data and then aggregating the results using GDP weights.[8] *SD* is the standard deviation of this aggregate series, whereas *SD** denotes the GDP-weighted standard deviation of individual country series around the aggregate.

Both demand and supply shocks are larger for Australia than for any other country. There is reason to think that the Australian case is different from that of the other economies in the sample, as we explain below. Both shocks are relatively small in Great Britain, the country at the center of the gold standard system.

The data on the size of aggregate disturbances (*SD*) indicates a decline over time in the size of demand shocks and an increase in the size of supply shocks after 1890. The dispersion across countries of supply and demand disturbances (*SD**) is relatively stable, except for a decrease in the dispersion of demand shocks after 1902. The fall in the size and dispersion of aggregate demand disturbances plausibly reflects the solidification of the gold standard system, while the increase in the size of aggregate supply disturbances after 1890 may be associated with the increasing disruptiveness of financial crises in the United States and the reduced efficiency of financial intermediation that they implied.

We use the impulse response functions associated with these regressions to plot the aggregate demand and short-run aggregate supply curves in price–output space. For the aggregate demand curve this is the path traced out by prices and output in response to a supply shock. For the aggregate supply curve it is the line segment marked off by the initial equilibrium on one end and the level of output and prices in the first period following a demand shock on the other. This is the impact effect of a shift in aggregate demand, which traces out a movement up or down the short-run supply curve. The remainder of the adjustment to a demand shock can be thought of as a movement along the new demand curve, with prices rising and output demand falling.

The simulated supply and demand schedules are shown in the top half of figure 6.2. The left-hand panel shows the schedules themselves, the right-hand panel their stylized counterparts. These are derived from estimates using aggregate data for the sum of our seven countries, constructed using 1900 GDP weights. Two features are noteworthy. First, the short-run aggregate supply schedule is quite steep, as if much of the adjustment of prices and quantities to shocks was completed within a year. Second, the aggregate demand curve is upward-sloping, confirming the paradoxical finding of previous authors.

Various explanations have been advanced for this counterintuitive result. Keating and Nye invoke the Tobin effect, which suggests that demand shocks that cause inflation could induce agents to substitute capital for

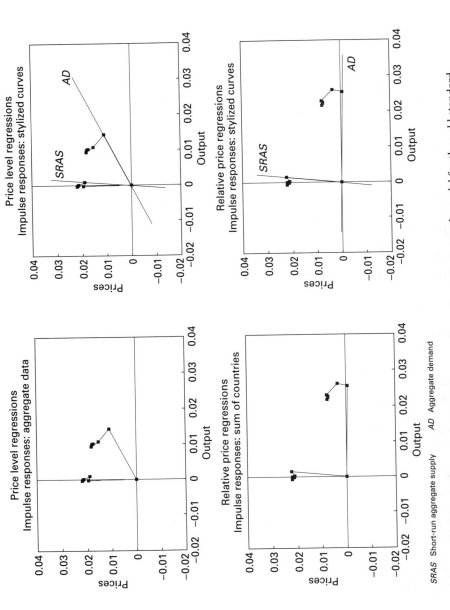

Figure 6.2 Alternative estimates of the aggregate demand, aggregate supply model for the gold standard

SRAS Short-run aggregate supply   *AD* Aggregate demand

labor, raising the capital/labor ratio and increasing output permanently. Why this effect should have operated more powerfully in the gold standard period, however, is not clear. (Indeed, the fact that inflation was less likely to be persistent under the gold standard than the fiat money regimes that followed should have weakened the operation of the Tobin effect, other things being equal.) Keating and Nye mention the possibility that negative demand shocks could have led to a permanent deterioration in levels of human and physical capital, as in recent hysteresis models, although again it is not clear why hysteresis effects should have operated more powerfully before 1914. They suggest that there may have existed multiple equilibria in late 19th-century economies, with demand shocks permanently shifting them from one equilibrium to another. Insofar as subsequent reductions in transactions costs facilitated the efforts of agents to coordinate on the superior equilibrium, technological progress could have worked to eliminate the multiplicity problem. Finally, there is the possibility that econometric techniques are incapable of distinguishing highly persistent temporary disturbances from permanent ones when applied to relatively short time series.

Our explanation rests on the importance of arbitrage in international commodity and factor markets during the gold standard years and on the tendency for the money supply to adjust endogenously to shocks. Recall that the aggregate demand curve is traced out by subjecting the system to a permanent (aggregate supply) shock. In a closed economy this would tend to raise output and lower prices as in panel (c) of figure 6.1, tracing out a negatively-sloped demand curve. Under the fixed rates of the gold standard, however, commodity market arbitrage should have prevented domestic and foreign prices from diverging substantially. If goods produced at home and abroad were imperfect substitutes in consumption, some relative price movement was still possible. In the limiting case of perfect substitutability, arbitrage would drive domestic prices back to the level of foreign prices, a process which may take time or, if no unexploited arbitrage profits are assumed to exist (as in McCloskey and Zecher, 1984), occur instantaneously. The point is that in a commodity standard the money supply will adjust through the balance of payments to restore equilibrium to both asset and commodity markets.

The close connection of prices across countries implied by a commodity standard provides an intuitive explanation for why aggregate supply shocks appear associated with increases in prices. It is a well known characteristic of the pre-1914 period that expansions in the world gold stock were associated with both increases in prices and robust levels of world output growth, while declines in prices were associated with more modest overall economic expansion. As prices across countries were closely linked, the estimation results could reflect this association between overall world prices and the level of output. Such a relationship would not be a concern in postwar data as national price levels were not bound together in the long run in the same manner.

This suggests that the relevant way of measuring the aggregate demand curve under the gold standard is in output–relative price space, where the domestic price level is measured relative to the foreign price level. We re-estimated the same bivariate VARs using domestic output and this relative price variable. The price level is measured relative to the aggregate price level (a GDP weighted aggregate of individual country price levels). Australia was excluded from the aggregate for reasons we describe below.

The lower half of figure 6.2 shows the results from this decomposition. The aggregate demand curve now slopes downwards in the short run, after which domestic prices recover to world levels. In fact, domestic prices more than recover to world levels. An interpretation of this last finding is that many of the positive supply shocks experienced by these industrial economies took the form of declines in the prices of imported primary products, which raised the relative price of manufactured goods in the long run. That the countries (aside from Australia) for which prices do not rise in the long run are Denmark and Italy, the two economies in our sample specializing most heavily in the production of agricultural products, supports this interpretation.

One country for which these adjustments fail to remove the anomaly is Australia, where the aggregate demand curve when plotted in output–relative price space continues to display a positive slope. Australia was more dependent on gold production than any other country in our sample, which may account for the positive price response to aggregate supply shocks. Positive supply shocks which take the form of gold discoveries and increased gold production would have tended to raise prices even in the short run (by raising the amount of gold and hence the amount of money in the economy). From this point of view the persistence of a positive price response to supply shocks is no paradox.

Comparisons of the gold standard with other regimes

A noteworthy feature of the impulse response functions for the pre-1914 gold standard is the combination of a strikingly flat aggregate demand curve with a steep aggregate supply schedule. In this section we contrast these slopes with comparable estimates for subsequent international monetary regimes and advance an explanation for the observed shifts.

We followed the same procedure for the interwar period as for the pre-1914 gold standard, using real GDP and relative price data to estimate bivariate VARs for the United States, Great Britain, Italy, Sweden, and Australia for the years 1919–1938 (see table 6.2).[9] Again, Australia yielded anomalous results, with prices rising in both the short and long runs in response to a positive supply shock. Insofar as money supplies were gold based for much of this period, we are inclined toward the same explanation as before.[10] For the postwar period, we followed previous work in estimating VARs using output and the domestic price level for each of the G7 countries, splitting the sample around the time of the breakdown of the Bretton Woods System of pegged exchange rates. The two subperiods were 1955–1970 and 1973–1988 (with an additional two annual observations to allow for lags). Data were collected from the OECD National Accounts.[11] We used 1970 GDP weights to construct the international aggregate from the individual country results.[12]

As can be seen from table 6.2, this comparative analysis lends little support to the hypothesis that disturbances were smaller under the pre-1914 gold standard than under subsequent international monetary regimes. Admittedly, the standard deviation of demand shocks to the gold standard aggregate is only about half as large as that to its interwar counterpart, consistent with the view that the gold standard imposed discipline on national economic policymakers. The difference in the ratio of the standard deviations of supply shocks is even larger, about one third as large during the gold standard period as between the wars. The largest shocks are those for the United States, the country whose industrial production declined most dramatically and which suffered the most severe financial crises in the 1930s. Further analysis of the interwar results also suggests a predominance of demand shocks in the 1920s and of supply shocks in the 1930s (Bayoumi and Eichengreen, 1994a), consistent with qualitative accounts of the period. Far and away the largest increase in the magnitude of supply shocks occurs in the United States, reflecting the exceptional severity there of the financial crisis and its negative supply-side repercussions through the loss of financial intermediation.[13]

The picture is very different when extended to the post-World War II years. The average supply shock was over twice as large under the pre-1914 gold standard as under Bretton Woods and the post-Bretton Woods float. Demand shocks, meanwhile, also appear to have been about twice as large under the pre-1914 gold standard. Similarly, the dispersion of supply and demand shocks across countries (SD^*) was larger than under either Bretton Woods or the post-Bretton Woods float. There is little support here, in other words, for the notion that the smooth operation of the gold standard, compared to modern international monetary arrangements, reflected the accommodating nature of the underlying environment.

Figure 6.3 juxtaposes the impulse response functions for all four periods,

Table 6.2 *Underlying disturbances across exchange rate regimes, 1880–1988, selected periods*[a]

	Gold standard 1880–1913	Interwar period 1919–1938		Bretton Woods 1955–1970	Post-Bretton Woods 1973–1988
Demand					
Aggregate *SD*	0.018	0.032	Aggregate *SD*	0.008	0.011
*SD**	0.014	0.020	*SD**	0.012	0.013
United States	0.024	0.050	United States	0.016	0.018
Great Britain	0.019	0.049	Japan	0.016	0.016
Germany	0.023	. . .	Germany	0.018	0.015
Italy	0.029	0.059	France	0.019	0.011
Australia	0.042	0.046	United Kingdom	0.010	0.021
Sweden	0.023	0.055	Italy	0.008	0.028
Denmark	0.022	. . .	Canada	0.025	0.021
Supply					
Aggregate *SD*	0.016	0.046	Aggregate *SD*	0.006	0.007
*SD**	0.020	0.016	*SD**	0.009	0.013
United States	0.027	0.065	United States	0.009	0.013
Great Britain	0.023	0.049	Japan	0.018	0.016
Germany	0.028	. . .	Germany	0.012	0.010
Italy	0.034	0.045	France	0.011	0.011
Australia	0.046	0.053	United Kingdom	0.011	0.030
Sweden	0.036	0.061	Italy	0.013	0.021
Denmark	0.026	. . .	Canada	0.005	0.021

Notes:
[a] Estimates are from preferred models. As a result, the results for the gold standard are not the same as in table 6.1.

together with the stylized supply and demand schedules. There is a clear tendency for short-run aggregate supply curves to become flatter over time and for aggregate demand curves to grow steeper. This flattening of supply curves suggests a declining short-run responsiveness of prices to demand shocks, and hence a growing tendency for demand shocks to displace output from long-run equilibrium levels. At the same time, the speed of adjustment along the curves slows over time. This is consistent with evidence presented by some previous investigators (e.g. Cagan, 1975; Sachs, 1980) of a tendency towards increasing nominal inertia.[14] The steepening of the demand curve has an obvious interpretation. Under fixed exchange rates domestic prices could not diverge significantly from prices in the rest of the world; as explained above, this meant that supply shocks resulted in a large ratio of output to price responses. By this explanation, the aggregate demand curve should have been flatter under the gold standard, when the exchange rates of the countries in our sample were essentially fixed, than under the Bretton Woods System, when they were pegged but could be adjusted periodically, and flatter under Bretton Woods than under the post-1972 float, when the link between domestic and foreign prices was further relaxed.

How the interwar period fits into this hierarchy is not clear. The countries in our sample were all back on the gold standard in the second half of the 1920s. Some of them, including the United States and Sweden, returned to gold even earlier, while others such as the United Kingdom and Australia behaved as if they had, managing their price levels to shadow those of the gold standard countries even before resuming convertibility. With the breakdown of the gold standard in the 1930s, few countries allowed their exchange rates to float freely. The United States repegged the dollar to gold, Australia joined the sterling area, and France maintained a fixed rate until 1936. While exchange rates were more flexible than under the pre-1914 gold standard, it is not clear how to categorize the interwar period relative to subsequent years. The short-run aggregate demand curve for this period is clearly flatter than that for Bretton Woods, as if countries attempted to maintain a high degree of exchange rate fixity in the short run. The long-run aggregate demand curve is nearly as steep as that for Bretton Woods, reflecting the fact that Bretton Woods was in fact characterized by some exchange rate variability over long intervals.[15]

The flattening of the short-run aggregate supply curve and the steepening of the aggregate demand curve may be connected. As the short-run aggregate supply curve becomes flatter, changes in aggregate demand have larger effects on output in the short run. As a result, governments have an incentive to adjust policy in a manner more responsive to deviations in output and less responsive to changes in prices, producing a steeper aggregate demand curve.

These ideas can be illustrated with a small macroeconomic model made up of a welfare function, an aggregate demand curve, an aggregate supply curve, and a monetary reaction function.

$$W = -\mathrm{var}(y) - \alpha\mathrm{var}(p) \qquad \text{Welfare function}$$
$$y + \beta p = \psi m \qquad \text{Aggregate demand}$$
$$y = \delta p + (1 + \beta)\epsilon_t \qquad \text{Aggregate supply}$$
$$m = \phi / \psi p \qquad \text{Monetary reaction}$$

W is welfare, y is output, p is the price level, m is the money supply (which is a proxy for all macroeconomic demand policies), ϵ_t is a random

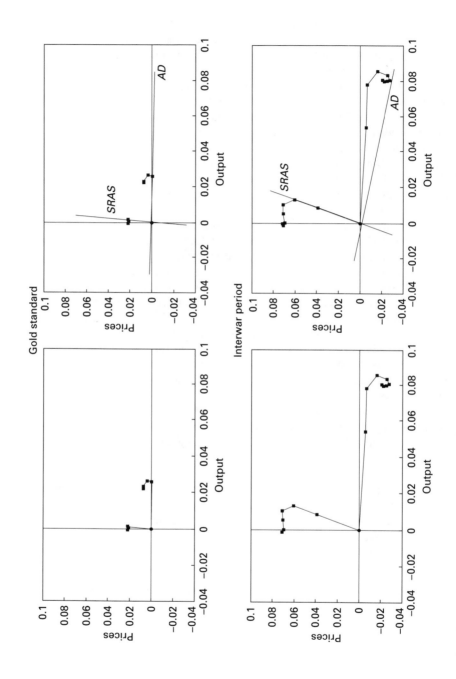

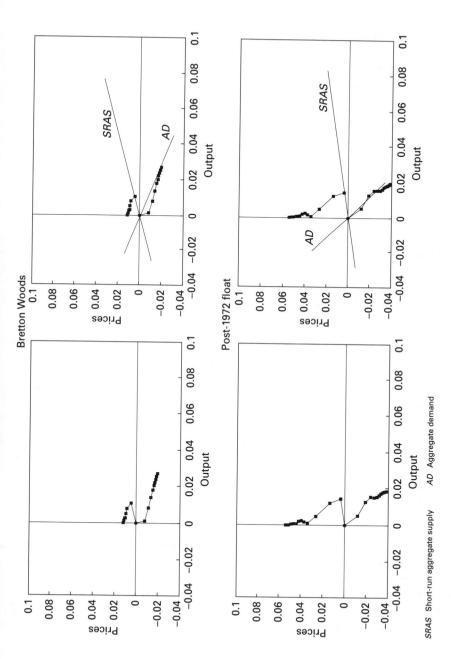

Figure 6.3 ADAS estimates across different regimes

SRAS Short-run aggregate supply   *AD* Aggregate demand

aggregate supply disturbance, and α, β, δ, ψ, and ϕ are coefficients. All variables are measured as deviations from desired levels, and all coefficients (except possibly ϕ) are positive.

The welfare function says that the government aims to minimize a weighted average of the variance of output and prices. The aggregate demand function, which can be shifted by changes in macroeconomic policy, incorporates the standard negative relationship between prices and output in the money market, while the aggregate supply curve shows the positive short-run relationship between prices and output in the goods market. Finally, the monetary response function shows the degree to which macroeconomic policy responds to fluctuations in prices.

Consider the response to an aggregate supply shock, ϵ_t. In the absence of a monetary response (i.e. if $\phi=0$) this disturbance would raise output by $\beta\epsilon_t$ and lower prices by ϵ_t. The government chooses the monetary response to such a disturbance, in other words the value of ϕ. From the aggregate supply curve it follows that a monetary rule will raise prices by $\phi\delta\epsilon_t$. Hence, output changes by $(\beta+\phi\delta)\epsilon_t$, prices by $(\phi-1)\epsilon_t$.

Given the welfare function, the optimal ϕ is that which minimizes:

$$(\beta+\phi\delta)^2\alpha(1-\phi)^2\sigma_\epsilon^2.$$

This value, ϕ^*, is:

$$\phi^*=(\alpha-\delta\beta)/(\alpha+\delta^2).$$

ϕ^* depends upon the slope of the aggregate supply curve. If the supply curve is vertical ($\delta=0$), so that policy affects prices but not output, the optimal ϕ is 1, the value that eliminates the fluctuations in prices. For very large values of δ (i.e. a very flat aggregate supply curve) so that policy only affects output, the optimal ϕ is $-\beta/\delta$, the value at which fluctuations in output are minimized. Intermediate values of δ produce responses which take account of both effects.

The slope of the observed aggregate demand curve is the ratio of the responses of output and prices:

$$(1-\phi)/(\alpha-\phi\delta).$$

It is easy to show that the slope of the aggregate demand curve under optimal government policy is horizontal when the aggregate supply curve is vertical and becomes steeper as the aggregate supply curve becomes flatter. This result obtains even though the welfare function and determinants of aggregate demand remain unchanged. The steepening of the aggregate demand curve is purely a function of the change in the optimal response of policy to disturbances produced by the flattening of the aggregate supply curve.

Clearly, this is a simple model lacking dynamics and taking no account of the fact that private sector responses may themselves change in response to government policy. Still, at a basic level it provides an intuitive explanation for the development of the international monetary system over time.[16] During the gold standard years, this argument runs, prices were relatively flexible, dampening the impact on output of disturbances even in the short run. With a steep short-run aggregate supply curve preventing output from being significantly displaced from long-run equilibrium levels, economic policy could be keyed to the maintenance of price stability. This was achieved through the operation of a fixed exchange rate regime in which the price level was linked to the rest of the world and largely insulated from domestic disturbances.

With the passage of time, economies came to display growing price inertia, magnifying the impact on output of macroeconomic disturbances. Consequently, policy was increasingly directed toward cushioning the impact of disturbances on output. This required more freedom for governments to pursue policies that might alter the price level; greater exchange rate flexibility was a necessary concomitant of this change in priorities. This trend is evident in the international monetary system's evolution from the relatively rigid exchange rates of the pre-1914 gold standard to the pegged but adjustable rates of the Bretton Woods System to the increasingly adjustable rates of the post-Bretton Woods float. Our analysis suggests that this evolution was a logical consequence of the growth of nominal rigidities which reduced the capacity of industrial economies to absorb macroeconomic disturbances without experiencing deviations of output and employment from normal levels in the short run.

Conclusion

In this chapter we have examined some popular explanations for the smooth operation of the pre-1914 gold standard. Along with the credibility of the policy rules followed by central banks and governments, such explanations focus on potentially stabilizing features of the underlying economic environment, such as the magnitude of disturbances to the participating economies and the latter's capacity to accommodate supply and demand shocks without suffering costly output and employment fluctuations. Our analysis confirms the findings of previous studies which have rejected explanations for the success of the gold standard based on an absence of destabilizing shocks. Rather, we find that the rapid adjustment of economies to such disturbances played an important role in stabilizing output and employment under the gold standard system.

Our methodological innovation is to introduce into the VAR framework used to analyze these questions arbitrage conditions linking domestic and foreign prices. This extension dispatches several perplexing findings that have emerged from earlier studies. Most notably, it eliminates the paradox of an upward-sloping aggregate demand curve in the short and intermediate runs. Rather, it suggests that the aggregate demand curve was flat in the gold standard years, consistent with the predictions of standard models of fixed exchange rate regimes, and that it grew progressively steeper with the evolution of the international monetary system toward greater exchange rate flexibility.

Finally, the simple aggregate supply–aggregate demand framework of the chapter suggests an explanation for the evolution of the international monetary system. Insofar as we find the short-run aggregate supply curve becoming progressively flatter, implying growing nominal inertia over time, this suggests that governments have had an incentive to opt for regimes permitting greater exchange rate flexibility, since the growth of output fluctuations gives them reason to sacrifice a modicum of price and exchange rate stability in return for freedom to use policy to stabilize output. Thus, the trend toward greater exchange rate flexibility following the gold standard years is a logical response of the change in policy priorities that is itself a consequence of changes in economic structure.

Appendix

The point of departure for our econometric analysis is the aggregate supply–aggregate demand diagram (figure 6.1). We estimate this model using a procedure proposed by Blanchard and Quah (1989) (using their equation numeration) for distinguishing temporary from permanent shocks to a pair of time series variables. Consider a system where the true model can be represented by an infinite moving average representation of a (vector) of variables, X_t, and an equal number of shocks, ϵ_t. Using the lag operator L, this can be written as:

$$X_t = A_0 \epsilon_t + A_1 \epsilon_{t-1} + A_2 \epsilon_{t-2} + A_3 \epsilon_{t-3} \cdots, \ = \sum_{i=0}^{\infty} L^i A_i \epsilon_t \qquad (3A.2)$$

where the matrices A_i represent the impulse response functions of the shocks to the elements of X.

Let X_t be made up of change in output and the change in prices, and let ϵ_t be demand and supply shocks. Then the model becomes:

$$\begin{bmatrix} \Delta y_t \\ \Delta p_t \end{bmatrix} = \sum_{i=0}^{\infty} L^i \begin{bmatrix} a_{11i} & a_{12i} \\ a_{21i} & a_{22i} \end{bmatrix} \begin{bmatrix} \epsilon_{dt} \\ \epsilon_{st} \end{bmatrix} \qquad (3A.2)$$

where y_t and p_t represent the logarithm of output and prices, ϵ_{dt} and ϵ_{st} are independent supply and demand shocks, and a_{11i} represents element a_{11} in the matrix A_i.

The framework implies that while supply shocks have permanent effects on the level of output, demand shocks only have temporary effects. (Both have permanent effects upon the level of prices.) Since output is written in first difference form, this implies that the cumulative effect of demand shocks on the change in output (Δy_t) must be zero. This implies the restriction:

$$\sum_{i=0}^{\infty} a_{11i} = 0. \tag{3A.3}$$

The model defined by equations (3A.2) and (3A.3) can be estimated using a VAR. Each element of X_t can be regressed on lagged values of all the elements of X. Using B to represent these estimated coefficients, the estimating equation becomes:

$$\begin{aligned} X_t &= B_1 X_{t-1} + B_2 X_{t-g} + \ldots + B_n X_{t-n} + e_t \\ &= (I - B(L))^{-1} e_t \\ &= (I + B(L) + B(L)^2 + \ldots) e_t \\ &= e_t + D_1 e_{t-1} + D_2 e_{t-2} + D_3 e_{t-3} + \ldots \end{aligned} \tag{3A.4}$$

where e_t represents the residuals from the equations in the VAR. In the case being considered, e_t comprises the residuals of a regression of lagged values of Δy_t and Δp_t on current values of each in turn; these residuals are labeled e_{yt} and e_{pt}, respectively.

To convert (3A.4) into the model defined by (3A.2) and (3A.3), the residuals from the VAR, e_t, must be transformed into demand and supply shocks, ϵ_t. Writing $e_t = C\epsilon_t$, four restrictions are required to define the four elements of the matrix C in the two-by-two case considered. Two are simple normalizations which define the variance of the shocks ϵ_{dt} and ϵ_{st}. A third comes from assuming that demand and supply shocks are orthogonal.

The final restriction, which uniquely defines the the matrix C, is that demand shocks have only temporary effects on output. This implies equation (3A.3). In terms of the VAR:

$$\sum_{i=0}^{\infty} \begin{bmatrix} d_{11i} & d_{12i} \\ d_{21i} & d_{22i} \end{bmatrix} \begin{bmatrix} c_{11} & c_{12} \\ c_{21} & c_{22} \end{bmatrix} = \begin{bmatrix} 0 & . \\ . & . \end{bmatrix} \tag{3A.5}$$

This allows C to be uniquely defined and the demand and supply shocks to be identified. Note from (3A.4) that the long-run impact of the shocks on output and prices is equal to $(I - B(1))^{-1}$. The restriction that the long-run effect of demand shocks on output is zero implies a simple linear restriction on the coefficients of this matrix.

This is where our analysis, based on Blanchard and Quah (1989), differs from other VAR models. The usual decomposition assumes that the variables in the VAR can be ordered such that all the effects which could be attributed to (say) either a_t or b_t are attributed to whichever comes first in the ordering, which is achieved by a Choleski decomposition.

Interpreting shocks with a permanent impact on output as supply disturbances and shocks with only a temporary impact on output as demand disturbances is controversial. Doing so requires adopting the battery of restrictions incorporated into the aggregate supply–aggregate demand model. One can think of frameworks other than the standard aggregate supply–aggregate demand model in which that association might break down. Moreover, it is conceivable that temporary supply shocks (for example, an oil price increase that is reversed subsequently) or permanent demand shocks (for example, a permanent increase in government spending which affects real interest rates and related variables) dominate our data. But here a critical feature of our methodology comes into play. While restriction (3A.5) affects the response of output to the two shocks, it says nothing about their impact on prices. The aggregate supply–aggregate demand model implies that demand shocks should raise prices while supply shocks should lower them. However, these responses are not imposed in estimation and hence can be used as an overidentifying restriction to see how well the responses correspond to those expected from the underlying model.

The Blanchard–Quah procedure has also come in for more general criticism. Lippi and Reichlin (1993), in a comment on the Blanchard–Quah paper, point out that the procedure includes the assumption that the error terms in the model are fundamental, and that nonfundamental representations can give different results. As noted by Blanchard and Quah (1993) in their reply, this is a very general issue which is not specific to VAR representations but covers virtually all dynamic analysis. Hence, while acknowledging that the assumption that the errors are fundamental is important to our procedure, we would note that this is a very general assumption in applied time series work. On a different tack, Faust and Leeper (1994) discuss the identifying restrictions required for long-run restrictions to provide reliable results, involving the relationship between long-run behavior and finite horizon data, aggregation across disturbances, and aggregation over time. These issues are clearly important; however, as in the case of Lippi and Reichlin, it remains unclear that these problems are peculiar to the structural VAR methodology. Overall, while we agree that it is important to understand the assumptions required to implement the technique, these papers do not convince us that the identifying assumptions required by the Blanchard–Quah approach are significantly different from those used in most other applied work.

Notes

This chapter does not necessarily represent the views of the International Monetary Fund.

1. Experience was very different in Latin America and other parts of the "periphery," as emphasized by Ford (1962), de Cecco (1984), and Bordo and Schwartz (1994).
2. Cooperation was repeated subsequently. In 1893 a consortium of European banks, with the encouragement of their governments, defended the US gold standard. In 1898 the Reichsbank and German commercial banks obtained assistance from the Bank of England and the Bank of France. In 1906 and 1907 the Bank of England, confronted by another financial crisis, again obtained support from the Bank of France and from the Reichsbank. The Russian State Bank shipped gold to Berlin to replenish the Reichsbank's reserves. In 1909 and 1910 the Bank of France again discounted English bills, making gold available to London. Smaller European countries such as Belgium, Norway, and Sweden also borrowed reserves from foreign central banks and governments.
3. On the concept of escape clauses and for applications to exchange rates, see Canzoneri (1985), Obstfeld (1991), Flood and Isard (1989) and de Kock and Grilli (1989).
4. For instance, there is Bloomfield's (1959) seminal study emphasizing central banks' violations of the "rules" of the gold standard "game."
5. Blanchard and Quah themselves formulated the model in terms of output and unemployment rather than output and prices. Keating and Nye estimate both variants of the model.
6. Aside for Australia, for which our data come from Butlin (1984), and the United States, for which they are drawn from Romer (1989), the source of these time series is Mitchell (1975).
7. Using the decomposition suggested in Bayoumi (1992).
8. Results using a decomposition from aggregate data are similar (Bayoumi and Eichengreen, 1994a).
9. Breaks in wartime and during the postwar hyperinflation prevented us from constructing comparable estimates for Denmark and Germany.
10. Global gold production rose and fell with the relative price of gold, particularly in the 1930s, and the supply response of the Australian mining industry contributed significantly to this variation.
11. For additional discussion of the data and results for the post-World War II period, see Bayoumi and Eichengreen (1994b).
12. The aggregate supply and aggregate demand schedules traced out by the impulse response functions generally accorded with the predictions of the

standard model. One exception was France in the post-1972 period, for which neither response had converged toward a new long-run equilibrium level even after twenty years. We therefore exclude France from the post-1972 aggregate plotted below.

13. Bernanke (1983).
14. Other writers, however, have failed to find increasing wage flexibility over time. For further discussion of the literature surrounding this point, see Barry Eichengreen's chapter 13 in this volume.
15. These results dissolve the paradox offered by Neumann (1993), since we generate the slopes of the relevant schedules directly on the basis of impulse response functions rather than inferring them from the variance of output and prices and some auxiliary assumptions.
16. We intend this story to apply only to the industrial countries whose experience is analyzed above.

References

Bayoumi, T. (1992). "The Effect of the ERM on Participating Economies." *IMF Staff Papers* 39 (June), 330–356

Bayoumi, T. and B. Eichengreen (1994a). "Economic Performance Under Alternative Exchange Rate Regimes: Some Historical Evidence," in P. Kenen, F. Papadia and F. Saccamoni (eds.), *The International Monetary System*, Cambridge: Cambridge University Press, 287–297

(1994b). "Macroeconomic Adjustment Under Bretton Woods and the Post-Bretton Woods Float: An Impulse-Response Analysis," *Economic Journal* 104, 813–827

Bernanke, B. S. (1983). "Nonmonetary Effects of the Financial Crisis in the Propagation of the Great Depression," *American Economic Review* 73 (June), 257–276

Blanchard, O. and D. Quah (1989). "The Dynamic Effects of Aggregate Demand and Aggregate Supply Disturbances," *American Economic Review* 79, 655–673

(1993). "Reply to Comment on the Dynamic Effects of Aggregate Demand and Supply Disturbances by Lippi and Reichlin," *American Economic Review* 83, 653–658

Bloomfield, A. I. (1959). *Monetary Policy Under the International Gold Standard*, New York: Federal Reserve Bank of New York

Bordo, M. (1993). "The Gold Standard, Bretton Woods and Other Monetary Regimes: A Historical Appraisal," *Federal Reserve Bank of St. Louis Review* 75, 123–191

Bordo, M. and F. Kydland (1996). "The Gold Standard as a Commitment Mechanism," chapter 3 in this volume

Bordo, M. and A. J. Schwartz (1994). "The Specie Standard as a Contingent Rule: Some Evidence for Core and Peripheral Countries, 1880–1990," NBER, *Working Paper* 4860 (September)

Butlin, N. G. (1984). "Select Comparative Economic Statistics 1900–1940," *Source Papers in Economic History* 4, Department of Economic History, RSSS, Australian National University

Cagan, P. (1975). "Changes in the Recession Behavior of Wholesale Prices in the 1920s and Post-World War II," *Explorations in Economic Research* 2, 54–104

Canzoneri, M. (1985). "Monetary Policy Games and the Role of Private Information," *American Economic Review* 75, 1056–1070

de Cecco, M. (1984). *The International Gold Standard: Money and Empire*, 2nd edn., London: Frances Pinter

de Kock, G. and V. Grilli (1989). "Endogenous Exchange Rate Regime Switches," NBER, *Working Paper* 3066

Eichengreen, B. (1992). *Golden Fetters: The Gold Standard and the Great Depression, 1919–1939*, New York: Oxford University Press

  (1994). "Central Bank Cooperation and Exchange Rate Commitments: The Classical and Interwar Gold Standards Compared," *Financial History Review* 2, 99–118

  (1996). "Déjà Vu All Over Again: Lessons from the Gold Standard for European Monetary Unification," chapter 13 in this volume

Faust, J. and E. Leeper (1994). "When do Long-run Identifying Restrictions Give Reliable Results?," Board of Governors of the Federal Reserve System, International Finance Division, *International Finance Discussion Paper* 462 (March)

Flood, R. and P. Isard (1991). "Monetary Policy Strategies," *IMF Staff Papers* 36 (September), 612–632

Ford, A. G. (1962). *The Gold Standard, 1880–1914: Britain and Argentina*, Oxford: Clarendon Press

Goodhart, C. (1992). "Economic and Monetary Union (EMU) in Europe: A UK Perspective," in E. Baltensperger and H.-W. Sinn (eds.), *Exchange-Rate Regimes and Currency Unions*, New York: St. Martin's Press, 183–199

Keating, J. W. and J. V. Nye (1991). "Permanent and Transitory Shocks in Real Output: Estimates from Nineteenth Century and Postwar Economies," *Working Paper* 160, Department of Economics, Washington University in St. Louis

Lippi, M. and L. Reichlin (1993). "Comment on the Dynamic Effects of Demand and Supply Disturbances," *American Economic Review* 83, 644–652

McCloskey, D. N. and J. Zecher (1984). "The Success of Purchasing-Power Parity: Historical Evidence and its Implications for Macroeconomics," in M. D. Bordo and A. J. Schwartz (eds.), *A Retrospective on the Classical Gold Standard, 1821–1931*, Chicago: University of Chicago Press for NBER, 121–170

Mitchell, B. R. (1975). *European Historical Statistics 1750–1970*, London: Macmillan

Neumann, M. J. M. (1993). "Commentary on the Gold Standard, Bretton Woods and Other Monetary Regimes: A Historical Appraisal," *Federal Reserve Bank of St. Louis Review* 75, 192–199

188 **Tamim Bayoumi and Barry Eichengreen**

Obstfeld, M. (1991). "Destabilizing Effects of Exchange Rate Escape Clauses,"
NBER, *Working Paper* 3606 (January)
Romer, C. (1989). "The Prewar Business Cycle Reconsidered: New Estimates of
Gross National Product, 1869–1908," *Journal of Political Economy* 97, 1–37
Sachs, J. (1980). "The Changing Cyclical Behavior of Wages and Prices,
1890–1976," *American Economic Review* 70 (March), 78–90

7 International adjustment under the Classical gold standard: evidence for the United States and Britain, 1879–1914

Charles W. Calomiris and R. Glenn Hubbard

Introduction

Links between disturbances in financial markets and those in real activity have been the focus of studies of economic fluctuations during the period prior to World War I. The standard "business cycle" analysis of the period emphasizes the importance of domestic monetary shocks in an environment of sticky prices and inelastic money supply. In this chapter, we provide evidence suggesting that those basic assumptions are at odds with the data from the period. Domestic autonomy was substantially limited by internationally integrated markets for gold, capital, and traded commodities. Such findings are likely to be important for studying business cycles during the period; for example, we have shown elsewhere (see Calomiris and Hubbard, 1989) that, when prices are flexible, observed cyclical movements can be related to a credit market transmission of deflationary shocks.

The focus on international linkages has been common in the literature; indeed, recent studies of the operation of the Classical gold standard have revived interest in the process by which macroeconomic shocks were transmitted internationally during this period (see Eichengreen, 1985; Bordo and Schwartz, 1984). The principal competing approaches differ according to the means by which international equilibrium is re-established after a disturbance occurs in capital, money, or commodity markets. According to the "price–specie–flow" mechanism, shocks which raise (lower) the gap between the domestic money supply and its equilibrium level raise (lower) the domestic price level; this in turn decreases (increases) the balance of trade, which leads to outflows (inflows) of gold and eventually equilibration of the system at commodity price levels roughly consistent with foreign prices. More recent models of international adjustment emphasize the roles of arbitrage and speculation in efficient markets for capital, currency, and commodities. This latter "internationalist" approach argues that interest rates and traded goods prices will maintain levels consistent with foreign interest rates and prices in the short run, while currency, capital, and

189

commodity flows adjust to achieve long-run changes necessary to restore equilibrium in all markets. The intuition for this result is that speculative demands or supplies for commodities, capital, and money place bounds on predictable short-run deviations of prices.

A representative view (e.g. that of Friedman and Schwartz, 1963) associated with the price–specie–flow mechanism posits the following – sluggish international gold movements, sticky commodity prices, the cyclical importance of money supply shocks (mainly shocks to the money multiplier), and the consequent potential for central banks to influence the aggregate money supply and (though it) interest rates and economic activity. In order to argue that money multiplier shocks and central bank interventions have more than fleeting influence on the real money supply, one must assume both that commodity prices are rigid and that the supply of high-powered money is inelastic. This general view is consistent with the price–specie–flow sequence of events: International adjustment to monetary shocks follows gradual domestic price adjustment which, through changes in the terms of trade, brings about trade deficits (surpluses) and hence balance of payments surpluses (deficits).

On the other hand, the "internationalist" approach implies far less domestic autonomy in the short run for interest rates, the money supply, and commodity prices. According to this view,[1] gold supply is highly elastic, capital markets for some securities (internationally traded commercial paper and bonds) are closely integrated internationally, and domestic traded goods' gold prices respond to international price movements in the short run within "narrow" band-widths of transaction cost (which includes transport and insurance fees, tariffs, and a fair rate of return to international commodity market speculators). These assumptions, in turn, imply demand determination of the real (and nominal) money stock, an internationally determined commercial paper rate (in gold units), and a minor role for any central bank with respect to its ability to influence the aggregate money supply or the rates of return on internationally traded securities.[2] The essential process of adjustment of traded goods' prices and interest rates does not depend on immediate synchronous changes in wages and nontraded commodity prices. In the absence of highly responsive (nontraded goods) prices, these results still hold, but the lagging adjustment of some domestic prices and wages to international price shocks entails real effects on the time path of output and the balance of trade.

Because the internationalist approach posits rapid endogenous gold movements, it places little emphasis on domestic money supply shocks as a source of output variation. Instead, it focuses on cyclical output responses induced by changes in autonomous influences on the IS curve, aggregate supply, or international changes in desired savings.

Essentially what is at issue in distinguishing these two views empirically is whether the deviations allowed by transaction and information costs in gold, capital, and commodity markets were sufficiently small to support the "close" short-run connections in prices and rates of return across the Atlantic which the internationalist approach posits. Were gold flows "sufficiently" elastic? Were interest rates "closely" linked?

Our chapter approaches these questions in two ways: first, in the next section, we measure directly the responsiveness of gold flows and the band-widths of tolerance for autonomous interest rate movements. While these measures provide some evidence in favor of close international links, alone they are insufficient evidence to conclude that the internationalist approach is superior to the monetarist price–specie–flow view. The narrowness of band-widths must be measured relative to the macroeconomic importance of relative price deviations. That is, even if autonomous interest rate movements were bounded by band-widths of 100 basis points, if autonomous domestic interest rate movements of, say, 50 basis points accompany large macroeconomic effects, then the price–specie–flow view may provide a superior description of the macroeconomic transmission of shocks. Thus we argue that macroeconomic simulation models are the best way to establish which of the two views is a more useful historical model for explaining events of the period.

In the third section, we employ a monthly data set for the United States and Britain for the pre-World War I period to evaluate the overall explanatory power of the respective frameworks. We compare the actual historical importance of shocks and the observed patterns of short-run adjustment to shocks with the predictions of each of the two models. Here we employ the "structural vector autoregression (VAR)" approach for simultaneous equations modeling developed by Blanchard and Watson (1986), Bernanke (1986), and Sims (1986). The fourth section concludes the chapter.

Evidence on international integration of capital markets

Gold flow responsiveness

Even an unsophisticated analysis of monthly gold flows leads one to question the so-called "stylized fact" of gold supply inelasticity (a formal treatment of the relationships among gold flows and other variables is presented in the next section). The mean and standard deviation of the monthly net gold outflow over the period 1885–1914 are $45,000 and $11 million, respectively. Positive net outflows have a mean of $8 million and a standard deviation of $7.6 million, while net inflows have a mean of $6.2 million and a standard deviation of $8.7 million. The ratio of the potential monthly

Table 7.1 *ARMA identification of monthly*
US net gold outflows (GLDFUS), *1885–1914*

Lag	Gold-flow autocorrelations	Partial autocorrelations
1	0.48	0.48
2	0.18	−0.07
3	0.04	−0.02
4	−0.02	−0.03
5	−0.11	−0.10
6	−0.06	0.05
7	−0.01	0.02
8	−0.01	−0.03
9	−0.04	−0.04
10	0.02	0.07
11	0.09	0.07
12	0.11	0.05

AR(1) and MA(2) specifications (standard errors
in parentheses)
AR(1):

$GLDFUS = -87855 + 0.509 \ GLDFUS_{-1} + \epsilon$
(466224) (0.048)

$DW = 1.87$
$R^2 = 0.24$.

MA(2):

$GLDFUS = -125324 + 0.545\epsilon_{-1} + 0.195\epsilon_{-2} + \epsilon$
(805923) (0.053)   (0.054)

$DW = 1.94$
$R^2 = 0.24$.

flow of gold to the existing stock of gold is high, as well – in December 1907
and January 1908, total net gold inflows amounted to $106 million, com-
pared to a stock of currency in circulation outside the Treasury of $3.07
billion, composed of $1.86 billion held by the public and $1.21 held by
banks, and a total money supply (M2) of approximately $11.6 billion.[3]

Autocorrelation and partial autocorrelation functions for monthly US
gold flows are presented in table 7.1. These patterns suggest an MA(2)
process, or possibly an AR(1). Under either specification, gold flows essentially adjust fully to disturbances within three months, with most of the
adjustment occurring in the first month. Coefficients, autocorrelation functions, and partial autocorrelation functions for residuals are presented in
table 7.2 for both specifications.

Table 7.2 *US gold flow residuals for AR(1) and MA(2) models*

Lags	Autocorrelations MA(2)	Partial autocorrelations MA(2)	Autocorrelations AR(1)	Partial autocorrelations AR(1)
1	0.00	0.00	0.04	0.04
2	0.02	0.02	−0.04	−0.05
3	0.04	0.04	−0.04	−0.03
4	0.00	0.00	0.00	0.00
5	−0.10	−0.10	−0.11	−0.12
6	−0.03	−0.03	−0.03	−0.02
7	0.03	0.03	0.04	0.03
8	0.02	0.03	0.04	0.03
9	−0.07	−0.07	−0.08	−0.08
10	0.02	0.00	0.00	0.00
11	0.05	0.04	0.05	0.04
12	0.07	0.08	0.08	0.08

The short time horizon for gold stock adjustment to demand shocks is confirmed by the response of gold flows to the panic of (October) 1907. The regional pattern of gold flows during the crisis supports the view of New York as an active entrepôt between the domestic interior and London, with elastic gold flows in both directions. For example, from October 18 to December 27, 1907, net shipments of gold from banks in New York to the US interior totalled $129 million. From January 3 to January 31, fully $69 million in net shipments had returned to New York. International accounts also show this rapid inflow and outflow of gold. From June through September 1907, net gold exports total $29 million; from October 1907 to April 1908, net gold imports totalled $122 million; from May to September 1908, net gold exports totalled $45 million.

Hence, in annual, – or, *a fortiori*, "business cycle" – time, the market for gold operated well enough that gold sluggishness *per se* cannot be faulted for persistent macroeconomic fluctuations. Second, the elasticity of gold movements within the country and across the Atlantic appear similar. Thus it seems arbitrary to use national borders to define regions of economic autonomy for the gold market.

These results are not surprising given the existence of the transatlantic cable, the markets for gold, and the available technology for transporting gold by steamship across the Atlantic in a matter of days. Officer (1986) carefully estimates the costs of international gold transport and finds that the observed gold price differentials virtually never violate his constructed cost band-widths which average roughly half of 1 percent.[4]

Interest rate arbitrage between New York and London

Another approach to measuring the extent to which money markets were linked across the Atlantic is to examine the tolerance for interest rate differentials between New York and London, and the speed with which large differences in interest rates were eliminated. One difficulty in comparing interest rates is that the financial instruments whose interest rates were quoted in New York and London were not identical. The most frequently used US interest rates are single-name and double-name commercial paper rates of high-quality paper. In England, as in the rest of the world, commercial paper was not an important money market instrument.[5] The money market instrument quoted in English financial newspapers is the prime discount rate on bankers' bills (bankers' acceptances). Commercial paper and bankers' acceptances may have differed in their degree of risk or liquidity. Differences in average risk and liquidity, or in the timing of changes in risk and liquidity premia over time attendant to these differences in the types of money market instruments, complicate comparisons of rates of return between New York and London.

Another problem of comparing existing British and American interest rates is "silver risk." Nominal interest rates in the United States during the 1890s reflected inflation uncertainty as well as the real (i.e. gold-denominated) required rate of return (Garber, 1986; Calomiris, 1993a).

Fortunately, both of these problems can be solved by using bill of exchange prices to measure US interest rates rather than rates on commercial paper. Bills of exchange entailed the exchange of gold dollars in the present for a promise to deliver gold British pounds in the future. Prices for two types of bills of exchange were quoted: "sight" bills, which were redeemable as quickly as a ship could travel from New York to London; and 60-day bills, which were redeemable only in 60 days. Because bills were traded for both delivery dates, and because bills did not suffer from silver risk (since they entailed the exchange of gold today for gold tomorrow), it is possible to derive an implicit New York gold interest rate from the relative price of sight and 60-day bills. Moreover, bills of exchange are international bankers' acceptances; thus the implicit interest rate from this calculation is more comparable to the bankers' acceptance rate quoted in London than would be a US commercial paper rate.

We use data on sight and 60-day New York bills from the National Monetary Commission (1910) for the period 1889–1909, taken from end-month quotations.[6] We chose the dates for these observations to correspond to the dates of publication of *The Economist*'s quotations of London prime bill discount rates. Prior to 1897, the London rates appear to represent that day's rate, while beginning in 1897, the London quotations are averages for the previous week.

We converted London discount rates into annualized yields. To calculate the New York annualized yield from bill of exchange prices, one must first estimate a delivery time for sight bills. We assume sight bills are deliverable ten days after they have been purchased (a rough estimate of the travel between New York and London). The difference of the dollar price of sight bills and 60-day bills, divided by the price of sight bills, provides a measure of a 50-day interest rate beginning ten days in the future. From this we derived an annualized 60-day rate, assuming that holding period returns for the first ten days are the same as returns for the following 50 days.

Figures 7.1 and 7.2 plot the gold-denominated interest rates on bankers' bills in New York and London, and the difference between the two. The rates are not identical; the average differential between them is 1.13 percent. With the exception of one observation, interest rates in New York are always higher than in London. The interest rate differential was not constant over time. For 1889–1893, the average differential was 1.60, while the average for 1894–1909 was 0.99.

Clearly, interest rate parity did not hold perfectly across the Atlantic. Three factors account for this. First, physical transaction costs created a tolerance for independent movements of interest rates. For example, a British investor faced a cost of moving funds from his British bank account to his American bank account. Even if these funds were transferred by wire, there was still a brokerage fee. And if funds were transferred by shipping gold abroad – as we will argue was sometimes necessary – then the foreign investor paid 0.5 percent of the gold shipment in transportation costs. It is also worth noting that a fund transfer via a gold shipment would not be riskless, since the American interest rate could fall once the gold was in transit.[7]

Second, if wire transfers were sometimes not feasible as a means for British investors to reap higher interest rates in New York, then shipments would sometimes have been required. During these episodes, the tolerance for real interest rate differences should have risen, due to the higher transportation cost and risk associated with capital market arbitrage via gold shipments. Given the risk of a reversal of the interest rate differential while the funds were in transit, it could conceivably have taken weeks or months for British investors to have been willing to send sufficient gold abroad to bring US rates down significantly.

Why would gold flows, rather than wire transfers, have been required of foreign investors seeking to reap higher rates of return in the United States?

A sufficient condition for this constraint would be that New York banks did not regard the deposits of foreign banks as perfect substitutes for gold deposits in New York. Most of the time, deposits held in London banks (which were virtually riskless) would have been regarded as close substitutes for gold by New York banks. But during a banking crisis in New York this would probably not have been the case. If New York banks faced the risk of large withdrawals of gold by depositors, and if those depositors were unwilling to accept checks written by the New York banks on London as a substitute form of payment, then New York banks would have preferred gold to deposits in London banks, and would have paid higher interest rates for gold deposits than they would have paid for wire transfers. Thus, during a period when the New York banks were threatened with a run, our measured interest rate differences could be significantly higher than otherwise.

Third, during times of financial strain, the acceptances of banks in New York or London may have become relatively riskier than before. Large money center banks in New York were among the US banks with the lowest risk of failure during this period, and London banks were the most stable financial intermediaries of their time. Nevertheless, during panic episodes, increased risk on bankers' acceptances of money center banks may have distorted interest rate comparisons between financial centers. In particular, during financial crises that threatened New York banks, and not London banks, one should expect to see a rise in the New York/London interest rate differential because of an increase in risk.

To sum up, the maximum allowable interest rate differential between London and New York should have reflected permanent and transitory factors. Physical costs of wire transfers imply a constant minimum tolerance for interest rate differences. Additionally, occasional changes in the cost of arbitrage that required gold shipments, and occasional increases in the riskiness of bankers' acceptances on New York, should have caused temporary increases in the allowable interest rate differential during financial crises. To the extent that bank risk caused the increase in the observed differential, the measured differential overstates the true (risk constant) differential between London and New York.

Thus it is useful to consider whether financial crises – defined by some measure other than interest rate movements themselves – witnessed unusual changes in the tolerance for interest rate differences. Calomiris and Gorton (1991) argue that during the period 1889–1909 there were four episodes that can be considered New York banking panics – defined as episodes when New York City Clearinghouse banks instituted formal measures to coordinate actions in response to their perception that a crisis was upon them. These were the panics of November 1890, June–August

1893, October 1896, and October 1907. Many other lesser panics have been identified in the literature on the basis of stock price movements or interest rate changes, but these four panics stand out as important times of strain for New York banks.

Figure 7.1 shows that during the panic of 1890 (November 1890–January 1891) there was an unusually large interest differential between New York and London. August 1893 also witnessed an unusually large differential. In 1896 and 1907, however, there is no evidence of any influence of the panics on the interest differential, although in both cases interest rates in New York and London rose in the months surrounding the panics.

With the exception of the panics of 1890 and 1893, the interest rate differential remained small. For the period 1889–1909, there are only three months in which the interest differential exceeded 2.5 percent. Two of these months occurred during the panics of 1890 and 1893; the third was October 1889. For 1889–November 1893, the interest differential exceeded 1.5 percent in 30 out of 59 months, and exceeded 2.0 in 10 months; for the 16-year period after November 1893, the interest rate differential exceeded 1.5 percent in only eight months, including the consecutive months of October–December 1899 (which Kemmerer, 1910, identifies as a "minor panic"), and never exceeded 2.0 percent. Even during the period of relatively high interest differentials (1889–1893), interest rate differentials in excess of 2.0 percent did not occur in consecutive months, except for the brief periods, October–November 1889 and November 1890–January 1891.[8]

To preserve the narrow differential between New York and London bankers' acceptance rates, interest rate levels often increased by large amounts in both countries simultaneously, as shown in figure 7.2. For example, in the wake of the panic of 1896 in the United States, London interest rates rose from 0.69 percent in July to 3.8 percent in December. In response to the panic of 1907, from July to December, London interest rates rose from 3.8 percent to 6.4 percent.

Seasonal patterns also confirm the potential for shocks originating in America to cause large increases in interest rates abroad. The seasonal demand for loans in the United States, which was associated with planting and marketing crops, produced seasonal fluctuations in interest rates, as shown in figure 7.3. These fluctuations, it should be noted, are substantially smaller than those apparent in nominal interest rates on other money market instruments discussed by Miron (1986), but are similar in magnitude to those found by Barsky *et al.* (1988). Figure 7.4 shows that Britain, which did not experience large domestic loan demand shocks from seasonal agricultural needs, nevertheless showed virtually identical seasonality of interest rates to the United States (see also Clark, 1986; Barsky *et al.*, 1988).

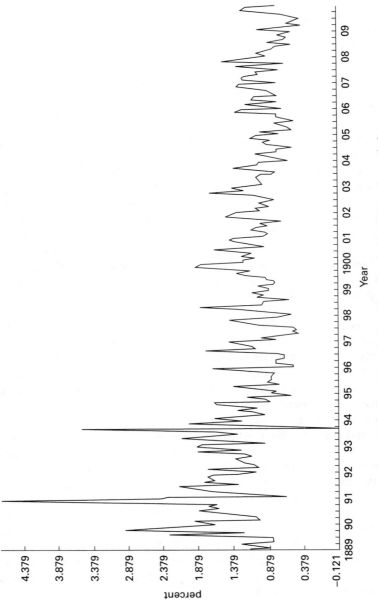

Figure 7.1 Interest rate differential between New York and London, 1889–1909, end-month data

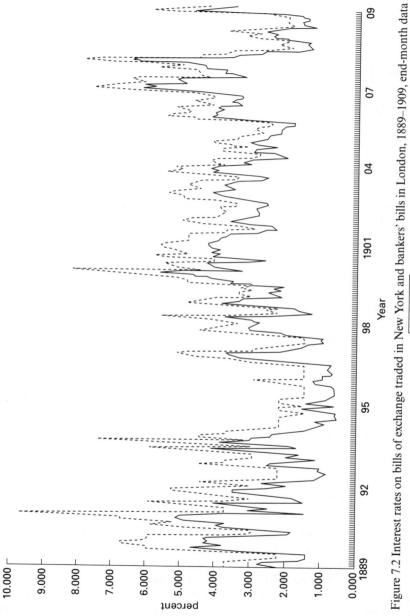

Figure 7.2 Interest rates on bills of exchange traded in New York and bankers' bills in London, 1889–1909, end-month data

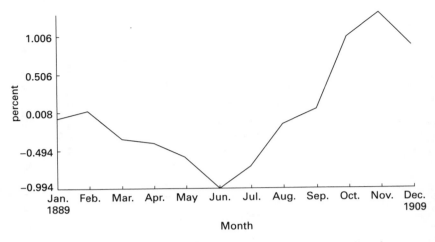

Figure 7.3 Average seasonal effects in New York: interest rates for bills of exchange traded in New York, 1889–1909, end-month data

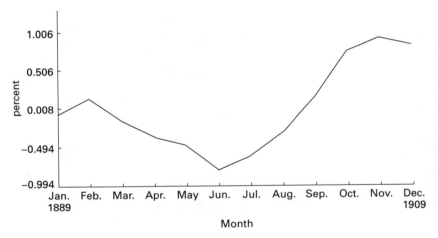

Figure 7.4 Average seasonal effects in London: interest rates on bankers' bills in London, 1889–1909, end-month data

As shown in figure 7.5, average differences in interest rates were only slightly higher in the Fall peak lending season.

To summarize, interest rate differentials typically were less than 1.5 percent. Interest rate differentials in excess of 1.5 percent did not last for long. With the exception of a panic episode (in 1890) – when larger interest differentials were expected – and autumn 1889, the interest rate differential

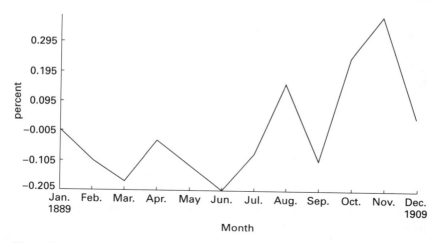

Figure 7.5 Average seasonal effect on interest rate differential between New York and London, 1889–1909, end-month data

never exceeded 2.0 percent for more than one consecutive month. Seasonal shocks to loan demand in the United States did not produce average seasonal differences between New York and London greater than 0.4 percent. It is worth emphasizing that the data on which all these calculations are based are bill of exchange prices observed on particular days at monthly intervals, so that these results do not reflect the smoothing of differentials that would result from constructing monthly averages of daily observations.

There are two small "surprises" from the above analysis of interest rate differences that are worthy of mention: First, interest rate differentials are unusually high in late 1889, given that this period did not coincide with a banking panic. Second, it is curious that the 1896 and 1907 panics had smaller effects on interest differentials than the panics of 1890 and 1893.

Particular historical circumstances may shed some light on what made 1889 special, and on why 1890 and 1893 witnessed seemingly less elastic gold flows than 1896 and 1907. While an informal discussion of the circumstances of these five episodes (1889, 1890, 1893, 1896, and 1907) "proves" nothing, it does raise some interesting questions about how policy within the United States, the policies of foreign central banks, and the state of the London market may have affected the degree and speed of adjustment in international markets for capital and gold. At issue here is the fundamental question of whether adjustment under the gold standard occurred "automatically," or whether policies of central banks, or circumstances peculiar to a regular trading partner, might have hindered or helped the adjustment process.

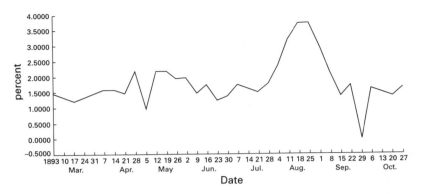

Figure 7.6 Interest rate differential between New York and London during the panic of 1893, March–October 1893, end-week data

During our period, the major policymakers in the international markets for capital and gold were the central banks of Europe (especially Britain, France, and Germany), and the US Treasury Department. Friedman and Schwartz (1963, 149–152) discuss the growing importance of the Secretary of the Treasury as a source of assistance to banks during the pre-Fed period. The Treasury acted to offset outflows of funds from banks by depositing Treasury reserves in the banking system. Friedman and Schwartz argue that this policy was pursued especially aggressively by Secretary Shaw during his tenure (1902–1906), although other Secretaries had initiated the policy much earlier. Apparently successful publicly announced interventions to offset interest rate increases were reported in the *Commercial and Financial Chronicle* regularly throughout our sample period. Delays in effective Treasury intervention were blamed for the protracted stringency of 1889.

Friedman and Schwartz's portrayal of the increasing aggressiveness of Treasury interventions over this period is consistent with the lower tolerance for interest rate differentials between New York and London in years after 1889–1893. This could explain why the panics of 1896 and 1907 elicited less of a differential than the panics of 1890 and 1893. This argument could also explain why, after 1902, the interest differential never exceeded 1.54 percent (its value during October 1907).

On the other hand, there are alternative explanations for these facts, and there have been challenges to the claim that Treasury intervention was effective. Allen (1986) questions whether Secretary Shaw's policies helped to stabilize the New York money market. Allen shows that call loan interest rate seasonality actually increased during his tenure, and that Shaw's announced willingness to intervene was associated with declines in New

York banks' desired excess reserve holdings. Allen argues that Shaw's policy ultimately was counterproductive because it reduced the available stock of gold in New York banks. Furthermore, Shaw's successor was not as willing to intervene to assist banks. Allen argues that the unannounced change in policy, combined with the low level of excess reserves, may have contributed to producing the panic of 1907.

In part, differences in the extent and duration of interest rate spreads across panics may simply have reflected differences in the severity of the events. The panic of 1896 was the mildest of the major shocks to the New York banks. During this panic, unlike all the others, the New York banks were never forced to actually issue Clearinghouse certificates.

Another possible explanation for differences across the panic episodes is the actions of central bankers abroad. French, British, and German central banks effectively coordinated the transfer of gold to New York during the panic of 1907 (Eichengreen, 1992, 50–57), but during the stringency of 1889 and the Baring crisis of 1890, they were not willing to sponsor the shipment of gold to the United States. Financial commentators in the *Commercial and Financial Chronicle* noted the low supply of gold in Britain during the stringency of 1889. In the case of the Baring crisis of 1890, the Bank of England and the commercial banks of London were in no position to send resources to New York, since they were borrowing heavily from the Bank of France to shore up their own resources (Clapham, 1958, 326–339). It may have been that during those episodes the effective cost of importing gold was higher, since it had to come from more distant, less coordinated, and less closely related, financial centers in Europe.

It is hard to say whether foreign central bank coordination was important for explaining differences in the tolerance for high interest differentials across the various episodes. Rich (1989) argues that Canadian–American linkages in international credit markets were crucial for stabilizing the New York market, particularly during the panic of 1907. These connections were entirely private, as neither Canada nor the United States had a central bank. This evidence, along with Dick and Floyd's (1991) analysis of the rapid international adjustment process in Canada during the Classical gold standard, seems to argue for the strength of "automatic," private mechanisms of international adjustment (see also chapter 8 in this volume).

Whatever the causes of rapid international adjustment and close ties across countries, the comovement of interest rates between London and New York raises the possibility that American money supply shocks may have produced cyclical change within and outside the United States through their effects on world interest rates. But despite the fact that American seasonal and cyclical loan demand shocks seem to have been capable of moving British interest rates by large amounts at monthly frequency, that does not imply that money supply shocks originating in the United States were important sources of world or US business cycles, for three reasons.

First, interest rate disturbances may not all reflect monetary shocks. Second, for interest rate shocks related to monetary disturbances to have been important at business cycle frequencies, they should have persisted in their effect on interest rates (and been expected to persist) for several months. Otherwise, their influence on aggregate demand should have been minimal. It may be that the high elasticity of endogenous international capital and gold flows shortened the duration of high-interest rate episodes, and thus limited the impact of monetary shocks on the business cycle. Third, the measurement of tolerances for interest rate differentials above does not answer the fundamental question of how important money supply disturbances – or other disturbances affecting interest rates – were for output, because a simple measurement of interest rate differences does not consider the linkages between these disturbances and output. To investigate the potential importance of domestic money supply disturbances, therefore, requires a dynamic model of the US economy in the context of trans-Atlantic markets for capital and gold.

Simulation of the macroeconomic importance of domestic and international shocks

Our goal here is to measure the relative importance of domestic and international shocks in financial and commodity markets for influencing output, interest rates, prices, gold flows, and the balance of trade. For example, were domestic money supply shocks an important source of macroeconomic disturbances? How do money supply shocks compare in importance to disturbances in money demand, or other macroeconomic disturbances? How important are changes in the terms of trade for short-run movements in the balance of trade? In order to answer these questions, we construct a model of the US economy and its international linkages.

Data and econometric approach

Our results so far imply potentially rapid adjustment of interest rates, prices, and commodity and gold flows. In order to capture important features of shocks and responses, we construct a monthly data set which includes US and British interest rates and wholesale price indices, and US data on exports, imports, gold flows, and output (using pigiron as an output proxy).[9] Our measure of the British interest rate is the monthly average of weekly quotations for the prime rate on bankers' bills, plotted on p. 199. As our measure of the US interest rate we use the monthly average of the double-name, choice New York commercial paper rate (Macaulay, 1938). This variable has several advantages over other interest rates: it is a rate paid by firms for credit as well as a measure of portfolio opportunities for investors, and it is available as a monthly average over a long period. The chief disadvantage of using this, or any other, nominal interest rate is that prior to 1897 "silver risk" complicates the interpretation of the interest rate. For this reason, we begin our sample in January 1897. Our sample ends in June 1914, before the outbreak of war.

Despite the exclusion of the panics of 1890, 1893, and 1896 from our sample, our sample still contains many episodes which have been identified as severe monetary contractions. Kemmerer (1910) identifies December 1899, May 1901, March 1903, and October 1907 as "major panics," and March 1898, September 1899, July 1901, September 1901, September 1902, December 1904, April 1905, April 1906, March 1907, and September 1908 as "minor panics."

In order to analyze dynamic adjustment to disturbances, we adopt the "structural VAR" approach developed by Blanchard and Watson (1986), Bernanke (1986), and Sims (1986) as an alternative to recursive (nonstructural) identification of disturbances. The "structural VAR" approach permits one to solve a simultaneous equations model of the shocks to each series in which orthogonalized shocks and their interrelations are associated with behavioral functions rather than variables. The first stage of the structural VAR model is identical to a standard VAR – lagged values of all variables are included to estimate reduced form predictions, and to derive series of unpredicted innovations (which are correlated across variables). In the next stage, one posits a matrix of contemporaneous functional relationships, which can be tested, and which imply time series of orthogonalized shocks to the hypothesized functions.

One then calculates impulse responses of each variable in the system to shocks that originate in particular functions, and decompositions of each variable's forecast variance, which attribute the uncertainty regarding the future of any particular variable to each of the functional shocks. Impulse responses and variance decompositions together permit one to infer the time path of a given shock's influence on all variables, as well as its economic importance.

A simultaneous equations macroeconomic model for the United States

We posit seven functional relationships for our seven-variable model: an equilibrium-output equation for the United States, an exogenously determined international (British) riskless interest rate, US money supply and money demand equations, demand functions for US imports and exports, and a desired short-run capital flow equation, which we set equal to the balance of trade net of gold flows. These functions are described in equations (1)–(7) below.

$$i_t^L = i_t^{L*} \qquad \text{(International interest rate)} \qquad (1)$$

$$i_t^{NY} = a_1 i_t^L + a_2 G_t + i_t^{NY*} \qquad \text{(US money supply)} \qquad (2)$$

$$X_t - M_t - G_t = a_3 i_t^L - a_4 i_t^{NY} + X_t^* \qquad \text{(Desired net savings)} \qquad (3)$$

$$Y_t = -a_5 i_t^{NY} + a_6 P_t + Y_t^* \qquad \text{(Equilibrium output)} \qquad (4)$$

$$M_t = a_7 P_t - a_8 i_t^{NY} + a_9 Y_t + M_t^* \qquad \text{(Import demand)} \qquad (5)$$

$$P_t = -a_{10} X_t \pm a_{11} i_t^L + P_t^* \qquad \text{(Export demand)} \qquad (6)$$

$$G_t = a_{12} Y_t + a_{13} P_t - a_{14} i_t^{NY} + G_t^* \qquad \text{(US money demand)}, \qquad (7)$$

where all variables are defined as innovations, and where Y denotes the growth rate of output, i^{NY} and i^L are the New York commercial paper rate and London open market discount rate, respectively, G is US net imports of gold, X and M are US commodity exports and imports, and P is the log ratio of US to British wholesale price indices. All disturbance terms with an asterisk are mutually orthogonal. i^{L*} is the innovation in the British open market discount rate. i^{NY*} is the orthogonal money supply shock. X^* is the disturbance to desired net savings (which might include IS shocks and supply side credit shocks). M^* is the shock to the demand for imports. P^* is the export demand disturbance. G^* is the innovation in US demand for money (gold).

By setting $i^L = i^{L*}$ we do not mean to suggest that British interest rate were unrelated to American rates, or that Britain was the source of all comovement between the two. Rather, i^{L*} is simply a statistical construct that combines shocks originating abroad with those originating in the United States that moved interest rates abroad. This definition is useful for modeling gold flows between countries, and for defining "autonomous" movements in US interest rates (those unrelated to foreign interest rates).

The US money supply equation assumes that net gold imports respond positively to US and negatively to British, interest rate innovations. International influence on domestic money supply takes the form of gold movement induced by interest differentials. Autonomous movements in i^{NY*}, by construction, are unrelated to these international effects, and thus are best viewed as capturing the effects of domestic money multiplier shocks on interest rates, holding other functions unchanged.

The savings equation (3) posits that US desired short-run net savings responds positively to foreign, and negatively to US interest rate changes.

Our specification of the output equation (4) assumes negative interest elasticity in the IS curve, as well as a positive relative terms of trade response in aggregate supply. Y^* will be a mixture of supply and IS disturbances.

The US demand for imports (5) is assumed to depend positively on P and Y, and negatively on i^{NY}. We write export demand as a negative function of P, and an indeterminate function of i^L. The sign on i^L in (6) depends on whether foreign interest rate innovations are associated mainly with expansion or contraction abroad.

The money demand equation (7) assumes a standard formulation in which shocks to desired money balances, and hence net gold inflows, are related to disturbances in price, income, and the interest rate.

There are two criteria against which to measure the reasonableness of this identification of functional disturbances. One is the estimated coefficients (and standard errors) of the matrix of contemporaneous disturbances – i.e. how many coefficients are of the "right sign"? The other involves the time paths of the impulse response functions to each functional disturbance. If, for example, negative shocks to the supposed money supply innovation equation (positive i^{NY*} shocks) imply positive output and negative interest rate responses, it would be difficult to believe that one had properly identified a money supply disturbance.

Estimation results

We regress each of the original seven variables in our model on six lagged values of all variables, monthly dummies, a time trend, and the tariff on pigiron. We include the tariff in order to abstract from relative supply shifts, given our use of pigiron as the output proxy. We saved these reduced form equations for use in simulation and defined their residuals as the innovations Y, i^{NY}, i^L, X, M, P, and G, modeled in system (1)–(7).

The results for the simultaneous equations model in innovations are given below (standard errors appear in parentheses):

$$i_t^{NY}=0.252 i_t^L+0.110 G+i_t^{NY*} \tag{2}$$
$$(0.050) \quad (0.070)$$

$$X_t - M_t - G_t = 0.112 i_t^L - 0.048 i_t^{NY} + X_t^* \tag{3}$$
$$(0.269) \quad (0.462)$$

$$Y_t = -0.136 i_t^{NY} + 0.700 P_t + Y_t^* \tag{4}$$
$$(0.120) \quad (0.335)$$

$$M_t = -0.019 i_t^{NY} + 0.321 Y_t + 3.190 P_t M_t^* \tag{5}$$
$$(0.205) \quad (0.112) \quad (0.580)$$

$$P_t = -0.021 i_t^L - 0.099 X_t + P_t^* \tag{6}$$
$$(0.022) \quad (0.019)$$

$$G_t = -0.344 i_t^L - 0.117 Y_t + 2.66 P_t + G_t^*. \tag{7}$$
$$(0.614) \quad (0.140) \quad (0.93)$$

Only one of the coefficients in this system of equations contradicts our model – the sign on Y in the money demand equation is negative. All 13 other estimated coefficients are of the right sign and some are measured precisely. As Sims (1986, 12) notes, however, the method we use for constructing standard errors need not be very accurate since it is based on an approximate second derivative matrix.

As we noted before, the coefficients in the contemporaneous association matrix are not conclusive by themselves. The best way to verify functional identification of disturbances is to examine the "reasonableness" of simulated responses to shocks.

At the same time, not all impulse responses merit equal weight in determining the reasonableness of our identification. Rather, one wishes to ascertain whether the *important* sources of disturbances in the model are consistent with our identification matrix. The importance of disturbances for influencing any variable's future may be measured by the forecast variance decomposition of that variable. For example, functional disturbances in export demand are important for gold inflows if they play a large role in explaining future uncertainty about gold inflows.

Simulation results

Forecast variance decompositions which describe the percentage contribution from each functional disturbance to each variable in the system at time horizons of 3, 12, and 20 months are given in table 7.3. Beside these figures, we indicate whether the sign of the impulse response at that time horizon is positive ($+$), negative ($-$), or essentially zero (N), defined roughly as a cumultive response of less than one tenth of the initial standard deviation shock. Table 7.3 allows us to examine whether important sources of disturbances have effects consistent with our model.

At the same time, table 7.3 allows us to assign relative importance to domestic and international factors in the determination of output, prices, interest rates, gold flows, and foreign trade. In particular, one can ascertain whether: exports and imports are responsive in the short run to international relative price changes; prices or income respond importantly to money supply shocks; and shocks to desired net foreign savings, and export and import demand, contribute greatly to short-run price and interest rate variation, as the internationalist approach predicts.

It is important to note that the diagonal elements of the forecast variance matrix in table 7.3 are always the largest single contributor to forecast variance. This is not a coincidence. Shocks to variables not captured by the functional relationships posited in the model (unexplained errors) will appear as diagonal disturbances, and may have persisting autoregressive explanatory power. Thus diagonal forecast variances will overstate the relevance of diagonal functional shocks.

The signs of impulse responses are supportive of our identifying assumptions. US autonomous money supply contractions not explained by gold flows – those due to money multiplier shocks – are captured in i^{NY*}. Such shocks produce unimportant contractions in output and have a less persistent effect on i^{NY} than do changes in international interest rates (i^{L*}). Autonomous money supply shocks have a persistent, positive effect on gold flows, but this accounts only for roughly 4 percent of gold flow forecast variance. Autonomous US money supply shocks have virtually no effect on relative international prices in the short, or long, run. This provides strong evidence against the causal role of autonomous money supply shocks for US business cycles.

To what extent can one argue that US money supply shocks (autonomous or not) mattered for US output? The effects of monetary shocks should be captured either in i^{NY*} or in i^{L*}. Even if all of the variation in i^{L*} were caused by shocks from the US money supply, the total effect of both shocks on US output is too small to indicate an important influence from US money supply shocks.

Furthermore, i^{L*} shocks are at least partly associated with expansions in economic activity abroad (e.g. positive IS shocks in Britain). British interest rate innovations produce lagging, but important, positive effects on US exports. The negative impact of higher foreign interest rates on output may reflect either interest rate parity, or a US source of some i^{L*} shocks.

Innovations in desired net saving (X^*) play an important role in determining the US interest rate, short-run commodity price movements (which dampen quickly), imports, and exports. All of these effects are of the predicted sign – a desire to save more leads to a period of high exports, low commodity and gold imports, low relative domestic prices, and a lower US interest rate. The response of output to the savings shock is harder to explain. The initial negative, and subsequent positive, response of output may reflect a very short-run "Keynesian" contraction followed by a longer-run "equilibrium" expansion in response to a reduction in the propensity to consume.

Shocks coming from domestic aggregate supply and the IS function (Y^*), which are unrelated to monetary disturbances, saving preferences, international interest rate disturbances and the demands for imports and exports, play an important role in short-run domestic interest rate determination. Imports respond positively to income innovations, as do interest rates. The positive response of both interest rates and income to these output shocks may reflect a positive correlation between aggregate supply and demand disturbances. In Calomiris and Hubbard (1989), we

Table 7.3 Simulation results for the simultaneous equations model

Shocks originating in:	time horizon (months)	Cumulative responses of:												
		i^L		i^{NY}		X		Y		M		P		G^x
		(a)^a	(b)^b	(a)^a	(b)^b	(a)^a	(b)^b	(a)^a	(b)^b	(a)^a	(b)^b	(a)^a	(b)^b	(a)^a (b)^b
World interest rate (i^L)	3	90.0 +		19.0 +		1.5 +		2.2 –		0.4 +		0.6 –		1.9 +
World interest rate	12	62.1 +		19.7 +		7.3 +		4.1 –		3.2 –		7.5 –		4.3 +
World interest rate	20	53.0 N		17.9 N		7.4 N		4.2 –		3.7 N		8.8 –		4.4 +
US money supply (i^{NY})	3	2.6 +		68.0 +		0.4 N		1.9 –		0.6 +		3.0 +		4.9 +
US money supply	12	2.7 +		34.6 +		0.4 N		4.5 –		4.5 –		1.2 N		6.2 +
US money supply	20	3.1 N		31.7 N		3.9 N		4.5 –		4.7 N		1.1 N		6.2 +
US desired savings (X)	3	1.4 N		2.6 –		47.9 +		6.1 –		16.9 –		32.4 –		7.8 N
US desired savings	12	3.9 N		10.7 –		37.7 +		8.0 +		15.6 N		26.1 –		7.7 –
US desired savings	20	4.1 N		10.1 N		35.6 N		8.1 +		16.2 N		23.2 N		7.8 –
Equilibrium–output (Y)	3	3.0 +		0.3 +		0.3 +		81.5 +		8.6 +		0.7 +		5.7 –
Equilibrium–output	12	15.8 +		13.0 +		3.8 +		65.1 +		13.4 N		2.9 –		9.6 –
Equilibrium–output	20	15.5 N		13.4 N		4.2 +		64.3 N		12.5 N		4.0 –		9.9 N
US import demand (M)	3	2.1 +		0.3 +		16.6 +		2.5 N		52.4 N		9.4 –		2.0 –
US import demand	12	12.3 +		8.9 +		16.8 +		10.2 N		41.9 N		10.2 –		4.3 +
US import demand	20	14.4 +		11.4 +		16.8 N		10.6 –		37.7 N		11.4 –		4.5 +
US export demand (P)	3	0.4 N		4.6 +		12.8 +		4.2 +		16.2 +		39.9 +		5.4 +
US export demand	12	1.4 N		9.3 +		14.5 N		5.6 N		15.8 N		40.3 +		9.9 –
US export demand	20	4.9 –		9.9 N		15.7 N		5.7 N		18.3 N		39.2 +		9.8 –

Table 7.3 (*cont.*)

Shocks originating in:	time horizon (months)	Cumulative responses of:												
		i^L		i^{NY}		X		Y		M		P		G^c	
		(a)[a]	(b)[b]	(a)[a]	(b)[b]	(a)[a]	(b)[b]	(a)[a]	(b)[b]	(a)[a]	(b)[b]	(a)[a]	(b)[b]	(a)[a]	(b)[b]
US money demand (G)	3	0.5	+	5.3	–	20.5	+	1.6	–	5.0	–	14.0	–	72.3	+
US money demand	12	1.9	+	3.8	+	16.0	+	2.5	+	5.6	+	11.9	–	58.0	+
US money demand	20	4.9	+	5.5	+	16.4	N	2.6	–	6.9	N	12.3	–	57.4	+

Notes:

[a] Column (a) represents the percentage contribution of a functional shock to a variable's forecast variance at the given time horizon.

[b] Column (b) provides the sign of the impulse response at the given time horizon. *N* denotes that the sign is essentially zero at that horizon.

[c] Column (b) impulse response signs are described for accumulated gold flows.

argue that disturbances to credit markets will be a source of positive correlation between aggregate supply and demand shocks.

The negative response of gold flows to output innovations – which mirrors the negative estimated coefficient on Y in (7) appears puzzling and is a relatively important contributor to future gold flows. We offer two possible explanations for this anomaly.

One way to explain this finding is to appeal to the relationship between current output innovations and predictable *future* changes in the money multiplier. If current positive innovations in output lead to increased money demand and predict a greater increase in the money multiplier, then output innovations may be negatively associated with current gold flows because of reductions in anticipated gold demand. Evidence for comovements between output growth and the money multiplier appears in Cagan (1965, p. 25). Cagan finds that at peaks and troughs money multiplier changes are more closely associated with income than variations in high-powered money, and that movements in the money multiplier are pro-cyclical. Our use of monthly data precludes a direct test of this hypothesis since we lack data on the currency/deposit and reserve/deposit ratios at that frequency.

Another explanation – which also relies on a supposed negative correlation between output shocks and the money multiplier – emphasizes the role of *credit*, as opposed to money shocks. In an environment of imperfect capital markets, the effects of money multiplier shocks may not be fully captured by money supply shocks (i^{NY*}). In this case, output movements (Y^*) will contain marginal information regarding current money multiplier shocks, over and above i^{NY*}. In this case gold flows are not *anticipatory*; rather it is *current* money multiplier shocks that account for the correlation between Y^* and G.

This does not imply that Y^* should be interpreted as a money supply disturbance in disguise. Money supply shocks, *per se*, should be fully reflected in the shadow price of liquidity (i^{NY}). Y^* may contain additional information, however, related to *credit* shocks which follow from reductions in the money multiplier. Unlike markets for gold, bankers' acceptances, and commercial paper, markets for bank lending often involve local relationships. Foreign suppliers of bank credit, therefore, will not be able to supply bank loans to firms as easily as they can ship gold, wire funds to banks, or purchase commercial paper. Thus close international linkages in traded commodities and financial instruments that limit price and interest rate fluctuations may not limit variation in the supply of bank credit or its cost. For an extended discussion of this point, see Bernanke (1983) and Calomiris and Hubbard (1989).

These potential connections between output movements and money multiplier shocks raise the possibility that – contrary to our model's restriction – G^* and Y^* should be correlated, because of the omission of the money multiplier from the model. In this case, (7) will properly measure gold demand, but not money demand defined more broadly. G^* shocks have effects on US prices and interest rates consistent with viewing (7) as a gold demand function.

Innovations in export and import demand – which may reflect, *inter alia*, changes in preferences, tariff changes not captured by price indices, or measurement errors due to price aggregation – provide strong support for our model. Impulse responses to a positive shift in import demand imply the predicted negative US relative price response, a lesser response in exports and a rise in the interest differential between US and British securities, which implies a consistent movement along the net foreign savings function.

Response patterns to shocks from export demand provide further support for the model. Export demand shocks raise relative US prices, and produce a positive response in commodity imports and gold inflows.

In summary, our results provide substantial evidence in favor of elastic responses to relative commodity prices. Moreover, shocks to desired savings and export and import demands explain between 70 and 75 percent of the forecast variance of relative price at all time horizons. Export and import demands by themselves account for roughly 50 percent. This contrasts sharply with the relatively small contributions to relative prices from Y^* or autonomous money supply shocks. Furthermore, disturbances relating to the balance of trade – desired net savings and the supply of exports (demand for imports) – prove to be the most important sources of output fluctuations other than Y^*.

Conclusions and implications

We have presented evidence that supports close direct asset and commodity price linkages between the United States and Great Britain in the short run. Gold flows respond rapidly to the demand for gold. Interest rate differentials, adjusted for risk, remained small (less than 2 percent).

Our results indicate that domestic money supply shocks, *per se*, were not an important source of output variation. Domestic money supply shocks did influence exports and gold flows, presumably by affecting incentives for money accumulation. The short-run price elasticities of import and export demand functions are a significant and important channel of influence from international disturbances to domestic output and prices.

Though a more thorough treatment of the sources of unexplained disturbances in output is beyond the scope of this chapter, we argue elsewhere

(Calomiris and Hubbard, 1989) that disturbances in credit markets in an environment of imperfect information account for much of the variation in output which characterizes pre-World War I business cycles. We find this approach fruitful for explaining the priority of price to output shocks noted by DeLong and Summers (1986), and for providing a rationale for the predictive role of money for nominal income. Money stock changes may proxy for *real* changes in bank loan supply.

Data appendix

US commodity imports and exports: US Department of Commerce, *Historical Statistics of the United States, 1789–1945*, 1st edn., 1949, 339–341; original data taken from *Monthly Summary of Commerce and Finance of the United States*, various issues

British interest rate: London open market discount rate; weekly data from *The Economist*

US interest rate: Double-name, choice commercial paper rate in New York City; US Department of Commerce, *Historical Statistics of the United States, 1789–1945*, 1st edn. 1949, 346–347; original monthly averages taken from F. R. Macaulay, *The Movement of Interest Rates, Bond Yields, and Stock Prices in the United States Since 1856*, NBER, 1938

US net gold exports: Department of Commerce, *Monthly Summary of the Foreign Commerce of the United States*, various issues

US pig iron output: US Department of Commerce, *Historical Statistics of the United States, 1789–1945*, 1st edn., 1949, 332–333; original data taken from F. R. Macaulay, *The Movement of Interest Rates, Bond Yields, and Stock Prices in the United States since 1856*, NBER, 1938

US sight and 60-day bill of exchange prices: National Monetary Commission, *Statistics for the United States, 1867–1909*, 1910, 188–208

Notes

We are grateful to Barry Eichengreen and participants in seminars at Berkeley, Harvard, Northwestern, Stanford, the Cliometric Society meetings, and the NBER for helpful comments. John Keating, John Shea, and Venere Vitale provided excellent research assistance. Christopher Sims generously provided invaluable technical advice.

1. In the late 1920s, advocates of the classical price–specie–flow view noted that the priorities of adjustment of prices and quantities seemed often to contradict their model (see, for example, Taussig, 1927, 286–290), but it was not until Whale's (1937) work on direct linkages that a theoretical framework capable of explaining these phenomena emerged.

2. It is important to note that these assumptions do not imply the irrelevance of central bank lending to domestic banks – merely that the influence such loans may have does not come from an effect on the money supply *per se*. In Calomiris and Hubbard (1989), we argue that capital market imperfections (and hence the well-being of banks and borrowers) played an important role in propagating pre-World War I business cycles. For further evidence that financial intermediation, but not money *per se*, was important for output determination, see Rush (1985).

3. Gold flows are defined as the difference between gold imports and exports (see data appendix, p. 214). Currency holdings of banks and individuals, and total money supply, are taken from Friedman and Schwartz (1970, p. 402 and p. 65, respectively).

4. Officer reports costs which vary over time and depending on country of origin. Because the British had lower interest rates, which enter into the cost of shipping, gold export costs for the United States are typically higher than half a percent, with an average of 0.65 percent over the period 1890–1904. Officer's calculations slightly overstate the gold cost of US exports, however, because he interprets US interest rates to be gold interest rates. As we show below, US interest rates in gold terms were closer to British levels once one adjusts for silver devaluation risk.

5. Unit banking in the United States seems to have been the essential institutional difference that produced the American commercial paper market. In other countries banks' operating branches provided financing to customers through bankers' acceptances, which did not become important in the United States until the 1920s (see Calomiris, 1993b).

6. For 1889–1895 the data are described as "posted" rates of exchange; for 1896–1909 the data are described as "actual" rates of exchange.

7. For example, in response to the gold inflows after the panic of 1893, the New York interest rate fell precipitously from 7.5 percent on August 25 to 3.0 percent on September 29. Gold shipments that had been sent to New York from London during the interim would have proved a disappointing investment.

8. To see whether the conclusions about tolerances for interest rate differentials or their persistence were sensitive to the specific dates chosen, we collected additional data at weekly frequency for 1893 and 1896, and found no differences.

9. The well-known Persons (1931) index of industrial production relies mainly on bank clearings and other variables of questionable relevance for output. Another alternative, the level of imports, is unattractive for our purposes because price effects on imports are contaminated by the terms of trade effect. Pigiron is highly correlated (with a correlation coefficient of 0.84 in *growth rates*) with total nonagricultural commodity output, on an annual basis. Hull

(1911) argues that iron is the "barometer of trade" because of its ubiquitous presence as an input.

References

Allen, A. T. (1986). "Private Sector Response to Stabilization Policy: A Case Study," *Explorations in Economic History* 23 (July), 253–268

Barsky, R. B., N. G. Mankiw, J. A. Miron and D. N. Weil (1988). "The Worldwide Change in the Behavior of Interest Rates and Prices in 1914," *European Economic Review* 32, 1123–1154

Bernanke, B. S. (1983). "Nonmonetary Effects of the Financial Crisis in the Propagation of the Great Depression," *American Economic Review* 73 (June), 257–276

(1986). "Alternative Explanations of the Money–Income Correlation," *Carnegie-Rochester Conference Series on Public Policy* 25 (Autumn), 49–100

Blanchard, O. J. and M. W. Watson (1986). "Are All Business Cycles Alike?," in R. J. Gordon (ed.), *The American Business Cycle: Continuity and Change*, Chicago: University of Chicago Press

Bordo, M. D. and A. J. Schwartz (eds.) (1984). *A Retrospective on the Classical Gold Standard, 1821–1931*, Chicago: University of Chicago Press for NBER

Cagan, P. (1965). *Determinants and Effects of Changes in the Stock of Money, 1875–1960*, New York: NBER

Calomiris, C. W. (1993a). "Greenback Resumption and Silver Risk: The Economics and Politics of Monetary Regime Change in the United States, 1862–1900," in M. D. Bordo and F. Capie (eds.), *Monetary Regimes in Transition*, Cambridge: Cambridge University Press, 86–132

(1993b). "Regulation, Industrial Structure, and Instability in US Banking: An Historical Perspective," in M. Klausner and L. J. White (eds.), *Structural Change in Banking*, Homewood, IL: Business One Irwin, 19–116

Calomiris, C. W. and G. Gorton (1991). "The Origins of Banking Panics: Models, Facts, and Bank Regulation," in R. G. Hubbard (ed.), *Financial Markets and Financial Crises*, Chicago: University of Chicago Press, 109–173

Calomiris, C. W. and R. G. Hubbard (1989). "Price Flexibility, Credit Availability, and Economic Fluctuations: Evidence for the United States, 1894–1909," *Quarterly Journal of Economics* 104 (August), 429–452

Clapham, J. (1958). *The Bank of England: A History*, Cambridge: Cambridge University Press

Clark, T. A. (1986). "Interest Rate Seasonals and the Federal Reserve," *Journal of Political Economy* 94 (February), 76–125

DeLong, J. B. and L. H. Summers (1986). "The Changing Cyclical Variability of Economic Activity in the United States," in R. J. Gordon (ed.), *The American Business Cycle: Continuity and Change*, Chicago: University of Chicago Press

Dick, T. J. O. and J. E. Floyd (1991). "Balance of Payments Adjustment under the International Gold Standard: Canada, 1871–1913," *Explorations in Economic History* 28 (April), 209–238

Eichengreen, B. (1985). *The Gold Standard in Theory and History*, New York: Methuen
  (1992). *Golden Fetters: The Gold Standard and the Great Depression, 1919–1939*, New York: Oxford University Press
Friedman, M. and A. J. Schwartz (1963). *A Monetary History of the United States, 1867–1960*, Princeton: Princeton University Press for NBER
  (1970). *Monetary Statistics of the United States: Estimates, Sources and Methods*, New York: Columbia University Press for NBER
Garber, P. M. (1986). "Nominal Contracts in a Bimetallic Standard," *American Economic Review* 76 (December), 1012–1030
Hull, G. H. (1911). *Industrial Depressions*, New York: Frederick A. Stokes Co.
Kemmerer, E. W. (1910). *Seasonal Variations in the Relative Demand for Money and Capital in the United States*, National Monetary Commission, Document 588, 61st Congress, 2nd session, Washington, DC: US Government Printing Office
Macaulay, F. R. (1938). *The Movement of Interest Rates, Bond Yields, and Stock Prices in the United States since 1856*, New York: NBER
Miron, J. A. (1986). "Financial Panics, the Seasonality of the Nominal Interest Rate, and the Founding of the Fed," *American Economic Review* 76 (March), 125–140
National Monetary Commission (1910). *Statistics for the United States, 1867–1909*, Document 570, 61st Congress, 2nd session, Washington, DC: US Government Printing Office
Officer, L. H. (1986). "The Efficiency of the Dollar–Sterling Gold Standard," *Journal of Political Economy* 94 (October), 1038–1073
Perkins, E. J. (1974). "The Emergence of a Futures Market for Foreign Exchange in the United States," *Explorations in Economic History* (Spring)
Persons, W. M. (1931). *Forecasting Business Cycles*, New York: John Wiley
Rich, G. (1989). "Canadian Banks, Gold, and the Crisis of 1907," *Explorations in Economic History* 26 (April), 135–160
Rush, M. (1985). "Unexpected Monetary Disturbances During the Gold Standard Era," *Journal of Monetary Economics* 15 (May), 309–321
Sachs, J. (1980). "The Changing Cyclical Behavior of Wages and Prices, 1890–1976," *American Economic Review* 70 (March), 78–90
Sims, C. A. (1986). "Are Forecasting Models Usable for Policy Analysis?," Federal Reserve Bank of Minneapolis, *Quarterly Review* (Winter), 2–16
Taussig, F. W. (1927). *International Trade*, New York: Macmillan
Whale, P. B. (1937). "The Working of the Prewar Gold Standard," *Economica* (February), 18–32

8 Balance of payments adjustment under the gold standard policies: Canada and Australia compared

Trevor J. O. Dick, John E. Floyd and David Pope

Introduction

The operation of the Classical gold standard has recently received renewed attention by scholars as a potential source of arguments for and against a commodity standard and of clues to the propriety of fixed versus flexible exchange rates. History has not provided a widespread monetary experiment of this kind since the gold standard effectively ended with the onslaught of World War I. The gold standard era also provides a history of shocks that permit us to explore a full range of scenarios in the mechanism of balance of payments adjustment.

Because 1870–1914 was an era of growth in the international economy when international capital and labor as well as commodity flows were abundantly occurring between the center and the periphery – between the established economy of Great Britain and areas of recent settlement – there is a unique opportunity to study the impact of capital mobility under fixed exchange rates. This was only incompletely appreciated by Taussig (1966 [1927]) and many of his students and followers (Williams, 1920; Viner, 1924; White, 1933; Beach, 1935; Ford, 1962) who first accepted the challenge of understanding these issues. Little agreement has been reached even now on exactly how the gold standard worked (Bordo, 1984).

Canada and Australia provide two notable examples of countries that participated in the gold standard, engaged in international trade, and had major dealings in the international capital market centered on London between 1870 and 1913. Although the history of their cases differed in detail, the two countries shared the same mechanism of interaction with Great Britain (Thomas, 1973, 258) and made similar kinds of financial adjustments in their growth processes. During significant though different subperiods of their histories the money supplies and gold stocks expanded in both countries, and balance of trade deficits arose to finance the net capital inflows and enable the repatriation of debt service balances.

Although the gold standard era has been the subject of much scrutiny in recent years (McCloskey and Zecher, 1976, 1984), and efforts to reinterpret the evidence for both Canada and Australia have been made (Dick and Floyd, 1991, 1992, 1993; Pope, 1993), it remains to bring the gold standard experience of both these countries under the umbrella of a single consistent and unified theory that can form the basis for our reinterpretation of how the gold standard really worked. The present chapter seeks to re-examine the Australian and Canadian cases by applying the same portfolio equilibrium framework to each while adding some theoretic and data refinements to the authors' earlier work.

The balance of payments adjustment process that results from our theory departs sharply from the traditional Classical interpretation. According to the latter, capital inflows caused a balance of payments surplus, an inflow of gold, and a consequent rise in the domestic price level. This made domestic goods more expensive in world markets and produced a deficit in the balance of trade. Our study of Australia and Canada essentially establishes that the opposite occurred. When investment expanded to feed domestic growth, it was that expansion, not the inflow of monetary reserves that raised the domestic price level. This had two effects. First, imports rose relative to exports causing the trade balance to deteriorate to match the net capital inflow. Second, the increase in domestic output increased the demand for nominal money by domestic residents who maintained their portfolio equilibrium by exchanging assets for money on the international market at world interest rates. The domestic banking systems were, in effect, forced to provide the increased money domestic residents wanted to hold.

The chapter is organized in four main sections. First, the background conditions of Australian and Canadian monetary history and their participation in the international economy are outlined. Second, the details of the portfolio and price–specie–flow mechanisms of adjustment are explained and related to the historical settings being studied. Third, the empirical evidence used to discriminate between these two interpretations of adjustment is presented and the operation of the gold standard in the Australian and Canadian economies compared. Finally, we conclude with an evaluation of the evidence as a basis for our reinterpretation of the operation of the gold standard and as a key to what further research may be useful.

Canada, Australia and the international economy, 1871–1913

Canada and Australia were widely separated and important participants in the expansion of the international economy from the mid-19th century to World War I, interacting with Great Britain in similar ways as the trade in goods and factors of production between the periphery and the center

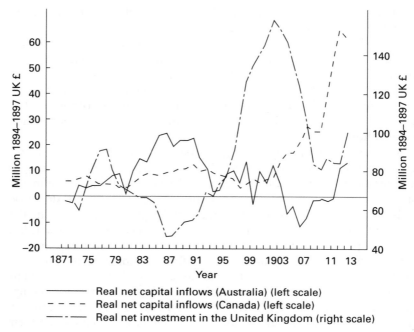

Figure 8.1 Real net capital inflows, Australia and Canada, and real net investment in the United Kingdom, 1871–1913
Source: See data appendix

expanded (Kenwood and Lougheed, 1992, chapter 9; Green and Urquhart, 1976). During our period of analysis both countries were subject to major inflows of immigrants and capital that accompanied the early settlement of vast hitherto vacant areas capable of producing and exporting major staple products. Both countries experienced important differences between domestic savings and domestic investment demand that bore an inverse relationship to contemporaneous differences in Great Britain (Thomas, 1973, 256–260; Edelstein, 1982, chapters 11–12; Hall, 1968, chapters 6–7; Eichengreen, 1990). Investment in Great Britain peaked in the 1870s and again around 1900. A surplus of British savings were absorbed in the 1880s by Australia, to which migrants were drawn by gold discoveries and the development of the wool trade, and in the early 1900s by Canada, to which people and capital were drawn by the prospects of wheat production and exports (Pomfret, 1981; Butlin, 1964; Thomas, 1973, p. 115).

Differences in the timing of the international flows to which the Canadian and Australian balance of payments had to adjust, shown in figure 8.1, were a function of differences at the periphery rather than at the center of the developing international economy. The flows to Australia were influenced by the early gold discoveries and a kinked age distribution of the population that persisted across generations as a result of early migration attracted by gold and helped to raise the savings rate (Hall, 1963b; McLean, 1991). A temporary slump in the growth of the savings rate in the 1880s after having attained 11 percent in the 1870s, combined with investment opportunities in wool, led to major expansion based on capital imports that in retrospect were excessive (Pomfret, 1991, 145; Edelstein, 1982, 268). A major slowdown followed, with recovery eventually beginning after 1904 based on more diverse opportunities. The domestic savings rate rose to 14 percent by World War I, and this was sufficient to preclude further major attraction of foreign capital. Canada, by contrast, experienced only relatively slow growth prior to the 1890s combined with a savings rate of only 9 percent (Urquhart, 1986; McLean, 1991). Despite a rise in the savings rate to 16 percent by World War I, investment opportunities appeared so great in Canada after 1896 that the growing surplus of British savings over home investment opportunities were attracted to Canada rather than to Australia in the decade or so before 1914. Although Australia appeared to make a significant pull on British savings in the 1880s and Canada a similar pull after 1900, push forces were also at work in as much as overinvestment also appears to characterize both booms at the periphery (Edelstein, 1982; Paterson, 1976).

The changing balance between savings and investment opportunities at the center and periphery was also influenced by the nature of the developing capital markets at the periphery. Australia and Canada present some contrasts as well as similarities. Although the branch banking system grew in both countries, banks were much less regulated in Australia (Drummond, 1991). The similar patterns of long-run increases in the savings rate in Australia and Canada (McLean, 1991) were differently accommodated. In Australia there was no sustained counterpart to the Bank of Montreal that consistently operated as the government's fiscal agent and handled all government long-term loans in the London market. Before 1890 a number of Australian banks performed this function, although the two largest maintained their head offices in London. After 1890, Australia used English banks in London for this purpose (Gilbert, 1971). In addition, a much greater fraction of Australian capital formation was financed by government loans than in Canada, and a new issue market developed in Australia much earlier than in Canada. Australian governments, both states and municipalities, exploited this market before 1914 in a way that had no counterpart in Canada. The Dominion and provincial governments in Canada before 1914 were generally reluctant to borrow at home. It appears that the development of the new issue market in Australia after 1895 and the general absence of Australian flotations in London left the London market open to absorb Canadian securities (Drummond, 1959).

The international payments system under which the British, Australian, and Canadian economies operated in the 1870–1913 period was the gold standard (Kenwood and Lougheed, 1992, chapter 7). Britain had been on the gold standard since 1821. In Australia, a branch of the Royal Mint was opened in 1855. Money in circulation consisted of gold, silver and bronze coins, notes and deposit liabilities of the trading banks, and by 1893, Queensland treasury notes (legal tender in Queensland only). The trading banks maintained gold convertibility of their notes and Queensland maintained convertibility of its notes. After 1910, Australian notes (government issue) replaced all trading bank notes and Queensland notes, and were also convertible into gold (Butlin, 1986; Butlin, Hall and White, 1971). In Canada, the money supply consisted of notes and deposit liabilities and deposit liabilities of the chartered banks, Dominion notes issued by the government, and token coinage. The chartered banks maintained convertibility of their notes and deposits into gold, and the Dominion government maintained convertibility of Dominion notes into gold. US gold pieces and UK pounds also circulated in Canada, tradable at fixed rates with the Canadian dollar. Except for inconvertibility in the United States during the greenback era before 1879, both the United States and the United Kingdom maintained convertibility of their currencies into gold.

The circulation of government notes came about gradually in Canada by the requirement that Dominion notes be the only permitted denominations under $5. In Australia, apart from a small circulation of Queensland notes, government notes were not introduced until 1910, after which new issues of all other notes were prohibited. Notes of the trading banks and Queensland notes were completely replaced by Australian notes by the end of our study period. Compared to Canada, therefore, there was only a short period (1893–1910) when both bank and government notes circulated together, and this happened only in Queensland. For the entire period in Canada the monetary base consisted of gold and secondary reserves held by the chartered banks plus gold reserves of the Dominion government held as backing for Dominion notes. In Australia the monetary base consisted of gold and secondary reserves of the trading banks alone until the early 1890s. This base was augmented by the Queensland government's gold backing for its notes after 1893, and then gradually replaced after 1910 by the Commonwealth government's gold reserves that backed Australian notes.

The mechanism of balance of payment adjustment under the gold standard that accommodated international capital flows to Australia and

Canada in 1870–1913 has been in dispute from the time the topic was first studied. Whatever this mechanism was, the only agreement seems to have been that it worked relatively smoothly. The standard interpretation, articulated by Taussig ([1927] 1966) and his students, rests on the Classical price–specie–flow mechanism. According to this view, long-term capital inflow and the associated new investment resulted in a balance of payments surplus and an inflow of gold and secondary reserves. An increase in the monetary base and money and money supply then produced a rise in the domestic price level, discouraging exports and encouraging imports, thereby deteriorating the trade balance to finance the inflow of capital.

The most emphatic case ever made for this approach is probably that of Viner (1924) who studied Canada's experience from 1900 to 1913. His view was questioned from the outset for lack of evidence showing a clear sequence from gold and secondary reserve change to the Canadian money supply and prices (Angell, 1925a, 1925b, 1925c). More recently Dick and Floyd (1991, 1992, 1993) have shown that an alternative portfolio theory, extending the monetary approach to the balance of payments, is more consistent with the evidence. In Australia, there has been difficulty in showing that capital inflow had the appropriate price effects to make a case similar to Viner (Wilson, 1931). The problem is compounded by the fact that unlike Canada, which experienced a massive capital inflow shock after 1900, it is the effects of an opposite shock at about the same time in Australia that have to be explained (Cain, 1970, 101). As elsewhere, gold movements do not seem to have had a time path that support the price–specie–flow story (Kennett, 1972). Pope (1993), in a first attempt to apply a monetary approach, finds limited support for it and concludes that the price–specie–flow story is inadequate.

Competing theories of gold standard adjustment

In this section we first develop a modern portfolio theory of balance of payments adjustment under a gold standard and then compare it with the standard Classical price–specie–flow mechanism. This sets the stage for empirical tests of the two theories with Canadian and Australian data.

The portfolio theory

Three basic propositions underlie our portfolio theory of balance of payments adjustment.

1. First, economic agents make decisions about the form in which they hold their wealth and the disposition of the income from that wealth on the basis of rational choice.

2. Second, agents are free to exchange a wide variety of assets in an international market.
3. And third, the markets for goods and assets must be in equilibrium, subject to the usual resource constraints.

Our portfolio theory of balance of payments adjustment follows from a rigorous interpretation of the implications of proposition 2 in terms of propositions 1 and 3.

The proposition that individuals are free to buy and sell a wide range of assets (though not necessarily every asset) across international boundaries constrains the domestic interest rate in relation to interest rates in the rest of the world according to the familiar relationship

$$i = i^* + \rho + E_\pi \tag{1}$$

where i and i^* are the domestic and rest of the world nominal interest rates, ρ is the risk premium on domestic assets and E_π is the expected rate of change of the nominal exchange rate, with the latter defined as the price of foreign currency in terms of domestic currency. When convertibility into gold is not in doubt, E_π will equal zero. (1) has its counterpart in the relation between the two countries' real interest rates. The two Fisher equations can be written

$$i = r + E_P \tag{2}$$

$$i^* = r^* + E_{P*} \tag{3}$$

where r and r^* are the domestic and foreign real interest rates and E_P and E_{P*} are the expected inflation rates. Substitution of these into (1) yields

$$r = r^* + \rho - E_q \tag{4}$$

where E_q is the expected rate of change of the real exchange rate. The real exchange rate is defined as

$$q = \frac{P}{\pi P^*} \tag{5}$$

where P and P^* are the price levels of domestic and foreign output and π is the nominal exchange rate. The real exchange rate is the relative price of domestic output in terms of foreign output. (1) and (4) derive from market efficiency and interest rate parity and appear as Euler equations in all properly constructed intertemporal maximization models.[1] The risk premium ρ would be zero if there were "perfect capital mobility." This would occur where every asset is tradable internationally and all assets are perfect substitutes in the portfolios of a sufficient number of individuals. The importance of (4) lies in its constraining effect on domestic real and monetary equilibrium.

To explore the nature of this constraining effect, begin with the budget constraint

$$X = C + I + B_T \tag{6}$$

where X equals domestic output, C is real consumption of domestic and foreign goods (on both private and government account), I is real investment of domestic and foreign goods (on both private and government account), and B_T is the balance of trade. Adding the debt service balance to both sides of (6), we get

$$Y = X + DSB = C + I + B_T + DSB, \tag{7}$$

where Y is domestic real income and DSB is the debt service balance (interest and dividends received from foreign residents *minus* interest and dividends paid to foreign residents). Subtracting $C + I$ from both sides of (7) yields

$$Y - C - I = B_T + DSB \tag{8}$$

which can be written as

$$S - I = B_T + DSB \tag{9}$$

where S is domestic real savings. Since $S - I$ is the net capital outflow and $B_T + DSB$ is the current account balance, (9) implies that the capital account deficit must equal the current account surplus.

It is important to note that (9) can be viewed as an equilibrium condition as well as an identity. Viewed as an identity, it must hold as a consequence of standard book-keeping regardless of what determines C, I, Y, B_T, and DSB. Viewed as an equilibrium condition, it must hold in the sense that for the demand for domestic output to equal the supply, the "desired" or "planned" magnitudes of C, I, Y, B_T, and DSB must satisfy (9). Certain variables in the economy must adjust continually to maintain equilibrium. In a closed economy (where B_T and DSB equal zero), adjustment falls on r and Y. When there is price flexibility and full employment, the interest rate must adjust to equate desired savings and desired investment. When there is some form of wage rigidity, both output (income) and the interest rate adjust. In an open economy, the real exchange rate provides a third avenue for adjustment.

To see how equilibrium is attained, modify (9) by expressing the balance of trade as a function of domestic and foreign incomes and the real exchange rate:

$$S - I = B_T[q, Y, Y^*] + DSB. \tag{10}$$

A rise in domestic income increases imports relative to exports, a rise in foreign income increases exports relative to imports, and a rise in the real exchange rate (i.e. an increase in the relative price of domestic output in terms of foreign output) shifts both domestic and rest of the world demand away from domestic goods towards foreign goods and reduces the balance of trade. DSB is determined, of course, by past capital movements.

Although there are differences across models, the excess of domestic savings over investment is generally held to depend upon real income, the real interest rate, and exogenous shift variables reflecting time preference, productivity, expectations about the future profitability of investment, and other forces:

$$N[Y,r,\Omega] = B_T[q, Y, Y^*] + DSB, \tag{11}$$

where Ω represents the collection of shift variables. A rise in income unaccompanied by any change in Ω increases savings relative to investment but a rise in income that occurs in association with an increase in Ω (due to, say, a shift in the consumption or investment function) will be associated with an increase in investment relative to savings. Similarly, a rise in the real interest rate unaccompanied by any change in the productivity of domestically employed capital associated with changes in Y or Ω increases savings relative to investment. An equation similar to (11) can also be constructed for the rest of the world, but our small open economy assumption enables us to omit it. In intertemporal maximization models, separate and interrelated equations like (11) emerge for each period in the time horizon.

Either q, Y, or r must continually adjust to maintain the aggregate demand for domestic output equal to the aggregate supply. Their roles are evident from the conditions of asset equilibrium. One of those conditions has already been defined by (4) – relative domestic and foreign interest rates must adjust so that world asset holders in the aggregate have no incentive to reallocate their portfolios among the outstanding stocks of claims to domestic and foreign employed capital. The second condition is that the demand for money equal the supply:

$$M = P \cdot L[r, r^*, Ep, Y], \tag{12}$$

where M is the nominal quantity of money. The real quantity of money demanded depends on the real returns from holding domestic and foreign assets as well as the expected rate of domestic inflation. Monetary equilibrium is assumed to hold in the rest of the world but that equilibrium condition can be omitted because we make a small-country assumption. (12) implies that, ignoring human capital, the aggregate demand for non-monetary assets equals the aggregate supply because any excess demand or supply of nonmonetary assets in the aggregate has to be reflected in a corresponding excess supply or demand for money balances.[2]

After eliminating q by substituting (5) into (11) to obtain

$$N[Y,r,\Omega]=B_T\left[\frac{P}{\pi P^*},Y,Y^*\right]+DSB,\tag{13}$$

we can describe domestic macroeconomic equilibrium by (4), (12), and (13). These three equations solve in gold standard and other fixed exchange rate regimes for the three variables, M, r, and either P or Y, in terms of the exogenously determined levels of output, prices and the interest rate in the rest of the world and the shift variable Ω.[3] The nominal money stock is endogenous because of the constraining effect of world capital market equilibrium on the domestic interest rate in (4). Substituting the latter equation into (11) and rearranging to bring q to the left, we can formally express the real exchange rate as follows:

$$q=q[Y,\Omega,DSB,\rho,E_q,r^*,Y^*].\tag{14}$$

Then this together with (5) determines the domestic price level:

$$P=\frac{q(Y,Y^*,\Omega,DSB,\rho,E_q,r^*)}{\pi P^*}\tag{15}$$

This equation can also be obtained by substituting (4) into (13). Note that the domestic money stock does not appear in (15). The only possible effects of domestic money on domestic prices would occur through its effect on ρ. Modern asset pricing theory views ρ as determined by the covariance structure of output and asset returns and establishes no presumption that an increase in the supply or demand for money in any given period will affect that covariance structure – the money shock need only be a draw from the random process defining that covariance structure (Merton, 1971; Kouri, 1977; Lucas, 1978, 1982; Stulz, 1984; Pasula, 1992). The domestic price level is thus determined by monetary conditions abroad, which determine P^*, and the set of domestic and foreign real factors – technology, savings propensities, and the international distribution of investment opportunities – that determine the real exchange rate.

If the banking system creates, through its domestic loan and discount policies, less money than domestic residents want to hold, domestic residents re-establish portfolio equilibrium by selling nonmonetary assets in the world market. As the foreign currency acquired is converted into domestic currency at the banks the domestic banking system is forced to create additional domestic money balances to meet the demand for them and to acquire international reserves in the process. The banking system controls its reserve levels by appropriately adjusting domestic credit policies. It has *no* control over the domestic money supply. The latter always equals whatever domestic residents want to hold. The banks can only control the division of their asset portfolios between domestic loans and discounts and international reserves. The country's stock of international reserves thus depends on the public's desired money holdings, which determine the banking system's note and deposit liabilities, and on the various factors, such as interest rates, that affect the profit maximizing reserve ratios of the commercial banks.[4]

Changes in international reserves have no causal effect on the domestic price level. Indeed, the opposite is the case. Increases in the domestic price level emanating from real forces of demand and supply and/or monetary developments in the rest of the world cause the public to hold more money which in turn causes the banks to create that money and hold larger reserves. It also follows from the analysis above that changes in domestic monetary conditions have no effect on the balance of trade. (11) and (13) imply that the ratio of the domestic to the foreign price levels (i.e. the real exchange rate) will adjust to bring the trade balance into line with the (autonomous *plus* induced) net capital flow – in a world of less than full employment, changes in domestic income may also play a role in this adjustment process in the short run. But the portion of the total net capital flow comprising induced monetary gold and reserve asset flows plays no part in real goods market equilibrium. The sole function of reserve flows is to finance an endogenous adjustment of the domestic money supply to bring it into line with domestic residents' demand for money balances. It also follows from (14) that there is no reason why purchasing power parity as it is conventionally defined should hold. The equilibrium real exchange rate will vary through time in response to changes in domestic and foreign technology and tastes – the fact that there is little trend in the real exchange rate over periods of 100 years or more can be interpreted to mean simply that shocks to technology, taste, and other factors were just as often positive as negative so that their effects tended to average out to zero. Mean reversion was not rapid enough to justify a conclusion that real exchange rate movements were monetary phenomena. We view mean reversion as a statistical phenomenon rather than evidence of a tendency to return to long-run equilibrium in any economic sense.

Building on (4) and (12), the stock of foreign exchange reserves can be formally expressed

$$R = \delta M = \delta PL[r^*, \rho + E_q, E_p, Y], \tag{16}$$

where δ is the equilibrium ratio of international reserves to the money supply and R is the net stock of gold and reserve assets convertible into gold held by the public and the banking system (including, where appropriate, the government). The reserve flow or balance of payments surplus is obtained by differentiating (or differencing) this expression with respect to time.

$$dR/dt = \delta L(...)dP/dt + \delta PL_{r*}dr^*/dt + \delta PL_Y dY/dt + PL(...)d\delta/dt, \quad (17)$$

where L_{r*} and L_{Y*} are the partial derivatives of $L(...)$ with respect to r and Y.

The balance of payments surplus can also be expressed in more conventional terms. We can split aggregate real savings in (10) into two components: the country's accumulation of international reserves, measured in units of domestic output, and all other accumulations of assets by domestic residents on both private and public account, denoted by S'

$$S = \frac{1}{P}\frac{dR}{dt} + S'. \quad (18)$$

Substitution of this into (10) yields

$$\frac{1}{P}\frac{dR}{dt} = B_T[q, Y, Y^*] + DSB + I - S'. \quad (19)$$

(19) represents the balance of payments surplus as the excess of autonomous receipts over autonomous payments. Nevertheless, as (18) indicates, the entire source of variation in the induced net capital flow is S', which varies only as a result of shifts in the rate of growth of desired money holdings, given by the left-hand side of (17). The balance of trade and debt service balance are unrelated to factors affecting the real reserve flow for the reasons discussed above.

It is evident from the role played by ρ in the above analysis that the condition for balance of payments equilibrium – and the *process* by which balance of payments adjustments occur – is fundamentally the same whether capital is perfectly or imperfectly mobile internationally. Even if the risk premium varies through time, a change in the surplus or deficit in the balance of payments results from a change in autonomous relative to total saving as a direct consequence of a change in the desired rate of domestic money accumulation and corresponding change in the accumulation of domestic bank reserves. Domestic interest rates will not change unless there is a change in the risk premium. Modern consumption based asset pricing theory suggests that the difference between domestic and foreign interest rates should depend on the differences between the covariances of domestic and foreign returns on real capital with the marginal utility of consumption.[5] Domestic credit expansion can affect the domestic covariance and risk premium only if it signals a change in the pattern of future variations in domestic output and asset returns.

The price–specie–flow mechanism

The Classical price–specie–flow theory has a long history dating back at least to Hume (Hume, [1752] 1898, 330–41 and 343–5).[6] The standard text-book version of the adjustment mechanism equates the international gold flow to the balance of trade, sometimes including long-term capital flows as an exogenous additive item. When gold flows occur, the quantity of money and price level fall in the country losing gold and increase in the recipient country, thereby making the goods of the deficit country relatively more attractive. This process leads to an adjustment of the balance of trade until the gold flow is eliminated. In more sophisticated discussions of the adjustment mechanism, short-term capital flows are incorporated as a response to international interest rate differentials. An outflow of gold and the resultant tightening of domestic money causes the interest rate to rise relative to the interest rate abroad. This attracts capital, moderating the gold loss and smoothing out the adjustment process. More theoretically sophisticated treatments also allow for the effects on the balance of trade of small movements of the exchange rate between the gold export and import points and of spending effects that are negative in the country losing gold and positive in the country accumulating it.

The classical view can be represented formally in terms of the equation

$$\frac{1}{P}\frac{dR}{dt}=B_T[q,Y,Y^*]+DSB+N_L+N_S[r-r^*], \tag{20}$$

where N_L is the exogenous net inflow of long-term capital and $N_S[r-r^*]$ is the net inflow of short-term capital, expressed as an increasing function of the differential of domestic over foreign real interest rates.

In essence, (2) is simply (19) with the constraint imposed that

$$I-S'=N_L+N_S[r-r^*]. \tag{21}$$

The equilibrium of the domestic economy is then determined by (12), (13); and (20) instead of (12), (13), and (4).

(4) connects the domestic and foreign interest rates on the basis of risk adjusted arbitrage in an open international capital market. (20) imposes a relationship between the interest rate differential and the magnitude of the autonomous international flow of short-term capital. In the Classical system, the domestic interest rate is determined by domestic real and mon-etary conditions. A capital flow is then generated by the interest differen-tial leading, along with the balance of trade surplus or deficit, to reserve flows and consequent adjustments in the domestic money supply until a new domestic equilibrium is established consistent with a zero gold flow. This process of re-establishing balance of payments equilibrium involves

temporary changes in prices, incomes, and the balance of trade. In contrast, domestic interest rates are determined in the portfolio theory by the condition that, given free international trade in assets, asset prices must adjust at every point in time until the aggregate stocks of domestic and foreign assets are willingly held by world asset holders. Domestic residents then adjust their money holdings to the desired level by exchanging money and assets with foreign residents at this equilibrium vector of world interest rates and the associated equilibrium levels of domestic income and prices.

The essential difference between the two theories lies in different interpretations of what is meant by "imperfect capital mobility." The portfolio theory treats imperfect capital mobility as the absence of perfect substitutability of domestic and foreign assets in portfolios. As a result, world wealth holders attach different risks and different interest rates to domestic and foreign securities. Capital does not flow between countries in response to interest rate differentials. Higher interest rates in a country will indeed cause individual wealth owners whose risk perceptions are unchanged to shift part of their portfolios in the direction of that country's securities. While an individual agent can do this, all wealth owners acting together cannot. Attempts of all asset holders to sell assets in the low-interest rate country and buy them in the high-interest rate country will cause asset prices in the two countries to adjust until the interest rate differential has been eliminated. Interest rate differentials can change only when wealth owners' perceptions of the relative riskiness of the two countries' securities has changed.

Under the specie–flow theory, domestic and foreign interest rates diverge by an amount that depends on the magnitude of the autonomous net capital flow. It is as though there is a per unit transaction or frictional cost of transferring assets into and out of domestic hands that increases with the quantity of assets transferred per unit time. Since interest rates must diverge sufficiently to cover these increasing transactions costs, the domestic interest rate must exceed the foreign interest rate by an amount (additional to any risk premium and allowance for expected change in the real exchange rate) that depends directly on the rate through time at which foreigners are acquiring nonmonetary assets from domestic residents. Because the friction cost per unit of capital increases with the *flow* of capital into the country, the cost of making instantaneous stock adjustments at a point in time becomes prohibitive. Excess money holdings on the part of domestic residents thus lead to a bidding down of the interest rate on domestic assets relative to the interest rate on foreign assets until domestic agents willingly hold the excess money – no one-shot exchange of foreign exchange reserves for nonmonetary assets can occur.

The fundamental argument of the portfolio theory is that the simple perfect capital mobility model can be used without essential modification when capital is not perfectly mobile internationally. Under usual circumstances where assets are imperfect but nevertheless good substitutes in portfolios, movements of the interest rate differential, relative price levels and the balance of trade can occur. For example, an expansion of domestic credit resulting from a decision of the commercial banks to reduce their desired reserve ratios will find them selling international reserves and adding domestic loans and other assets to their portfolios, with private asset holders increasing their loan liabilities (reducing net domestic asset holdings) and increasing their reserve assets by the same amounts. If domestic and foreign assets are not perfect substitutes in portfolios, one might expect a fall in ρ to arise because the commercial banks will have to give the public an inducement to alter its portfolio mix. This is not the relationship predicted by the price–specie–flow mechanism, however, because any interest rate and balance of trade changes are permanent, not temporary. Moreover, an examination of both the Canadian and Australian data indicates that reserve flows typically made up less than 2 percent of GNP. Assuming that income from nonhuman capital was, say, 15 percent of GNP and that the real interest rate was 5 percent, the stock of nonhuman capital would have been about three times GNP, making reserve flows considerably less than 1 percent of the stock of nonhuman capital, and a trivial fraction of total wealth. Given the magnitudes of reserve flow movements in relation to the size of the aggregate portfolio, one might expect any effects they had on interest rate differentials and relative price levels to be too small to be observable in the data.

The empirical evidence

We turn now to our empirical tests of the two theories, beginning with an examination of the relationship between the real net capital inflow and the real exchange rate. Then, after presenting estimates of the demand function for money, we turn to tests of balance of payments adjustment under the specie–flow and portfolio theories. The specie–flow theory is examined first. Tests of cross-equation restrictions implied by the two theories are then made, using the equations suggested by the specie–flow theory estimated as a system of seemingly unrelated regressions. Then the reserve flow equation suggested by the portfolio theory is estimated and its standard error compared to the standard error of the reserve flow equation under the price–specie–flow theory. The section concludes with a set of nonnested hypotheses tests.

Capital flows and real exchange rate movements

Figure 8.2 plots the real exchange rate movements and real net capital inflow for Canada and Australia. The main flow of capital into Australia occurred during the boom of the late 1800s whereas the inflow of capital into Canada was concentrated in the years of prairie expansion after 1900. The real exchange rate follows the major movements of the combined net capital inflow and debt service balance. There is an obvious positive relationship between the real net capital inflow *plus* debt service balance and the real exchange rate.

The effects on the real exchange rate of real factors other than shifts in world investment are complex. As indicated in (11), a shift of world investment into the domestic economy increases aggregate demand and raises the price level. The price level must rise sufficiently relative to the price level abroad, switching demand off domestic and onto foreign goods, to produce a deterioration of the trade balance equal to the increased net inflow of capital. Changes in the allocation of world investment among countries, however, do not exhaust those factors that typicaly affect real exchange rates nor are such changes easily isolated from the other factors (Edwards, 1989; Johnston, 1992). For example, an exogenous shift of the function $B_T[q, Y, Y^*]$ due to a change in tastes or technology in the absence of exogenous changes in savings and investment will result in a change in the real exchange rate without any change in the balance of trade or net inflow of capital – the real exchange rate will adjust to bring the balance of trade back into equality with the net capital flow plus debt service balance. Indeed, if the demand for imports happens to shift exogenously upward at the same time as an exogenous increase in investment in the domestic economy leads to an increased net inflow of capital, the observed relationship between the real capital inflow plus debt service and the real exchange rate could be negative. The desired increase in imports may be more than the net capital inflow at the initial real exchange rate so the real exchange rate will have to fall to maintain equality between the excess of desired imports over exports and the new level of net capital inflow. Consider, for example, a rise in domestic income due to technological change in the domestic economy. The rise in income results from increased production of both traded and nontraded goods. At the same time, it increases the demand for both traded and nontraded goods. Either a rise or fall in the real exchange rate can result, depending upon the shift of the demand relative to the supply of nontraded goods, the prices of traded goods being determined in the world market. Similarly, a rise in foreign real income may be associated with a shift in the relative price of nontraded in terms of traded goods abroad in either direction, with a rise in the relative price of foreign nontraded goods

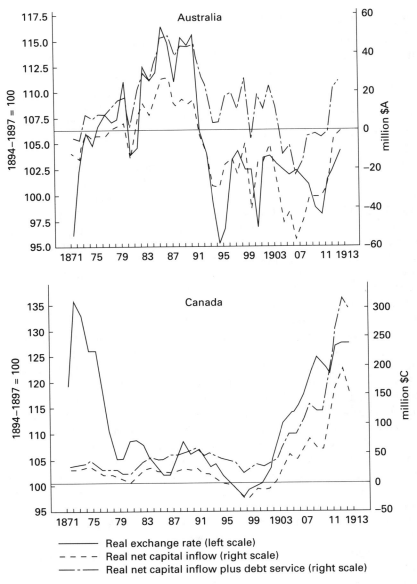

Figure 8.2 Real exchange rate and real net capital inflow and real net capital inflow plus debt service, 1871–1913
Source: See data appendix

leading to a decline in the domestic real exchange rate. The net effect on a country's real exchange rate of ongoing worldwide technological growth will thus depend upon the effect of that technological change on the relative costs of producing nontraded in terms of traded goods in the separate countries as well as on the income elasticities of demand for both countries' nontraded and traded goods.

A further complexity arises because a country's export goods may rise or fall in price relative to its import goods, even though the country is small and all traded goods prices are determined in the world market. This will depend on how worldwide technological change affects the relative costs of producing the different traded goods and the location of resources that can be exploited with the new technology. A rise in the price of a country's exports relative to the price of its imports – i.e. an improvement in its terms of trade – will lead *ceteris paribus* to an increase in that country's real exchange rate if domestic export production exceeds import goods production. These real exchange rate movements arising from the effects of world technological change on the terms of trade may be either reinforced or offset by the effects of technological change and resultant real income growth on the relative prices of nontraded in terms of traded goods. Since we cannot model the growth of technology in a satisfactory manner, we cannot identify and separate the relationship between real income changes on the real exchange from the relationship between terms of trade changes and the real exchange rate. We can only expect to observe a positive relationship between the net capital inflow and the real exchange rate if the effects of shifts of investment into and out of the country are large relative to the effects of other factors that we cannot observe and account for. Some of these other factors can, of course, be proxied by including domestic and foreign real incomes and the terms of trade in estimating equations for the real exchange rate. We can expect the coefficients of these latter variables to take either sign for the reasons noted above.

Columns (1) and (3) of table 8.1 present regressions of the real exchange rate on the real net capital inflow *plus* debt service balance for Canada and Australia respectively. The capital flow *plus* debt service balance explains 44 percent of the variance of the real exchange for Canada and 61 percent for Australia. That simple linear relationships of this sort can be observed suggests that exogenous capital movements have been very important relative to other factors that affected the two countries' real exchange rates. In columns (2) and (4), domestic and foreign real incomes and the terms of trade are added to the regressions. These variables proxy technological change, resource discovery, and the whole range of income and terms of trade related factors that affected the real exchange rate. They improve the fit substantially in Canada, raising the R^2 from 0.44 to 0.79, and only slightly

Table 8.1 *Real exchange rates and real net capital inflows* plus *debt service, 1871–1913*

| | Real exchange rate[b,c] | | | |
| | Canada | | Australia | |
	(1)	(2)	(3)	(4)
Constant	107.32	151.73	107.22	92.90
	(75.00)	(13.92)	(178.70)	(14.77)
Real net capital inflow *plus*[c]	0.14	0.20	0.21	0.20
debt service	(5.63)	(4.23)	(8.01)	(4.84)
Domestic real income[a,b]		−0.36		0.03
		(−1.96)		(0.62)
Rest of world real income[a,b]		0.68		−0.04
		(2.66)		(−0.49)
Terms of trade		−0.83		0.11
		(−6.50)		(2.38)
Observations	43	43	43	43
R^2	0.44	0.79	0.61	0.67
Standard error	7.91	5.05	3.51	3.36
DW	0.30	1.02	1.15	1.28

Notes:
[a] The real exchange rate is the consumer price index divided by an index of the rest of the world income deflator for Canada and the domestic GDP deflator divided by an index of the rest of the world income deflator for Australia.
[b] All income and real exchange rate variables are indexes on the base 1894–1897=100.
[c] The net capital inflow *plus* debt service variables are the negatives of the respective trade account balances with gold exports included as a trade balance item. These variables are deflated by the consumer price index in the Canadian case and the GDP deflator in the Australian case. Both variables are in million 1894–1897 domestic dollars.
The figures in brackets are *t*-ratios.
Sources: See data appendix (p. 251).

in Australia, where the R^2 increases from 0.61 to 0.67. All the added variables are significant in the Canadian case but only the terms of trade variable is significant for Australia. The fact that the terms of trade variable has a positive sign for Australia and a negative sign for Canada and the income variables are insignificant in Australia suggests strongly that the factors affecting the real exchange rate during the period were very different in the two countries. The low DW statistics in regression (2) and (4) suggest that the real incomes and terms of trade do not adequately proxy all the technological and other factors affecting the real exchange rates.

The observed relationships between the real net capital inflows and real exchange rates of the two countries are consistent with both the price–specie–flow and portfolio theories of balance of payments adjustment.

The demand for money

Demand function for money estimates for the two countries are presented in table 8.2. The results are pretty much as one would expect. The Australian savings deposit rate has a negative effect on the quantity of M1 demanded by residents of that country and a positive effect on the quantity of M2 demanded – the latter positive effect arises because the savings deposit rate represents a return and not a cost of holding savings deposits. No statistically significant effect of the savings deposit rate on the M3 aggregate is observed. Both domestic long-term rates and UK short-term rates have the expected negative effects on the real quantities of M2 demanded in both countries. Dummy variables for income and the constant term for the period 1871–1889 were included for Canada because earlier investigation (Dick and Floyd, 1992, chapter 4) indicated a sharp increase in money holdings, a shift toward deposit banking, and a general decline in interest rates in Canada relative to Great Britain in the years before 1890.

Balance of payments adjustments – price–specie–flow theory

Neither the real exchange rate nor demand for money evidence enables us to distinguish between the two theories. Since the process of balance of payments adjustment is very different under the two approaches, the empirical evidence on the determination of international reserve flows sets up the required direct confrontation. We begin by estimating the model of real international reserve flows implied by the price–specie–flow theory. The appropriate estimating equation is (2) with an error term added.

$$RRF = \alpha_0 + \alpha_1 q + \alpha_2 Y + \alpha_3 Y^* + \alpha_4 DSB + \alpha_5 N_L + \alpha_6 (r - r^*) + u_t, \quad (22)$$

where $RRF\,(= 1/P \cdot dR/dt)$ is the real reserve flow or real balance of payments surplus and u_t is an error term. It is also useful to estimate the balance of trade as a function of the real exchange rate, domestic and foreign incomes and the real long-term net capital inflow

Table 8.2 *Demand for money regressions, 1871–1913*

	Australia			Canada
	(1) Real M1	(2) Real M2	(3) Real M3	(4) Real M2
Constant	−4.06 (−11.12)	−4.73 (−9.48)	−5.01 (−10.61)	−3.99 (−17.35)
Domestic long-term bond rate	−0.12 (−3.52)	−0.27 (−5.49)	−0.20 (−4.45)	−0.18 (−7.09)
Domestic savings deposit rate	−0.17 (−5.95)	+0.08 (2.05)	−0.03 (−0.93)	
UK treasury bill rate	−0.04 (−2.75)	−0.12 (−5.71)	−0.11 (−5.67)	−0.055 (−5.44)
Domestic real income	0.85 (17.74)	1.08 (16.48)	1.20 (19.32)	1.53 (45.77)
Real income dummy[a]				−0.50 (−7.09)
Constant dummy[a]				3.11 (6.64)
Observations	43	43	43	43
R^2	0.97	0.95	0.97	0.997
Standard error	0.08	0.11	0.10	0.05
DW	1.22	0.88	0.85	2.49

Notes:
Figures in brackets are *t*-ratios.
All variables but interest rates are in logarithms.
[a] The dummy variable takes a value of 1.0 for 1871–1889 and a value of zero for the remaining years.
Sources: See data appendix (p. 251).

$$RBT = \beta_0 + \beta_1 q + \beta_2 Y + \beta_3 Y^* + \beta_4 N_L + v_t, \tag{23}$$

where RBT is the real balance of trade and v_t is an error term. The inclusion of the long-term real net capital flow in the balance of trade regression takes account of direct effects of real investment flows on exports and imports. The two theories have the same predictions about the effects of relative price levels and incomes on the balance of trade. The portfolio theory also predicts that $\alpha_1 = \alpha_2 = \alpha_3 = \alpha_4 = \alpha_5 = \alpha_6 = 0$, while the price–specie–flow theory predicts that $\alpha_1 = \beta_1, \alpha_2 = \beta_2$, and $\alpha_3 = \beta_3$. These latter predictions arise because under the specie–flow theory the balance of trade and real net capital inflow are additive components of the balance of payments, each determined by separate factors, whereas under the portfolio theory the balance of payments surplus is matched exclusively by an excess of actual savings over autonomous savings resulting from banks' desired real reserve accumulations.

The results are presented in table 8.3. The real balance of trade equations for Australia in columns (1) and (2) indicate the expected significant negative coefficients for the real exchange rate variable as well as significant and correctly signed coefficients for the domestic and rest of world income variables. The real long-term net capital inflow variable is also statistically significant with the expected negative sign. The results for Canada in columns (6) and (7) show all the independent variables but the long-term real net capital inflow variable correctly signed and significant – the latter variable is not statistically significant.

The real reserve flow equation for Austalia in column (3) indicates insignificance of all variables except the long-term interest rate differential, although the signs are as predicted by the specie–flow theory. In the Canadian real reserve flow regression in column (8) the real exchange rate variable is insignificant as expected, but the two real income variables and the real net capital flow are significant with the signs predicted by the specie–flow theory. The long-term interest rate differential was used instead of the short-term interest rate differential because no appropriate domestic short-term rates were available for either country. It is questionable whether the Montreal call loan rate, the only available rate for Canada, is a short-term rate at all, and the only available Australian short-term rate is a savings deposit rate which is not comparable with the UK treasury bill rate. While some of the signs are as predicted by the price–specie–flow theory, and significant coefficients are obtained for the real income and long-term real net capital inflow variables in the Canadian case and the long-term interest rate differential in the Australian case, one cannot describe the fit as a good one, given R^2 values in 0.2 to 0.35 range (columns (8) and (3) respectively in table 8.3).

Tests of cross-equation restrictions

Because the portfolio and specie–flow theories have quite different implications with respect to the coefficients of the real exchange rate and income variables in the balance of trade and balance of payments equations it is useful to test the restrictions proposed by the two theories. Accordingly, the real reserve flow and balance of trade equations were estimated as a system using the seemingly unrelated regression (SUR)

Table 8.3 *Real reserve flow regressions, price–specie–flow theory, 1872–1913*

	Australia					Canada				
	Real trade account balance		Real reserve flow	SUR[b]		Real trade account balance		Real reserve flow	SUR	
				trade balance	reserve flow				trade balance	reserve flow
	(1)	(2)	(3)	(4)	(5)	(6)	(7)	(8)	(9)	(10)
Constant	151.5 (3.79)[c]	150.6 (4.09)	0.24 (0.01)	148.5 (4.05)	0.24 (0.01)	34.33 (1.07)	35.15 (1.08)	31.83 (−0.67)	55.91 (1.54)	−31.83 (−0.74)
Real exchange rate	−1.53 (−4.38)	−1.46 (−4.53)	−0.20 (−0.83)	−1.42 (−4.81)	−0.20 (−0.91)	−1.06 (−4.75)	−1.09 (−4.75)	0.03 (0.10)	−1.12 (−4.46)	0.03 (0.11)
Domestic real income	−0.39 (−2.94)	−0.29 (−2.30)	0.08 (0.89)	−0.22 (−1.92)	0.08 (0.98)	−2.60 (−10.24)	−2.70 (−7.17)	−1.03 (−2.00)	−2.52 (−6.45)	−1.03 (−2.20)
Rest of world real income	0.62 (3.64)	0.50 (3.11)	−0.01 (−0.06)	0.31 (2.00)	−0.01 (−0.06)	3.42 (8.59)	3.53 (6.90)	1.36 (1.91)	3.26 (6.02)	1.36 (2.09)
Real long-term net capital inflow		−0.45 (−2.80)	1.00 (0.77)	−0.64 (−4.03)	1.00 (0.85)		0.04 (0.38)	0.33 (2.26)	0.07 (0.64)	0.36 (2.47)
Long-term interest rate differential[a]			11.67 (3.02)	−2.11 (−0.44)	11.67 (3.30)			−4.06 (−0.27)	−5.99 (−0.525)	−4.06 (−0.30)
Net repatriated earnings			−0.09 (−0.47)	−0.62 (−2.54)	−0.01 (−0.51)			0.007 (0.021)	0.176 (0.73)	0.007 (0.023)
Observations	42	42	42	42	42	42	42	42	42	42
R^2	0.76	0.80	0.33	0.83	0.33	0.92	0.92	0.22	0.92	0.22

Table 8.3 (cont.)

	Australia					Canada				
	Real trade account balance		Real reserve flow	SUR[b] trade balance	SUR[b] reserve flow	Real trade account balance		Real reserve flow	SUR trade balance	SUR reserve flow
	(1)	(2)	(3)	(4)	(5)	(6)	(7)	(8)	(9)	(10)
Standard error	8.81	8.11	5.67	7.67	5.67	12.57	12.70	15.40	12.88	15.40
DW	1.29	1.49	2.20	1.83	2.20	1.69	1.67	2.53	1.65	2.53

Notes:

[a] The long-term interest rate differential equals long-term Australian rates *minus* long-term UK rates.

[b] Regressions obtained using the seemingly unrelated regression (SUR) technique.

[c] Figures in brackets are *t*-ratios.

Sources: See data appendix (p. 251).

Table 8.4 *Tests of cross-equation restrictions, price–specie–flow theory, 1872–1913*

	Australia	Canada
The coefficients of the real exchange rate and real income variables are the same in the balance of trade and balance of payments equations	$\chi^2(3)=41.72\ (0.00000)$	$\chi^2(3)=23.07\ (0.00004)$
The coefficients of all variables in the balance of payments equation except the constant term are zero	$\chi^2(6)=20.81\ (0.002)$	$\chi^2(6)=12.15\ (0.060)$
The coefficients of the real exchange rate and real income variables in the balance of payments equation are zero	$\chi^2(3)=9.24\ (0.026)$	$\chi^2(3)=4.97\ (0.174)$

Notes:
Figures in brackets are the *P*-values.

technique. The regression results for Australia are shown in columns (4) and (5) of table 8.3 and those for Canada are shown in columns (9) and (10). The results of the tests of restrictions are presented in table 8.4. The portfolio theory hypothesis that the coefficients of the real exchange rate and real income variables in the balance of payments equation are zero can be rejected for Australia but not for Canada. The portfolio theory hypothesis that the coefficients of all variables in the balance of payments equation except the constant term are zero is rejected for Australia but cannot be rejected for Canada. Finally the hypothesis that the coefficients of the real exchange rate and real income variables are the same in the balance of trade and balance of payments equations is overwhelmingly rejected for both countries. On balance, this evidence provides support for the portfolio theory and not for the price–specie–flow theory.

Balance of payments adjustments – portfolio theory

(17) can be reworked to obtain an estimating equation for the portfolio theory by converting it into first differences, dividing all terms by P_{t-1}, and

transforming the partial derivatives of the demand function for money with respect to Y and r_t^* into elasticity form

$$\frac{(R_t - R_{t-1})}{P_{t-1}} = \frac{R_{t-1}}{P_{t-1}} \frac{(P_t - P_{t-1})}{P_{t-1}} + \eta \frac{R_{t-1}}{P_{t-1}} (r_t^* - r_{t-1}^*) + \epsilon \frac{R_{t-1}}{P_{t-1}} \frac{(Y_t - Y_{t-1})}{Y_{t-1}}$$
$$+ \frac{R_{t-1}}{P_{t-1}} \frac{(\delta_t - \delta_{t-1})}{\delta_{t-1}} + u_t \qquad (24)$$

where η is the interest semi-elasticity of demand for money (relative change in the quantity of money demanded for a given absolute change in the interest rate differential), ϵ is the income elasticity of demand for money, and u_t is an i.i.d. error term with zero mean and constant variance. For the reasons noted earlier, a dummy variable taking a value of unity for 1871–1889 and zero for 1890–1913 is also included in the Canadian regressions.

Estimates of (24) are presented in table 8.5. In regressions (1), (2), (9), and (10) the money multiplier variable is dropped. These regressions determine the reserve flow as a function of changes in interest rates and real income. The regressions that include a money multiplier variable allow that variable to take care of the influence of changes in the public's desired cash/deposit ratio and the banking system's desired reserve/deposit ratio on reserve flows, leaving the interest rate and income variables to explain only the influence on real reserve flows of changes in desired money holdings. The results for Canada are exactly as the portfolio theory would predict, although the dummy variable is insignificant. The coefficient of the price variable is insignificantly different from unity in regressions (9) and (11) and the results change very little when it is constrained to equal unity in regressions (10) and (12). The coefficient of the money multiplier variable is insignficantly different from minus unity in regressions (11) and (12), indicating that proportional changes in the multiplier lead to proportional changes in reserve flows in the opposite direction. This suggests that variations in the money multiplier tended to be independent of those variations in the demand for money that are not explained by real income and the interest rate. Positive shifts of the demand function for money, for example, that tend to occur simultaneously with decreases in the money multiplier will result in observed increases in reserves that are proportionally greater than the decrease in the money multiplier. When the money multiplier is dropped, the coefficient of the interest rate variable gets larger in absolute value and more significant and the coefficient of the income variable gets smaller and less significant.

In the Australian regressions that include a money multiplier variable, the broad money multiplier variables are insignificantly different from minus unity while the M1 multiplier is significantly above minus unity. The

Table 8.5 *Real reserve flow regressions – portfolio theory, 1872–1913*

	Australia								Canada			
	(1)	(2)	(3)	(4)	(5)	(6)	(7)	(8)	(9)	(10)	(11)	(12)
Constant	3.28 (3.05)	2.55 (2.08)	2.70 (3.34)	2.44 (3.04)	1.96 (3.17)	1.73 (2.87)	2.33 (4.33)	2.25 (4.35)	4.16 (1.88)	4.64 (2.16)	3.71 (2.68)	3.78 (2.83)
Price level variable	−0.70 (−1.57)	1.0	0.42 (1.08)	1.0	0.60 (2.07)	1.0	0.84 (3.20)	1.0	1.89 (2.09)	1.0	1.13 (1.97)	1.0
Interest rate variable	0.05 (2.72)	0.02 (1.27)	0.02 (1.37)	0.01 (0.75)	0.002 (0.16)	−0.01 (−0.61)	−0.004 (−0.35)	−0.007 (−0.78)	−0.23 (−5.93)	−0.23 (−6.00)	−0.11 (−3.98)	−0.11 (−4.03)
Real income variable	0.004 (0.02)	−0.01 (−0.05)	0.03 (0.19)	0.03 (0.18)	0.10 (0.73)	0.10 (0.75)	0.15 (1.18)	0.15 (1.22)	0.47 (0.92)	0.70 (1.52)	1.17 (3.50)	1.20 (4.13)
M1 multiplier variable			−0.68 (−5.57)	−0.78 (−7.29)								
M2 multiplier variable					−0.89 (−9.16)	−0.96 (−11.18)					−1.001 (−7.67)	−1.001 (−7.92)
M3 multiplier variable							−0.97 (−10.85)	−0.99 (−13.40)				
Dummy variable[c]									−1.29 (0.87)	−1.71 (−1.19)	−0.32 (−0.34)	−0.38 (−0.42)
Observations	42	42	42	42	42	42	42	42	42	42	42	42
R^2	0.18	0.04	0.55	0.60	0.75	0.78	0.80	0.82	0.56	0.53	0.83	0.83

Table 8.5 (*cont.*)

	Australia								Canada			
	(1)	(2)	(3)	(4)	(5)	(6)	(7)	(8)	(9)	(10)	(11)	(12)
Standard error	6.02	6.99	4.50	4.57	3.38	3.42	2.99	2.96	11.32	11.31	7.07	6.98
DW	1.91	1.84	1.47	1.44	1.22	1.24	1.17	1.21	2.31	2.22	2.63	2.61

Notes:
[a] The dummy variable takes a value of 1.0 for 1872–1889 and a value of zero for the remaining years.
The independent variables are obtained as indicated in (22).
Figures in brackets are *t*-ratios;
Sources: See data appendix (p. 251).

price level variable is always insignificantly different from unity in these regressions. The interest rate and income variables are always insignificant. When no money multiplier variable is included and the price level coefficient is constrained to unity, neither the income nor interest rate variables are significant. When the price level is not constrained to equal unity it is significantly less than unity and the interest rate variable becomes significant with the wrong sign. The standard errors of all real reserve flow regressions that include a money multiplier variable are lower than those in the price–specie–flow real reserve flow regressions in table 8.3, indicating that the portfolio theory explains real reserve flows better than the specie–flow theory. The Australian regressions that exclude the money multiplier produce higher standard errors than the specie–flow regressions in table 8.3. This is an indication that the real income and interest rate variables do a perverse job of explaining the evolution of bank reserves and the public's cash holdings.

The poor performance of the interest rate and income variables in the Australian regressions suggests that the differencing implicit in (24) removes much of the low-frequency variation in the data and amplifies the noise. Accordingly, it is useful to estimate a real reserve stock equation of the form suggested by (16), regressing the real stock of reserves on the UK treasury bill rate, real income and the money multiplier. Then by dropping the money multiplier variable, the real reserve stock can be estimated strictly as a function of the UK treasury bill rate and income, assigning these variables the task of explaining not only the quantity of money demanded but the money multiplier as well. The results are shown in table 8.6. For comparability of the results with the demand for money estimates in table 8.2, an Australian regression that includes the domestic short-term and long-term interest rates but not a money multiplier variable is shown in column (2). The fit in all cases is excellent except for specification error indicated by the low DW-statistics. Dickey–Fuller-tests indicate that the residuals are marginally stationary or better in all cases.[7] Of course, the results in table 8.6 cannot be used to directly compare the portfolio and specie–flow theories since the dependent variables in tables 8.3 and 8.6 are different.

Nonnested hypotheses tests

A final set of tests of the relative performance of the two theories in explaining the data is the nonnested hypotheses tests summarized in table 8.7. These are performed by pooling the independent variables of (22) and (23) to give a single estimating regression for real reserve flows. Two categories of tests are made: (a) that under the null hypothesis that the portfolio theory

Table 8.6 *Real reserve stock regressions[a] – portfolio theory, 1872–1913*

	Australia					Canada	
	(1)	(2)	(3)	(4)	(5)	(6)	(7)
Constant	−7.08	−1.46	−0.05	−0.57	−0.66	−9.87	−4.56
	(−9.39)[b]	(−1.63)	(−0.09)	(−0.84)	(−1.18)	(−10.75)	(−9.35)
UK treasury bill rate	−0.21	−0.19	−0.03	−0.14	−0.10	−0.20	−0.61
	(−3.80)	(−5.32)	(−1.12)	(−5.07)	(−4.29)	(−4.85)	(−3.38)
Domestic short-term rate		−0.32					
		(−4.64)					
Domestic long-term rate		−0.23					
		(−2.63)					
Domestic real income	2.03	1.42	0.734	1.06	1.15	2.12	1.52
	(15.59)	(11.83)	(7.21)	(9.79)	(13.80)	(5.26)	(23.50)
M1 multiplier			−1.51				
			(−14.8)				
M2 multiplier				−1.10			−0.99
				(−11.21)			(−15.25)
M3 multiplier					−1.37		
					(−13.90)		
Constant dummy[b]						6.31	1.39
						(3.79)	(1.99)
Real income dummy[b]						−0.97	−0.25
						(−3.75)	(−2.38)
Observations	42	42	42	42	42	42	42
R^2	0.87	0.95	0.98	0.97	0.98	0.96	0.99
Standard error	0.30	0.19	0.11	0.14	0.12	0.19	0.07
DW	0.46	1.10	1.22	0.63	0.84	1.31	1.20

Notes:
[a] The dependent variable is the log of the real stock of international reserves.
[b] The constant dummy variable takes a value of 1.0 for 1872–1889 and a value of zero for the remaining years. The real income dummy equals the real income variable for the years 1872–1889 and takes a value of zero otherwise.
Figures in brackets are *t*-ratios.
All variables but interest rates are in logarithms.
Sources: See data appendix (p. 251).

Table 8.7 *Nonnested hypotheses tests, 1872–1913*

	Australia		Canada	
(a) Null hypothesis: portfolio theory				
–F-test of means				
using M1	$F(6,31)=1.70$	(0.15)		
using M2	$F(6,31)=2.10$	(0.08)	$F(6,30)=4.15$	(0.004)
using M3	$F(6,31)=4.58$	(0.002)		
–J-test of conditional variance				
using M1	$F(1,36)=6.08$	(0.019)		
using M2	$F(1,36)=0.099$	(0.75)	$F(1,35)=17.68$	(0.000)
using M3	$F(1,36)=0.404$	(0.53)		
–CPE-test				
using M1	$F(6,37)=1.52$	(0.20)		
using M2	$F(6,37)=1.78$	(0.13)	$F(6,36)=2.72$	(0.03)
using M3	$F(6,37)=2.90$	(0.02)		
(b) null hypothesis: price–specie–flow theory				
–F-test of means				
using M1	$F(4,31)=7.69$	(0.000)		
using M2	$F(4,31)=21.33$	(0.000)	$F(5,30)=44.62$	(0.000)
using M3	$F(4,31)=42.14$	(0.000)		
–J-test of conditional variance				
using M1	$F(1,34)=30.54$	(0.000)		
using M2	$F(1,34)=84.15$	(0.000)	$F(1,34)=177.35$	(0.000)
using M3	$F(1,34)=146.41$	(0.000)		
–CPE-test				
using M1	$F(4,35)=4.36$	(0.006)		
using M2	$F(4,35)=6.42$	(0.000)	$F(5,36)=6.17$	(0.000)
using M3	$F(4,35)=7.39$	(0.000)		

Notes:
Figures in brackets are the *P*-values.

is true, the Classical variables contribute nothing beyond what the portfolio variables explain, and (b) that under the null hypothesis that the Classical theory is true, the portfolio variables contribute nothing beyond what the Classical variables explain. These categories represent the predictions of each of the respective theories about coefficients in the other theory. Within each category, three tests are performed – *F*-tests on the means, *J*-tests on the conditional variances, and complete parameter encompassing (CPE) tests on the means and conditional variances combined.[8] Evidence supporting our theory is evidence that rejects (b) but not (a) or rejects (b) more strongly than it rejects (a).

The null hypotheses (b) is overwhelmingly rejected for both countries. The evidence does not support the predictions of the price–specie–flow theory. The evidence also rejects at the 5 percent level the predictions of the portfolio theory in null hypothesis (a) in every test for Canada and for Australia in the J-test when the M1 money multiplier is used and in the other two tests when the M3 money multiplier is used. In all cases in table 8.7 where (a) is rejected, the corresponding rejection of (b) is possible at much lower significance levels. These results, therefore, provide strong evidence against the price–specie–flow theory and in favor of the portfolio theory.

We also test a further hypothesis: that the coefficient of the price variable suggested by the portfolio theory is unity and the coefficients of all variables suggested by the price–specie–flow theory are zero. We tested in table 8.4 the hypothesis that all variables in the specie–flow theory were zero, but this was in a regression that did not include the portfolio theory variables. Similarly, we tested in table 8.5 the hypothesis that the price variable is unity in the portfolio theory regressions but those regressions did not include the price–specie–flow variables. Here we test the hypothesis that the price level coefficient implied by the portfolio theory is unity and the coefficients of the price–specie–flow variables are all zero in a regression that contains both the portfolio and price–specie–flow variables. This hypothesis can be rejected for Canada but, except where the M3 money multiplier is used, not for Australia.[9]

It is interesting that these nonnested hypotheses tests provide more support for the portfolio theory for Australia than they do for Canada. This is in contrast to the tests of restrictions which provided more support for the portfolio theory in Canada than they did in Australia. Overall, the tests come out quite strongly in favor of the portfolio theory over the price–specie–flow mechanism.

Conclusions

This study has reinterpreted Australian and Canadian monetary experience between 1870 and 1913 in terms of a portfolio model of balance of payments adjustment that treats asset markets in a worldwide general equilibrium framework with imperfect capital mobility. Both the Australian and Canadian evidence is shown to be more consistent with the portfolio than the price–specie–flow mechanism of adjustment.

It is notable that Australia and Canada both shared close economic ties with Great Britain and experienced similar kinds of shocks, though at different times, within the 1870–1913 period. Canada enjoyed her biggest surge of capital imports only after 1900 while Australia absorbed her largest capital inflow in the 1880s – in both cases the capital imports coincided with different episodes of weak investment demand in Great Britain. Notwithstanding these differences in timing, the same process of balance of payments adjustment appears to have been at work. While there are some differences in the details of relative price experience between the two countries, it remains the case for both that net capital inflow dominated the movement of the real exchange rate supporting the notion that there was a positive real relative price effect from net capital inflow in capital receiving countries. In the tests designed to discriminate between the two approaches to balance of payments adjustment, the most comprehensive tests (CPE tests) show that the Australian evidence supports the portfolio approach even more strongly than does the Canadian evidence.

The possibility that the adjustment processes for Australia and Canada were jointly dependent, inasmuch as both shared the same capital market and traded substantially with Great Britain, was considered. Although little statistical evidence of interdependence was found, it remains plausible that Canada became a substitute outlet for surplus British savings in the early 20th century. Extension to incorporate still other contemporaneous gold standard experiences may well reveal correlations among equation disturbances as more of the world capital market is taken into account.

The result that both Canada and Australia together provide strong evidence in support of the portfolio approach provides considerably stronger warrant for a reinterpretation of how the gold standard really operated than previous separate and unintegrated studies for these two countries that used somewhat less refined data and lacked a common theoretical approach. Serious doubt is cast on the long-standing view that governments or central banks played by "the rules of the game." Money supplies in small countries like Canada and Australia, where no banks were performing central banking functions in our period, were endogenous under the gold standard so that gold flows could not have been sterilized. The gold standard, in effect, imposed a constraint on these countries making their price levels virtually independent of their control in both the long and short runs. Prices were not unchanging during the gold standard era, but it was the international mobility of capital rather than adherence to any rules that made the system function smoothly (Dick and Floyd, 1992, 170–174). The results of our study give one plausible interpretation of the role of capital mobility and endogenous money akin to that first suggested by Ford (1962) who sparked an ongoing debate over the role played by the Bank of England in the operation of the gold standard (Broadberry and Crafts, 1992, 1–9).

The conclusions here are also supported by those of Calomiris and Hubbard in chapter 7 in this volume. They found that gold flows between the United States and the United Kingdom responded rapidly to shocks to the demand for gold and that interest rate differentials remained small, even in the presence of seasonal demand for money fluctuations in the United States. Their vector autoregression (VAR) results also indicated that shocks to the domestic gold supply were not an important source of output and price level variations.

It is also significant that both Canada and Australia remained on the gold standard throughout the period notwithstanding the fact that Australia suffered what amounted to a secular depression at the end of 19th century not matched by Canada's experience before 1900 (Green and Urquhart, 1987, 195). The combined results for both countries transcend the traditional distinction between long and short runs and demonstrate a speed of adjustment using annual data that is consistent with the portfolio theory for both countries. Such an outcome invites consideration of yet more extreme examples, like Argentina, where the setback experienced in the 1890s was severe enough to drive the economy off the gold standard. How this experience may have been related to international capital mobility and what factors made the gold standard a less durable monetary regime in this case are worthwhile topics for further research. Both Australia and Argentina had serious banking crises in the 1890s that Canada avoided, yet the Argentine economy behaved very differently to Australia with respect to the gold standard (Dick and Floyd, 1993; Pope, 1987a; Della Paolera, 1988; Taylor, 1992; Calomiris, 1992).

Data appendix

Real output series for Canada and Australia are based on the nominal output estimates of Urquhart (1986) and Butlin (1962) respectively with deflation based, for Canada, on historical series of traded and nontraded goods' prices from Dick and Floyd (1992), and for Australia, on an implicit deflator from Butlin (1962). The Canadian output series are based on extensive work of revision by Urquhart (1986, 1993). Real GNP data and the corresponding implicit deflator for the rest of the world rely on aggregates that include the United States, the United Kingdom, Italy, Germany, France, Norway, and Sweden as described in the appendixes of Dick and Floyd (1992).

The balance of payments data are drawn mainly from the national accounts estimates augmented by some additional series for international capital flows. For both countries, net capital flows are an indirect estimate based on the negative of the trade and debt service balances combined. For

Canada, long-term autonomous inflows are new estimates based on Urquhart (1986). For Australia, autonomous long-term capital inflow was less clearly isolated in the national accounts estimates. A series of company and new issues floated in London appeared to meet this defintion best (Hall, 1963a).

Money stock data for Canada are provided by Rich (1988). Money (an M2 definition) consists of Canadian dollar bank deposits held by Canadian residents, chartered bank notes held by the public and the Government of Canada, and Dominion notes held by the public in Canada. Data for the Australian money supply include series for M1 (private bank and Queensland treasury notes, gold, silver and bronze coin in the hands of the public *plus* current deposits of the trading banks), for M2 (M1 *plus* fixed deposits of the trading banks), and for M3 (M2 *plus* savings bank deposits) as reconstructed from official sources by Pope (1986, 1987b) and Schedvin (1973), and first assembled by Butlin, Hall and White (1971). The rest of the world money supply is a weighted sum of indexes of nominal money in the United States, the United Kingdom, France, Germany, Italy, Norway, and Sweden constructed from Mitchell (1975). The components of this aggregate typically include government notes and currency, demand and time deposits of banks, and savings bank deposits.

International reserves for both Australia and Canada consist of both primary (gold and foreign exchange) and secondary (short-term liquid claims on foreign banks) components. For Australia, gold flows are tabulated in the balance of payments (Butlin, 1962), and secondary reserves before 1877 can only be measured by London funds (Pope, 1986; Schedvin, 1973; Butlin, Hall and White, 1971). After 1877, we use adjusted foreign cash balances as estimated by Pope (1986) using Sheppard (1971). For Canada, Rich (1988) provides revised data on gold, while secondary reserves are based on call loans of banks held abroad *plus* net claims on foreign banks as tabulated by Rich (1988).

Interest rates were selected to proxy the rate payable on Canadian and Australian securities marketed in London, the primary source of long-term capital. For Canada, we use the average rate on Canadian sterling bonds reported in Neufeld (1972). There is no appropriate short-term rate. For Australia, we use long-term government bond yields and proxy the short-term rate with a savings bank deposit rate. Both Australian interest rate series are provided by Pope (1987b). World interest rates are taken to be the average of the rates obtained in New York and London, as described in Dick and Floyd (1992).

The real exchange rates are based on the ratio of domestic to the rest of the world prices brought to domestic currency using nominal exchange rates. The Canadian price level is a consumer price index assumed to proxy aggregate output prices while the price levels for Australia and the rest of the world are income deflators. The Canadian and Australian price series are described in Dick and Floyd (1992) and in Butlin (1962). The nominal exchange rates between the Canadian and Australian dollars and the rest of the world are based on trade weighted indexes of exchange rates for the US dollar and UK pound. These remained unchanged over the period except for the greenback era from 1871 to 1879 when the variability was based on the gold premium recorded by Mitchell (1908).

Terms of trade data were taken from Urquhart and Buckley (1965) and from Bambrick (1970).

Notes

We would like to thank Gordon Anderson, Jack Carr, Allan Hynes, Gary Koop, and Angelo Melino for helpful comments.

1. Interest parity implies that
    $$i - i^* = \psi + \rho_X,$$
    where ψ is the forward discount on domestic currency and ρ_X is the premium for political and security-specific risks. Efficient markets implies that
    $$\psi = \rho_T + E_\pi,$$
    where ρ_T is the risk premium on forward domestic currency. These two equations plus the Fisher equations yield (1) and (4) above, with the consolidated risk premium equal to
    $$\rho = \rho_X + \rho_T.$$
    This relationship is derived many places in the international monetary economics literature (e.g. Obstfeld, 1986; Cumby, 1988).

2. Our approach differs from a number of contemporary models of international portfolio equilibrium (See, for example, Dornbusch, 1975; Frankel, 1983; Branson and Henderson, 1985; and Frenkel and Mussa, 1985). These models formulate issues in terms of a wealth aggregate composed of four assets consisting of domestic money, foreign money, domestic bonds, and foreign bonds, where the quantities of all aggregates are defined as their present values. Demand functions for the respective assets are then constructed with interest rates and the aggregate present value of wealth as arguments. Given the exogenously determined (in the short run) supplies of the assets, the system of equations solves for the domestic and foreign interest rates and the portfolio shares. This type of formulation focuses on the effects of changes in government debt and official reserve holdings in a world of Ricardian nonequivalance. It largely ignores international exchange in real capital assets. Our purposes do not require an explicit definition of aggregate wealth. Moreover, we deal with a time period in which foreign exchange reserves were largely private assets both in Australia and Canada and fiscal policy involving substitutions of bond for tax finance was of little consequence in either country. Government gold holdings accounted for less than 15 percent of foreign exchange reserves in Canada before

1890, rising to 30 percent by 1907 and 35 percent by 1913. In Australia, government gold holdings constituted a trivial fraction of international reserves before 1910 but rose to 100 percent shortly thereafter. The usual wealth effects that drive contemporary models were therefore not present, and international capital transfers took the form of direct or indirect claims on real capital.

3.   In a classical world the equations solve for P, and in a simplified Keynesian world for Y. More generally, of course, a relationship between P and Y can be incorporated to allow the two variables to be solved for simultaneously and incorporate deeper issues regarding so-called "price stickiness." Our analytical framework is consistent with a wide variety of alternative models of wage and price setting, requiring only that any "unemployment" represent an equilibrium, however short-term and nonoptimal.

4.   In neither country did the government have any control over the stock of money through its note issue. The quantity of government notes held depended on the public's and the banking system's demand for them – any excess would be converted into gold. This convertibility enables us to apply our theoretical model without explicitly separating government and private note issue.

5.   For a review of this point see Blanchard and Fischer (1989, 510–512) as well as the references cited in n. 1.

6.   For a useful historical survey, see Viner (1937, chapters 6 and 7).

7.   For details on the application of these tests see Dickey and Fuller (1981) and Engle and Granger (1987).

8.   See Mizon and Richard (1986) for details about the construction and interpretation of CPE tests. For details on the use of J-tests, see Davidson and MacKinnon (1981).

9. $F(7,31)$ values of 1.20, 1.31, and 3.50 are obtained in the cases where the M1, M2, and M3 multipliers are used for Australia. The corresponding P-values are 0.331, 0.277, and 0.007. An $F(7,30)$ value of 3.59 and a corresponding P-value of 0.006 is obtained for Canada.

References

Angell, J. W. (1925a). "The Effects of International Payments in the Past," in *The Inter-Ally Debts and the United States*, National Industrial Conference Board, New York: NICB, 138–189

(1925b). "Review of Canada's Balance of International Indebtedness 1900–1913," *Political Science Quarterly* 40 (June), 320–322

(1925c). *The Theory of International Prices: History, Criticism and Restatement*, Cambridge, MA: Harvard University Press

Bambrick, S. (1970). "Australia's Long-run Terms of Trade," *Economic Development and Cultural Change* 19 (October), 1–5

Beach, W. (1935). *British International Gold Movements and Banking Policy, 1881–1913*, Cambridge, MA: Harvard University Press

Blanchard, O. J. and S. Fisher (1989). *Lectures on Macroeconomics*, Cambridge, MA: MIT Press, 279–283, 506–512

Bordo, M. D. (1984). "The Gold Standard: The Traditional Approach," in M. D. Bordo and A. J. Schwartz (eds.), *A Retrospective on the Classical Gold Standard, 1821–1931*, Chicago: University of Chicago Press for NBER, 23–199

Branson, W. H. and D. Henderson (1985). "The Specification and Influence of Asset Markets," in R. W. Jones and Peter B. Kenen (eds.), *Handbook of International Economics, II*, Amsterdam: North-Holland, 749–805

Broadberry, S. N. and N. F. R. Crafts (1992). "British Macroeconomic History 1870–1939: Overview and Key Issues," in S. N. Broadberry and N. F. R. Crafts (eds.), *Britain in the International Economy, 1870–1939*, New York: Cambridge University Press, 1–27

Butlin, N. G. (1962). *Australian Domestic Product, Investment and Foreign Borrowing 1861–1938/39*, Cambridge: Cambridge University Press

   (1964). *Investment in Australian Economic Development 1861–1900*, Cambridge: Cambridge University Press

   (1987). "Australian National Accounts," in W. Vamplew (ed.), *Australian Historical Statistics*, Sydney: Fairfax, Syme & Weldon, 126–144, 453–454

Butlin, S. J. (1986). *The Australian Monetary System 1851–1914*, Sydney: Reserve Bank of Australia

Butlin, S. J., A. R. Hall and R. C. White (1971). "Australian Banking and Monetary Statistics 1817–1945," Reserve Bank of Australia, *Occasional Paper* 4A, Sydney

Cain, N. (1970). "Trade and Economic Structure at the Periphery: The Australian Balance of Payments, 1890–1965," in C. Forster (ed.), *Australian Economic Development in the Twentieth Century*, London: Allen & Unwin, 66–122

Calomiris, C. W. (1992). "Regulation, Industrial Structure, and Instability in US Banking: An Historical Perspective," in M. Klausner, and L. J. White (eds.), *Structural Change in Banking*, Homewood, IL: Business One Irwin, 19–116

Cumby, R. (1988). "Is it Risk? Explaining the Deviations from Covered Interest Parity," *Journal of Monetary Economics* 22, 279–299

Davidson, R. and J. G. MacKinnon (1981). "Several Tests for Model Specification in the Presence of Alternative Hypotheses," *Econometrica* 49, 781–793

Della Paolera, G. (1988). "How the Argentine Economy Performed During the International Gold Standard: A Reexamination," unpublished Ph.D. thesis, Department of Economics, University of Chicago

Dick, T. J. O. and J. E. Floyd (1991). "Balance of Payments Adjustment under the International Gold Standard: Canada, 1871–1913," *Explorations in Economic History* 28 (April), 209–238

   (1992). *Canada and the Gold Standard: 1871–1913*, New York: Cambridge University Press

   (1993). "Canada and the Gold Standard, 1871–1914: A Durable Monetary Regime," in M. D. Bordo and F. Capie (eds.), *Monetary Regimes in Transition*, New York: Cambridge University Press

Dickey, D. A. and W. Fuller (1981). "Likelihood Ratio Statistics for Autoregressive Time Series with a Unit Root," *Econometrica* 49(4) (July), 1057–1072

Dornbusch, R. (1975). "A Portfolio Balance Model of the Open Economy," *Journal of Monetary Economics* 1, 3–20

Drummond, I. (1959). "Capital Markets in Canada and Australia, 1895–1914," unpublished Ph.D. thesis, Department of Economics, Yale University

(1991). "Banks and Banking in Canada and Australia," in R. Cameron and V. I. Bovykin (eds.), *International Banking, 1870–1914*, New York: Oxford University Press, 189–213

Edelstein, M. (1982). *Overseas Investment in the Age of High Imperialism: The United Kingdom 1850–1914*, New York: Columbia University Press

Edwards, S. (1989). *Real Exchange Rates, Devaluation, and Adjustment*, Cambridge, MA: MIT Press

Eichengreen, B. (1990). "Trends and Cycles in Foreign Lending," *Discussion Paper* 451, London: CEPR

Engle, R. F. and C. W. J. Granger (1987). "Co-integration and Error Correction: Representation, Estimation, and Testing," *Econometrica* 55(2) (March), 251–276

Ford, A. G. (1962). *The Gold Standard, 1880–1914: Britain and Argentina*, Oxford: Clarendon Press

Frankel, J. (1983). "Monetary and Portfolio Balance Models of Exchange Rate Determination," in J. Bhandari and B. Putnam (eds.), *Economic Interdependence and Flexible Exchange Rates*, Cambridge, MA: MIT Press, 84–115

Frenkel, J. A. and M. Mussa (1985). "Asset Markets, Exchange Rates, and the Balance of Payments," in R. W. Jones and P. B. Kenen (eds.), *Handbook of International Economics*, II, Amsterdam: North-Holland, 679–747

Gilbert, R. S. (1971). "London Financial Intermediaries and Australian Overseas Borrowing, 1990–1939," *Australian Economic History Review* 10 (March), 39–47

Green, A. and M. C. Urquhart (1976). "Factor and Commodity Flows in the International Economy of 1870–1914: A Multi-country View," *Journal of Economic History* 36 (March), 217–252

(1987). "New Estimates of Output Growth in Canada: Measurement and Interpretation," in D. McCalla (ed.), *Perspectives on Canadian Economic History*, Toronto: Copp, Clark, Pitman, 182–199

Hall, A. R. (1963a). *The London Capital Market and Australia 1870–1914*, Social Science Monographs, Canberra: Australian National University

(1963b). "Some Long Period Effects of the Kinked Age Distribution of the Population of Australia 1861–1961," *Economic Record* 39 (March), 43–52

Hall, A. R. (ed.) (1968). *The Export of Capital from Britain 1870–1914*, Debates in Economic History, London: Methuen

Hume, D. ([1752] 1898). "Of the Balance of Trade," in David Hume, *Essays, Moral, Political and Literary*, 1, London: Longmans Green, 1898, 330–341, 343–345

Johnston, J. W. (1992). "Real and Nominal Exchange Rate Determination in a Small Open Economy: An Empirical Investigation of the Canadian Case," unpublished Ph.D. dissertation, University of Toronto

Kennett, J. A. (1972). "The Australian Commercial Bank Managed Gold Exchange Standard: 1880–1913," Economic History IV thesis, University of Sydney

Kenwood, A. G. and A. L. Lougheed (1992). *The Growth of the International Economy, 1820–1990*, London: Routledge

Kouri, P. J. K. (1977). "International Investment and Interest Rate Linkages Under Flexible Exchange Rates," in R. Z. Aliber (ed.), *The Political Economy of Monetary Reform*, London: Macmillan, 74–96

Lucas, R. E., Jr. (1978). "Asset Prices in an Exchange Economy," *Econometrica* 46(6), 1426–1445

(1982). "Interest Rates and Currency Prices in a Two Country World," *Journal of Monetary Economics* 10, 335–360

McCloskey, D. N. and J. R. Zecher (1976). "How the Gold Standard Worked, 1880–1913," in J. A. Frenkel and H. G. Jonnson (eds.), *The Monetary Approach to the Balance of Payments*, London: Allen & Unwin, 357–385

(1984). "The Success of Purchasing-Power Parity: Historical Evidence and its Implications for Macroeconomics," in M. D. Bordo and A. J. Schwartz (eds.), *A Retrospective on the Classical Gold Standard, 1821–1931*, Chicago: University of Chicago Press for NBER, pp. 121–170

McLean, I. W. (1991). "Australian Saving Since 1861," in P. J. Stemp (ed.), *Saving, Policy and Growth: Conference Proceedings*, Canberra: Center for Economic Policy Research, Australian National University, 1–29

Merton, R. (1971). "Optimum Consumption and Portfolio Rules in a Continuous Time Model," *Journal of Economic Theory*, 3, 373–413

Mitchell, B. R. (1975). *European Historical Statistics, 1750–1970*, London: Macmillan

Mitchell, W. C. (1908). *Gold, Prices and Wages Under the Greenbacks Standard*, Berkeley, CA: University of California Press

Mizon G. E. and J. F. Richard (1986). "The Encompassing Principle and its Application to Non-nested Hypotheses," *Econometrica*, 54, 657–678

Neufeld, E. P. (1972). *The Financial System of Canada*, New York: St. Martin's Press

Obstfeld, M. (1986). "Capital Mobility in the World Economy: Theory and Measurement," in K. Brunner and A. Meltzer, (eds.), *The National Bureau Method, International Capital Mobility, and Other Essays*, Amsterdam: North-Holland

Pasula, K. (1992). "The Balance of Payments, The Balance of Trade, and Monetary Independence Under Bretton Woods: Perspectives from Stochastic, Maximizing Models," unpublished Ph.D. dissertation, University of Toronto

Paterson, D. G. (1976). *British Direct Investment in Canada, 1890–1914*, Toronto: University of Toronto Press

Pomfret, R. (1981). "The Staple Theory as an Approach to Canadian and Australian Economic Development," *Australian Economic History Review* 21 (September), 131–146

Pope, D. (1986). "Australian Money and Banking Statistics," *Source Papers in Economic History* 11, Canberra: Australian National University

(1987a). "Bankers and Banking Business, 1860–1914," *Working Paper* 85, Canberra: Australian National University

(1987b). "Private Finances," in W. Vamplew (ed.), *Australians: Historical Statistics*, Sydney: Fairfax, Syme & Weldon, 238–253, 456–457

(1993). "Australia's Payments Adjustment and Capital Flows Under the International Gold Standard, 1870–1913," in M. D. Bordo and F. Capie (eds.), *Monetary Regimes in Transition*, New York: Cambridge University Press

Rich, G. (1988). *The Cross of Gold: Money and the Canadian Business Cycle, 1867–1913*, Ottawa: Carleton University Press

Schedvin, C. B. (1973). "A Century of Money in Australia," *Economic Record* 49 (December), 588–605

Sheppard, D. K. (1971). *The Growth and Role of UK Financial Institutions 1880–1962*, London: Methuen

Stulz, R. (1984). "Currency Preferences, Purchasing Power Risks, and the Determination of Exchange Rates in an Optimizing Model," *Journal of Money, Credit and Banking* (August), 302–316

Taussig, F. W. ([1927] 1966). *International Trade*, New York: Kelly

Taylor, A. M. (1992). "Argentine Economic Growth in Comparative Perspective," unpublished Ph.D. thesis, Department of Economics, Harvard University

Thomas, B. (1973). *Migration and Economic Growth*, 2nd edn., Cambridge: Cambridge University Press

Urquhart, M. C. (1986). "New Estimates of Gross National Product, Canada, 1870–1926: Some Implications for Canadian Development," in R. Gallman and S. L. Engerman (eds.), *Long-term Factors in American Economic Growth, NBER Studies in Income and Wealth*, Chicago: University of Chicago Press, 9–94

(1993). *Gross National Product, Canada 1870–1926, The Derivation of the Estimates*, Kingston and Montreal: McGill–Queen's University Press

Urquhart, M. C. and K. A. H. Buckley (eds.) (1965). *Historical Statistics of Canada*, Cambridge: Cambridge University Press

Viner, J. (1924). *Canada's Balance of International Indebtedness: 1900–1913*, Cambridge, MA: Harvard University Press

(1937). *Studies in the Theory of International Trade*, New York: Harper & Bros, chapters VI and VII

White, H. D. (1933). *The French International Accounts 1880–1913*, Cambridge, MA: Harvard University Press

Williams, J. H. (1920). *Argentine International Trade Under Incontrovertible Paper Money, 1880–1913*, Cambridge, MA: Harvard University Press

Wilson, R. (1931). *Capital Imports and the Terms of Trade*, Economic Series, Melbourne: Melbourne University Press

IV

Monetary issues

9 Money demand and supply under the gold standard: the United Kingdom, 1870–1914

Forrest H. Capie and Geoffrey E. Wood

Introduction

This chapter is concerned with the behavior and determination of money demand and money supply in a particular monetary regime, the gold standard, and in a particular country, the United Kingdom. Restriction to one country plainly raises concern over how representative of the regime the results we set out may be. Although such concern is inevitable, it should not be overdone. This is partly because restriction to one country is to an extent forced on us by the data – for the United Kingdom has for this period higher-quality, more consistent and complete, data than exist for other countries under gold standard regimes. But there are more and better reasons than that for accepting the results as representative. First, they are completely unsurprising; they are as theory would lead one to expect. Second, they are from a period of comparative economic tranquillity in the United Kingdom; there is thus little chance that the results are dominated by some extraordinary, important but unique, event. There is every reason to think that the findings are what should be expected qualitatively (and quantitatively in one important respect, homogeneity of money demand with respect to the price level) in every other gold standard country.

Nonetheless, there are some institutional features which are important, and should be set out before the detailed findings are examined. These institutional features relate to the UK banking system, and to the gold standard itself. We discuss them in that order.

In the years covered in this chapter, 1870–1914, the UK banking system was evolving quite rapidly; towards the system of a few banks with nationwide branching (although some still retained a regional bias) that the United Kingdom has today. There were also changes, first in practice and then in law, regarding the disclosure of information on banks' balance sheets. These features, and the influence of them on the money supply, are captured by the base multiplier framework of analysis. This framework is set out in detail below, but it is necessary here to defend its use as the approach is unfashionable, indeed has often been rejected as inappropriate, in the United Kingdom in recent years.

The criticism commonly encountered is that reserve ratios are not imposed on British banks, and that the Bank of England does not operate by controlling the supply of monetary base. Neither of these criticisms bears on the present issue. First, the approach can be viewed simply as an accounting framework, one which shows how the banks' attitude to reserve holding and the public's to the use of cash, both varying over time, interacted in an accounting sense to determine the money supply supported by a given amount of gold. But we would argue more strongly for the period under review; banks *did* have a clear cut view of the reserves they wished to hold relative to deposits, and the public's cash holding was influenced by economic considerations (see the discussion below).

These factors do, of course, only determine the money supply given the base. Is analysis of the supply of and demand for money of any particular interest in a genuinely fixed exchange rate regime such as the gold standard? After all, in such a regime, monetary conditions are out of the hands of the domestic money authorities. Although that is often taken as meaning that the money supply is unimportant, that extension of the point is incorrect. The exchange rate regime determines the *source* of money base change, but does not render it unimportant. Changes in the quantity of money, however produced, will affect income. While income fluctuations will produce accommodating monetary flows, it is equally true (and important) that monetary flows will produce accommodating income fluctuations; we discuss this further below (p. 273).

The gold standard was different from most other regimes not only in being a fixed exchange rate system; it was different also in the way in which it influenced expectations. The price level behaved in a very stable and predictable way, moving little from year to year and, over a long period of years, moving in long swings, their length determined by variations in the demand for and supply of gold, about a level trend (see Cagan, 1984; Mills, 1990; Mills and Wood, 1992, for a discussion of this). Prices were, no doubt in part as a result of this experience, expected to be stable. This is suggested by the stability of long-term interest rates relative to short (discussed further below) and is crucial to the explanation of the Gibson Paradox (for a review and examination of all the explanations of this phenomenon, see Mills and Wood, 1992). As will emerge below price expectations play little part in explaining the demand for money under the gold standard, and the short rate is often a more satisfactory explanatory variable than the long rate; the above discussion suggests why.

Finally in this Introduction we briefly outline the structure of the chapter. There is first a discussion of the money supply data. This provides one of the reasons for their being so many estimates of a money demand relationship for this period; for, as will emerge, the data have in recent years changed substantially. Several money demand equations are then surveyed, and their similarity discussed. We then turn to the money supply and examine in turn the base multiplier framework; the determination of the money supply given the base, and how and why these determinants varied over time; and the impact of financial crises and the lender of last resort (LLR) actions to contain them on the behavior of the money supply. The chapter ends with a brief concluding overview of the main findings.

Money demand under the gold standard

The demand for money under the gold standard is in principle no different from the demand for money under any other money supply regime. The demand is determined by the convenience yield of money in its various uses, and is a demand for *real money balances* – purchasing power – not for nominal balances. Nevertheless, money demand under the gold standard is a subject both deserving separate study from other periods, and providing a benchmark which can assist interpretation of results from other periods. The reason for this is that 1870–1914, the classic years of the gold standard, is a period particularly well suited to testing the basic theory of money demand. They were years of financial stability in the United Kingdom. The economy grew steadily; prices moved slowly and indeed started and ended the period at almost the same level; and both short and long interest rates moved within a modest range. Table 9.1 and figures 9.1–9.4 summarize these data.

Further, the financial system was stable. There were no major bank failures or panics; banking spread steadily through the United Kingdom, and the banking system evolved gradually towards the form it was to take very soon after the end of World War I, a few large banks with extensive branch networks. Financial innovation, at least at the retail level, was essentially nonexistent. Hence none of the problems such innovation can cause for money demand studies was present. And finally, the data allow – or perhaps compel – a major simplification. There is little choice over which definition of money to use – one can use notes and coin, or notes and coin *plus* bank deposits. Bank deposits cannot be subdivided into interest bearing and noninterest bearing – the data are not available (see Capie and Webber, 1985).

Accordingly, money demand studies of this period test basic money demand theory, with results uncontaminated by many of the factors that have caused problems in recent years. This relative simplicity does not mean there have been few such studies. There have been several, in good part

Table 9.1 *Economic performance, United Kingdom, 1870–1914*

Year	GNP (1)	DEF (2)	Real GNP (3)	GNP (percent) (4)	RPI (5)	RPI (percent) (6)	Short (7)	Long (8)
1870	1081	92	11.75		108		3.276	3.246
1871	1184	95	12.46	6.07	111.00	2.78	2.62	3.235
1872	1244	101	12.32	−1.17	118.00	6.31	3.927	3.239
1873	1285	104	12.36	0.32	120.00	1.69	4.438	3.235
1874	1325	101	13.12	6.18	113.00	−5.83	3.5	3.242
1875	1290	97	13.30	1.37	109.00	−3.54	2.87	3.195
1876	1274	95	13.41	0.84	108.00	−0.92	1.771	3.155
1877	1251	93	13.45	0.31	108.00	0.00	2.427	3.141
1878	1238	91	13.60	1.14	102.00	−5.56	3.683	3.15
1879	1161	87	13.34	−1.91	99.00	−2.94	1.589	3.07
1880	1306	90	14.51	8.74	103.00	4.04	2.328	3.041
1881	1277	88	14.51	0.00	101.00	−1.94	2.875	2.997
1882	1318	90	14.64	0.92	100.00	−0.99	3.396	2.977
1883	1363	89	15.31	4.58	100.00	0.00	3.004	2.962
1884	1315	86	15.29	−0.16	95.00	−5.00	2.38	2.972
1885	1277	84	15.20	−0.58	89.00	−6.32	2.052	3.021
1886	1272	82	15.51	2.04	87.00	−2.25	2.062	2.967
1887	1340	83	16.14	4.08	86.00	−1.15	2.344	2.941
1888	1361	83	16.40	1.57	86.00	0.00	2.37	2.762
1889	1408	84	16.76	2.22	87.00	−1.16	2.752	2.779
1890	1455	85	17.12	2.12	87.00	0.00	3.698	2.849
1891	1498	84	17.83	4.18	87.00	0.00	2.563	2.868
1892	1470	84	17.50	−1.87	88.00	1.15	1.568	2.845
1893	1452	84	17.29	−1.22	87.00	−1.14	2.375	2.793
1894	1504	83	18.12	4.83	83.00	−4.60	1.008	2.716
1895	1530	82	18.66	2.97	81.00	−2.41	0.844	2.588
1896	1596	81	19.70	5.60	81.00	0.00	1.539	2.47
1897	1617	82	19.72	0.08	83.00	2.47	1.885	2.442
1898	1720	83	20.72	5.09	86.00	3.61	2.607	2.474
1899	1842	84	21.93	5.82	84.00	−2.33	3.274	2.574
1900	1926	90	21.40	−2.41	89.00	5.95	3.664	2.764
1901	1989	89	22.35	4.43	88.00	−1.12	3.198	2.921
1902	1964	87	22.57	1.01	88.00	0.00	3.013	2.909
1903	1963	87	22.56	−0.05	89.00	1.14	3.375	2.83
1904	1977	87	22.72	0.71	90.00	1.12	2.646	2.829
1905	2030	88	23.07	1.51	90.00	0.00	2.655	2.775
1906	2095	88	23.81	3.20	91.00	1.11	4.06	2.833
1907	2145	90	23.83	0.11	93.00	2.20	4.49	2.971
1908	2080	90	23.11	−3.03	91.00	−2.15	2.206	2.899

Table 9.1 (*cont.*)

Year	GNP (1)	DEF (2)	Real GNP (3)	GNP (percent) (4)	RPI (5)	RPI (percent) (6)	Short (7)	Long (8)
1909	2150	90	23.89	3.37	92.00	1.10	2.304	2.981
1910	2239	90	24.88	4.14	94.00	2.17	3.175	3.087
1911	2326	92	25.28	1.63	95.00	1.06	3.019	3.153
1912	2393	94	25.46	0.69	98.00	3.16	3.618	3.279
1913	2542	100	25.42	−0.15	100.00	2.04	4.365	3.391
1914	2572	95	27.07	6.51	101.00	1.00	2.951	2.991

Sources: Cols. 1, 2, and 5 from Capie and Webber (1985, table III.12).
Cols. 7 and 8 from Capie and Webber (1985, table III.10).

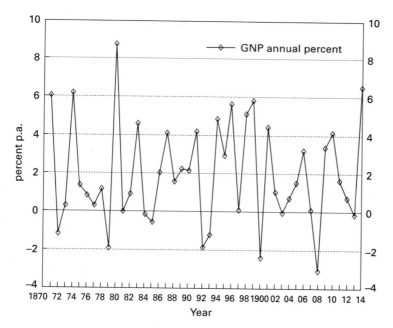

Figure 9.1 UK GNP, annual change, 1870–1914
Source: Capie and Webber (1985), tables III.12 and III.10

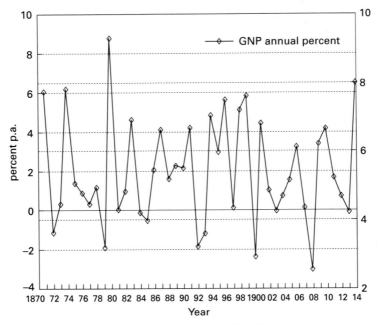

Figure 9.2 UK real GNP, annual change, 1870–1914
Source: Capie and Webber (1985), tables III.12 and III.10

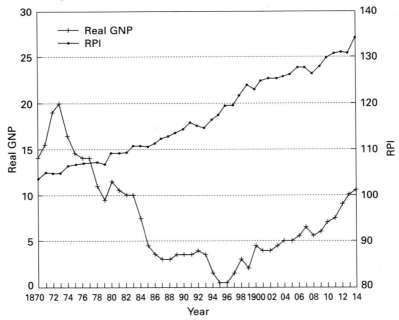

Figure 9.3 UK real GNP and RPI, 1870–1914
Source: Capie and Webber (1985), tables III.12 and III.10

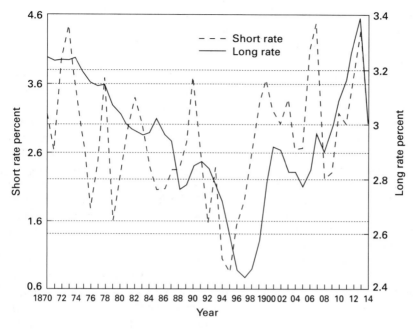

Figure 9.4 UK short and long rates, 1870–1914
Source: Capie and Webber (1985), tables III.12 and III.10

because the data – particularly the measures of the money stock, but also the interest rates – have changed. The next section briefly discusses why these data revisions were made. We then turn to reviewing some of the studies of money demand in this period.

Data revisions

Monetary series prior to Capie and Webber (1985) were constructed largely on the basis of published data (there was no "official" series). This reliance on published data introduced two deficiencies. First, the figures which were published were not very informative. Banks were not required to publish complete balance sheets. Only joint stock banks had any obligation – that being to publish information relating to shares, capital, and dividends. All UK bank deposit series for the late 19th century used the printed balance sheets of the banks that chose to make their accounts public. These were published both individually and in the aggregate in the half-yearly edition of *The Economist*'s Banking Supplement.

The chief defect this introduced into the monetary series resulted from more and more banks publishing every year. This caused *The Economist*'s series to increase – but the increase resulted not only from growth in the stock of money, but from growth in the part of it which was reported. Not only was there a spurious trend; there was also a spurious step. From 1891 onwards, private banks (i.e. non-joint stock) started to publish their figures. Those figures, too, appeared in *The Economist*. So the series suddenly jumped upwards in 1891.

These were the two major problems. There was also a variety of others. Because different banks published at different times, the figures aggregated in *The Economist* could be for balance sheets months apart. Sometimes when a bank was absorbed by another its figures were (correctly) dropped, but were sometimes not added to those of the other banks. The figures were swollen by double counting – mainly of the interbank deposits the provincial, Scottish, and Irish banks held with their London agents. Finally, most banks "window dressed" their accounts; this increased the amount of interbank and customers' deposits.

These problems were well known, and those who constructed UK money data attempted to deal with them. The Capie and Webber (1985) series was, however, produced with the aid of access to previously unpublished balance sheets. It was thus able to solve the problems created by the spurious trend, and the spurious step of 1891. A detailed account of the work of previous scholars, and of Capie and Webber's revisions, can be found in Capie and Webber (1985, chapters 2 and 11).

Harley (1976) revised the consol yield series. The most widely used series (reproduced for example in Sheppard, 1971) is misleading for two reasons. It does not take account of the possibility of conversion (or redemption) on the yield of consols when their price rose above par – as the price of 3 percent consols did in 1881. Harley suggests that $2\frac{1}{2}$ percent consols are a better guide to yields. Second, he argues that the yield on Goschen consols, issued in 1888, was miscalculated in the standard sources (for the years before 1903) because it did not properly allow for the 1903 reduction in the coupon from $2\frac{3}{4}$ percent to $2\frac{1}{2}$ percent. All work subsequent to Harley's paper has (so far as we know) used his data. But as will emerge below, the results seem insensitive to data revision.

The demand equation

All the studies discussed below follow the same general theoretical framework.The model relates the amount of money demanded to the price level, real income, a short-term interest rate, and a long-term interest rate. The own rate on money should of course also be an argument in the demand function, and one study (Friedman and Schwartz, 1982) reports estimates containing a measure of that own yield. Friedman and Schwartz use the measure proposed in Klein (1970), derived on the assumption of a competitive banking system leading banks to pass on to their customers the net return on bank assets, and calculating this return on the basis of market interest rates. This leads to the return on deposits being a fraction of the market rate, the fraction being equal to

$$1 - \frac{R}{D}$$

where R/D is the reserve/deposit ratio, and reserves are noninterest bearing. Income per unit of money would then be a weighted average of that rate and the zero rate on currency (the weights are determined by the currency/deposit (C/D) ratio).

There can be no doubt that the argument is right in principle. Before proceeding to the results of the empirical work, the variable should therefore be discussed further, so that we can understand its lack of success. Most important, it presumes a competitive banking system. In the British banking system of these years there was some degree of cartelization – in particular, there were agreements which prevent interest being paid on deposits, or restricted it to below the competitive level. These agreements were certainly not all-pervasive, but they did produce deviations from competitive behavior (see Goodhart, 1972, 178–188; Griffiths, 1973). (There are in principle also statistical problems with the measure; but they may well not be problems in practice; see Friedman and Schwartz, 1982, n. 46, 270–274.)

The equations we discuss below broadly fall into two groups – those which examine the demand for money in this period as part of a longer study, and those which consider the period in isolation. We briefly discuss the first group, and then, in more detail, the latter. It is worth noting at the outset, though, how similar the results of the various studies are. Without exception, three features stand out very clearly in every study. First, the function is stable. A change in income, the price level, or the interest rate (or rates) has the same effect on the amount of money demanded at whatever time we are in the period; and at any given level of these variables, the amount of money demanded is the same, regardless of when the observations occur. Second, the income elasticity of demand is very close to unity. Third, the demand is for real balances: double the price level, and the demand for nominal balances doubles; double nominal balances, and the price level doubles.

This stability and simplicity of the money demand function is of the greatest importance for interpreting the behavior of the British economy in those years, for it means that there can be no doubt when there was an excess supply of or excess demand for money. Clarification of the influence of money on the economy is therefore greatly simplified.

Now to a selection of the studies which have produced this simplification. Two studies not readily comparable with the others are those contained in Friedman and Schwartz (1982), and a commentary on it by Hendry and Ericsson (1991). Friedman and Schwartz estimated a function that was stable, after allowing for some special factors, over a century from 1870. A discussion of these special factors highlights just how stable the function was in the gold standard years, and also suggests why.[1] Apart from that, the special factors allowed for are war and its immediate aftermath, and the depression and associated uncertainty of the interwar years.[2] Note that *none* of these special factors was important in the United Kingdom before 1914. This reinforces our earlier suggestion that the stability of the estimated function in the gold standard period is a reflection of the stability of the period, allowing us to see how the money holding behaves in the absence of shocks.

The Friedman and Schwartz study was examined somewhat critically by Hendry and Ericsson (1991), their criticism being directed at the statistical methods used. Friedman and Schwartz (1991) replied; in part of their reply, they point out that Hendry and Ericsson's findings were actually the same as theirs. Hence the Friedman–Schwartz study is not inconsistent with our opening general summary of how money demand behaved in this period in the United Kingdom.

Turning now to studies which concentrate exclusively on the gold standard years, we note first the study by Mills and Wood (1982), and then turn to Klovland's (1987) paper, which comprehensively reviewed previous work on the subject. The Mills and Wood study was an attempt to discriminate statistically between various measures of the money stock then available. That aspect of the paper is now superseded, as all the series they examined have been displaced by Capie and Webber (1985). What is now notable about the paper's results is that all *four* measures of money used (Sheppard's, 1971, series for UK bank deposits and UK money supply; Nishimura's, 1973, measure of bank deposits; and a measure comprising Nishimura's bank deposits *plus* Sheppard's net coin and currency outside banks) yielded results for all purposes identical in the important aspects of income, interest rate, and price elasticities (see Mills and Wood, 1982, p. 272.) In view of the differences in the series, this is perhaps somewhat surprising; but no explanation has as yet been given.

Another paper worthy of note before we turn to a general review is Capie and Rodrik-Bali (1985). This paper followed the method suggested in Hendry (1979) "intended over-parameterisation with data-based simplification." The resulting specification was in general consistent with the other studies surveyed here. But there are some interesting minor differences. The demand for money was affected by permanent income – not surprising, although not generally examined in this period. But what the authors did note as a puzzle was that the demand for money depended negatively (*ceteris paribus*) on the real growth rate. This has been found elsewhere (Hendry and Mizon, 1978) but it is not common. Otherwise the results display the robustness to changes in econometric techniques and minor data changes that we have already noted as characterizing this period – the income elasticity of demand was unity, the demand was homogeneous in the general level of prices, and the interest elasticity of demand was negative, albeit low.

Now to Klovland's study. As well as presenting his own work, he gathered the results of four previous papers. These, together with his preferred equation, comprise table 9.2. (The equations differ slightly from the original versions, as for the sake of consistency Klovland re-estimated them all using his preferred money stock data.) The long-run price level homogeneity with respect to nominal money is rejected for Mills and Wood (1982), and Capie and Rodrik-Bali (1985) (it is not rejected on the data those authors use) but retained in all other equations. Longbottom and Holly (1985) have the long-run income elasticity different from unity, but not significantly so. As Klovland notes, the short-run dynamics differ between the models – perhaps not surprisingly, as each uses a different opportunity cost variable. Every one of these, though, was a short rate. The consol yield appeared (and then insignificantly) in only two equations – *HE* and *LH*. This insignificance is highly likely (as Mills and Wood, 1982, suggested) to be the result of the stability of the long rate over these years as a result of the low actual and expected inflation produced by the gold standard regime.

Klovland concludes his survey by noting that despite the data changes all the main results that we noted in the opening of the section were reproduced. He, too, contrasts the stability of the function and its robustness to data changes with evidence from later periods, but offers no explanation.[3]

To conclude this section, the result seems to be that the money demand function in the gold standard years was stable and well behaved. Interpretation of the role of money in these years should therefore be relatively straightforward. Furthermore, this stability helps interpret the apparent instability of the demand function in later periods.[4]

Money supply

Under the gold standard the quantity of money lies outside the control of the monetary authorities, though some modification to this statement is

Table 9.2 *Alternative demand for money equations, 1878–1913*

A *Coefficient estimates* (MW) Mills and Wood (1982, (9))

$$\Delta_1(m-p)_t = 0.209\Delta_1 y_t - 0.434\bar{\Delta}_1 p_t - 0.032 r_t^{TB} - 0.103(m-p-y)_{t-1}$$
$$\quad\quad\quad (0.159)\quad\quad (0.226)\quad\quad (0.013)\quad\quad (0.083)$$
$$+0.027$$
$$(0.013)$$

(*HE*) Hendry and Ericsson (1983, table VIII (i))

$$\Delta_1(m-p)_t = -4.94\Delta_2 RL_t + 0.880\bar{\Delta}_4 y_t - 0.692\Delta_1^2 p_t - 0.196\Delta_1^2 p_{t-2}$$
$$\quad\quad\quad (3.52)\quad\quad\quad (0.138)\quad\quad (0.074)\quad\quad (0.091)$$
$$+0.467\Delta_1^2(m-p)_{t-1} - 0.093\Delta_1^2(m-p)_{t-2} - 0.708 RS_t$$
$$(0.046)\quad\quad\quad\quad (0.080)\quad\quad\quad\quad (0.230)$$
$$-0.149(m-p-y)_{t-4} - 0.069$$
$$(0.048)\quad\quad\quad\quad (0.032)$$

(*LH*) Longbottom and Holly (1985, (7))

$$\Delta_1(m-p)_t = -0.042\Delta_2 r_t^L - 0.708\Delta_1^2 p_t - 0.260\Delta_1 p_{t-1} + 0.512\Delta_1(m-p)_{t-1}$$
$$\quad\quad\quad (0.034)\quad\quad (0.065)\quad\quad (0.097)\quad\quad (0.083)$$
$$-0.124\Delta_1^2(m-p)_{t-2} - 0.018 r_t^N + 0.261 y_t - 0.281(m-p)_{t-1}$$
$$(0.037)\quad\quad\quad\quad (0.006)\quad\quad (0.034)\quad\quad (0.042)$$
$$-0.012$$
$$(0.061)$$

(*CRB*) Capie and Rodrik-Bali (1985)

$$\Delta_1(m-p)_t = -0.195\Delta_1\ln(1+RS/100)_t + 0.082(\Delta_1 y_t + \Delta_1 y_{t-3}) - 0.627\Delta_1^2 p_t$$
$$\quad\quad\quad (0.524)\quad\quad\quad\quad\quad (0.082)\quad\quad\quad\quad (0.196)$$
$$-0.515\Delta_1 p_{t-1} - 0.904\ln(1+RS/100)_{t-2} - 0.123(m-p-y)_{t-1}$$
$$(0.231)\quad\quad (0.482)\quad\quad\quad\quad\quad (0.087)$$
$$+0.025$$
$$(0.013)$$

(*K*) Klovland (6)

$$\Delta_1(m-p)_t = 0.007(\Delta_1 r_t^D - \Delta_2 r_t^S) + 0.613\bar{\Delta}_2 y_t - 0.702_1^2 p_t - 0.421\Delta_1 p_{t-1}$$
$$\quad\quad\quad (0.004)\quad\quad\quad\quad\quad (0.057)\quad\quad (0.039)\quad\quad (0.053)$$
$$-0.113\Delta_1^2(m-p)_{t-2} - 0.035(r^{S*}+r^{L*})_t + 0.040(r^D-r^S)_{t-3}$$
$$(0.023)\quad\quad\quad\quad (0.004)\quad\quad\quad\quad (0.011)$$
$$-0.425(m-p-y)_{t-2} - 0.173$$
$$(0.033)\quad\quad\quad\quad (0.022)$$

B *Summary statistics*	MW	HE	LH	CBR	K
Γ	36	36	36	36	36
k	5	9	9	7	9
s	0.0182	0.0103	0.0097	0.0194	0.0063
R^2	0.445	0.844	0.411	0.943	
LA $(4,T-k-4)$ 1.58	0.30	0.74	3.49	0.67	
ARCH	3.75	0.21	2.83	1.62	
NORM	3.37	0.95	0.02	1.04	0.24
CHOW $(8,T-k-8)$	0.30	0.95	0.29	0.17	

Table 9.2 (*cont.*)

Long-run elasticities					
Short rate	−0.305	−0.134	−0.063	−0.187	−0.177
Consol rate				−0.082	
Own rate			0.063	0.095	

required in the case of the large or dominant economy in the system. The relationship of the money stock to real income is complex. There is nevertheless still interest in examining the relationship between the broad money stock and the monetary base. This part of the chapter outlines the basic theoretical framework and then considers the second part of this question, the role of the public and the banks in the process. As a starting point take a fixed exchange rate system and leave aside that it was commodity based. In such a system, money would move *after* changes in (real or nominal) income, and not before. The explanation is straightforward. Assume the monetary authorities expand the money supply by lowering short-term interest rates. Since there is no concern about exchange rate risk, money flows abroad to obtain a higher interest rate there, and the monetary expansion is negated.[5] Conversely, an expansion of *real* income in a country increases the amount of money demanded.

By various channels,[6] including a rise in interest rates as there is initially excess demand for money, money is attracted into the economy until the excess demand is eliminated and interest rates are again at the world level. In such a setting, then, money can *follow* fluctuations in real income, but does not lead them. Money *following* income does not mean that money is unimportant for movements in income. As Friedman and Schwartz (1982, 325, n. 14) put it:

in a fixed exchange rate regime the quantity of money is endogenous, and cannot be determined, except for brief periods, by the monetary authorities. Monetary policy cannot affect the quantity of money except temporarily; nonetheless changes in the quantity of money, however produced, will affect income. Indeed, it is precisely because they do that a gold standard or other fixed exchange rate regime is self-adjusting . . .
The exchange rate regime does not affect the existence of a "causal" link from money to income; it affects the forces determining the quantity of money and thereby whether the situation is one of largely unidirectional influence from money to income or of simultaneous determination and interaction.

The full force of this argument can be understood by moving from a fixed exchange rate to a gold standard. In such a system the money supply in Britain could expand (for more than a brief period) for *two* reasons: income expansion in Britain, producing a monetary inflow as described above; or a gold discovery (outside Britain). This gold is spent on goods, services, and assets, and thus finds its way into circulation in every country of the world. Some flows into Britain, and produces effects – so in this case, the money flow precedes changes rather than follows them. And even if the money flow followed rather than initiated a change, this need not mean it has no subsequent effects; for the ratio of nominal money to income will be higher if the money flows than if it does not, and this in turn will have consequences.

A third should be added to these two possible money income relationships. If the economy is sufficiently large then monetary fluctuations originating there, although spilling over to the rest of the world, nevertheless affect that country's money stock by having a significant effect on the *world's* money stock. While Britain was not a gold producer, this last possibility is not ruled out, if the banking system evolved so as to support a larger money stock on an unchanged gold base. It has also been argued that the size of the British economy and the fact that sterling was a key currency meant the Bank of England was in a position to use its discount rate and influence the world distribution of gold.

Money supply process

The useful framework referred to above for examining the money supply process is that of the money multiplier that places the behavior of the banks alongside the monetary authorities and the public. The simplest expression of this is the following:

$$M = mB,$$

where m is the money multiplier, B is the monetary base, and M is the money stock. The money multiplier can be shown as:

$$\frac{\dfrac{C}{D}+1}{\dfrac{R}{D}+\dfrac{C}{D}}$$

and this brings out the fact that the public who hold currency (C) in relation to deposits (D) can influence the size of the money stock if they change the ratio in which they hold cash as against deposits. Equally, the banks choose to hold cash reserves (R) as cover for their deposit liabilities. When they feel the need to raise that cover, they dampen down the total money stock. This way of examining the money supply process brings out that there are three parties influencing the total money stock – the monetary authorities, the banks, and the public. There are generally good reasons for believing that the behavior of the banks and the public is relatively stable, leaving the outcome of the money stock largely in the hands of the monetary authorities or at least as the product of the monetary base, however that is determined. But although the behavior of the banks and public was stable and predictable, it could vary.

In Britain in this period there were no legal restrictions on the reserve-deposit (R/D) ratio and the variation from bank to bank could be quite considerable. Indeed, the idea of a reserve ratio was not clearly articulated at the beginning of this period, though obviously banks worked with some idea of requisite cover or they were in danger of going out of business. There is evidence that the first consciously stated reserve ratio was self-imposed by the Lincoln Bank in 1872 and that in the course of the next twenty years or so most English banks came to employ an announced minimum ratio. Contemporary estimates of the size of the ratio lend support to our own estimates. According to one survey of 75 nonclearing banks the range was 9–17 percent. An estimate of twelve London clearing banks gave a range of 10.4–16.8 percent. Our own estimates for the system as a whole show that it fluctuated between 8.5 percent and 12.5 percent (with a mean of 10.4 percent and standard deviation of 1.1 percent) (Capie and Webber, 1985). After some initial erratic behavior in the 1870s, from the early 1880s onwards the R/D ratio was on a gently upward trend. That is, the banks held a growing quantity of reserves in relation to deposits. This must therefore have been a factor holding down the growth of the broad money stock. This growth of the R/D ratio is on the face of things slightly perplexing. A jump in the proportion of reserves could indicate fears of instability or financial uncertainty. It is not a jump, but rather a slow steady growth, that has to be explained and, in any case all the evidence for the period, particularly from the 1880s onwards, would seem to be against crises and instability. The last major financial crisis was in 1866 and economic stability, however measured, generally improved towards the end of the century.

It might be hypothesized that small banks would have held higher reserves than large banks since the latter acquired a certain soundness by virtue of size. But if this were the case the trend in R/D would have been *downwards* since small banks shrank as a proportion of total bank population. However, the rising ratio can be explained, and the explanation we offer would be as follows. Small banks in fact held smaller reserves than large banks. Turner (1972) found in his investigations that the lowest ratios of all were amongst the nonclearers. The reason for this is that private banks were not obliged to publish their accounts. As more and more banks published accounts there was therefore an increase in the ratio; the need to publish in itself provided a pressure to keep a higher ratio of reserves. And this move to publish coincided in time with the Baring crisis (of 1890), when it became accepted that the banks should hold a higher ratio.

One method (Friedman and Schwartz, 1963) of examining the contribution of each proximate determinant of the money supply gives the fraction of monetary change which was produced by each of the determinants between the beginning and the end of any selected period. Over the period as a whole it was high-powered money (the base) that explained by far the greatest part of the change in the broad money stock – some 70 percent. As already shown, R/D was acting to slow monetary expansion; the cash/deposit ratio (C/D) was acting to offset this. The effect of C/D was considerably stronger than that of R/D over the whole period, although within some periods the respective contribution of each of these factors was more or less the same. For the period 1897–1913 monetary base is the powerful explanation, R/D is strong and C/D has lost a little of its importance. In summary, in spite of the considerable changes that took place in this period, the monetary base was the prime determinant of money supply in this period.

What also stands out in this period is the considerable growth and changing structure of the banking system. This deserves some comment, for not only was it an important element in the relative stability of the financial system and in producing an environment in which there were no banking panics or financial crises, but it clearly had enormous potential for changing the money stock.

We have already hinted at how the structure was important in reducing monetary volatility and hence played a part in reducing the likelihood of monetary shocks affecting output. Some further comment on the changing structure may be useful. By 1870 British banking had already evolved to close to its modern form with a number of commercial banks, the largest of which had many branches across the country. Table 9.3 shows how this form developed over the next fifty years.

As early as 1870 there were 2,728 bank offices in the country (0.87 offices per 10,000 population). Although the total number of banks in all categories fell fairly steadily throughout the period there were still over 100 banks in 1914 and there were around 8,000 bank offices at that point (1.63 per 10,000 population). The fall in the total number of banks was in part the result of a growing concern for size, associated as it was with greater reserves, security and prestige; hence came the mergers/acquisitions that took place at an accelerating pace in the 1890s. But the main point to make is that there was a great growth, from an already substantial base in 1870, of this branching network. This meant that any one bank, usually with headquarters in London, had loans and sources of funds in most if not all parts of the country covering the whole spectrum of industry, agriculture,

Table 9.3 *Bank branching, United Kingdom, 1870–1920*

Year	London banks Banks	Branches	Provincial banks Banks	Branches	All UK banks Banks	Branches	Bank branches per 10,000 population
1870	56	84	299	1092	387	2728	0.87
1880	65	109	258	1396	358	3454	1.00
1890	65	149	200	1795	303	4347	1.16
1900	39	135	108	1875	188	5822	1.44
1910	27	36	47	1516	112	7565	1.68
1920	29	31	21	949	75	9668	2.08

Source: Capie and Webber (1985).

and services. This branch network meant that if a branch, or even several branches, were in trouble in an area adversely affected by a fall in demand for its product, the resources of the bank could readily be diverted to ease the pressure. This could be done without any indication being given to a wider public and so could remove an important potential source of apprehension for the depositor.

There were nonetheless still many banks in Britain without branches and there were fairly frequent bank failures; and there were also regular new entrants to the system every year. The failures did not result in runs; they were simply accepted as part of the normal pattern of business enterprise. There were even occasionally quite large bank failures such as that of the City of Glasgow Bank in 1878. This was a badly managed bank, with corrupt practices, which was clearly insolvent and was allowed to fail. It had close connections with a number of other banks, all of which were affected. But there was no run on banks, no banking panic, no financial crisis (although it may have been a near miss), no significant rise in C/D or R/D ratios.

Short-run problems

The gold standard was demonstrably a provider of long-run stability. But what happened in the short run? What happened when, for example, the financial system was threatened and there was the prospect of a consequent collapse in the stock of money? This should be differentiated from "financial distress" or "pseudo-crises" which may threaten the wealth of one group in society, but do not threaten the prosperity of the entire economy. For example, in Britain there was undoubtedly financial distress when the City of Glasgow Bank failed. Shareholders suffered, but there was no run on the banking *system*. (For a discussion of the distinction between real and pseudo-crises, see Schwartz, 1986.)

A financial crises is a run to cash by depositors nationwide. The switching of funds from one institution to another undoubtedly causes distress to the first institution, and could cause it to fail, but does not threaten the financial *system* or the economy as a whole. What is notable about this aspect of British monetary experience in the years studied in this chapter is the absence of a crisis. There was none. This is a quite different experience from that of either continental Europe or the United States. In both of these, genuine crises on the above definition occurred. This contrast of experience suggests that an explanation for the absence of crises in Britain must be sought not in a claim that the whole world was stable, but in something unique to British experience.

Two features of the British financial system provide much of the explanation: the structure of banking and the Bank of England acting as lender of last resort. We consider them in turn. A classic cause of a bank's failing is a problem affecting local industry. Suppose, for example, there is a crop failure in one area of the country, or some manufacturing industry suddenly loses its market because of an exogenous shock such as a foreign war or a tariff. Loans cannot be repaid, or even serviced. The bank's assets deteriorate, while liabilities remain unchanged; and some depositors lose their wealth. If this is recognized as being a purely local event, it may not spread to other banks. But in the absence of good information it could spread – even if thought to be due to a local event people elsewhere might still run for cash to be absolutely safe.

Such an episode could occur under unitary banking, but was unlikely under branch banking. Branching allows diversification (as does the scale usually associated with branched but not with unitary systems). Hence these shocks are unlikely to affect the entire branch network simultaneously. A shock to one branch is withstood with the help of others not adversely affected. Depositors at the branch which suffered loan defaults do not lose their deposits, so no bank run starts. The structure of British banking in the years before World War I was such as to reduce the likelihood of a banking crisis.

The attitude and action of the Bank of England constitute the second feature. The Bank of England acted as *lender of last resort*. It had acted in this way before 1870, and it is worth looking at the outcome of these actions, for this will highlight both what the Bank did and the reasons why it never needed to do so in subsequent years. A financial crisis occurs because an event has triggered a run from bank deposits to cash. The way to curtail such a run is to supply the cash. The central bank supplies it to banks in exchange for securities, and the banks then supply it to their customers. The central bank has lent "to the market" – that is to say, to any institution which offers securities at the discount window. The ready availability of cash reassures the public, the run ends, and the crisis comes to an end. That was how the Bank acted in the crises of 1847, 1857, and 1866. The market got nervous, panic broke out, and there was an immense demand for cash. The Bank was allowed to suspend the 1844 Act, allowing an expansion of the fiduciary issue, and more cash was forthcoming. From then on the knowledge that the Act could be suspended prevented panic, for people knew they could get cash.

Walter Bagehot is often credited with convincing the Bank of England of the need to act as lender of last resort.[7] That was plainly unnecessary; what he in fact did was to urge it to commit itself in advance to doing so. This, he argued, would eliminate the fear that cash could not be obtained and so would prevent crises from arising. It appears, then, that we cannot distinguish between the Bank's precommitment and the structure of the banking system as the cause of the absence of banking crises in Britain. Both may have contributed; perhaps either would have been sufficient.

In this period there were three occasions when crises have been identified. The first was 1878, the second the "Baring crisis," and the third the panic at the outset of the 1914–18 war.

In 1878 a number of banks got into difficulties following the collapse of the City of Glasgow Bank. Not all were directly or even indirectly connected with that bank but there were undoubtedly fears in the market of widespread difficulties. As noted above, the City of Glasgow Bank was allowed to fail. There was no bail-out. But neither did a crisis develop. That can be seen from the behavior of the C/D ratio and the R/D ratio.

Baring's difficulties in 1890 derived from involvement in Argentina. The flow of remittance from Argentina stopped. The Bank of England organized a rescue – a lifeboat. In contrast to the Chancellor of the Exchequer (Goschen), who was reluctant to provide government assistance lest Baring prove to be insolvent, the Bank thought that the problem was one of illiquidity. It persuaded other banks to agree, on the basis of a report which concluded that Baring was fundamentally sound but needed some £10 million in liquidity. Baring was put into liquidation and there was a modest rise in the demand for cash. Baring was reconstituted as a limited liability company with a new chairman and the Argentinian debt written off. Although both the Bank and the City were busy, there was no crises. Note that there was not a classic lender of last resort operation – one was not needed.[8]

Finally, in 1914 the prospect of imminent war caused plunging stock prices and a failure of remittance from overseas. A rush for liquidity began and the banks called in their loans to the Stock Exchange and the discount market, further weakening the former and driving the latter to the Bank of England. Fortunately all this occurred just before a bank holiday – which was extended. Assistance was provided to the stock market under a scheme proposed by the clearing banks, and the Bank of England gave assistance to the discount market. There may have been a subsequent inflation (see Goodhart, 1986) but that was to some extent intertwined with the exigencies of war finance. This eposide exemplifies the problem of explaining UK financial stability in these years. The consequences of large well-diversified banks are inextricable from those of having a precommitted lender of last resort.

Summary

The experience of the gold standard in the years 1870–1914 has frequently been cited as a model of exchange rate and price stability. The world economy prospered. Britain was at the center of the system, and her experience, while mixed in terms of output growth (Feinstein, 1972), was nevertheless one of price and general stability. The British experience could, however, have been unique, since Britain was a large economy in the international trade sense and exercised considerable influence in the world economy over capital flows. In that now well known phrase Britain was the "conductor of the international orchestra."

As far as the role of money in the British economy goes it is clear that fluctuation in the supply of money relative to income was the long-run determinant of the behavior of the general level of prices. In other words the view that there was serious economic depression, and that collapsing agricultural prices were the cause of the general price level movement, can be rejected. There was of course as is well known a depression in southern agriculture (in arable farming), and there was a more general prolonged downturn in the economy in the 1880s. But the trend rate of growth of output over the whole period, while declining, was fairly steady.

The general level of prices declined slowly but steadily from 1873 to 1896 (the period formerly referred to in the literature as the Great Depression), and then rose slowly but steadily until 1913 when they were back more or less where they had been in 1870. (Indeed, the whole 19th century was a period of when prices were more or less flat, insofar as they can be measured.) A relationship between cyclical fluctuations in money and fluctuations in output is elusive for the United Kingdom in this period, a finding which contrasts with the United States. For the United States, Friedman and Schwartz found a relationship. But it was a case of *major* fluctuations in output being associated with major fluctuations in money. Monetary stability in Britain may in part be explained by the structure and maturity of the banking system – one that had a small number of large banks with countrywide branch networks. The other element in the stability was the acceptance, in this period, by the Bank of England of its responsibility to act as lender of last resort in the classic fashion – that is, lending to the market as a whole rather than bailing-out individual institutions; and it did so in a precommitted way – it indicated in advance its willingness to do so.

The remarkable monetary stability that prevailed in all probability contributed to the stability of the money demand function in this period; while supply and demand have separate determinants, the behavior of demand was influenced by the behavior, and expected behavior, of supply.

Notes

1. For the United States they included a term to allow for increasing financial sophistication before 1903. In the United Kingdom there was as noted above a developed, stable, nationwide banking system by 1870. For detailed discussion of the effect of this on the demand for money, see Bordo and Jonung (1981); Capie and Wood (1986a).
2. In his discussion of these, Goodhart (1982) suggests that rather than treating these episodes by use of dummy variables it would be worthwhile attempting to explain money holding behavior during them in more detail. This interesting suggestion has not yet been implemented.
3. In his concluding paragraph Klovland remarks, erroneously, that, because money was endogenous "the evidence from this time period does not fit well into a framework which assigns a major causal role to the stock of money under a fixed exchange rate regime." His confusion is that he does not distinguish between the causes of money growth and the consequences of that growth. See Friedman and Schwartz (1982, 325).
4. A most interesting discussion of this apparent instability can be found in Christ (1993). These issues are also discussed in a most useful recent paper by Taylor (1993).
5. In fact some of the monetary expansion will remain; the proportion will depend on the share of the originating country in the world economy.
6. See McCloskey and Zecher (1984) for a detailed discussion of these.
7. His advice appeared in *The Economist*, which he edited and in "Lombard Street." For a detailed discussion of this issue, see Rockoff (1986).
8. It may be that concerned with the dangers of fostering "moral hazard," the Bank Governor had been determined that financial institutions should not feel that they could always turn for rescue to the Bank. There was therefore, not a classic lender of last resort operation – but the collective guarantee instead. Although the Baring crisis had the effect of permanently enhancing the Bank's authority, the Bank's aim had been to throw the banking system on to its own resources in case of banking crises, rather than on to the Bank: Bagehot upside down?

References

Bordo, M. D. and L. Jonung (1981). "The Long Run Behaviour of the Income Velocity of Money in Five Advanced Countries 1870–1975: An Institutional Approach," *Economic Inquiry* 19

Bordo, M. D. and A. J. Schwartz (eds.) (1984). *The Retrospective on the Classical Gold Standard 1821–1931*, Chicago: University of Chicago Press for NBER

Cagan, P. (1984). "War, Prices and Interest Rates: A Martial Solution to Gibson's Paradox," in M. D. Bordo and A. J. Schwartz (eds.), *A Restrospective on the Classical Gold Standard 1821–1931*, Chicago: University of Chicago Press for NBER

Capie, F. H. and G. Rodrik-Bali (1985). "The Money Adjustment Process in the UK 1870–1914," *Economica* 52, 117–122

Capie, F. H. and A. Webber (1985). *A Monetary History of the United Kingdom 1870–1982*, vol. 1: *Data, Sources, Methods*, London: George Allen & Unwin

Capie, F. H. and G. E. Wood (1986a). "The Long Run Behaviour of Velocity in the UK," *Monetary History Discussion Paper* 23, City University Business School

(1986b). *Financial Crises and the World Banking System*, London: Macmillan

Christ, C. F. (1993). "Assessing Applied Econometric Results," *Federal Reserve Bank of St. Louis Review* 75(2), 71–94

Eichengreen, B. (1985). *The Gold Standard in Theory and History*, London: Methuen

Feinstein, C. H. (1972). *National Income, Expenditure and Output of the United Kingdom 1855–1965*, Cambridge: Cambridge University Press

Friedman, M. and A. J. Schwartz (1963). *A Monetary History of the United States, 1867–1960*, Princeton: Princeton University Press for NBER, 119–134

(1982). *Monetary Trends in the United States and in the United Kingdom 1870–1970*, Chicago: University of Chicago Press for NBER

(1991). "Alternative Approaches to Analysing Economic Data," *American Economic Review* 81, 39–99

Goodhart, C. A. E. (1972). *The Business of Banking 1891–1914*, London: Weidenfeld & Nicolson

(1982). "Monetary Trends in the UK and the US," *Journal of Economic Literature* 20, 1540–1591

(1986). "Comment on Seabourne," in F. H. Capie and G. E. Wood (eds.), *Financial Crises and the World Banking System*, London: Macmillan

Griffiths, B. (1973). "The Development of Restrictive Practices in the UK Monetary System," *Manchester School* 4 (March) 3–13

Harley, C. K. (1976). "Goschen's Conversion of the National Debt and the Yield on Consols," *Economic History Review* 34(1) (February), 101–106

Hendry, D. F. (1979). "Predictive Failure and Econometric Modelling in Macro Economics: The Transaction Demand for Money," in P. Ormerod, *Economic Modelling*, London: Heinemann

Hendry, D. F. and N. R. Ericsson (1991). "An Econometric Analysis of UK Money Demand in Monetary Trends in the US and UK," *American Economic Review* 81, 8–38

Hendry, D. F. and G. E. Mizon (1978). "Serial Correlation as a Convenient Simplification, not as a Nuisance: A Comment on a Study of the Demand for Money by the Bank of England," *Economic Journal* 88, 549–563

Klein, B. (1970). "The Payment of Interest on Commercial Bank Deposits and the Price of Money: A Study of the Demand for Money," Ph.D. dissertation, University of Chicago

Klovland, J. T. (1987). "The Demand for Money in the United Kingdom 1875–1913," *Oxford Bulletin of Economics and Statistics* 49 (August), 251–271

Longbottom, A. and S. Holly (1985). "Econometric Methodology and Monetarism: Professor Friedman and Professor Hendry on the Demand for Money," London Business School, *Discussion Paper*

McCloskey, D. and J. R. Zecher (1984). "The Success of Purchasing-Power Parity: Historical Evidence and its Implications for Macroeconomics," in M. D. Bordo and A. J. Schwartz (eds.), *A Retrospective on the Classical Gold Standard 1821–1931*, Chicago: University of Chicago Press for NBER, 121–170

Mills, T. C. (1990). A Note on the Gibson Paradox Under the Gold Standard," *Explorations in Economic History* 27, 277–286

Mills, T. C. and G. E. Wood (1978). "Money, Income, and Causality under the Gold Standard," *Federal Reserve Bank of St. Louis Review* (2), 22–27

(1982). "Econometric Evaluation of Alternative UK Money Stock Series, 1870–1913," *Journal of Money, Credit and Banking* (May), 265–277

(1992). "The Gibson Paradox Re-examined," in S. N. Broadberry and N. F. R. Crafts (eds.), *Money, Trade and Business Cycles: Essays in Honour of A. G. Ford*, Cambridge: Cambridge University Press

Nishimura, S. (1973). "The Growth of the Stock of Money in the UK 1870–1913," Hosei University, *Discussion Paper*, unpublished

Rockoff, H. (1986). "Walter Bagehot and the Theory of Central Banking," in F. H. Capie and G. E. Wood (eds.), *Financial Crises and the World Banking System*, London: Macmillan

Schwartz, A. J. (1986). "Real and Pseudo Financial Crises," in F. H. Capie and G. E. Wood (eds.), *Financial Crises and the World Banking System*, London: Macmillan

Sheppard, D. K. (1971). *The Growth and Role of UK Financial Institutions 1880–1962*, London: Methuen

Taylor, M. (1993). "Modelling the Demand for UK Broad Money, 1871–1913," *Review of Economics and Statistics* 75 (February), 112–117

Thomas, B. (1984). "Discussion of S. Easton's Paper," in M. D. Bordo and A. J. Schwartz (eds.), *A Retrospective on the Classical Gold Standard 1821–1931*, Chicago: University of Chicago Press for NBER, 544–546

Turner, A. J. (1972). "The Evolution of Reserve Ratios in English Banking," *National Westminster Bank Quarterly Review* (February), 52–63

10   Stability and forward-looking behavior: the demand for broad money in the United Kingdom, 1871–1913

Mark P. Taylor and Geoffrey E. Wood

Introduction

The demand for money in the United Kingdom during the heyday of the international gold standard, 1870–1913, has been studied quite intensively. Some studies (notably Friedman and Schwartz, 1982; Bordo and Jonung, 1987; Hendry and Ericsson, 1991) have examined a whole century of data from 1870, while others (Mills and Wood, 1978; Capie and Rodrik-Bali, 1985), have concentrated on the gold standard years. In this chapter we follow the latter group of authors; for, despite extensive study, there remain important unresolved questions about money demand in this period. In particular, although there is broad similarity among long-run estimates, estimated short-run demand functions appear to differ significantly. One of the aims of this chapter is to estimate more precisely than before the short-run function by applying recent econometric techniques to the best currently available data. We also test a forward-looking model of money demand on this data, which goes some way towards explaining the form of the short-run dynamics.

We address these issues by application of a number of recently developed econometric techniques. In particular, we apply the Johansen (1988) method of estimating cointegrating vectors (Engle and Granger, 1987) to estimate the parameters of a long-run UK money demand function for the gold standard period, and to test economic hypotheses such as long-run price and income homogeneity in money demand.

The cointegration results are then used to derive a dynamic error correction representation of the money process (applying the Granger Representation Theorem – Engle and Granger, 1987), which we interpret as a short-run dynamic money demand function. The resulting equation is then compared with and tested against equations which have been estimated for this period by previous authors.

We also use our cointegration results to test a particular hypothesis concerning money demand – the forward-looking model of Cuthbertson and

Taylor (1987) – which, we demonstrate, can be viewed as a restricted version of the error correction form.

The remainder of the chapter is set out as follows. In the next section we give a brief description of our main econometric techniques and of the strategy employed in modeling money demand. The data are described in the third section. The fourth section contains our cointegration results. These results are then further developed to obtain a dynamic short-run money demand function, which is reported in the fifth section, and tested against competing models in the sixth. In the seventh section we apply our cointegration results to test the Cuthbertson–Taylor forward-looking model. A final section summarizes our findings.

Long-run money demand, cointegration, and error correction

The concept of cointegration was introduced into the economics literature by Engle and Granger (1987) (see also chapter 2 in this volume). It may be briefly defined as follows. If a variable x_t has to be differenced d times before it becomes stationary, it is termed "integrated of order d," $x_t{\sim}I(d)$. Thus, if $x_t{\sim}I(d)$, then $\Delta^d x_t{\sim}I(0)$. Generally, any linear combination of $I(d)$ variables will also be $I(d)$. If however, there is some linear combination which is integrated of order $d-b$ $(b>0)$ then the variables are said to be cointegrated of order d, b. Generally, the most interesting case in economics is where a set of variables are individually $I(1)$ but a linear combination exists which is $I(0)$. For then, although each of the variables tends to drift over time, there is a sense in which the variables have a stable long-run relationship. To be concrete, suppose money, m_t, and the elements of a vector $z_t=$(prices, income, interest rates) are individually nonstationary and in fact $I(1)$. If the concept of a stable, long-run money demand function relating these variables is to have empirical content, then m_t and z_t must be cointegrated:

$$m_t - \gamma' z_t {\sim} I(0).$$

Otherwise, money, prices, income and interest rates will tend to drift apart over time, rather than settle down together.

If we are considering only two $I(1)$ variables, it is easy to demonstrate that, if it exists at all, the cointegrating linear combination must be unique. But in general, for q variables there can be up to $q-1$ cointegrating vectors (Engle and Granger, 1987). This nonuniqueness has been something of a problem with empirical applications of cointegration until recently since, although Stock (1987) showed that ordinary least squares (OLS) provides "super consistent" estimates of the cointegrating vector, possible nonuniqueness is clearly a worry. Johansen (1988) has, however, developed a maximum likelihood technique of estimating *all* of the cointegrating vectors and for testing which are statistically significant. The Johansen technique is based on the vector autoregressive representation of the variables (a brief summary of the technique is given in the appendix to Johansen, 1988). An added advantage of the Johansen technique is that it also allows linear restrictions on the cointegrating parameter vector to be tested.

If a cointegrating relationship is identified, e.g.

$$e_t = m_t - \gamma' z_t \sim I(0),$$

then, according to the Granger Representation Theorem (Engle and Granger, 1987), there must exist an error correction representation relating current and lagged first differences of m and the elements of z, and at least one lagged value of e, e.g.

$$\Delta m_t = \alpha_0 + \sum_{i=1}^{q} \alpha_i \Delta m_{t-i} + \sum_{i=1}^{s} \delta_i' \Delta z_{t-i} + \theta(m - \gamma' z)_{t-1} + u_t. \tag{1}$$

Indeed, (1) has proved a popular and successful family of empirical models for UK money during the international gold standard period (Mills and Wood, 1978; Capie and Rodrik-Bali, 1985; Klovland, 1987; see also Hendry and Ericsson, 1989). In long-run steady state equilibrium (Δm_{t-i}=constant, Δz_{t-i}=vector of constants, for all i), the long-run money demand function $m_t = \gamma' z_t$ is recovered (subject to a constant intercept).[1] In the short run, money demand responds, *inter alia*, to deviations from long-run equilibrium. In order to achieve parsimony, it is common to include current dated values of Δz on the right-hand side in equations like (1) (see the studies cited above). While this will not affect the long-run properties of the model it will have a bearing on the imposition of restrictions implied by the forward-looking model, as discussed on p. 300 below (see also Campbell and Shiller, 1988).

Our strategy in modeling the demand for money is as follows. We first of all check for the order of integration of our variables. We then apply the Johansen (1988) estimation procedure to estimate the parameters of the long-run money demand function and to test linear restrictions on them (price and income homogeneity). The error correction term can then be formed using the estimated long-run parameters, and a short-run demand function of the kind (1) tested for. We then apply these results to test the forward-looking model of Cuthbertson and Taylor (1987) as an explanation of the behavior of UK broad money during the gold standard.

Data

The data are annual, for the period 1871–1913; more frequent money supply and interest rate data are available, but we are forced to use annual observations because income (which we use, in real terms, as a scale variable in the absence of any wealth data) is available only annually. This series (GDP at factor cost) was taken from Feinstein (1972), together with a series for prices (implicit GDP deflator).

The underlying theoretical framework we adopt is that of Friedman and Schwartz (1982), but our data are quite different from theirs. Our data on broad money, M3, are drawn from Capie and Webber (1985); largely as a result of eliminating a specious trend, this series differs from those which have been generally used previously[2] (see Capie and Webber 1985, chapter 5; see also chapter 9 in this volume).

Following Friedman and Schwartz, we considered three interest rates: one long, one short and one as a measure of the own rate of return on money. The long-term interest rate was the yield on consols. Harley (1976) notes that standard series for the consol rate (Mitchell and Deane, 1962; Sheppard, 1971; Capie and Webber, 1985), is an overestimate of the true nominal yield on consols for the years 1880–1903. This overestimation arose for two reasons (Harley, 1976; Capie and Webber, 1985, 317–318). The first was the failure to take account of the possibility of redemption at par when the market price rose above par. The second reason is that the yield on Goschen consols issued in 1888 was miscalculated in sources before 1903 because of the reduction in the coupon rate from 2¾ percent to 2½ percent. Accordingly, we used the revised consol yield series given in the appendix to Harley (1976). The short-term interest rate is the discount on three-month prime bank bills, from Capie and Webber (1985, table III(10)), which were originally collected from *The Economist*.

Friedman and Schwartz (1982) use a measure of the own return on money suggested by Klein (1974). Denoting broad money as M, the high-powered stock as H, the short rate as RS and the own rate of return as RO, the formula for this is: $RO = RS(1 - H/M)$. For this to be a valid measure of the own rate of return, one has to assume perfect competition among banks, so that marginal profits from banks' deposit accounts are passed on to depositors (Klein, 1974) There were, however, cartel arrangements with respect to deposit account interest rates during this period (Keynes, 1930; Goodhart, 1972; Griffiths, 1973) so this assumption may be unwarranted. The extent and the rigidity of these cartel arrangements is not established, and it does seem clear that they were much less important outside London; but nevertheless their existence must give rise to reservations about use of the Klein measure. Moreover, since RO is a (nonlinear) function of the current value of broad money, it may generate econometric problems if used as an explanatory variable in an equation explaining broad money (Carlson and Frew, 1980). Since the rate of interest on deposit accounts was available (Capie and Webber, 1985, table III(10), again originally from *The*

Economist), we decided to use this as a direct measure of the own rate of return.

Data on money, prices and income were converted to natural logarithms. We adopt the following notation throughout the chapter: m=logarithm of nominal M3; p=logarithm of GDP deflator; y=logarithm of real GDP; RD=interest rate on deposit accounts (percent per annum); RPB=interest rate on prime three-month bank bills (percent per annum); RL=consol yield (percent per annum).

Figures 10.1–10.6 are graphs of m, y, p, RL, RD and RPB, respectively. Both money and output show steady secular growth over the period (figures 10.1, 10.2), while prices show a steady secular decline until 1896, followed by an equally steady rise to World War I (figure 10.3). A similar pattern of decline and rise, with a floor around 1896–1897 is also in evidence for the consol rate (figure 10.4). This positive relationship between long interest rates and the *level* of prices is an example of the Gibson Paradox (see Friedman and Schwartz, 1982).

The interest rate on deposit accounts and the yield on prime three-month bank bills are graphed in figures 10.5 and 10.6, respectively. Unlike the consol rate, and notwithstanding a discernible decline in the mid-1890s, these interest rates appear to be rather more stable – in terms of an apparently stable mean – than the consol rate. This is probably due in large measure to the fact that these rates were linked to an administered interest rate – Bank Rate – for much of this period (Goodhart, 1972).

Estimating long-run money demand

Table 10.1 lists tests of $I(1)$ behavior for all of the variables under consideration. We applied the Dickey–Fuller-test suggested by Fuller (1976) and a likelihood ratio-test due to Johansen (1988). Where the null hypothesis of $I(1)$ behavior in levels could not be rejected, the tests were carried out for the data in first differences.

The Dickey–Fuller- and Johansen-statistics are in uniform agreement. Money, prices, income and the consol yield appear to be $I(1)$ series, while the deposit rate and prime bank bill rate appear to be $I(0)$.

Since we found strong evidence that the deposit rate and prime three-month bank bill rate were stationary ($I(0)$) variables, they were not included in the cointegration analysis (although we did not rule out the possibility that they might appear in the short-run demand function – see below), since their long-run effect will be implicitly captured by including an intercept term.

We thus began by estimating a VAR for m, p, y and RL, summary diagnostics for which are reported in table 10.2a; a lag depth of 2 seemed adequate in terms of generating satisfactory equation diagnostics.

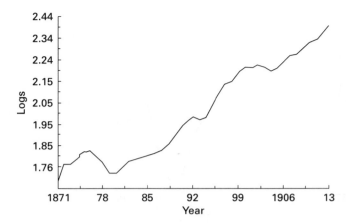

Figure 10.1 Log of nominal M3, 1871–1913

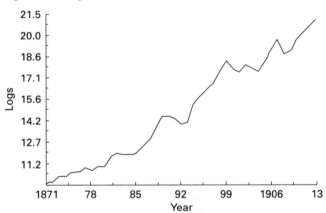

Figure 10.2 Log of real GDP, 1871–1913

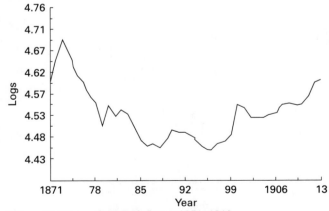

Figure 10.3 Log of GDP deflator, 1871–1913

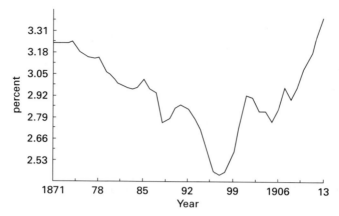

Figure 10.4 Consol yield, 1871–1913

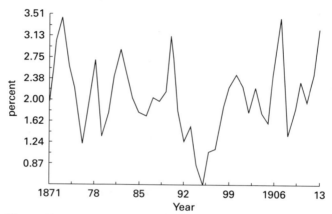

Figure 10.5 Interest rate on deposit accounts, 1871–1913

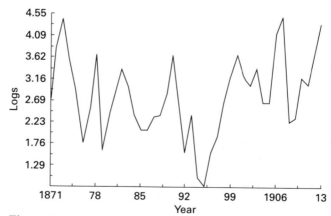

Figure 10.6 Interest rate on prime bank bills, 1871–1913

Table 10.1 *Unit root tests*[a]

Variable	Dickey–Fuller-statistic	Johansen-statistic
m_t	1.00	1.04
Δm_t	−4.21	16.80
p_t	−1.60	1.66
Δp_t	−5.03	22.97
y_t	−0.32	0.28
Δy_t	−3.82	21.82
RL_t	−0.68	2.24
ΔRL_t	−3.54	9.87
RD_t	−3.68	14.35
RPB_t	−3.30	11.69

Notes:
[a] The null hypothesis in each case is that the variable in question is $I(1)$; the 5 percent rejection region for the Dickey–Fuller-statistic is $\{DF<-2.93\}$ (Fuller, 1976, 373); the 5 percent rejection region for the Johansen-statistic is $\{J>8.18\}$ (Johansen, 1988, 239).

We then applied the Johansen procedure to obtain test statistics for the number of significant cointegrating vectors (table 10.2b). The results were encouraging: the null hypothesis of zero cointegrating vectors is strongly rejected at the 5 percent level, while the hypothesis that the number is less than or equal to one cannot be rejected – i.e. there is a unique statistically significant cointegrating vector. This is reported (table 10.2c) as the unrestricted cointegrating vector. Again the results are encouraging: the estimated long-run price and income elasticities (after normalizing on m) are close to unity and the long-run interest rate semi-elasticity is of the correct sign and of a plausible magnitude. We also report estimates of the cointegrating vector with price and income homogeneity imposed – the likelihood ratio statistic for the restrictions is insignificant at the 5 percent level (table 10.2c).

Given that the consol yield failed to Granger-cause money in the VAR (table 10.2a), we also tested the restriction that RL does *not* appear in the long-run money demand function: the exclusion restriction is easily rejected.

Thus, the results of this section suggest that there is a unique cointegrating vector relating m, p, y and RL which corresponds closely to our economic priors concerning long-run money demand. In particular, we

Table 10.2 *Results of Johansen maximum likelihood estimation applied to m, p, y, and* RL[a]

a VAR diagnostics (lag length=2)

Variable	Q(18)	R^2	m	p	y	RL
m	20.86	0.99	—	2.78 (0.08)	9.78 (0.5E-3)	2.33 (0.11)
p	16.82	0.91	1.21 (0.31)	—	2.61 (0.09)	0.73 (0.49)
y	18.81	0.99	5.38 (0.01)	5.60 (0.8E-2)	—	4.26 (0.02)
RL	13.42	0.94	0.03 (0.97)	0.58 (0.57)	0.14 (0.86)	—

b Tests for cointegration

Null hypothesis	Likelihood ratio-statistic	5% critical value
Number of cointegrating vectors ≤3	0.04	8.18
Number of cointegrating vectors ≤2	7.61	17.95
Number of cointegrating vectors ≤1	22.72	31.52
Number of cointegrating vectors=0	71.40	48.28

c Estimated cointegrating vector (largest latent root only)

(i) unrestricted
$$m_t=1.19p_t+0.98y_t-0.077RL_t$$
(ii) with homogeneity restrictions
$$m_t=p_t+y_t-0.050RL_t$$
Likelihood ratio-statistic: $LR(2)=4.57$
$$(0.10)$$
(iii) with exclusion restriction on RL
$$m_t=0.78p_t+1.01y_t$$
Likelihood ratio-statistic: $LR(1)=16.23$
$$(5.62E-5)$$

Notes:
[a] Figures in parenthesis under test-statistics are marginal significance levels; Granger causality-statistics in a are $F(2, 32)$ under the null hypothesis; $Q(18)$ is the Ljung–Box-statistic applied to the equation residuals at eighteen autocorrelations; R^2 is the coefficient of determination; Critical values in b are from Johansen (1988); the $LR(n)$ statistics are asymptotically $\chi^2(n)$ under the null hypothesis.

have found strong evidence of long-run price and income homogeneity in money demand.

Note, however, that long-run money demand may also be partly determined by the long-run means of $I(0)$ variables – short-term interest rates in particular – although their influence will not be explicitly detected by cointegration analysis. In the next section, we apply our results on *long-run* demand to model the *short-run* dynamics of money demand.[3]

Modeling the short-run dynamics and allowing for $I(0)$ explanatory variables

The next step was to model the short-run dynamics. We formed the error correction variable corresponding to the cointegrating vector with price and income homogeneity imposed:

$$e_t = m_t - p_t - y_t + 0.05RL_t.$$

In moving to a consideration of the short-run dynamics, it is legitimate (statistically and economically) to consider $I(0)$ variables. Since these variables are stationary, their long-run effect will be felt only through their constant *means*; they are thus implicitly allowed for in the Johansen procedure by including a constant term in the VAR. When modeling the short run, however, they should be considered explicitly. Given that we are modeling the time series behavior of broad money, economic theory suggests that the own rate of return, RD, and the short-term interest rate, RPB, should be tested for explanatory power.

Given that a second order VAR appeared adequate in describing m, p, y and RL, we thus started with an error correction form consisting of: Δm as the explanatory variable, with 1 lag of itself and current and 1 lagged value of Δp, Δy and ΔRL on the right-hand side, as well as 1 lag of the error correction term e. To this were added current and 2 lagged values of RD and RPB. We then tested down to find a parsimonious empirical equation, reported in table 10.3.

The equation reported in table 10.3 is very satisfactory: all of the coefficients have large t-ratios and are of economically plausible signs and magnitudes, and the equation fits well and passes a range of diagnostic tests.

Given the quite different behavior of prices and long interest rates before and after 1896–1897 (figures 10.3 and 10.4), it was of some interest to test for a structural break in the model after 1896. The HF-statistic (table 10.3) is a test-statistic obtained by estimating the model on data up to 1896, using the estimates to forecast one–seventeen years ahead, 1897–1913, and then comparing the squared forecast errors with the in-sample residual variance (Hendry, 1979). The statistic is clearly insignificant at standard test sizes

Table 10.3 *Parsimonious error correction form for m*[a]

$$\Delta m_t = -2.036 + 0.399\Delta m_{t-1} + 0.359\Delta y_t + 0.010(RD_{t-2} - RPB_{t-1})$$
$$\quad\;\; (0.302)\quad(0.085)\qquad\;(0.056)\quad\;(0.002)$$

$$\quad\; -0.405(m - p - y + 0.05RL)_{t-1}$$
$$\quad\;\; (0.060)$$

$DW = 1.93;\qquad SE = 0.97(\%);\qquad AR(4,31) = 0.57;$
$$\qquad\qquad\qquad\qquad\qquad\qquad\qquad\;\; (0.69)$$

$ARCH(2,32) = 0.33;\qquad HET(8,26) = 0.69;\qquad WHITE(14,20) = 0.57;$
$$\qquad\qquad (0.72)\qquad\qquad\qquad (0.70)\qquad\qquad\qquad\qquad (0.86)$$

$B\text{--}J(2) = 2.02;\qquad HF(17) = 14.45;\qquad CHOW(17,18) = 0.74$
$$\qquad\; (0.36)\qquad\qquad (0.64)\qquad\qquad\qquad\; (0.73)$$

$R^2 = 0.87$

Notes:
[a] Period of estimation is 1874–1913; DW is the Durbin–Watson-statistic SE is the standard error of the regression; figures in parenthesis below coefficient estimates are heteroskedasticity consistent standard errors (White, 1980), those below test-statistics are marginal significance levels; AR is a Lagrange multiplier test for up to fourth order serial correlation; $ARCH$ is a test-statistic for up to second order ARCH effects (Engle, 1982); HET is a heteroskedasticity test-statistic, based on the squares of the regressors; $WHITE$ is White's (1980) test-statistic for general heteroskedasticity or functional misspecification; $B\text{--}J$ is the (1982) Bera–Jarque-statistic for normally distributed residuals; HF and $CHOW$ are Hendry's (1979) and Chow's (1960) test-statistics for predictive failure and parameter stability respectively, when the model is estimated up to 1896 and forecasts are made for one–seventeen years ahead. Test-statistics with one figure in brackets should be referred to the χ^2 distribution with the indicated degrees of freedom; those with two figures are F-statistics. R^2 is the coefficient of determination.

and reveals the structural stability of the model. This is further confirmed by a (1960) Chow-test for parameter stability (table 10.3). Apart from these formal tests, the parameters estimates for data up to 1896 are quite similar to those reported in table 10.3:

$$\Delta m_t = -2.231 + 0.329\Delta m_{t-1} + 0.316\Delta y_t + 0.011(RD_{t-2} - RPB_{t-1})$$
$$\quad\;\; (0.382)\quad(0.094)\qquad\;(0.058)\quad\;(0.002)$$

$$\quad\; -0.443(m - p - y + 0.05RL)_{t-1}$$
$$\quad\;\; (0.076)$$

$R^2 = 0.86;\qquad DW = 1.60;\qquad SE = 1.04(\%);\qquad AR(1,17) = 0.56;$
$ARCH(2,15) = 0.08;\qquad HET(8,9) = 0.64;$
$WHITE(14,3) = 0.21;\qquad B\text{--}J(2) = 1.38.$

The equation reported in table 10.3 can be solved for its long-run, steady state solution by setting $\Delta RL_t=0$, by letting the other $I(1)$ variables enter steady state growth:[4]

$$\Delta x_t=g_x, x=m, p, y$$

by setting the $I(0)$ variables equal to their long-run means,

$$x_t=\bar{x}, x=RD, RPB,$$

and noting that $x_{t-1}=x_t-g_x$ and $g_m=g_p+g_y$ (by long-run homogeneity). This yields:

$$m_t=k+p_t+y_t-0.05RL_t \tag{2a}$$

$$k=-5.027-1.484g_p-0.598g_y+0.025\overline{RD}-0.025\overline{RPB}. \tag{2b}$$

The long-run elasticities and semi-elasticities in (2a and 2b) are all of a plausible magnitude and sign – in particular, the influence of the mean short rate and deposit rate on long-run demand has now been estimated explicitly (rather than included implicitly in the intercept term as in the cointegration analysis). The negative long-run inflation effect can be rationalized as resulting from substitution between monetary and real assets as the relative rate of return shifts. Also, since the rate of growth of output can be viewed as a proxy for the return to physical investment (see e.g. Friedman and Schwartz, 1982) the coefficient of g_y is also economically meaningful: at an annual growth rate of 1.8 percent (the average for the period), the long-run elasticity is -0.011, which is correctly signed and, as one might expect, small.

Comparison with previous studies

As a point of comparison, we compared our model with two empirical money demand equations which have appeared in the literature: that of Mills and Wood (1982), and that of Hendry and Ericsson (1989). The Mills–Wood and Hendry–Ericsson equations have $\Delta(m-p)_t$ as the variable to be explained. Since, however, they include Δp_t as an explanatory variable, the properties of the equation are unaffected if Δm_t is used as the variable to be explained (i.e. Δp_t is effectively added to both sides of the equation).

Using our data set, the Mills–Wood equation was estimated with Δm_t as the explanatory variable (1874–1913):

$$\Delta m_t=-2.091+0.389\Delta p_t+0.378\Delta y_t-0.010RPB_t \tag{3}$$
$$(0.341)\,(0.155)\quad(0.085)\quad(0.004)$$

$$-0.0409(m-p-y)_{t-1}$$
$$(0.066)$$

Table 10.4 *Encompassing tests*[a]

Test	Ho: Model 1 encompasses Model 2 (i)	Ho: Model 2 encompasses Model 1 (ii)	Ho: Model 1 encompasses Model 3 (iii)	Ho: Model 3 encompasses Model 1 (iv)
Ericsson (1983)	$N(0,1)=1.67$ (0.09)	$N(0,1)=6.75$ (0.1E−10)	$N(0,1)=1.44$ (0.15)	$N(0,1)=7.21$ (0.6E−12)
Sargan (1964)	$\chi^2(3)=3.22$ (0.36)	$\chi^2(3)=21.41$ (0.9E−4)	$\chi^2(6)=8.64$ (0.19)	$\chi^2(3)=20.38$ (0.1E−3)
Joint model	$F(3,32)=1.08$ (0.37)	$F(3,32)=16.74$ (0.1E−5)	$F(6,28)=1.59$ (0.19)	$F(3,28)=17.91$ (0.1E−5)

Notes:
[a] Model 1 is the equation reported in table 10.3; Model 2 is the Mills–Wood equation reported as (3); Model 3 is the Hendry–Ericsson equation reported as (5). Figures in parenthesis denote marginal significance levels.

$$R^2=0.57; \quad DW=1.12; \quad SE=1.49(\%); \quad AR(4,31)=3.33;$$
$$ARCH(2,33)=0.16; \quad HET(8,26)=1.86; \quad WHITE(14,20)=1.89;$$
$$B-J(2)=0.10; \quad HF(17)=19.55; \quad CHOW(17,18)=0.76.$$

(See note to table 10.3 for a guide to the diagnostics.)

The equation performs reasonably well, particularly as the Mills–Wood equation was originally estimated on a different data set; the coefficients are well determined and plausible, and most of the diagnostic tests are passed, although there is some sign of serial correlation. Table 10.4 contains the results of a number of formal encompassing tests for the two models (Mizon, 1984). Column (ii) reports test-statistics for the equation reported in table 10.3 ("Model 1") to encompass (3) ("Model 2"), whilst column (iii) reports a test of (3) to encompass the equation of table 10.3. The "joint model" test is simply derived by estimating an equation containing all of the explanatory variables for each equation (the joint model) and testing the restrictions necessary to get to each model by an *F*-test. The (1964) Sargan-test is a test for overidentifying exclusion restrictions on the instruments of the alternative model. It is asymptotically distributed as central χ-square with n degrees of freedom for n valid overidentifying restrictions. The Ericsson instrumental variables test is described in Ericsson (1983). It is distributed as asymptotically standard normal under the maintained hypothesis. The three pairs of encompassing test-statistics are uniform in their implications: the equation reported in table 10.3 encompasses the Mills–Wood equation, but the converse is not true.

Hendry and Ericsson (1989), using data for 1870–1970, start by attempting to estimate a long-run demand function by OLS. The analogous equation, estimated on our data (1871–1913) is:

$$(m-p-y)_t = -5.126 - 0.026 RPB_t \tag{4}$$

$$R^2 = 0.40; \qquad SE = 2.88(\%); \qquad DW = 1.09.$$

Hendry and Ericsson then take the residuals from the regression of velocity on the short interest rate, u_t, and proceed to estimate a highly nonlinear error correction model. Proceeding in this fashion, we have, from (4):

$$u_t = (m-p-y)_t + 0.5126 + 0.026 RPB_t$$

and their preferred equation, estimated on our data (1875–1913) is:

$$\Delta m_t = 0.002 + 0.716 \Delta(m-p)_{t-1} - 0.241 \Delta^2(m-p)_{t-2} \tag{5}$$
$$ (0.004)\,(0.125) (0.075)$$

$$+ 0.302 \Delta p_t + 0.784 \Delta p_{t-1} + 0.001 \Delta RPB_t$$
$$ (0.167) (0.148) (0.004)$$

$$- 0.025 \Delta_2 RL_t - 21.103(u_{t-1} - 0.2)u_{t-1}^2$$
$$ (0.014) (13.306)$$

$$R^2 = 0.63; \quad DW = 1.85; \quad SE = 1.47(\%); \quad AR(4,27) = 0.36;$$
$$ARCH(2,32) = 0.20; \quad HET(13,17) = 0.87; \quad WHITE(26,4) = 0.89;$$
$$B\text{–}J(2) = 0.51; \quad HF(17) = 17.00; \quad CHOW(17,14) = 0.70.$$

Again, the model clearly performs reasonably well, although the numerically large coefficient estimate for the nonlinear error correction term (-21.103) is so different from Hendry and Ericsson's (-2.55) as to suggest instability in the equation. The encompassing tests for this model ("Model 3") versus our own preferred equation ("Model 1") are also given in table 10.4. As with the Mills–Wood equation, our preferred equation easily encompasses the Hendry–Ericsson equation but the converse is not true.

Testing the forward-looking model

Cuthbertson and Taylor (1987) develop a forward-looking, rational expectations model of money demand, which can be tested on our data by applying our cointegration results and an extension of the method developed by Campbell and Shiller (1987, 1988) for testing present value models.

The forward-looking model essentially results from a generalization of the one-period quadratic costs of adjustment model (Chow, 1966) which yields the partial adjustment form widely used in empirical money demand studies (Judd and Scadding, 1982; Laidler, 1985). Specifically, agents are assumed to minimize the expected discounted present value of an infinite-period cost function measuring costs of being away from long-run equilibrium, and costs of adjustment, conditional on information at time t:

$$C = E_t \sum_{i=0}^{\infty} D^i \left[a_0(m_{t+i} - \gamma' z_{t+i})^2 + a_1(m_{t+i} - m_{t+i-1})^2 \right],$$ (6)

where E_t is the conditional expectation operator given information at time t, $\gamma' z_t$ is again taken to represent long-run money demand, D is a discount factor $(0 < D < 1)$, and a_0 and a_1 are positive, constant weights.

Minimization of (6) is a standard exercise in the discrete time calculus of variations (Sargent, 1979; Hansen and Sargent, 1980), and yields the forward-looking demand function:

$$m_t = \lambda m_{t-1} + (1-\lambda)(1-\lambda D) \sum_{i=0}^{\infty} (\lambda D)^i E_t \gamma' z_{t+i},$$ (7)

where λ is the stable root of the system $(0 < \lambda < 1)$.

Now suppose we partition the z vector, $z_t' = (z_{1t}', z_{2t}')$, such that $z_{1t} \sim I(1)$ and $z_{2t} \sim I(0)$, and let $\gamma' = (\gamma_1' \, \gamma_2')$ be a conformable partition of the long-run coefficient vector. (7) can be reparameterized:

$$\Delta m_t = (\lambda - 1)(m_{t-1} - \gamma_1' z_{1t-1}) + (1-\lambda) \sum_{i=0}^{\infty} (\lambda D)^i E_t \gamma_1' \Delta z_{1t+i}'$$ (8)

$$+ (1-\lambda)(1-\lambda D) \sum_{i=0}^{\infty} (\lambda D)^i E_t \gamma_2' z_{2t+i}.$$

If $m_t \sim I(1)$, and since, by assumption $\Delta z_{1t} \sim I(0)$, $z_{2t} \sim I(0)$, (8) demonstrates that money must be cointegrated with the $I(1)$ components of the long-run demand function, with a (normalized) cointegrating vector equal to the long-run parameters.

(8) also demonstrates neatly why, if the forward-looking model is correct, error correction money demand models will fit the data well (if expectations of Δz_{1t+i} and z_{2t+i} are conditioned on past values).

Now write the error correction term as e_t:

$$e_t = m_t - \gamma_1' z_{1t}.$$

Then since Δm_t, e_t and $\gamma_2' z_{2t}$ are stationary, they must have an infinite order moving average representative (by Wold's decomposition, Hannan, 1970). This can be approximated in finite samples by an nth order VAR:

$$\begin{pmatrix} \Delta m_t \\ e_t \\ \gamma_2' z_{2t} \end{pmatrix} = \sum_{i=1}^{n} \Phi_i \begin{pmatrix} \Delta m_{t-i} \\ e_{t-i} \\ \gamma_2' z_{2t-i} \end{pmatrix} + \begin{pmatrix} u_t \\ v_t \\ w_t \end{pmatrix},$$ (9)

where the Φ_i are deterministic (3×3) coefficient matrices and $(u_t\ v_t\ w_t)'$ is a vector white noise innovation.[5] The VAR (9) can be reparameterized into first order form:

$$
\begin{bmatrix}
\Delta m_t \\
e_t \\
\gamma_2' z_{2t} \\
\Delta m_{t-1} \\
e_{t-1} \\
\gamma_2' z_{2t-1} \\
\vdots \\
\vdots \\
\Delta m_{t-n+1} \\
e_{t-n+1} \\
\gamma_2' z_{2t-n+1}
\end{bmatrix}
=
\begin{bmatrix}
\begin{array}{ccc|c}
\Phi_1 & \Phi_2 & \cdots & \Phi_n \\
\hline
 & I & & \\
 & & & 0
\end{array}
\end{bmatrix}
\begin{bmatrix}
\Delta m_{t-1} \\
e_{t-1} \\
\gamma_2' z_{2t-1} \\
\vdots \\
\vdots \\
\vdots \\
\Delta m_{t-n} \\
e_{t-n} \\
\gamma_2' z_{2t-n}
\end{bmatrix}
+
\begin{bmatrix}
u_t \\
v_t \\
w_t \\
\\
0
\end{bmatrix}
$$

where I is an identity matrix of order $(3n-3)$. This can be written more compactly as;

$$X_t = \Phi x_{t-1} + W_t. \tag{10}$$

Let f, g and k be $(3n\times1)$ selection vectors with unity in the first, second, and third elements respectively, and zeros elsewhere. Then we can write:

$$\Delta m_t = f' X_t \tag{11}$$

$$e_{t-1} = g' X_{t-1} \tag{12}$$

$$\gamma_2' z_{2t} = k' X_t. \tag{13}$$

Let H_t be an information set consisting of current and lagged values of Δm_t, e_t and $\gamma_2' z_{2t}$,

$$H_t = \{\Delta m_t,\ \Delta m_{t-1},\ e_t,\ e_{t-1},\dots,\ \gamma_2' z_{2t},\ \gamma_2' z_{t-1}\dots\}.$$

Then

$$E(X_{t+i}|H_t) = \Phi^i X_t \tag{14}$$

Thus, using (12), (13), (14):

$$E\left[\sum_{i=0}^{\infty}(\lambda D)^i \gamma_2' z_{2t+i}\,\Big|\,H_t\right] = k'[I+\lambda D\Phi+(\lambda D)^2\Phi^2+\dots]X_t \tag{15}$$

$$= k'[I-\lambda D\Phi]^{-1}X_t$$

$$E\left[\sum_{i=0}^{\infty}(\lambda D)^i\gamma_1\Delta z_{1t+i}\bigg|H_t\right]=(f-g)'[I-\lambda D\Phi]^{-1}X_t+g'[I-\lambda D\Phi]^{-1}X_{t-1}. \quad (16)$$

Thus, projecting both sides of (8) onto X_t:

$$E(\Delta m_t|H_t)=\Delta m_t^*$$
$$=(\lambda-1)g'X_{t-1}+(1-\lambda)(f-g)'[I-\lambda D\Phi]^{-1}X_t$$
$$+(1-\lambda)g'[I-\lambda D\Phi]^{-1}X_{t-1}$$
$$+(1-\lambda)(1-\lambda D)k'[I-\lambda D\Phi]^{-1}X_t. \quad (17)$$

(17) gives the "theoretical" level of money demand growth. Since, however, Δm_t is an element of H_t, we should have:

$$\Delta m_t=\Delta m_t^*. \quad (18)$$

Projecting both sides of (17) onto H_{t-1} using (11), we have;

$$f'\Phi X_{t-1}=(1-\lambda)\{-g'+(f-g)'[I-\lambda D\Phi]^{-1}\Phi+g'[I-\lambda D\Phi]^{-1} \quad (19)$$
$$+(1-\lambda D)k'[I-\lambda D\Phi]^{-1}\Phi\}X_{t-1}.$$

From (19) we can then deduce $3n$ nonlinear restrictions which the forward-looking model imposes on the parameters of the VAR:

$$f'\Phi-(1-\lambda)\{g'[I-\lambda D\Phi]^{-1}+(f-g+(1-\lambda D)k)'[I-\lambda D\Phi]^{-1}\Phi-g'\}=0'. \quad (20)$$

Since estimating a closed form solution for the forward-looking equation involves computationally burdensome, highly nonlinear estimation (Cuthbertson and Taylor, 1987), (20) provides a neat way of testing the model while only having to estimate a linear VAR (so long as a Wald test is used, which requires only unrestricted estimates).

Note, however, that λ and γ must be estimated in advance. An estimate of γ is available from the long-run solution of our error correction model (table 10.3); that model can be viewed as an unrestricted version of (8). From (8), it is clear that $(\lambda-1)$ is the error correction coefficient in the equation for Δm in the VAR for Δm, Δp, Δy, and ΔRL augmented by e_{t-1} (i.e. the error correction representation for cointegrated variables). The equation reported on p. 294 achieved parsimony by including a current-dated value of Δy on the right-hand side. Although this will not, asymptotically, affect the long-run solution, it will affect the magnitude of the error correction coefficient (see Campbell and Shiller, 1988, 515). An estimate of the error correction coefficient can, however, be obtained as a by-product of the Johansen (1988) maximum likelihood procedure. Using this technique, an estimate of 0.337 was obtained, implying an estimate of λ of 0.663. Since these estimates are consistent, they will not affect the asymptotic properties of the Wald test of the restrictions (the estimate of the cointegrating vector will in fact be "super consistent", Stock, 1987).

The above framework can be used to evaluate the forward-looking model not only formally – by testing the restrictions (20) – but also informally, by comparing the movement over time of Δm_t and Δm_t^*. If these two series move closely together, then there is clearly some truth in the forward-looking model, even if its restrictions are rejected formally (Campbell and Shiller 1987, 1988). (18) shows that, as the forward-looking model has been derived above, the theoretical and actual values of money demand growth should coincide – i.e. it is an "exact linear rational expectations model," (Hansen and Sargent, 1980). It is plausible, however, that Δm_t will differ from Δm_t^* by a small amount either because of unforeseen difficulties in implementing plans (Cuthbertson and Taylor, 1987) or because money balances contain an additional "buffer stock" element which responds to innovations in prices, income and interest rates (Cuthbertson and Taylor, 1989).

These considerations suggest computing the variance ratio $\mathrm{var}(\Delta m_t)/\mathrm{var}(\Delta m_t^*)$. If the exact expectations model is correct, then this should be equal to unity (subject only to sampling error in estimating Δm_t^*). According to the above arguments, however, the model is capable of generating a value *slightly* in excess of unity, with only minor modifications. For example, suppose actual money growth is given by the "theoretical growth" Δm_t, *plus* a buffer stock element b_t which is orthogonal to Δm_t^* (Cuthbertson and Taylor, 1989):

$$\Delta m_t = \Delta m_t^* + b_t,$$

so

$$\mathrm{var}(\Delta m_t)/\mathrm{var}(\Delta m_t^*) = 1 + \mathrm{var}(b_t)/\mathrm{var}(\Delta m_t^*) > 1.$$

Table 10.5 reports tests of the forward-looking model. Not only does the model appear to perform well informally (in terms of the variance ratio), it also *easily* passes the Wald test of the implied restrictions on the parameters of the VAR. With a sample value of 1.13, the deviation of the variance ratio from unity can be attributed either to sampling error or to small "buffer stock" elements in money demand. Figure 10.7 graphs the time series behavior of actual and theoretical money growth: again, at an informal level, the model appears to perform well.

Another noteworthy feature of our results is that the direction of Granger causality appears to run towards money growth from the error correction term and interest rates, rather than vice versa, suggesting that a money demand equation (rather than, say, an interest rate equation) has been discovered.

Table 10.5 *Tests of the forward model*[a]

Variable	$Q(18)$	R^2	Δm_t	e_t	$\gamma_2' z_{2t}$
				Granger causality-tests	
a VAR diagnostics (lag length=2)					
Δm_t	14.44	0.62		9.13	3.09
	(0.69)			(0.7E−3)	(0.06)
e_t	14.91	0.67	2.00	−	1.20
	(0.67)		(0.15)		(0.32)
$\gamma_2' z_{zt}$	17.50	0.58	2.99	2.60	−
	(0.49)		(0.06)	(0.09)	−

b Test of forward model restrictions

Wald-statistic: $1.87 \sim \chi^2(6)$
         (0.93)

var $(\Delta m_t)=0.47\text{E}-3$
var $(\Delta m_t^*)=0.38\text{E}-3$
Variance ratio: var(Δm_t)/var$(\Delta m_t^*)=1.22$

Notes:
[a] $e_t=(m_t-p_t-y_t+0.05RL_t)$, $\gamma_2' z_{2t}=0.025(RD_t-RDB_t)$; for the Wald-test, $\lambda=(1-0.337)$; $D=(1+0.03)^{-1}$. Figures in parenthesis are marginal significance levels. See note to table 10.2 for other definitions.

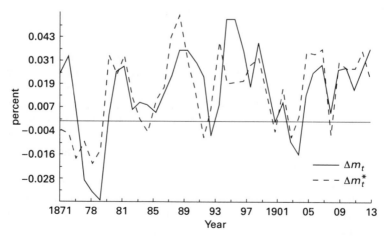

Figure 10.7 Time series behavior: actual and theoretical money growth, 1871–1913

We would not, however, wish to push the favorable interpretation of these results too far. In particular, the forward-looking cost function (6) has not been derived in an explicitly utility maximizing framework – a flaw it shares with the simpler, myopic, one-period cost functions used by previous researchers (Chow, 1966) and of which it is a generalization. The fact that the model is still able to yield favorable test results may however underline the importance of allowing for forward-looking behavior in modeling the demand for financial assets.

Conclusion

In this chapter we have applied best-practice econometric techniques to the best currently available data to investigate the demand for broad money in the United Kingdom during the period 1871–1913.

Our results were encouraging on a number of fronts. First, we discovered a unique, statistically significant long-run money demand function relating broad money, prices, real income and the long-term interest rate, which displayed price and income homogeneity and a long-run interest rate semi-elasticity of −0.05. We then used our cointegration estimates to model short-run adjustment in money demand in which short-term interest rates and the own rate were found to be important, and which returned the long-run estimates as the steady state solution. This short-run demand function was found to be superior to previous estimates for this period on statistical grounds. It fits well with well determined coefficients and shows no sign of structural instability after 1896, even though the behavior of prices and long-term interest rates alters dramatically after that year.

We also extended the methodology of Campbell and Shiller (1987, 1988) to show how the cointegration results could be used to test a particular hypothesis of money demand – the Cuthbertson–Taylor (1987) forward-looking model – for this period. The forward-looking interpretation was shown to stand up well to both formal and informal tests, and suggests the importance of allowing for forward-looking expectations in modeling money demand.

Notes

1. The long-run characteristics of stochastic difference equations such as (1) are discussed in Currie (1981) and Patterson (1984).
2. Mills and Wood (1982) analyze several money stock series and suggest that a series based on Nishimura's unpublished estimates of bank deposits was to be preferred. Most other studies of this period (Hendry and Ericsson, 1989) have used the Friedman–Schwartz data, with the notable exception of Klovland (1987), which uses the same money stock series as the present study.

3. Goodfriend (1985) argues that the role of lagged variables, and in particular of lagged dependent variables, in empirical money demand relationships may be simply to "soak up" serially correlated measurement error in the observed data series. It is, however, easy to demonstrate that, so long as the measurement error is $I(0)$, the cointegration estimates will still be superconsistent. Viewed in this light, our cointegration estimates can be viewed as estimates of a *short-run*, static money demand function.

4. There are good empirical and theoretical reasons for setting the steady state growth rate of RL to zero. On empirical grounds, the ΔRL_t process appears to have a zero mean, since the following MA(3) model was identified and fitted (1873–1913, standard errors in parenthesis):
$$\Delta RL_t = 0.607\text{E}-2 + (0.571 + 0.372L + 0.352L^2)u_t$$
$$(0.243\text{E}-1)\ (0.155)\ (0.170)\ (0.154)$$
    which clearly has an intercept insignificantly different from zero at least at the 5 percent level. Moreover, with a constant steady state rate of inflation, steady state growth in RL translates into steady state growth in the *real* long-term interest rate, which seems counterintuitive on theoretical grounds. In addition, given a constant steady state short-term interest rate, this would also imply a continously steepening yield curve.

5. Constant terms are excluded from (9) for expositional purposes; they were included in all of the empirical work.

References

Bera, A. K. and C. M. Jarque (1982). "Model Specification Tests: A Simultaneous Approach," *Journal of Econometrics* 20, 59–82

Bordo, M. D. and L. Jonung (1987). *The Long-Run Behaviour of the Velocity of Circulation: the International Evidence*, New York: Cambridge University Press

Campbell, J. Y. and R. J. Shiller (1987). "Cointegration and Tests of Present Value Models," *Journal of Political Economy* 95(5), 1062–1088

    (1988). "Interpreting Cointegrated Models," *Journal of Economic Dynamics and Control* 12, 505–522

Capie, F. and G. Rodrik-Bali (1985). "The Money Adjustment Process in the United Kingdom: 1870–1914," *Economica* 52, 117–22.

Capie, F. H. and A. Webber (1985). *A Monetary History of the United Kingdom, 1870–1982*, vol. 1, *Data, Sources, Methods*, London: George Allen & Unwin

Carlson, J. A. and J. R. Frew (1980). "Money Demand Responsiveness to the Rate of Return on Money: A Methodological Critique," *Journal of Political Economy* 88, 598–607

Chow, G. C. (1960). "Tests of the Equality Between Two Sets of Coefficients in Two Linear Regressions," *Econometrica* 28, 561–605

    (1966). "On the Long-Run and Short-Run Demand for Money," *Journal of Political Economy* 74, 111–131

Currie, D. (1981). "Some Long-Run Features of Dynamic Time Series Models," *Economic Journal* 91, 704–715

Cuthbertson, K. and M. P. Taylor (1987). "The Demand for Money: A Dynamic Rational Expectations Model," *Economic Journal* 97, 65–76

(1989). "Anticipated and Unanticipated Variables in the Demand for M1 in the UK," *Manchester School,*

Engle, R. F. (1982). "Autoregressive Conditional Heteroscedasticity with Estimates of the Variance of UK Inflation," *Econometrica* 55, 251–276

Engle, R. F. and C. W. J. Granger (1987). "Co-integration and Error Correction: Representation, Estimation and Testing," *Econometrica* 55(2) (March), 251–276

Ericsson, N. R. (1983). "Asymptotic Properties of Instrumental Variables Statistics for Testing Non-Nested Hypotheses," *Review of Economic studies* 50(2), 287–304

Feinstein, C. H. (1972). *National Income, Expenditure and Output of the United Kingdom 1855–1965,* Cambridge: Cambridge University Press

Friedman, M. and A. J. Schwartz (1982). *Monetary Trends in the United States and in the United Kingdom 1870–1970,* Chicago: University to Chicago Press for NBER

Fuller, W. A. (1976). *Introduction to Statistical TimeSeries,* New York: John Wiley

Goodfriend, M. (1985). "Reinterpreting Money Demand Regressions," in K. Brunner and A. H. Meltzer (eds.), *Understanding Monetary Regimes, Carnegie–Rochester Conference Series on Public Policy,* Amsterdam: North-Holland, 207–241

Goodhart, C. A. E. (1972). *The Business of Banking, 1891–1914,* London: Weidenfeld & Nicolson

Griffiths, B. (1973). "The Development of Restrictive Practices in the UK Monetary System," *Manchester School* 41, 3–18

Hannan, E. J., (1970) *Multiple Time Series* , New York: Wiley

Hansen, L. P. and T. J. Sargent (1980). "Formulating and Estimating Dynamic Linear Rational Expectations Models," *Journal of Economic Dynamics and Control* 2, 7–46

Harley, C. K. (1976). "Goschen's Conversion of the National Debt and the Yield on Consols," *Economic History Review* 34(1) (February), 101–106

Hendry, D. F. (1979). "Predictive Failure and Econometric Modelling in Macroeconomics: The Transactions Demand for Money," in P. Ormerod (ed.), *Economic Modelling: Current Issues in Macroeconomic Modelling in the UK and the US,* London: Heinemann, 217–242

Hendry, D. F. and N. R. Ericsson (1991). "Monetary Trends in the United States and in the United Kingdom," *American Economic Review* 81(1), 8–38

Johansen, S. (1988). "Statistical Analysis of Cointegration Vectors," *Journal of Economic Dynamics and Control* 12, 231–254

Judd, J. P. and T. Scadding (1982). "The Search for a Stable Demand for Money Function," *Journal of Economic Literature* 20(3), 993–1023

Keynes, J. M. (1930). *A Treatise on Money,* vol. II, *The Applied Theory of Money,* London: Macmillan

Klein, B. (1974). "Competitive Interest Payments on Bank Deposits and the Long-Run Demand for Money," *American Economic Review* 64, 931–949

Klovland, T. C. (1987). "The Demand for Money in the United Kingdom 1875–1913," *Oxford Bulletin of Economics and Statistics* 49(3) (August), 251–271

Laidler, D. E. W. (1985). "The Demand for Money: Theories, Evidence and Problems," 3rd edn., New York: Harper & Row

Mills, T. C. and G. E. Wood (1978). "Econometric Evaluation of Alternative Money Stock Series, 1880–1913," *Journal of Money, Credit and Banking* 14, 265–277
  (1982). "Econometric Evaluation of Alternative UK Money Stock Series, 1870–1913," *Journal of Money, Credit and Banking* (May), 265–277

Mitchell, B. R. and P. Deane (1962). *Abstract of British Historical Statistics*, Cambridge: Cambridge University Press

Mizon, G. E. (1984). "The Encompassing Approach in Econometrics," in D. F. Hendry and K. F. Wallis (eds.), *Econometrics and Quantitative Economics*, Oxford: Basil Blackwell

Patterson, K. D. (1984). "Some Properties of Consumption Functions with Integral Correction Mechanisms," *Manchester School* 52, 347–362

Sargan, J. D. (1964). "Wages and Prices in the United Kingdom: A Study in Econometric Methodology," in P. E. Hart, G. Mills and J. K. Whittaker (eds.), *Econometric Analysis for National Economic Planning*, London: Butterworth

Sargent, T. J. (1979). *Macroeconomic Theory*, New York: Academic Press

Sheppard, D. K. (1971). *The Growth and Role of UK Financial Institutions 1880–1962*, London: Methuen

Stock, J. H. (1987). "Asymptotic Properties of a Least Squares Estimator of Cointegrating Vectors," *Econometrica* 55, 1035–1056

Taylor, M. (1993). "Modelling the Demand for UK Broad Money, 1871–1913," *Review of Economics and Statistics* 75 (February), 112–117

White, (1980). "A Heteroskedasticity-consistent Covariance Matrix Estimator and a Direct Test for Heterosicedasticity," *Econometrica* 48 (January), 55–68

V

Exchange rate behavior

11 The dollar/pound real exchange rate and fiscal policy during the gold standard period

Graciela L. Kaminsky and Michael Klein

Introduction

More than a century has passed since the widespread adoption of the gold standard in 1879 and almost 80 years stand between its demise at the beginning of World War I and the present day. Economists look back to the gold standard period as a time when international markets in goods and capital operated efficiently and effectively. This view has served to make the gold standard period a benchmark for studying the experience of the interwar period or the post-World War II period with respect to issues such as international integration and international policy coordination.

The gold standard period has also come to serve as a benchmark for exchange rate experience since it was largely characterized by stable nominal exchange rates. For example, the British pound was worth 4.86 US dollars during the entire 35 years of the gold standard while the pound was devalued twice against the dollar during the shorter Bretton Woods era. There was also relative stability in the real exchange rate between the United States and United Kingdom during the gold standard period as compared to other times. The bilateral dollar/pound real exchange rate fluctuated within a range of about 20 percent during the 35 years of the gold standard and its level a few years after the resumption of the gold standard by the United States was very close to its level at the outset of World War I. In contrast, the Bretton Woods period saw an ongoing loss of competitiveness of the British pound with respect to the dollar. Britain's bilateral real exchange rate against the dollar appreciated by more than 30 percent between 1950 and 1973 despite the 16 percent nominal pound devaluation in 1967.

In this chapter we look back to the gold standard period to consider the link between fiscal variables and the real exchange rate between the United States and the United Kingdom during the period from the United States' resumption of the gold standard in 1879 to the outbreak of World War I in 1914. Recent empirical studies of the determinants of the real exchange rate in the post-Bretton Woods era have focused on the role of fiscal variables under floating nominal parities (Feldstein, 1986) and under the semi-fixed parities of the European Monetary System (EMS) (Froot and Rogoff, 1991). As with other topics in international economics, the gold standard era can serve as a type of benchmark for studying the real exchange rate, since it was marked by relative stability.

A benchmark must not diverge too much from that to which it is compared, however, or the comparison will be too riddled with differences to make it meaningful. There are manifold differences in the economic profiles of the United States and the United Kingdom between the gold standard period and more recent times, and some of these are directly related to a study of the real exchange rate and fiscal policy. One obvious difference is that governments had a much smaller role in economies in the late 19th and early 20th centuries as compared to today. Government expenditures in the United States and the United Kingdom were a much smaller proportion of national income during this period than in recent times but these low levels of expenditures were punctuated by wars in each country, increased public works spending in the United States in the early 1890s and a naval military build-up in the United States after the turn of the century. A major source of government revenue in the United States at that time, tariff revenues, represents an inconsequential part of today's budget. The modern period has been characterized by persistent inflation and has not had the steep deflations of the late 19th century. Finally, as mentioned above, there was a stable nominal parity during the gold standard period while the post-World War II period included devaluations and a switch from a fixed dollar/pound parity to a floating exchange rate.

While these differences between the Classical gold standard period and the present day hardly need repeating, there are some striking similarities. The extent to which the United States and the United Kingdom were open to international trade in goods and assets during the period from 1879 to 1914 is more similar to the present day than to the intervening half-century. The steady growth in trade as a proportion of national income for the United States and the United Kingdom since World War II has served to return these proportions near levels that were observed in the late 19th century.[1] The high degree of international capital mobility during the gold standard period ended with World War I and was not to be seen again until the present day.[2] Also, while the period from 1879 to 1914 did not see a change in the international monetary system similar to the switch from the Bretton Woods System to a float in 1973, the maintenance of the gold standard was not without dispute. The United States was riven by the debate over the maintenance of the gold standard in the 1890s and the presidential election of 1896 largely centered on this issue.

The list of similarities and differences between eras discussed above are wide-ranging since movements in the real exchange rate reflect a range of economic factors. The simple model of the real exchange rate presented in the next section helps frame the empirical discussion that follows by showing how different factors affect the real exchange rate. This model captures both the equilibrium real exchange rate and the dynamics of its adjustment. The third section provides a historical context for the subsequent empirical analysis by presenting a chronology of the evolution of the real bilateral dollar/pound exchange rate and the relevant economic and political events of the time. The fourth section presents the empirical results. The analysis is based upon an econometric model which decomposes the movements in the real exchange rate into those associated with movements in fiscal variables, as well as those arising due to productivity shocks and shocks to the assets market. This model provides us with a variance decomposition of the real exchange rate, an impulse response relationship and a historical decomposition of its movements. The fifth section presents some conclusions.

A simple two-country model of the real exchange rate

In this section we provide a framework for the empirical discussion that follows by sketching a simple stochastic flexible price model of the real exchange rate for two countries with a fixed nominal parity. The model shows how factors such as government expenditures and supply shocks affect the equilibrium level of the real exchange rate. It also provides insight into the effect of an expected change in the nominal parity. This is important for our study since, as we will discuss below, there were several episodes when there was some likelihood that the United States would abandon the gold standard. We also discuss an extension of the model based upon the slow adjustment of relative prices.

The model, which describes the equilibrium conditions in the goods and money markets, is presented below:

$$\bar{y}_t = f_t + \sigma(m_t - p_t) \tag{1}$$
$$m_t + s_t = \lambda(_t s_{t+1} - s_t) + v_t, \tag{2}$$

where all variables represent UK variables relative to US variables. All variables are in logarithms. For example, $\bar{y}_t = \bar{y}_t^{uk} - \bar{y}_t^{us}$ is the UK full employment output relative to the US full employment output, s_t is the nominal exchange rate between the dollar and the pound (in dollars per pound), $_t s_{t+1}$ is the expected nominal exchange rate in period $t+1$ conditional on information known in period t, $f_t = f_t^{uk} - f_t^{us}$ is the UK fiscal shock relative to the US fiscal shock, which is interpreted as UK government spending relative to the US government spending, $m_t = m_t^{uk} - m_t^{us}$ is the UK money supply relative to US money supply, and $p_t = p_t^{uk} - p_t^{us}$ is the UK price index relative to the US price index. Later on, we will also refer to the real exchange rate, q_t, defined as $q_t = s_t + p_t$.

(1) is the equilibrium condition in the goods market. Since it is assumed that prices and wages are fully flexible, output is always at the full employment level, $\bar{y}_t$. The right-hand side of (1) reflects the demand for goods by the government sector, f_t, and the household sector, $\sigma(m_t - p_t)$. We think of the government as just purchasing domestic goods, thus a change in UK government spending relative to US government spending will equally change relative demand for UK goods.[3] We assume that households, as in the money in advance literature, must hold a stock of monetary balances to purchase goods. We further assume, as is traditional in international economics, that households need dollars to purchase US goods and pounds to purchase UK goods (see, for example, Helpman 1981). Thus, household demand for UK goods relative to US goods will be proportional to relative real money balances, $m_t - p_t$.

(2) is the condition for portfolio equilibrium. Investors are assumed to have available a choice between only two assets: US money and UK money. Both currencies bear zero nominal interest. To reflect the fact that capital markets in the United States and the United Kingdom during the period studied were closely integrated, it is assumed that the holdings of pounds relative to dollars are proportional to the expected rate of depreciation of the dollar, $_t s_{t+1} - s_t$.[4] Demand for relative money also depends on v_t, which we interpret as financial innovations that increase demand for money in the United Kingdom relative to the United States. According to Friedman and Schwartz (1982) financial innovations were the main factor behind the increase in the demand for dollars during the gold standard period.[5]

In order to examine the path of the real exchange rate over time, we have to postulate the process followed by the fiscal shock, the financial innovation, and the output supply shock. As an example, we postulate the following processes:

$$\bar{y}_t = \bar{y}_{t-1} + \mu_t^{\bar{y}} \tag{3}$$

$$f_t = f_{t-1} + \mu_t^f \tag{4}$$

$$v_t = v_{t-1} + \mu_t^v, \tag{5}$$

where the μs are uncorrelated innovations. In (3)–(5) we assume that supply, fiscal, and financial innovation shocks are of a permanent nature. This is just a useful simplification reflecting the highly persistent nature of the shocks.

The government foregoes control over the money supply when it pegs the exchange rate and faces highly-integrated world capital markets. For example, if the government issues more domestic money than the private sector is willing to hold, people will trade domestic money for foreign currency with the central bank. The central bank must accept the domestic money in exchange for the foreign currency to maintain the peg. The acceptance of this currency by the central bank, however, nullifies the initial expansionary monetary policy. Thus the equilibrium relative stock of money is determined by (2).

(2) is general enough to allow for different likelihoods of the maintenance of the fixed exchange rate regime. If the private sector believes that the fixed exchange rate regime will be maintained then the expected depreciation term $(_ts_{t+1} - s_t)$ will be zero. The expected depreciation may not be zero, however, if events suggest to the market that there is a likelihood of a change in nominal parities. For example, when the government runs a persistent deficit financed by issuing money there will be a persistent loss of foreign reserves from the central bank. In time, a crisis will develop when people buy up the remaining reserves of the central bank in anticipation of a devaluation and thereby force the devaluation to occur.[6] In this section we allow expectations of a devaluation to be nonzero although we do not relate those expectations to a particular process followed by the government deficit. In particular, we assume that expectations of depreciation are described by:

$$_ts_{t+1} - s_t = \mu_t^s, \tag{6}$$

where μ_t^s is an uncorrelated shock. In (6) investors expect a devaluation of the dollar of size μ_t^s. Naturally, if, for example, expectations of depreciation are generated by a continuous government deficit, expectations of depreciation will in general be correlated over time. Thus, (6) only provides a useful benchmark to examine the effects of an expected depreciation on the real exchange rate.

The equilibrium real exchange rate in the flexible price model, $\bar{q}_t$, is given in (7)

$$\bar{q}_t = \lambda\mu_t^s + v_t + \frac{1}{\sigma}[f_t - \bar{y}_t]. \tag{7}$$

An increase in the relative level of government spending by the United Kingdom increases the relative demand for UK goods because we assume that governments concentrate their spending on goods from their own countries. Therefore the dollar depreciates in real terms with increases in f_t. Conversely, the pound depreciates with a supply shock that increases the supply of UK goods relative to American goods (i.e. an increase in $\bar{y}_t$). The third determinant of the equilibrium real exchange rate is the expected devaluation of the dollar (μ_t^s). When investors expect the dollar to be devalued they sell dollars for pounds, lowering the level of the money supply in the United States relative to United Kingdom (see (2)). The lower relative money supply in the United States lowers the relative demand for US goods (1). This results in a reduction of the relative price of US goods and therefore in a depreciation of the dollar in real terms. Thus an expected future nominal devaluation causes a real depreciation in the present. Finally, an increase in v_t, increases the stock of relative real monetary balances in the United Kingdom, increasing the demand for UK goods relative to US goods, and depreciating the dollar in real terms.

For our empirical estimation, we allow also for the possibility of slow adjustment in prices. We assume the following price setting equation:

$$p_t = {}_{t-1}\bar{p}_t + \theta(y_t - \bar{y}_t),\tag{8}$$

where $\bar{p}_t$ is the equilibrium relative price that will prevail in a flexible price model and y_t is the demand determined level of output in the short run when price adjustment is sluggish. The pricing rule in this equation encompasses the outcomes of a broad set of models. At one extreme, it allows for fully flexible prices in a frictionless neoclassical model with output always at the full employment level ($\theta=\infty$). At the other extreme, prices are set at the beginning of the period and do not adjust to supply or demand shocks ($\theta=0$), but can be adjusted after a period.[7]

The equilibrium real exchange rate with slowly adjusting prices is:

$$q_t = \bar{q}_t + \frac{1}{1+\theta\sigma}\frac{1}{\sigma}[(\mu_t^{\bar{y}} - \mu_t^f) - \mu_t^v - \lambda\mu_t^s + (s_t - s_{t-1} - \mu_{t-1}^s)].\tag{9}$$

The dollar/pound real exchange rate in a slowly adjusting price model will increase in response to a fiscal shock, μ_t^f, a financial innovation shock, μ_t^v, an expectation of a future dollar depreciation, μ_t^s, but by less than does the real exchange rate in the flexible price model. Conversely, the dollar will appreciate in real terms if there is a positive supply shock, $\mu_t^{\bar{y}}$, but by less than does $\bar{q}_t$.

Finally, when prices are not fully flexible, expectations of depreciation of the dollar at the moment in which prices are set, μ_{t-1}^s, will also affect the real exchange rate if these expectations turn out to be wrong *ex post* (i.e. if $s_t - s_{t-1} - \mu_{t-1}^s \neq 0$). The intuition is straightforward. Prices are assumed to be set at $t-1$ so that they clear the market if expectations turn out to be correct. When prices are set in period $t-1$ prior to knowing the nominal exchange rate, s_t, they will incorporate price setters' expectations of the nominal exchange rate. Thus, if individuals expect that a dollar devaluation will occur next period, prices in the United States will rise accordingly. If in period t the devaluation is not made effective, there will be an appreciation

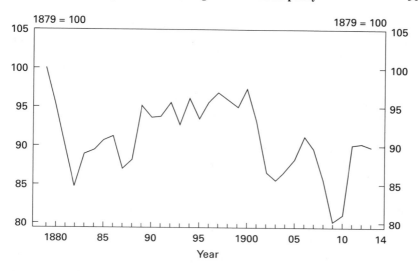

Figure 11.1 Dollar/pound real exchange rate, 1879–1913

of the dollar real exchange rate and excess supply of goods in the United States.

The real exchange rate and fiscal policy during the gold standard

As suggested by the model above, movements in the real exchange rate may reflect changes in a wide range of underlying fundamentals. A study of the bilateral real exchange rate between the United States and United Kingdom during the gold standard period is particularly interesting since there were many economic and political events at that time which played a role in the determination of the real exchange rate. To put the econometric analysis presented below into historical context, we discuss in this section the time path of the dollar/pound real exchange rate between 1879 and 1914 as well as relevant economic and political events of the period. We first present the time series of the real exchange rate, fiscal variables in each country, and UK relative to US output, as well as the interest rate differential, which can provide a measure of expectations of changes in the dollar/pound parity. This is followed by a narrative of the chronology of the path of the real exchange rate and concurrent relevant economic and political events.[8]

Figure 11.1 presents the logarithm of the real exchange rate between United Kingdom and the United States over the period from 1879 to 1914.[9] The range of the real exchange rate's movement during this period was about 20 percent. The most depreciated value of the dollar/pound real exchange rate was at the outset of the period and its most appreciated value was towards the end of the period. As shown in figure 11.1, however, the fact that the extreme values of the real exchange rate were at the beginning and the end of this era does not imply a steady appreciation over the almost four decades covered by the sample. Instead, there were periods of sharp appreciation and sharp depreciation that saw near 10 percent movements in the real exchange rate over the course of a few years.

The time series of some of the factors that may have contributed to the path of the real exchange rate during this period are presented in figures 11.2 and 11.3. Fiscal variables in the United Kingdom and the United States are presented in the six panels in figure 11.2. These six figures include government purchases relative to GNP (11.2a), the average tariff rates and the government deficits (corrected for the inflation erosion of the public debt) relative to GNP for each country (11.2b, 11.2c).[10] The figures demonstrate the differences across countries in the range of these variables. Government purchases were on average much larger in the United Kingdom than in the United States. Likewise, the UK real budget deficit rose at times to over 4 percent of national income while in the United States it never reached 2 percent (11.2c).[11] Finally, average tariff rates in the United States were orders of magnitude greater than those in United Kingdom.

Figure 11.3 presents relative output (11.3a) and interest rate differentials (11.3b) between the United Kingdom and the United States over the sample period. The figures demonstrate that the UK real output relative to that of the United States fell by about 30 percent over the sample, most of this change coming in the second half of the sample. The interest rate differential figure demonstrates that the interest rate in the United Kingdom was consistently below that of the United States, with the largest differential in the first half of the 1890s corresponding to the time of the greatest strength of the Free Silver Movement in the United States.

The data presented here, along with other information on relevant economic and political events of the times, allows us to develop a chronology of the evolution of the real exchange rate and its probable proximate causes over our sample. This informal description provides a historical context for the econometric analysis offered in the next section. The sample begins with an appreciation of the real value of the dollar of more than 15 percent within two years after resumption. This probably reflects the effect of substantial gold inflows at that time. The United States gold stock rose from $210 million in mid-1879 to $439 million two years later. The concurrent movement in the UK gold holdings is reflected in the loss of 40 percent of the Bank of England's reserves during this period. In response, the Bank of England raised the bank rate from 2.5 percent in 1879 to 6 percent by 1881.

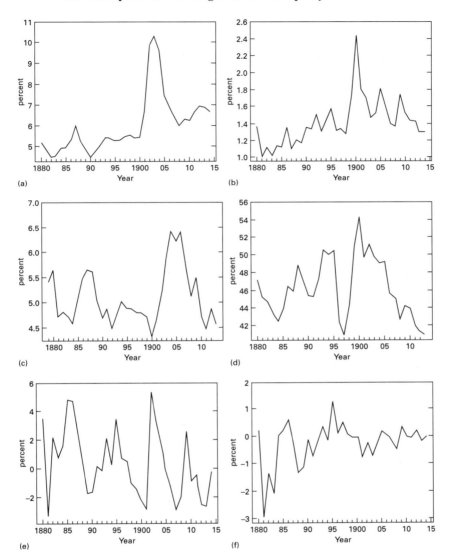

Figure 11.2 Fiscal factors, 1879–1913
(a) Great Britain, government purchases/GNP
(b) United States, government purchases/GNP
(c) Great Britain, average tariff
(d) United States, average tariff
(e) Great Britain, real government deficit/GNP
(f) United States, real government deficit/GNP

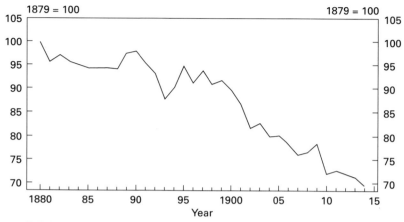

Relative output = ln (Great Britain GNP/United States GNP) taken at constant prices

(a)

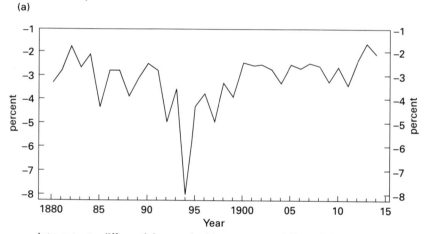

Interest rate differential = nominal interest rate of Great Britain - nominal interest rate of the United States

(b)

Figure 11.3 Other market factors, 1879–1913
(a) Relative output
(b) Interest rate differential

The subsequent real depreciation of the dollar from 1882–1886 reflects the 20 percent deflation in the United States and the smaller, 12 percent, deflation in Great Britain. During this time there was a financial panic in the United States (in May 1884) and silver purchases weakened confidence in the maintenance of the gold standard.

The latter half of the 1880s saw a depreciation of the dollar real exchange rate. This may have been due to a relatively contractionary fiscal policy in the United States since other factors, such as the revival of the United Kingdom lending to the United States, would have put pressure on the dollar to appreciate. The US government surplus, equal to $64 million in 1885, rose over the next few years, reaching a peak of $111 million in 1888 before falling again at the close of the decade. In the late 1880s, the administration of Grover Cleveland favored reducing this surplus through tariff reductions rather than through increased spending. This led, however, to a political backlash and as a consequence the protectionist McKinley Tariff was passed in 1890. One of the most important fiscal implications of the McKinley Tariff was its provision which put sugar on the "free list." This reduced tariff revenues and shrank the government's budget surplus. The surplus was further affected by Congressional authorization of increased government spending for pensions, rivers, and harbors.[12]

The real exchange rate fluctuated within a fairly narrow range of less than 5 percent during the 1890s. This quiescence belies the economic and political turbulence of the decade and reflects forces working in opposite directions on the real exchange rate. The decade began with a financial crisis when the English banking house of Baring Brothers failed in 1890. The potential panic and economic consequences due to this event, however, were averted through timely gold purchases by the Bank of England. A variety of events created incipient pressure for dollar appreciation in the 1890s. As discussed above, the McKinley Tariff and the Pension Act of 1890 had adverse fiscal implications. The McKinley Tariff may also have contributed to the fall in UK exports in the first half of the 1890s, when they were 10 percent lower than their average over the previous five years. At the end of the decade the Dingley Tariff in 1897 represented the highest tariffs in the United States up until that point. In the United Kingdom the Great Depression continued after a four-year hiatus. UK prices fell over the first part of the decade and reached a trough in 1896. Other events during the 1890s tended to cause an incipient dollar depreciation. In May 1893 there was a financial panic in the United States as gold reserves fell below $100 million, the level thought to be the minimum required for maintaining the parity. Reserves continued to fall and reached $66 million at the beginning of 1894 and, despite the efforts of the Morgan syndicate, $50 million by the beginning of 1896. The political events of this time also brought into question the maintenance of the gold standard by the United States. The Free Silver forces gained strength up until the election of 1896. None of these forces seemed to dominate the others, however, and the real exchange rate ended the century at a level close to that found over the full decade of the 1890s.

The steep dollar appreciation at the beginning of the new century foretold the higher real exchange rate volatility in the final years of the sample as compared to most of the earlier period. The dollar appreciated by about 10 percent in the first years of the 20th century. This may partially reflect increased confidence in the maintenance of the gold standard by the United States due to the second failure of the presidential aspirations of William Jennings Bryan as well as the passing of the Gold Standard Act of 1900, which made it the duty of the Secretary of the Treasury to maintain the gold parity. The period around the turn of the century also saw an increase in government expenditures associated with wars by each country. The United States fought the Spanish–American War in 1898, and this raised government expenditures by 50 percent. The United Kingdom was engaged in the more protracted Boer War from 1899 to 1902 and this was associated with a spike in UK government expenditures. While an increase in taxes and the limited length of the Spanish–American War resulted in a small change in the American government's budget deficit, the UK deficit rose dramatically after the turn of the century; this may have contributed to the depreciation of the dollar after 1902. The dollar appreciated again after 1905; though the exact timing of this is difficult to conclusively link to fiscal causes, this period did see an end to the UK war spending and an increase in US government expenditures to pay for a larger navy and to purchase the Panama Canal. The appreciation after 1905 may also have been fueled by the marked expansion in foreign investment by UK investors with the United States being one of the main recipients of these funds. The severe contraction in the United States in 1908 in the wake of the 1907 financial panic may have partly reduced the appreciation of the dollar in the late 1900s. The sample ends with a real dollar depreciation from 1909 to 1911 and then a stable real exchange rate in the final two years. The contraction in the American business cycle from its peak in January 1910 to its trough in January 1912 occurred at a time when the UK economy was in the midst of a five-year expansion that had begun in 1908.

While fiscal factors, supply and demand shocks, asset market shocks and political factors could all have played a part in the determination of the real exchange rate during the gold standard period, a narrative account is insufficient for decomposing the effects of the movements in the real exchange rate into parts attributable to each factor. For this reason we next turn to an econometric model in order to gauge the relative contribution of different factors to the time path of the real exchange rate under the gold standard.

Empirical evidence

The model developed above and the narrative provided in the previous section suggest the effect of economic fundamentals such as supply shocks or government expenditures on the real exchange rate. In this section we empirically explore the links between economic fundamentals and the real exchange rate between United Kingdom and the United States for the gold standard period from 1879 to 1914. We estimate a structural vector auto-regression (VAR) model with variables that represent the differences between UK macroeconomic variables and their US counterparts. We present estimates of the parameters of this structural VAR and then employ it to consider the variance decomposition of the shocks to the real exchange rate, the impulse responses of the real exchange rate to a variety of shocks, and a historical forecast error decomposition of the real exchange rate.

The model estimated is based upon the model introduced in the second section with a minor modification because we allow three different fiscal shocks to possibly affect the real exchange rate: (1) government spending, (2) import tariffs, and (3) fiscal deficit. Thus the fiscal shock f_t is now a vector of dimension (3×1), $f_t = [g_t, \tau_t, d_t]'$. The model is now rewritten as follows:[13]

$$q_t = a_{12} y_t + \sum_{j=1}^{r} A_j^q X_{t-j} - \eta_t^{\tilde{y}} \tag{10a}$$

$$y_t = -a_{21} q_t + a_{23}(s_{t+1} - s_t) + a_{24} g_t + a_{25} \tau_t + a_{26} d_t + \sum_{j=1}^{r} A_j^y X_{t-j}$$
$$+ \eta_t^v \tag{10b}$$

$$(_t s_{t+1} - s_t) = -a_{34} g_t + \sum_{j=1}^{r} A_j^s X_{t-j} + \eta_t^s \tag{10c}$$

$$g_t = -a_{42} y_t + \sum_{j=1}^{r} A_j^g X_{t-j} + \eta_t^g \tag{10d}$$

$$\tau_t = a_{54} g_t + \sum_{j=1}^{r} A_j^\tau X_{t-j} + \eta_t^\tau \tag{10e}$$

$$d_t = -a_{61} q_t + a_{63}(_t s_{t+1} - s_t) + a_{64} g_t - a_{65} \tau_t + \sum_{j=1}^{r} A_j^d X_{t-j} + \eta_t^d. \tag{10f}$$

We have already defined most of the variables in the second section. The new variables introduced in this section are defined as follows: $g_t = g_t^{uk} - g_t^{us}$ is UK government spending relative to US government spending (as a share of GNP), $\tau_t = \tau_t^{uk} - \tau_t^{us}$ is UK average import tariff relative to the US average import tariff, and $d_t = d_t^{uk} - d_t^{us}$ is UK real government deficit relative to the

US real government deficit (as a share of GNP). As we noted in the third section, the expected depreciation of the dollar, $({}_t s_{t+1} - s_t)$, is measured using the interest rate differential, $i_t^{us} - i_t^{uk}$. In the above equations we define X_t as follows: $X_t = [q_t, y_t, ({}_t s_{t+1} - s_t), g_t, \tau_t, d_t]'$. Finally, the η_ts are the policy or "structural" innovations, which buffet the system and cause fluctuations. We have already described most of these shocks in the second section. We should note that μ_t^y cannot be identified as a financial innovation shock. In fact, μ_t^y can represent any shock that increases demand for British goods relative to US goods (including financial innovations) and leads to an appreciation of the pound.[14] Thus, from now on, we will refer to μ_t^y as an "aggregate demand" shock. The fiscal shocks are now the shock to government expenditure η_t^d.

We capture the dynamics in the model introduced in the second section by allowing each variable in the system to depend on past realizations of all the variables in the system. The A_js for $j > 0$ capture the propagation mechanism of the economy over time. We impose no restrictions on these matrices (except by specifying the maximum lag length).

We concentrate on modeling the contemporaneous relationships based basically on the model described in the second section. The matrix A_0, whose nonzero elements are denoted by a_{ij} in (10a)–(10f), captures these contemporaneous relations. We now describe more thoroughly these within the period responses. (10a) is the price setting equation ((8) in the second section). As in that section, a demand determined increase in output generates a within the year hike in prices. On the contrary, a supply shock, η_t^y, will push prices downward.[15] The aggregate demand equation in (10b) is basically (1), in which we substituted away relative money balances, m_t, using (2). Since relative UK real balances increase with expectations of depreciation of the dollar and financial innovations in the United Kingdom, the relative demand for UK goods will increase with positive shocks to these variables. Conversely, since an increase of UK relative prices (a deterioration of the dollar in real terms) reduces UK real balances, demand for UK goods will decrease with a deterioration of the dollar in real terms. As in the second section, demand for goods increases with government spending, g_t. We should note that in (10b) we also allow tariffs and government deficits to affect demand for goods. (10b) postulates that demand for UK goods will increase with increases in UK tariffs relative to US tariffs, τ_t, and with increases in the UK relative real government deficit, d_t.[16]

(10c) models the response of expectations of changes in the dollar/pound parity to market fundamentals. This equation postulates, as in the literature of balance of payments crisis, that an expansionary fiscal policy in the United Kingdom may indicate future money creation in that country and a possible devaluation of the pound, which is reflected in investors' expectations. (10d)–(10f) model the behavior of the fiscal variables as a function of policy shocks – η_t^g, η_t^τ, and η_t^d. (10d) allows the government spending share in output to respond contemporaneously to fluctuations in output. Since during the period of analysis tariffs were the most important source of revenue of the government, (10e) allows tariffs to increase with increases in government spending. Finally, (10f) postulates that the government deficit decreases with unexpected inflation shocks, which reduce the costs of borrowing, and with increases in tariff revenues; and it increases with increases in government expenditures – purchases and interest payments. Fiscal policy innovations in (10d)–(10f) – η_t^g, η_t^τ, η_t^d – are designed to capture shocks to policy variables unrelated to other fundamental macroeconomic influences, such as military spending shocks due to the country engaging in a war or increases in tariffs due to a protectionist sentiment surge such as the adoption of the McKinley Tariff Act of 1890.[17]

We write the model using matrix notation as follows:

$$X_t = \sum_{j=0}^{r} A_j X_{t-j} + \eta_t, \tag{11}$$

where A_0, as defined in (10a)–(10f), can be written as follows:

$$A_0 = \begin{bmatrix} 0 & a_{12} & 0 & 0 & 0 & 0 \\ -a_{21} & 0 & a_{23} & a_{24} & a_{25} & a_{26} \\ 0 & 0 & 0 & -a_{34} & 0 & 0 \\ 0 & a_{42} & 0 & 0 & 0 & 0 \\ 0 & 0 & 0 & a_{54} & 0 & 0 \\ -a_{61} & 0 & a_{63} & a_{64} & -a_{65} & 0 \end{bmatrix}.$$

To summarize, the real exchange rate movements in the above model are explained by a supply and aggregate demand shocks, $\eta_t^{\bar{y}}$, η_t^y, a shock to expectations of devaluation of the dollar, η_t^s, and three fiscal shocks – η_t^g, η_t^τ, η_t^d. These "structural" disturbances are uncorrelated over time and have a variance covariance matrix $E(\eta_t \eta_t') = \Sigma$, which is assumed to be diagonal. The matrix A_0 captures the contemporaneous interaction of the variables. Their dynamic relationship is given by the matrices A_j (for $j > 0$). The theoretical source of the dynamic propagation mechanism of the economy is the slow adjustment in prices discussed in the second section.

Following Bernanke (1986) and Blanchard (1989), we estimate the system in (10) in two steps: First, we estimate a reduced form relating X_t to its lagged values:

$$X_t = \sum_{j=1}^{r} B_j X_{t-j} + \epsilon_t, \tag{12}$$

Table 11.1 *Estimated contemporaneous effects*

$\epsilon_t = A_0 \epsilon_t - \eta_t$

$$\epsilon^q = 0.325\epsilon^y + \eta^{\bar{y}}$$
$$(0.343)^a$$

$$\epsilon^y = 0.652\epsilon^s - 0.919\epsilon^g + 0.823\epsilon^\tau + 2.766\epsilon^d + \eta^y$$
$$(1.389)\quad(4.200)\quad(0.750)\quad(1.712)$$

$$\epsilon^s = -0.522\epsilon^g + \eta^s$$
$$(0.324)$$

$$\epsilon^g = -0.072\epsilon^y + \eta^g$$
$$(0.037)$$

$$\epsilon^\tau = \eta^\tau$$

$$\epsilon^d = -0.499\epsilon^q + 1.893\epsilon^g - 0.121\epsilon^\tau - 0.006\epsilon^s + \eta^d$$
$$(0.260)\quad(0.797)\quad(0.177)\quad(0.349)$$

Likelihood ratio test of overidentification: $\chi^2(4)=5.56$

Significance level: $=0.23$

Note:

[a] Standard errors are in parentheses.

where $B_j = (I - A_0)^{-1} A_j$ and ϵ_t is a serially uncorrelated vector of residuals, which is observed by the econometrician. Second, we estimate the parameters of A_0 using the reduced vector of residuals and the method of moments.[18] The estimation of A_0 will allow us to recover the "structural shocks," η_t, since the following condition holds:

$$\epsilon_t = A_0 \epsilon_t + \eta_t. \tag{13}$$

We estimate the model in (12) and (13) with the variables in levels using annual data for the period 1879–1913.[19] The order of the lag is 2, a value based upon the results of likelihood tests. We first report the estimates of the contemporaneous relationships between the variables in the system. Afterwards we examine the dynamic transmission of the shocks throughout the system.

The estimated contemporaneous relations

The estimate of the matrix A_0 is reported in table 11.1. These estimates show how shocks contemporaneously affect the economy. We should note at the outset that not all of the coefficients in A_0 (shown in (10a)–(10g)) turn out to be significantly different from zero, as indicated by the likelihood ratio test of overidentification, shown at the bottom of table 11.1. Thus in table

11.1 we do not report estimates of the coefficients a_{21} and a_{54}, which we restrict to be zero.

The estimated price setting equation is relatively flat (10a). This implies little relation between innovations to q_t and innovations to y_t, suggesting that fluctuations in demand have a small contemporaneous effect on relative prices and the real exchange rate and a large effect on output. The aggregate demand function, (10b), suggests that aggregate demand within the year strongly increases with positive shocks to deficit but is little affected by changes in interest rates and tariff policy. As it was just noted, the within the year response of demand to changes in the real exchange rate, a_{21}, turns out to be not statistically different from zero and thus it is constrained to be zero in table 11.1. Surprisingly, contrary to conventional wisdom, increases in government purchases have a negative impact effect on aggregate demand. The estimated parameter, however, is not statistically different from zero. The government spending equation indicates that the government spending share is highly countercyclical. Contrary to expectations, tariffs do not seem to respond to changes in government spending (at least contemporaneously). Thus, we restrict the within the year response of tariffs to fluctuations in government spending to be zero. The government deficit (10g), shows the deficit increasing with government spending and decreasing with increases in import tariffs. Unexpected shocks to inflation reduce the cost of borrowing of the government and hence negatively affect the government deficit.

Dynamic effects of structural shocks

While we estimate the VAR for the entire set of variables, the focus of our work is the determinants of the real exchange rate. Therefore, we only examine the dynamic effect of the structural shocks on the real exchange rate. The main source of the fluctuations of the real exchange rate over time and the dynamic effects of shocks can be examined in a variety of ways. We first examine the variance decomposition which demonstrates the contribution of each source of innovations to the variance of the n-year ahead forecast error for the real exchange rate. Afterwards, we report impulse responses and a historical forecast error decomposition.

Variance decomposition

Variance decompositions are reported in table 11.2. Three main findings here are:

1. Innovations to aggregate supply, $\eta_t^{\bar{y}}$, account for most of the variance of the real exchange rate at short horizons, reflecting that relative prices do not respond immediately to aggregate demand shocks.

Table 11.2 *Importance of different shocks in explaining real exchange rate fluctuations*

	Variance decomposition of the real exchange rate					
Years ahead	$\eta^{\bar{y}}$	η^{v}	η^{s}	η^{g}	η^{τ}	η^{d}
1	74.41	15.17	0.15	2.00	0.30	7.97
2	58.02	23.26	11.99	1.91	1.21	3.60
3	48.91	22.96	19.13	4.30	1.11	3.58
4	44.81	21.22	25.03	4.60	1.07	3.27
5	44.69	20.01	26.60	4.32	1.24	3.13
6	44.53	19.20	26.31	4.36	1.34	4.26
7	44.06	18.61	25.81	4.27	1.30	5.95
8	43.48	18.11	25.69	4.15	1.45	7.11
9	42.96	17.91	26.03	4.11	1.50	7.48
10	42.58	17.86	26.46	4.03	1.47	7.60
11	42.42	17.65	26.65	3.92	1.55	7.80
12	42.42	17.24	26.57	3.79	1.68	8.30

2. At longer horizons, demand innovations, shocks to expectations of devaluation and deficit innovations account for a larger fraction of the variance of the real exchange rate. The three innovations jointly account for 50 percent of the variance at medium and long horizons.
3. Government purchases cannot explain any of the fluctuations in the real exchange rate. The inability of government purchases to explain movements in the real exchange rate may be related to the fact that our series only account for central government spending, which accounts for less than 50 percent of total government expenditures.

Impulse responses

The impulse responses of the real exchange rate to innovations in each of the six structural shocks are presented in figure 11.4a–f. The results of the variance decomposition above suggest the importance of the responses to $\eta_t^{\bar{y}}$, η_t^{v}, η_t^{s} and η_t^{d} and accordingly we focus on these results though we also briefly discuss responses to the other innovations.

The panel representing the impulse response of the real exchange rate to a positive supply shock (a positive supply shock in the United Kingdom relative to a supply shock in the United States) in figure 11.4a demonstrates an appreciation in the real dollar exchange rate for about three years. Thereafter, its effect on the real exchange rate is very small. The response of the real exchange rate to output supply shocks may capture in part the

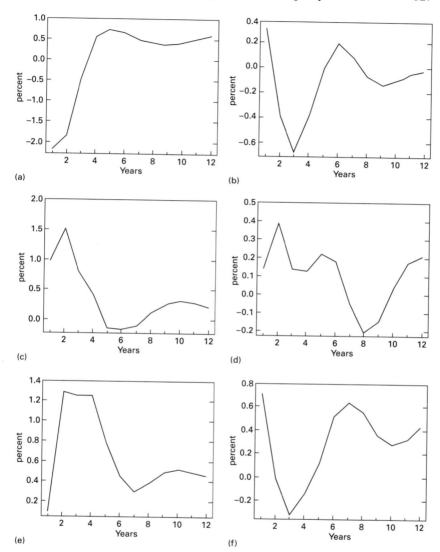

Figure 11.4 Response of the real exchange rate to a one standard deviation shock in the structural innovations
(a) Aggregate supply shock   (b) Government purchases shock
(c) Aggregate demand shock   (d) Tariff shock
(e) Shock to expected dollar depreciation
(f) Government deficit shock

response of the real exchange rate to large transitory fluctuations in agricultural output that occurred in this period, such as the unusually large crops in the United States in 1880–1881 and 1891–1892. In these years, American production was the largest on record and so were exports of crude foodstuffs. This generated a large gold inflow which, in turn, caused over time a spurt in the US money stock and a subsequent rise in US whole-sale prices, reversing the initial dollar real depreciation due to the positive US supply shock.

Figure 11.4c shows that a 3 percent aggregate demand shock leads to between ½ and 1½ percent depreciation of the dollar in the short and medium run (1–4 years) and disappears slowly over time. As we described before, this shock includes shocks to money demand and shocks to preferences.

It is interesting to examine in detail the response of the real exchange rate to an increase in expectations of changes in the dollar/pound parity (figure 11.4e). As postulated in the second section, the expectation of a dollar depreciation, which is manifested in an increase in the US interest rates relative to those in the United Kingdom leads to a depreciation in real terms of the dollar. The estimate suggests that an 80 basis points shock to expectations of depreciation of the dollar has basically no effect on the real exchange rate on impact but leads to a 1 percent real depreciation of the dollar in the medium run. Since expectations of a dollar devaluation, measured using interest rate differentials, were larger in absolute values in the disturbed decade of the 1890s, this impulse response reflects in large part the response of the real exchange rate to the agitation over silver. As is discussed in the third section, during the 1890s there was a general distrust of the maintenance of the gold standard, originating with the passing of the Sherman Silver Purchase Act in mid-1890. This distrust was manifested in a on-average large outflow of gold in 1892. The Senate's approval in July 1892 of a Free Silver Coinage bill, which never became a law, reinforced such fears. Moreover, the run on the banks in the financial crisis of 1893 reinforced those fears further, increasing capital outflows. These capital outflows reduced the money supply and prices and led to a real depreciation of the dollar.

The estimated dynamic effect of a shock to deficit policy (figure 11.4f) is consistent with the traditional Mundell–Fleming model. An increase in UK deficit relative to the deficit in the United States leads to an appreciation of the pound in real terms. A one standard deviation innovation in the deficit, which increases the relative deficit by 1/10 percentage point permanently, appreciates the pound by at most 0.5 percent in the medium and long run.

Finally, we discuss very briefly the two other impulse responses. A ½ percentage point increase in government purchases in the United Kingdom relative to the United States generates, as expected, a within the year depreciation of the dollar of about 0.5 percent (figure 11.4b). However, in contrast to the model in the second section, a relatively expansionary fiscal policy in the United Kingdom generates a depreciation of the pound in the medium run. This effect is consistent with results in the literature of balance of payments crisis, where an expansionary fiscal policy generates expectations of depreciation of the domestic currency. In turn the expectations of depreciation, in this case, of the pound make investors switch in favor of holding dollars against pounds, reducing the demand for UK goods and leading to a depreciation of the pound. The last impulse response shows the movements in the exchange rate after an increase in relative tariffs (figure 11.4d). This shock generates an increase in demand for goods in the United Kingdom leading to price increases in this country relatively to the United States. A positive one standard deviation shock to tariffs, which increases tariffs on impact by about 1.5 percentage points leads to a depreciation of the dollar in real terms of less than 0.3 percent after five years.

Historical decomposition
The six panels in figure 11.5 illustrate the roles played by the different shocks over different historical episodes. Each panel plots the forecast error of the real exchange rate at the four-year horizon and the portion of this forecast error attributable to each of the respective structural shocks. A closer tracking of the particular "structural" innovation (represented by the dashed line) to the overall real exchange rate innovation (represented by the solid line) suggests a larger role for that innovation as a source of the innovation of the real exchange rate.

Of the three fiscal shocks, the government deficit shock (figure 11.5f) seems to track the real exchange rate innovation somewhat better. At the end of the 1880s there were government surpluses in the United States. At this time, the total forecast error of the real exchange rate showing the unexpected real dollar depreciation is partly tracked by the error attributable to the relative fiscal constraint in the United States. These US fiscal surpluses were feared to be contractionary. Policy reversed this fiscal stance by 1894 with the revenue effects of the McKinley Tariff (which put sugar on the free list) as well as increased spending on pensions, rivers, and harbors. However, this time our decomposition does not pick up the fluctuations of the dollar. After 1895 the deficits of the United States and the United Kingdom began to diverge to a greater extent than in the earlier part of our sample. The deficit in the United States changed relatively little from 1895 to World War I but the deficit in the United Kingdom shifted dramatically, first falling with the end of the Boer War (1899–1902), rising with the

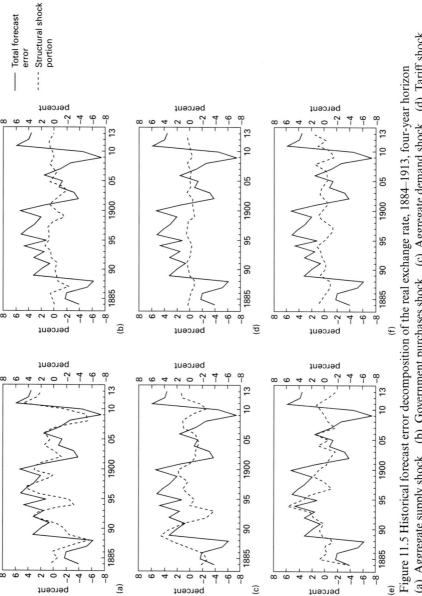

Figure 11.5 Historical forecast error decomposition of the real exchange rate, 1884–1913, four-year horizon

(a) Aggregate supply shock   (b) Government purchases shock   (c) Aggregate demand shock   (d) Tariff shock
(e) Shock to expected dollar depreciation   (f) Government deficit shock

income tax cut in 1907, and then decreasing basically until the end of the sample. Our decomposition shows that the effects of the relative deficit tracks the real exchange rate after 1908, with the pound first depreciating until 1909 and basically appreciating until the outbreak of World War I.

The contribution of the innovations of the other two fiscal factors to the total innovation of the real exchange rate appear relatively slight. Innovations to government purchases are only mildly associated with the overall innovation to the real exchange rate (figure 11.5e). The tariff shock makes the smallest contribution to the total real exchange rate innovation of any of the six innovations (figure 11.5f). Neither of the two changes in tariffs in the period studied, the McKinley Tariff of 1890 nor the Dingley Tariff of 1897, show up in the estimates as important explanations of the real exchange rate innovation in those years.

The innovation that accounts for the preponderance of the innovation in the real exchange rate is the output supply shock (figure 11.5a). This shock seems to explain relatively well the fluctuations in the real exchange rate around the turn of the century. One possible explanation can be traced to the favorable agricultural shock in the United States and unfavorable agri-cultural shock in Europe in 1897 and 1898. While initially these shocks exerted downward pressure on US commodity prices relative to British prices (a depreciation of the dollar in real terms), over time this trend was reversed. The reversion of the trend was brought about by the subsequent major shift in the recorded balance of merchandise trade in the United States, which was promptly reflected in gold movements – about 200 million during the 1897–1899 period. After some delay, in the 1899–1903 period, this shock was reflected in prices, which started to increase relative to those in England leading to a real dollar appreciation. After 1903 the real appreciation of the dollar was reversed with the dollar depreciating about 8 percent in real terms in the 1903–1906 period. Interestingly these years were characterized by strong industrial growth in the United States, of which the most obvious signs were the rapid growth of the output of coal and iron and of the volume of railroad traffic.

The innovation due to demand shocks tracks the overall real exchange rate innovation somewhat closely in the late 1890s during the recession in the United States after the banking panic of 1893 (figure 11.5c). Also, the vigorous and protracted expansion in the United States starting in 1904 explains in part the appreciation of the dollar in the 1906–1909 period, while the US banking panic in 1907 and the following recession generate a sharp depreciation of the dollar in the last years of the sample.

Finally, the expectations of devaluation shock seems to track the innova-tions to the real exchange rate over selected periods. It closely tracks the innovation in the real exchange rate in the early 1890s. This corresponds to the period of the rise and subsequent fall in the political strength of the Free Silver Movement. During the time when the Free Silver Movement was strongest the likelihood of the United States abandoning the gold standard was greatest.

Conclusions

There are three possible channels through which fiscal policy could have affected the bilateral dollar/pound real exchange rate during the gold standard period. The first is through the standard effect of government expenditures shifting the consumption pattern of the economy and affecting the relative price of domestic versus foreign goods. The second effect of fiscal policy is through tariffs which were an important souce of revenues for the United States during this period. Changes in government deficit are the third source of fiscal effects on the real exchange rate. Government deficits, as was discussed in the fourth section, may alter the behavior of households and therefore the equilibrium relative price of domestic goods. Although not modeled explicitly, persistent US government deficits may have affected the public's faith in the maintenance of the gold standard. We find that there is almost no empirical evidence that tariffs and government spending affected the real exchange rate. There is some stronger evidence that innovations in government budget deficits were associated with innovations to the real exchange rate. This is specially true with the large increases in deficits in the United Kingdom with the Boer War and the income tax cut in 1907.

Data appendix

Definitions

Government purchases=Government expenditure−Government interest payments−Government transfer payments
Government deficit=Government expenditure−Government revenue

$$g_t^j = \frac{\text{G. purchases}_t^j}{\text{GNP}_t^j} \times 100$$

$$\tau_t^j = \frac{\text{Custom duties}_t^j}{\text{GNP}_t^j} \times 100$$

$$d_t^j = \left[\frac{\text{Deficit}_t^j}{\text{GNP}_t^j} + \frac{\text{Debt}_{t-1}^j}{\text{GNP}_t^j} \times [1 - \frac{p_t^j}{p_{t-1}^j}] \right] \times 100$$

p_t^j=Country j producer price index in period t (in logs)

s_t=Dollar/pound nominal exchange rate in period t (in logs)

y_t^j=Country j real GNP in period t (in logs)

i_t^j=Country j short-term nominal interest rate in period t

Sources

Nominal exchange rate

1879–1884: Friedman and Schwartz (1982).
1885–1889: *Commercial and Financial Chronicle*, various issues.
1890–1910: National Monetary Commission (1910).
1911–1913: Pearson and Warren (1935), table 6, 158.

Producer price index

United States

1879–1913: Pearson and Warren (1935, table 1, 6–10).

United Kingdom

1879–1884: Mitchell (1988, table 4, Prices 725).
1885–1913: *Journal of the Royal Statistical Society*, various issues.

Real GNP, 1929 prices

United States

1879–1888: Romer (1986).
1889–1908: United States Bureau of the Census (1975, Series F3).
1909–1913: United States Bureau of Economic Analysis, (1981).

United Kingdom

1879–1913: Calculated as the ratio of nominal GNP to the GNP deflator.

Nominal GNP

United States

1879–1888: Estimated as real GNP×GNP deflator.
1889–1908: United States Bureau of the Census (1975, Series F1).
1909–1913: United States Bureau of Economic Analysis (1981).

United Kingdom

1879–1913: Capie and Webber (1985, table III(12)).

GNP Deflator

United States

1879–1913: Ratio of nominal to real income from Friedman and Schwartz (1982, table 4.8).

United Kingdom

1879–1913: Capie and Webber (1985, table III(12)).

Nominal interest rates

United States

1879–1890: United States Bureau of the Census (1975).
1890–1909: National Monetary Commission (1910, table 29, 4/6-month rates).
1909–1913: United States Bureau of the Census (1975).

United Kingdom

1879–1913: Capie and Webber (1985, table III(10), column V, 3-month bank bills).

Government expenditure

United States

1879–1913: United States Bureau of the Census (1975, chart Y457–469).

United Kingdom

1879–1913: Mitchell and Deane (1962, 397–399).

Government interest payments

United States

1879–1913: Mitchell and Deane (1962, 397–399).

United Kingdom

1879–1913: Mitchell and Deane (1962, 397–399).

Government transfer payments

United States

1879–1913: United States Bureau of the Census (1975, charts Y457–465, Y466–471).

United Kingdom

1879–1913: Mitchell and Deane (1962, social security payments, 400).

Government revenue

United States

1879–1913: United States Bureau of the Census (1975, chart Y258–263).

United Kingdom

1879–1913: Mitchell and Deane (1962, table 3, Public Finance, 393).

Government debt

United States

1879–1913: United States Bureau of the Census (1975, chart Y368–Y369).

United Kingdom

1879–1913: Mitchell and Deane (1962, table 5, Public Finance, 403).

Customs duties

United States

1879–1913: United States Bureau of the Census (1975).

United Kingdom

1879–1913: Mitchell and Deane (1962, 393–395).

Imports

United States

1879–1913: United States Bureau of the Census (1975, dutiable imports).

United Kingdom

1879–1913: Mitchell and Deane (1962, 283–284).

Notes

The views expressed in this chapter are those of the authors and should not be interpreted as reflecting those of the Federal Reserve System or other members of its staff. We thank Michael Bordo, Susan Collins, Barry Eichengreen, Tamim Bayoumi, and seminar participants at Rutgers University and at the 1995 Winter Meeting of the Econometric Society for helpful comments and Greg Belzer for excellent research assistance.

1. Krugman (1990, 194–196).
2. See, for example, Obstfeld (1993).
3. In this example, the fiscal shock, f_t, is assumed to capture just government spending. However, fiscal policy may affect demand for goods indirectly by affecting households' demand for goods. For example, the imposition of an import tariff may switch households' expenditure from foreign to domestic goods. Similarly, domestic fiscal expansions – an increase in the deficit of the domestic government – may affect households' net wealth, and thus modify households' consumption behavior. Thus, in the empirical estimation in the fourth section we extent the model and allow tariffs and government deficits to affect the relative demand for goods.
4. The left-hand side of (2) is the logarithm of the ratio of the stock of UK money (in dollars) to the stock of US money.
5. Friedman and Schwartz (1982) conclude that

   the doubling of real balances expressed in weeks of income in the United States in the course of the three decades from 1876 to 1906, during which United Kingdom balances fell by 7 percent, suggests that the change in relative financial sophistication of the United Kingdom and the United States from 1880 to 1906 was probably by all odds the single most important factor accounting for the divergent trends in real balances. (1982, 147)

6. See, for example, Krugman (1979) for a complete model of the timing of a balance of payments crisis.
7. We do not explicitly model the underlying source of stickiness here, although the rationale for the slow adjustment of prices in (8) can be provided by the small menu costs of price adjustment *à la* Akerlof and Yellen (1985) or Blanchard and Kiyotaki (1987).

8. This narrative draws from a number of sources including Clapham (1938), Dewey (1939), Eichengreen (1992), Friedman and Schwartz (1963), Jones and Pool (1940), Rostow (1948), and Studenski and Kroos (1963).

9. The real exchange rate is defined as the ratio of UK to US producer price indices (times the dollar/pound exchange rate), so an increase in this number represents a real depreciation of the dollar. The sources for these and all other series used in the chapter are presented in data appendix.

10. The data on government spending and government deficit only includes spending and deficits of the central government. Data on state and local finances for the United States are not available at annual frequencies during the period examined. Similarly for the United Kingdom, there is much less information on local than on central government finance until the end of the 19th century. The scattered information on local and state finances suggests that central government spending was about one third of total government spending in the United States and about half of total government spending in the United Kingdom.

11. Although some of the government imbalances in the United Kingdom were triggered by tax cuts, such as the 1907 income tax cut, or by increases in government purchases during the Boer War, some of the deficits in the 1880s and the beginning of the 1890s were the result of the large seemingly "unanticipated" deflation from the early 1880s to 1897, which substantially increased the real burden of the debt. In contrast, the effects of the deflation on the US real government deficit were quite small because of the relatively small size of the government debt.

12. For a discussion of the events of this period see Grilli (1990).

13. Since during the gold standard period the nominal exchange rate between the dollar and the pound remained constant, in what follows q_t will refer both to the real exchange rate and to relative prices interchangeably.

14. Disentangling financial innovations from other demand shocks requires the introduction of relative money balances as an additional variable in the system.

15. The influence of the expected flexible price on the price setting equation, $_{t-1}\bar{p}_t$ is captured by $\Sigma^r_{j=1} A^p_j X_{t-j}$.

16. Although there is basically general agreement that increases in domestic government spending generate increases in demand for domestic goods because most of government purchases are concentrated on domestic goods, there is less agreement concerning the effects of tariffs and government deficits. For example, the effect of tariffs depends, among other factors, on whether the tariff revenue is redistributed. When the tariff revenue is not redistributed, the tariff is a combination of an expenditure switching policy and an expenditure reducing policy. While the expenditure switching element increases demand for domestic goods, the income effect tends to reduce demand for domestic goods. In this case the effect of the tariff is ambiguous (See, for example, Ostroy and Rose, 1992). Similarly, the debate over whether government deficit matters is still unsettled. Some models rule out this connection by assuming an economy inhabited by an unchanged cohort of households. In this case, a budget deficit arising from a current tax cut requiring a corresponding rise in future taxes will

not affect present consumption and demand for domestic goods. In contrast, some other models (see, for example, Obstfeld, 1989) allow for changing cohorts of households, with the new-born cohort unconnected with the existing households. A budget deficit in this case transfers income from future generations (whose propensity to consume present goods is zero) to the current generation (whose propensity to consume is positive), creating more demand for present goods. To sum up, tariffs and deficits do not have clear-cut effects on output and on the real exchange rate. Thus, we should turn to the data for empirical evidence.

17. Fiscal policy in (10d)–(10f) also reacts to fluctuations in other variables in the economy but only with lags. Although the specification of fiscal policy in equations (10d)–(10f) is ad hoc, it is nonetheless quite general. For example, the tariff reaction function in (10f) is consistent with a variety of views on how tariffs are determined, such as countercyclical tariff policy, smoothing government deficits, or responding to imbalances in the foreign sector.

18. The covariance matrix of the reduced form contains 21 independent moments. Six of those moments are used to identify the standard deviation of the 6 structural shocks. We therefore can identify 15 additional parameters. The number of the parameters of A_0 in (10a)–(10g) is 13, indicating that the model is over-identified. When we estimate these parameters we will also test the over-identifying restrictions.

19. We perform unit root tests to determine the order of integration of the variables. Standard tests for stationary could not reject the presence of a unit root in all the variables with the exception of the deficit share in output. We also check for cointegration of q, y, $i^{us} - i^{uk}$ (which measures expectations of changes in the dollar/pound parity), g and τ. The tests of cointegration, allowing or not for a time trend in the cointegrating regression, show no evidence of cointegration. Since it is well known that both unit root tests and cointegration tests have low power in small samples, such as ours, we run the VAR in levels to capture any possible long-run relationship among the variables.

References

Akerlof, G. and J. Yellen (1985). "A Near-Rational Model of the Business Cycle, with Wage and Price Inertia," *Quarterly Journal of Economics*, Supplement 100, 823–838

Bernanke, B. (1986). "Alternative Explanations of the Money–Income Correlation," *Carnegie–Rochester Conference Series on Public Policy* 25 (Autumn), 49–100

Blanchard, O. (1989). "A Traditional Interpretation of Macroeconomic Fluctuations," *American Economic Review* 79 (December), 1146–1164

Blanchard, O. and N. Kiyotaki (1987). "Monopolistic Competition and the Effects of Aggregate Demand," *American Economic Review* 77 (September), 647–666

Capie, F. and A. Webber (1985). *A Monetary History of the United Kingdom, 1870–1982*, vol. 1, *Data, Sources, Methods*, London: George Allen & Unwin

Clapham, J. H. (1938). *An Economic History of Modern Britain*, New York: Macmillan

Commercial and Financial Chronicle, New York: W. B. Dana Co., various issues

Cooper, R. "The Gold Standard: Historical Facts and Future Prospects," *Brookings Papers on Economic Activity* 1, 1–45

Dewey, D. R. (1939). *Financial History of the United States*, 12th ed., New York: Longmans, Green & Co.

Eichengreen, B. (1992). *Golden Fetters: The Gold Standard and the Great Depression*, New York: Oxford University Press

Feldstein, M. (1986). "The Budget Deficit and the Dollar," *NBER Macroeconomics Annual*, Cambridge MA: MIT Press, 355–392

Friedman, M. and A. J. Schwartz (1963). *A Monetary History of the United States, 1867–1960*, Princeton: Princeton University Press for NBER

(1982). *Monetary Trends in the United States and in the United Kingdom 1870–1970*, Chicago: University of Chicago Press for NBER

Froot, K. and K. Rogoff (1991). "The EMS, the EMU, and the Transition of a Common Currency," *NBER Macroeconomics Annual*, Cambridge MA: MIT Press, 269–327

Giovannini, A. (1988). "The Real Exchange Rate, The Capital Stock, and Fiscal Policy," *European Economic Review* 32, 1747–1767

Grilli, V. (1990). "Managing Exchange Rate Crises: Evidence from the 1890s," *Journal of International Money and Finance* 9 (September), 258–275

Helpman, E. (1981). "An Exploration in the Theory of Exchange-Rate Regimes," *Journal of Political Economy* 89 (October), 865–890

Jones, G. P. and A. G. Pool (1940). *A Hundred Years of Economic Development in United Kingdom (1840–1940)*, London: Gerald Duckworth & Co.

Krugman, P. (1979). "A Model of Balance of Payments Crises," *Journal of Money, Credit, and Banking* (August), 311–332

(1990). *The Age of Diminished Expectations*, Cambridge, MA: MIT Press

Mitchell, B. R. (1988). *British Historical Statistics*, Cambridge: Cambridge University Press

Mitchell, B. R. and P. Deane (1962). *Abstract of British Historical Statistics*, Cambridge: Cambridge University Press

Mundell, R. (1963). "Capital Mobility and Stabilization Policy under Fixed and Flexible Exchange Rates," *Canadian Journal of Economics* 29 (November), 475–485

Obstfeld, M. (1989). "Fiscal Deficits and Relative Prices in a Growing Economy," *Journal of Monetary Economics* 23, 461–484

(1993). "International Capital Mobility in the 1990s," NBER, *Working Paper* 4534

Ostroy, J. and A. Rose (1992). "An Empirical Evaluation of the Macroeconomic Effects of Tariffs," *Journal of International Money and Finance* 11, 63–79

Pearson, F. and G. Warren (1935). *Gold and Prices*, New York: John Wiley

Perkins, E. (1978). "Foreign Interest Rates in American Financial Markets: A Revised Series of Dollar–Sterling Exchange Rates, 1835–1900," *Journal of Economic History* 37(2) (June)

Romer, C. (1986). "The Prewar Business Cycle Reconsidered. New Estimates of Gross National Product 1869–1918," NBER, *Working Paper* 1969 (July)

Rostow, W. W. (1948) *British Economy of the Nineteenth Century*, Oxford: Oxford University Press

Studenski, P. and H. E. Kroos (1963). *Financial History of the United States*, 2nd edn., New York: McGraw-Hill

United States Bureau of the Census (1960). *Statistical Abstract of the United States*, Washington, DC

(1975). *Historical Statistics of the United States*, Washington, DC

United States Bureau of Economic Analysis (1981). *The National Income and Product Accounts of the United States, 1929–1976*, Washington, DC

United States National Monetary Commission (1910). *Statistics for the United States 1867–1909*, Washington, DC: US Government Printing Office

12 Exchange rate dynamics and monetary reforms: theory and evidence from Britain's return to gold

Panos Michael, A. Robert Nobay and David A. Peel

Introduction

The appreciation of sterling prior to the return to gold in April 1925 was thought by economists of the period to be a consequence of the anticipation of the return to gold rather than an improvement in fundamentals. For instance, in a well known quotation, Keynes in "The Economic Consequences of Mr. Churchill" wrote:

> The movement away from equilibrium began in October last [1924] and has proceeded step by step with the improvement of the exchange brought about first by the anticipation, and then by the fact, of the restoration of gold, and not by an improvement in the intrinsic value of sterling. (Keynes, 1972, 209–210)

The pioneering contributions of Sargent (1986) and Flood and Garber (1983) have initiated a rich literature on credibility, monetary reform, and issues of exchange rate dynamics under alternative regimes. More recent extensions by Froot and Obstfeld (1991) and Smith (1989) now offer closed form solutions that allow for economic interpretations, as reflected in a growing literature on the application of the theory of stochastic process switching to the analysis of actual economic events and issues.

The example of Britain's return to gold in the Flood and Garber paper has been further considered by Miller and Sutherland (1994), Smith and Smith (1990), and Krugman and Rotemberg (1992). Relatedly, a number of authors have undertaken analysis of credibility and exchange rate behavior in target zones – see, for example, Miller and Weller (1989), Krugman (1991) and Smith and Spencer (1992).

A striking feature of the applications literature, when viewed in conventional econometric terms, is its lack of empirical content. To illustrate, consider the so-called Keynes/Treasury interpretation of sterling's appreciation prior to gold convertibility, as discussed in Moggridge (1972) and Skidelsky (1988). Miller and Sutherland (1992) presented a lucid theoretical analysis that allows for dynamics that are consistent with Keynes' "speculative

341

appreciation" conjecture. In commenting on their paper, Smith (1992) highlighted a crucial assumption there of a zero drift in fundamentals, and undertook a single nonparametric test of exchange rate data to challenge its empirical validity. Miller and Sutherland (1994) subsequently demonstrated that the assumption of an autoregressive evolution of fundamentals mimics Smith's empirical findings. This leaves open the possibility that Keynes' conjecture was right after all.

Yet, in principle, it should be the case that an episode such as Britain's return to gold, not unlike the German hyperinflation, should serve as a unique empirical testbed for theoretical advances. There remains, however, a striking contrast between the theoretical elegance of the analysis of Britain's return to gold, and its empirical underpinnings. This chapter is an attempt at redressing that balance. We tease out the distinctive empirical implications of three key features which result in variants of exchange rate dynamics, and confront these with the relevant data, these being the postulated evolution of fundamentals, the form of uncertainty surrounding monetary reform and the issue of price flexibility. The testable implications that are derived offer a clearer empirical evaluation than hitherto reported in the literature.

The chapter is structured as follows. The first section reviews the theoretical literature and highlights the distinctive set of empirical implications that arise. In the second section we undertake the relevant empirical analysis. This takes the form of both parametric and nonparametric analysis of exchange rate data, including the implied forward premiums, and the evolution of fundamentals. We also present error correction representations of the spot exchange rate, based on the purchasing power parity hypothesis. The third section reviews our empirical findings. To anticipate our conclusions, we show that the underlying nature of the dynamics of sterling in the approach to convertibility cannot be decided upon by simple tests of trends in fundamentals, or on the basis of the presumed stance of monetary policy.[1] We conclude in support of Keynes' hypothesis of speculative appreciation.

Implications of alternative assumptions

The basic monetary model can be written as follows:

$$m(t)-p(t)=\alpha_0+\alpha_1 y(t)-\alpha_2 r(t)+u(t) \tag{1}$$
$$m^*(t)-p^*(t)=\alpha_0^*+\alpha_1^* y^*(t)-\alpha_2^* r^*(t)+u^*(t) \tag{2}$$
$$p(t)=p^*(t)-e(t)+v(t) \tag{3}$$
$$r(t)=r^*(t)+E[\dot{e}(t)/i_t]+w(t), \tag{4}$$

where $m(t)$, $p(t)$, and $y(t)$ are the logarithms of the money supply, price level, and real income; $r(t)$ is the level of interest rate; * denotes foreign country variables; $e(t)$ is the logarithm of the exchange rate measured in dollars/pound; $u(t)$, $v(t)$, and $w(t)$ are random disturbance terms; and E denotes rational expectations.

(1) and (2) are the money demand functions for the United Kingdom and United States, respectively, while (3) and (4) are the purchasing power parity (PPP) and uncovered interest parity (UIP) conditions. Combining equations (1)–(4) yields

$$e(t)=K(t)+\alpha E[e(t)/I_t],\tag{5}$$

where $K(t)=\alpha_0^*-\alpha_0-\alpha_1 y(t)+\alpha_1^* y^*(t)+m(t)-m^*(t)-u(t)+u^*(t)+\alpha w(t)$, and it is assumed that $\alpha_2=\alpha_2^*=\alpha$.

It is clear from (5) that as long as α, the interest elasticity of money demand, is nonzero, expectations of future exchang rate changes influence the current exchange rate. In order to solve the model under rational expectations it is necessary to specify the process driving the relative fundamentals $K(t)$. We consider two alternative forms of this process, together with two alternative assumptions concerning the uncertainty of agents about the timing of the return to gold, as follows:

Assumption I(i): prior to the exchange rate being fixed, $K(t)$ follows a random walk with drift which, in continuous time, is

$$K(t)=K(0)+\mu t+\nu(t)\tag{6}$$

where μ is the drift rate and $\nu(t)$ is the driftless Wiener process with instantaneous variance σ^2.

Assumption I(ii): prior to the return to gold, $K(t)$ evolves according to an autoregressive process which, in the simplest case, can be written as

$$dK(t)=-\beta[K(t)-\bar{K}]dt+\sigma dz,\tag{7}$$

where β measures the speed of adjustment; $\bar{K}$ is the level of fundamentals consistent with the level of sterling at the return to gold ($\bar{e}=$(logarithm of) \$4.86²¹/₃₂); and z is a driftless Brownian motion process.

Assumption II(i): agents are uncertain of the precise date of the return to gold, but expect the exchange rate to be fixed permanently at $\bar{e}$ as soon as it reaches this level.

Assumption II(ii): agents believe that the authorities will return to gold at or before a known date T.

These two pairs of assumptions have been combined to produce a variety of solutions for the exchange rate, as outlined below. The first case was analyzed by Smith and Smith (1990), while the other three were considered by Miller and Sutherland (1992, 1994) – these authors spell out the derivation for the drift in the exchange rate.

Case A: assumptions I(i) and II(i). As shown in Flood and Garber (1983) and Smith (1989), given these assumptions the solution for the exchange rate is

$$e(t)=K(t)+\alpha\mu[1-\exp\{\rho[K(t)-\bar{K}]\}];\rho>0 \tag{A1}$$

Combining this with (5), we can obtain the following expression for the expected drift in the exchange rate:

$$\Im(t)\equiv E[\dot{e}(t)/I_t]=\mu[1-\exp\{\rho[K(t)-\bar{K}]\}] \tag{A2}$$

and by Itô's Lemma

$$E[\dot{\Im}(t)]=-\mu\rho(\mu+\rho\frac{\sigma^2}{2})\exp\{\rho[K(t)-\bar{K}]\} \tag{A3}$$

It can be seen from (A2) and (A3) that the drift $\Im(t)$ falls over time, which means that the expected value of sterling depreciates relatively as a consequence of the return to gold. This is the interesting insight of Smith and Smith (1990): a policy of fixing the price to gold when it reaches a level $\bar{e}$ lowers the current price of sterling, since agents understand that the price fixing switches off the drift in fundamentals at that parity and thus truncates the upper support of the expected future price.

Case B: assumptions I(i) and II(ii). The solutions in this case are given by:

$$e(t)=K(t)+\alpha\mu-[\alpha\mu+K(t)-\bar{e}+\mu(T-t)]\exp\{-\alpha^{-1}(T-t)\} \tag{B1}$$

$$\Im(t)=\mu-\frac{1}{\alpha}[\alpha\mu+K(t)-\bar{e}+\mu(T-t)]\exp\{-\alpha^{-1}(T-t)\} \tag{B2}$$

$$E[\dot{\Im}(t)]=-\frac{1}{\alpha^2}[\alpha\mu+K(t)-\bar{e}+\mu(T-t)]\exp\{-\alpha^{-1}(T-t)\}. \tag{B3}$$

As noted by Smith (1992), the total derivative in (B3) can have any sign so that the expected drift in the nominal exchange rate is not restricted by this model. However, as $K(t)$ approaches $\bar{e}$ the drift declines with time. If there is no drift in the fundamentals ($\mu=0$), then $E[\dot{\Im}(t)]>0$ so that the drift rises over time and the model is consistent with Keynes' view that the anticipated peg caused sterling to appreciate.

Case C: assumptions I(ii) and II(i), with solutions as follows:

$$e(t)=\bar{e}+\frac{1}{1+\beta\alpha}[K(t)-\bar{K}]\tag{C1}$$

$$\Im(t)=-\frac{\beta}{1+\beta\alpha}[K(t)-\bar{K}]\tag{C2}$$

$$E[\dot{\Im}(t)]=-\frac{\beta^2}{1+\beta\alpha}[K(t)-\bar{K}],\tag{C3}$$

where $\Im(t)>0$ and $E[\dot{\Im}(t)]<0$ for $K(t)-\bar{K}<0$. Note that the solutions (C2) and (C3) are obtained with or without an announcement of a return to gold. Essentially, the return (when $K(t)=\bar{K}$) removes as much downside as upside potential in future fundamentals, so that an announcement of a return at some future date has no impact.

Case D: assumptions (I(ii) and II(ii), with solutions as follows (for the case $\beta=1$):

$$e(t)=\bar{e}+\frac{1}{1+\alpha}[1-\exp\{-\lambda(T-t\}][K(t)-\bar{K}]\tag{D1}$$

$$\Im(t)=-\frac{1}{\alpha(1+\alpha)}[\alpha+\exp\{-\lambda(T-t)\}][K(t)-\bar{K}]\tag{D2}$$

$$E[\dot{\Im}(t)]=\frac{1}{\alpha^2(1+\alpha)}[\alpha^2-\exp\{-\lambda(T-t)\}][K(t)-\bar{K}],\tag{D3}$$

where $\lambda=(1+\alpha)/\alpha$. While $\Im(t)>0$ for $K(t)-\bar{K}<0$, the sign of (D3) depends on the value of α, with $E[\dot{\Im}(t)]>0$ for $\alpha>1$ and $E[\dot{\Im}(t)]<0$ for $\alpha>1$.

Within the context of the flexible price monetary model of the exchange rate, the solutions above illustrate how the different assumptions analyzed by Smith and Smith (1990) and Miller and Sutherland (1992) have different implications for the drift in the exchange rate over time. We may also note that a mixture of the above models could be relevant along the transition path to the return to gold. For example, an initial assumption of an uncertain date of return to gold (for a period of time) could at some point be replaced by the assumption of a return by a known terminal date. Similarly, the nature of the process driving the fundamentals could change following the announcement of the return to gold.

It is also possible to derive the univariate time series process for the instantaneous expected change in the exchange rate from the above solutions. Thus from (A2) and (A3), the expected exchange rate evolves as

$$E[\dot{\Im}(t)]=\rho(\mu+\rho\frac{\sigma^2}{2})[\Im(t)-\mu] \tag{A4}$$

and from the corresponding expressions for cases B, C, and D,

$$E[\dot{\Im}(t)]=\frac{1}{\alpha}[\Im(t)-\mu] \tag{B4}$$

$$E[\dot{\Im}(t)]=-\beta\Im(t) \tag{C4}$$

$$E[\dot{\Im}(t)]=-\frac{1}{\alpha}\frac{[\alpha^2-\exp\{-\lambda(T-t)\}]}{[\alpha+\exp\{-\lambda(T-t)\}]}\Im(t). \tag{D4}$$

The similarity of (A4) and (B4) suggests that, with random walk behavior of the fundamentals, the type of uncertainty over the timing of return to gold makes no qualitative difference to the univariate process even though it has different implications for the drift of the exchange rate over time. The positive relationship btween $\Im(t)$ and $E[\dot{\Im}(t)]$, of course, implies an explosive process. With autoregressive fundamentals and an uncertain date of return to gold the relationship in (C4) is negative; while with a known terminal date, the relationship in (D4) has an ambiguous sign depending on the magnitude of α and, unlike the other cases, is time dependent. These features of the univariate process for the expected exchange rate could, in principle, be exploited to provide additional tests of the various models suggested by Smith and Smith (1990) and Miller and Sutherland (1992).

All the predictions for the exchange rate set out above were derived from a model in which price adjustment is assumed to be perfectly flexible so that PPP holds period by period. It appears of interest to relax this assumption for two reasons. First, many economists of the period were of the *a priori* view that nominal prices were imperfectly flexible (see, e.g., Hicks, 1974). Second, empirical tests of PPP for this period using cointegration methods suggest imperfect price flexibility (though this analysis was conducted without formal allowance for any impact of the return to gold; see, e.g., Taylor and McMahon, 1988, Michael *et al.*, 1994).

Miller and Sutherland (1992) have analyzed some of the implications of the anticipation of a return to gold in models embodying price inflexibility. In their model there is a Phillips curve in which inflation is related to the level of real output. The inflation process is subject to a zero-mean white noise disturbance which is the only stochastic element in the model. In addition, output is demand determined where demand depends on the real interest rate, the real exchange rate and demand overseas. The other equations are as in the monetary model. For their particular representative model (there are no closed form solutions in general) the solution for the exchange rate for the time dependent path is given by:

$$e(t) = \bar{e}[1 - h(t)] + [p(t) - p^*(t)]h(t), \tag{8}$$

where $h(t)$, a function of time, equals zero at the return to gold $t = T$.

The central prediction of the theoretical models described above is that, whether prices are flexible or inflexible, a time dependent solution occurs when agents anticipate a regime switch by some known terminal date. In the next section we examine the time series properties of the exchange rate in the period between 1921 and the announcement of the return to gold, and relate this evidence to the theoretical predictions of the models outlined above. In addition, we consider the time series properties of the forward premium and the relationship of the exchange rate to fundamentals as measured by relative prices.

Empirical analysis

Previous empirical analysis of the impact on sterling of the return to gold has been of two kinds. Smith and Smith (1990) used simulation methods to compare the actual exchange rate with that which would have occurred if agents ignored the possibility of a return to gold. This simulation was conducted assuming (A1) above holds with particular values for μ, σ^2, and α. Naturally, the naive forecast was higher than the actual exchange rate observed, as theoretically implied from (A1). The actual exchange rate also exhibited a declining trend relative to the naive simulated value, but again this has to be the case theoretically. Consequently, whilst the Smith and Smith (1990) analysis is of great interest in providing empirical estimates of the process switching effect, it provides no evidence on the validity of the models generating the observed exchange rate.

This is not the case with the analysis of Smith (1992). He examines the univariate properties of changes in the daily spot exchange rate employing a nonparametric procedure. In particular, he regresses the rank of daily changes in the spot rate on a time trend. He finds no evidence of any significant trend in the rate of appreciation of the spot rate for the whole sample period, but evidence of a significant decline in trend after the Conservative Election victory of October 29, 1924. As Smith points out, this evidence is consistent with the Smith and Smith model but not with that of Miller and Sutherland (1992, 1994) with nonautoregressive fundamentals if $\mu = 0$ (Case B). It is also inconsistent with the views of Keynes. It was this evidence which in part motivated Miller and Sutherland to consider alternative specifications of the fundamentals which are consistent with Smith's empirical findings and with the views of Keynes. As Smith

348   Panos Michael, A. Robert Nobay and David A. Peel

notes, his test does not have high power. It therefore seems worthwhile to reconsider the univariate properties of the spot exchange rate employing a different nonparametric method as well as parametric methods.

Our nonparametric method is that proposed by Hastie and Tibshirani (1990). This method essentially allows the data to show the appropriate functional form between variables. This is achieved by fitting a scatter plot smoother. The scatter plot we employ is fitted using a cubic smoothing spline function which minimizes the residual sum of squares, penalized for curvature in the functional. Formally, we minimize the penalized residual sum of squares:

$$\sum_{i=1}^{n}[y_i-f(x_i)]^2+\gamma\int_a^b f''(x)dx, \tag{9}$$

where γ is a constant, and $a\leq x_1\leq...\leq x_n\leq b$. The first term in (9) measures closeness to the data while the second term penalizes curvature in the function. Hastie and Tibshirani show that (9) has a unique minimum which is the cubic spline with knots at the unique values of x_i. The parameter γ has the interpretation of the degree of smooth. As $\gamma\to\infty$ the penalty term dominates so that $f''(x)=0$ and the solution is the least squares regression. Alternatively, as $\gamma\to 0$ the penalty term becomes unimportant and the solution tends to an interpolating twice differentiable function. Our empirical estimation is undertaken using the GAIM package, details of which are in Hastie and Tibshirani (1990).

We first examine the univariate properties of daily, weekly and monthly spot exchange rates between 1921 and the announcement of the return to gold in April 1925. The data sources are described in the appendix (p. 359). Standard unit root-tests (augmented Dickey–Fuller and Phillips–Perron) do not reject the null hypothesis that the logarithm of the spot rate contains one unit root.

In figures 12.1–12.2 we present scatter plots of the relationship between the change in the logarithm of the spot rate and time. This is done for the daily, weekly and monthly data; for various sample periods; and for different degrees of smoothing.[2] The most striking feature of the scatter plots is the pronounced deterministic trends prior to Novemeber 1924, when the impact of the return to gold on the exchange rate is typically assumed to be at its least important. The second important feature of the scatter plots is that whilst the trend in the exchange rate is initially negative, from November 1924 there is evidence of it becoming positive.[3]

The cubic splines with little smoothing appeared significant on the basis of a χ^2 test. However, the asymptotic theory for these tests is as yet underdeveloped (see Hastie and Tibshirani, 1990). Consequently, we examine the parametric nature of the relationship between the logarithmic change

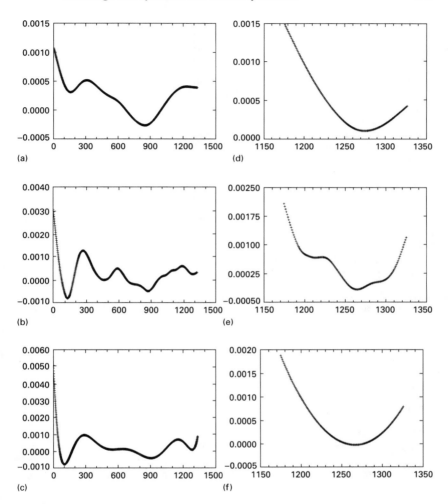

Figure 12.1 Nonparametric and parametric scatter plots, Δe against time,
λ=degrees of freedom, daily data
(a) $\lambda=6$ (b) $\lambda=16$ (c) Parametric
(d) $\lambda=2$ (e) $\lambda=6$ (f) Parametric

in the spot rate and time. A summary of the relationships is presented in table 12.1. The fitted relationships are displayed in figures 12.1c, f and 12.2c, f. These are consistent with the nonparametric findings discussed earlier. There are significant deterministic trends in exchange rates over the period. More specifically, from November 1924 the daily data show a

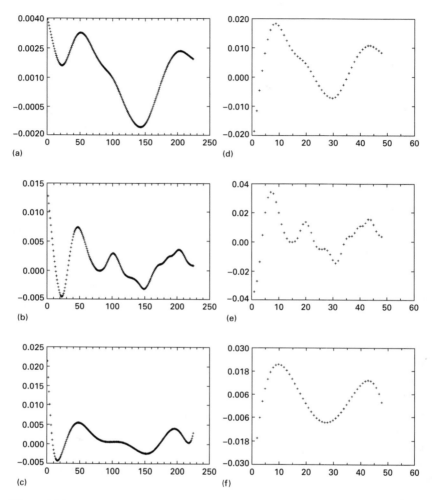

Figure 12.2 Nonparametric and parametric scatter plots, Δe against time,
λ=degrees of freedom, weekly and monthly data
(a) λ=6   (b) λ=16   (c) Parametric
(d) λ=6   (e) λ=16   (f) Parametric

marked U-shaped relationship, where the change in the spot rate remains
positive (see figures 12.1d–f).

The positive drift in the exchange rate in the period immediately prior to
the return to gold is consistent with the Miller–Sutherland (1992, 1994)
model with or without autoregressive fundamentals, though in the former

Table 12.1 *Parametric trends for the rate of change of the spot exchange rate* (Δe)

Sample period	N	Constant	Polynominal in time	$\bar{R}^2$	F	$Q(4)^a$
Daily:	1325	0.0002	–	–	–	8.11
01/3/1921–04/28/1925			1, 2,..., 8	0.03	6.15*[b]	7.06
Daily:	151	0.0005	–	–	–	14.00*
10/30/1924–04/28/1925			1, 2	0.07	6.75*	11.46
Weekly:	224	0.0012	–	–	–	17.28*
01/15/1921–04/25/1925			1, 2,..., 8	0.12	4.89*	6.28
Monthly:	48	0.0040	–	–	–	9.33
05/1921–04/1925			1, 2, 3, 4	0.21	4.28*	6.14

Notes:
[a] $Q(4)$ is the Box–Pierce-statistic and F is the usual test of the overall significance of the trend terms.
[b] * indicates significance at the 1 percent level.

case α is required to be less than unity. As suggested earlier, another possibility is that the key assumption underlying the Smith and Smith (1990) model, namely an unknown terminal date of return to gold, was valid initially but replaced by the Miller–Sutherland assumption of a known terminal date.

We next examine the behavior of the forward premium and forecast error. Standard unit root tests for the period December 1921–April 1925[4] suggest that the forward premium is nonstationary whilst the four-week forecast error ($e_{t+4}-f_t$) is stationary. Phillips–Perron test statistics are reported in table 12.2 for window length 4 (the results are qualitatively similar for other lag lengths). These results suggest that, for the whole period, any time varying risk premium is stationary (the implication of the stationarity of the forecast error), while the expected appreciation of the spot rate is nonstationary. The apparent contradiction implied by the nonstationarity of the forward premium and the stationarity of the rate of change of the spot rate can be reconciled if the noise in the actual

Table 12.2 *Phillips–Perron Tests*[a, c]

Variable	$Z(\tilde{\alpha})$	$Z(\tau_\tau)$	$Z(\phi_3)$	$Z(\phi_2)$	$Z(\alpha^*)$	$Z(\tau\hat{\mu})$	$Z(\phi_1)$
f–e	−5.9	−1.70	1.59	1.15	−4.4	−1.36	1.52
$\Delta(f$–$e)$	−199.0	−14.86	108.60	72.40	−199.2	−14.82	103.30
e_{t+4}–f_t	−41.8	−5.00	12.55	8.38	−42.0	−5.01	6.25
Critical values: [b]							
10 percent level	−18.3	−3.12	5.34	4.03	−11.3	−2.57	3.78
1 percent level	−29.5	−3.96	8.27	6.09	−20.7	−3.43	6.43

Notes:
[a] The notation used is that of Perron (1988).
[b] The critical values are from Fuller (1976) and Dickey and Fuller (1981).
[c] The data is weekly for the period 12/10/1921–04/25/1925.

change Δe masks the $I(1)$ behavior of the expected change (f–e) in small samples.

In table 12.3 we investigate further the univariate properties of the forward premium. We assume that the properties of the one-month forward premium will be similar to those derived for the instantaneous premium.[5] To make allowance for the time dependent solution obtained in the Miller–Sutherland model with autoregressive fundamentals, we approximate the functional by a Taylor expansion. This generates terms in time, time^2, etc. multiplied by the forward premium. It can be seen from table 12.3 that for the whole period the point coefficient on the lagged forward premium is less than unity in contrast with the explosive behavior implied by two of the models (see, (A4), (B4), p. 346); moreover, terms in time or interaction terms are insignificant in the presence of the lagged forward premium. For the period post-October 1924 the results change dramatically. When the lagged forward premium is the only independent variable, the point coefficient on the lagged forward premium falls to 0.58 and stationarity of the forward premium is not rejected. When the interaction terms are included they are both significant and the point coefficient on the lagged forward premium increases to 2.91. Terms in t and t^2 also appear to offer some additional explanatory power. Assuming that the effect of any risk premium, if it exists, is negligible these results are consistent with the type of model outlined by Miller and Sutherland (1994) with autoregressive fundamentals (see (D4), p. 346) where the interest elasticity of money demand is less than unity.

It appears of interest, therefore, to examine the behavior of fundamentals more directly.[6] We employ two different methods. First, we follow a method

Table 12.3 *Time series representations of the forward premium* $(f{-}e)^a$

Period	Constant	$(f{-}e)_{t-1}$	$t_*(f{-}e)_{t-1}$	$t_*^2(f{-}e)_{t-1}$	t_*	t_*^2	$\bar{R}^2$	Q(4)[c]	A(4)[c]
12/10/1921 -4/25/1925 (N=177)	0.000 (0.38)[b]	0.97 (50.02)					0.93	8.40	14.68
	-0.000 (1.74)	0.85 (0.13)	0.23 (0.38)	-0.10 (0.16)	0.0006 (1.54)	-0.005 (1.30)	0.93	7.91	13.66
11/01/1924 -4/25/1925 (N=26)	-0.000 (0.01)	0.58 (3.62)					0.35	2.07	1.31
	0.000 (1.55)	2.91 (5.37)	-58.38 (3.55)	287.95 (3.04)			0.66	1.50	2.01
	-0.000 (1.95)	1.62 (2.26)	-43.74 (2.68)	237.46 (2.66)	0.01 (2.49)	-0.07 (2.40)	0.68	3.76	0.96

Notes:
[a] The dependent variable is $(f{-}e)_t$ and the trend variable is measured as $t_*=(225-t)/225$, $t=49,...,225$.
[b] The numbers in brackets are t-ratios.
[c] Q(4) is the Box–Pierce-statistic and A(4) Engle's ARCH-statistic, both distributed as χ_4^2.

utilized by Flood *et al.* (1992): given weekly observations of the spot exchange rate and the forward premium, we obtain estimates of the fundamentals from (5) by postulating values of α, the interest elasticity of money demand. We consider a range of values including those employed by Smith and Smith (1990) (½, 6.5, 13). For all values of α, we cannot reject a unit root in our estimate of the fundamentals for the whole period. However, for values of $\alpha<1$ there is some evidence of autoregressive behavior of fundamentals for the period November 1924–April 1925. The illustrative results below are for the case $\alpha=0.5$, and the periods 12/10/1921–04/25/1925 ($N=177$) and 11/1/1924 04/25/1925 ($n=26$), respectively (t-ratios in brackets):

$$\Delta K_t = 0.04 \qquad -0.02 K_{t-1} \qquad \bar{R}^2=0.02$$
$$\qquad\qquad\qquad (2.20) \qquad\qquad (2.16)$$
$$\Delta K_t = 0.25 \qquad -0.16 K_{t-1} \qquad \bar{R}^2=0.38$$
$$\qquad\qquad\qquad (4.14) \qquad\qquad (4.09)$$

Second we examine the behavior of a measure of relative money supply to determine whether there is any evidence of autoregressive behavior. In figure 12.3 we plot the logarithm of the ratio of a monthly measure of UK and US money supplies (see the data appendix, p. 359, for sources). This indicates a downward trend in relative monies from 1922 onwards, which is consistent with the general appreciation of sterling over the period. In figures 12.4 and 12.5 we plot the difference in rates of change of UK and US money supply measured over 1 and 12 months, respectively. It can be seen that the annualized differences are negative from 1922 onwards. Also on an annualized basis there is evidence of UK money supply growing relatively less quickly from around March 1924 onwards.

Formal analysis suggests that the level of relative money supply is a nonstationary variable (for example, Augmented Dickey–Fuller t-statistic$= -0.24$) and that the first difference is stationary and also random. There is no evidence of significant mean reversion in relative money supplies for either the whole period or the large number of subperiods considered. For example, for the periods 02.1921–04.1925, 01.1924–04.1925 and 12.1924–04.1925 we obtain respectively (t-ratio in brackets):

$$\Delta M_t = -0.01 \quad +0.00 M_{t-1} \quad \bar{R}^2 = -0.02 \quad DW = 1.69$$
$$\qquad\quad (0.29) \qquad (0.12)$$

$$\Delta M_t = 0.13 \quad -0.10 M_{t-1} \quad \bar{R}^2 = -0.01 \quad DW = 2.36$$
$$\qquad\quad (0.89) \qquad (0.95)$$

$$\Delta M_t = 0.49 \quad -0.35 M_{t-1} \quad \bar{R}^2 = -0.17 \quad DW = 1.36.$$
$$\qquad\quad (0.63) \qquad (0.64)$$

We next examine whether there are significant deterministic trends in the spot exchange rate when allowance is made for the impact of relative prices on the exchange rate. As noted earlier, Miller and Sutherland have demonstrated (in a respresentative model) that when the boundary conditions involve time the spot exchange rate is a nonlinear function of both relative prices and a deterministic trend (see (8)). Utilizing monthly data (sources in the data appendix, p. 359) for the period January 1921–April 1925, we consider whether the exchange rate and wholesale prices are stationary. We employ Dickey–Fuller, Phillips–Perron and the rank test proposed by Granger and Hallman (1991). The test-statistics overall support the hypothesis of a unit root in each variable and are reported in Michael *et al.* (1994).

We initially consider whether the exchange rate is cointegrated with the relative price in the absence of a deterministic trend. A finding of cointegration would of course imply long-run PPP. For both a restricted regression, where the coefficient on relative price is imposed as unity, and an unrestricted regression, cointegration is rejected at normal levels of significance for the whole data period.[7] The absence of cointegration is also indicated

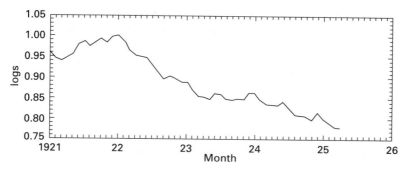

Figure 12.3 Relative money supply, United Kingdom/United States, 1921–1926, logs of ratio of money supplies

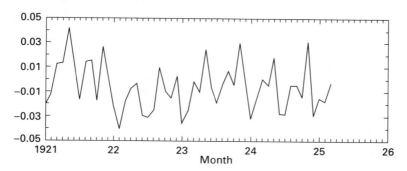

Figure 12.4 Relative money supply, United Kingdom/United States, 1921–1926, monthly rate of change

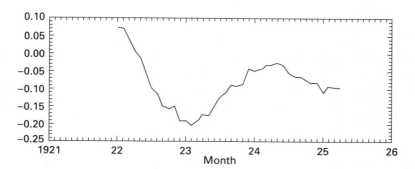

Figure 12.5 Relative money supply, United Kingdom/United States, 1921–1926, annual rate of change

by the insignificance of the cointegration residual in linear error correction models which were estimated with both exchange rates and prices as dependent variables. The most parsimonious linear error correction model with the exchange rate as dependent variable is reported as (10) below (sample period: 06.1921–04.1925):

$$\Delta e_t = 0.003 \quad -0.02\hat{u}_{t-1} \quad +0.44\Delta(p^*-p)_{t-1} \quad -0.50\Delta^2 p_{t-2}+0.29\Delta^2 e_{t-2} \quad (10)$$
$$(0.95) \quad (0.24) \qquad (2.75) \qquad\qquad (2.60) \qquad (3.05)$$

$$\left[\begin{array}{l} \bar{R}^2=0.36 \qquad s=0.017 \qquad DW=1.68 \qquad Q(4)=1.81 \\ J\!-\!B=0.02 \quad A(4)=1.49 \quad RE(2)=7.87 \quad F(6,36)=1.30 \end{array} \right],$$

where t-values are in parenthesis, RE=reset-test, $J\!-\!B$=Jarque–Bera-test, F=Chow predictive failure-test and $\hat{u}_{t-1}$=residual from the constrained PPP equation.

We now allow for any impact of deterministic trends on the exchange rate by estimating a cointegrating regression suggested by a Taylor expansion of (8). Our preferred specification is given by

$$e_t - p_t^* + p_t = 2.034 - 10.2t_* + 89.3t_*^2 - 264.6t_*^3 + 310.0t_*^4 - 125.1t_*^5$$
$$(180.0) \quad (3.33) \quad (3.94) \quad (4.23) \quad (4.17) \quad (3.85)$$

$$+\left\{ \begin{array}{l} -22.1t_* + 201.6t_*^2 - 608.4t_*^3 + 726.1t_*^4 - 298.8t_*^5 \\ (4.00) \ (4.90) \quad (5.56) \quad (5.81) \quad (5.74) \end{array} \right\}(p_t^* - p_t) + \hat{v}_t \quad (11)$$

$$[\bar{R}^2=0.90 \qquad s=0.012 \qquad DW=2.00],$$

where t-values are in parenthesis, and the trend is measured as $t_* = (52-t)/52;\ t=1, 2,... 52$.

(11) is an example of time varying parameter cointegration as discussed in Granger (1986). The regression has a form which implies that when the return to gold occurs ($t_*=0$) PPP will hold as a long-run equilibrium condition. The residual in this regression is comfortably accepted as white noise: $(\Delta\hat{v}_t = -1.00\ \hat{v}_{t-1})$
$\quad\quad (6.80)$

Clearly the cointegrating regression provides strong support for the hypothesis that the real and nominal exchange rates contain deterministic trends, as occurs in the time dependent model of Miller and Sutherland (1994). The actual and predicted levels of the spot exchange rate from constrained PPP and the time varying parameter cointegration regressions are shown in figure 12.6. It is observed that the predicted values from the time varying model are closer to the actual values, particularly in the period from mid-1924 onwards.

The estimates of the preferred error correction model corresponding to the time varying parameter cointegration regression gave

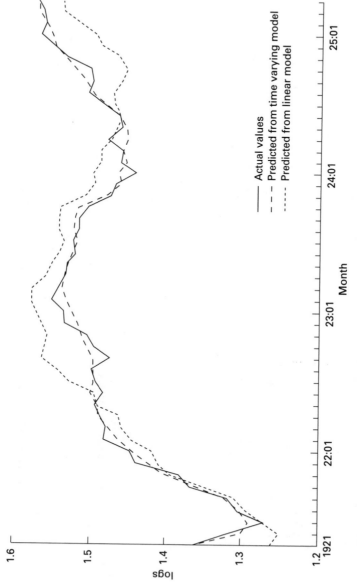

Figure 12.6 Actual and predicted levels of the nominal exchange rate, 1921–1926

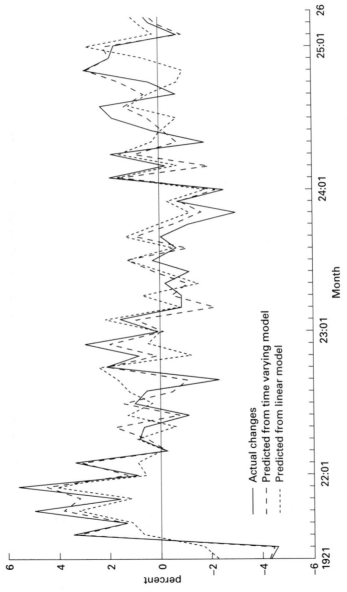

Figure 12.7 Actual and predicted changes in the nominal exchange rate, 1921–1926

$$\Delta e_t = 0.006 - 0.94\hat{v}_{t-1} - 0.61\Delta p^*_{t-2} + 0.50\Delta p_{t-3} + 0.32\Delta e_{t-1} + 0.41\Delta e_{t-2}$$
$$(0.87) \quad (5.44) \qquad (4.36) \qquad (3.28) \qquad (2.65) \qquad (4.58)$$
$$+0.07t_* - 0.88t_*^2 + 2.17t_*^3 - 1.43t_*^4$$
$$(0.56) \quad (1.50) \quad (2.10) \quad (2.42)$$
$$+(-6.1t_* + 51.1t_*^2 - 121.6t_*^3 + 83.9t_*^4)\Delta(p^* - p)_{t-1}$$
$$(0.95) \quad (1.45) \qquad (1.96) \qquad (2.42) \tag{12}$$

$$\begin{bmatrix} \bar{R}^2 = 0.77 & s = 0.010 & DW = 2.14 & Q(4) = 2.44] \\ J\text{-}B = 1.24 & A(4) = 2.06 & RE(2) = 8.65 & F(6,25) = 0.12 \end{bmatrix},$$

where the residual $\hat{v}_t$ and trend t_* are as in (11). The coefficient on the cointegration residual is highly significant with a point value close to unity, suggesting that adjustment to PPP is rapid when allowance is made for the influence of deterministic trends. Plots of the actual and predicted changes in the nominal exchange rate derived from both the linear and time varying parameter error correction processes are shown in figure 12.7. The predicted changes from the time varying error correction show close correspondence with the actual values, particularly in the period from November 1924 onwards.

Conclusions

In this chapter we have presented new empirical evidence in the behavior of the sterling/dollar exchange rate in the interwar floating period. A key finding of the chapter is that the exchange rate exhibited deterministic trends in the period; and in the period immediately preceding the return to gold, the drift in exchange rates was positive rather than negative as had been previously accepted.

The deterministic trends in the exchange rate remained highly significant when allowance was made for fundamentals, measured by relative prices. The empirical results in the chapter, on balance, appear supportive of the models developed by Miller and Sutherland (1992, 1994), in which time dependent terms occur in solutions for the spot rate, as a result of an expectation by market agents of a known terminal date to return to gold. Particularly interesting in this context were the results we reported on the time series behavior of the forward premium which exhibited explosive and time dependent behavior in the period preceding the return to gold.

Data appendix

Data on weekly spot and forward exchange rates from Einzig (1937). Monthly spot rates from Einzig – end-month quotation. Daily spot rates are the intra-day highs from *The Times*.

Wholesale prices from International Abstract of Economic Statistics 1919–1930, *International Conference of Economic Services* (London, 1934). The US money supply is currency held by the public, plus demand and time deposits at commercial banks, from Friedman and Schwartz (1970) and reported in Frenkel and Clements (1981). The UK money supply is the total deposits of the London clearing banks, from the Committee on Finance and Industry (1931) and reported in Frenkel and Clements (1981).

Notes:

A. R. Nobay acknowledges the research support from the H. G. B. Alexander Foundation, University of Chicago and the Financial Markets Group at the LSE. D. A. Peel acknowledges support from the Leverhulme foundation under Grant no. F/424/G.
1. See the discussion in Skidelsky (1988), and in Keynes' "The Economic Consequences of Mr. Churchill" (1972) on policy induced changes in relative prices and the consequent overvaluation of sterling.
2. All plots use a smoothing parameter corresponding to λ degrees of freedom as indicated in figures 12.1–12.2. For comparison, a least squares fit corresponds to one degree of freedom.
3. Using the rank of the change in the log of the spot rate in the nonparametric plots against time essentially replicates figures 12.1a–12.1c, thus confirming Smith's empirical finding.

    For the daily and weekly data we also estimated nonparametric smoothing using the residuals from bilinear models. As demonstrated in Brockett (1976), a bilinear model can approximate any nonlinear model to an arbitrary degree of accuracy. Our results (available on request) show that the deterministic trends remain qualitatively the same following this nonlinear transformation.
4. Weekly observations on the forward premium, whilst reported by Einzig (1937), are not comparable for the periods pre- and post-November 1921 since the contract prior to November 21 referred to the end of the month rather than the next calendar month.
5. In future analysis we hope to check this more formally using the methods outlined in Svensson (1991).
6. Direct estimation of (5) is not feasible. No monthly series for real output for the United Kingdom exists. Methods of interpolation based on quadratic deterministic trends as previously employed (see, e.g., Frenkel and Clements, 1981; Eichengreen, 1982) can produce seriously biased estimates as a result of proxying a potentially $I(1)$ variable by deterministic trends.
7. This empirical finding confirms that of Taylor and McMahon (1988), who also suggested that the absence of cointegration might be a result of the effect of speculation associated with the return to gold.

References

Brockett, R. W. (1976). "Volterra Series and Geometric Control Theory," *Automatica* 12, 167–172

Dickey, D. and W. A. Fuller (1981). "Likelihood Ratio Statistics for Autoregressive Time Series with a Unit Root," *Econometrica* 49, 1057–1072

Eichengreen, B. (1982). "Did Speculation Destabilize the French Franc in the 1920s?," *Explorations in Economic History* 19, 71–100

Einzig, P. (1937). *The Theory of Forward Exchange*, London: Macmillan

Flood, R. P. and P. M. Garber (1983). "A Model of Stochastic Process Switching," *Econometrica* 51, 537–552

Flood, R. P., A. R. Rose and D. J. Mathieson (1991). "An Empirical Exploration of Exchange Rate Target-zones," *Carnegie–Rochester Series on Public Policy* 35, 7–66

Frenkel, J. A. and K. W. Clements (1981). "Exchange Rates in the 1920s: A Monetary Approach," in M. J. Flanders and R. Assat (eds.), *Development in an Inflationary World*, New York, Academic Press, 283–318

Friedman, M. and A. J. Schwartz (1970). *Monetary Statistics of the United States: Estimates, Sources and Methods*, New York: Columbia University Press for NBER

Froot, K. and M. Obstfeld (1991). "Stochastic Process Switching: Some Simple Solutions," *Econometrica* 59, 241–50

Fuller, W. A. (1976). *Introduction to Statistical Time Series*, New York: John Wiley

Granger, C. W. J. (1986). "Developments in the Study of Cointegrated Economic Variables," *Oxford Bulletin of Economics and Statistics* 48, 213–228

Granger, C. W. J. and J. Hallman (1991). "Nonlinear Transformations of Integrated Time Series," *Journal of Time Series Analysis* 12, 207–224

Hastie, T. J. and R. J. Tibshirani (1990). *Generalized Additive Models*, London: Chapman & Hall

Hicks, J. (1974). *The Crisis in Keynesian Economics*, Oxford: Basil Blackwell

Keynes, J. M. (1972). "The Economic Consequences of Mr. Churchill," *The Collected writings of J. M. Keynes* vol. IX, *Essays in Persuasion*, London: Macmillan

Krugman, P. (1991). "Target Zones and Exchange Rate Dynamics," *Quarterly Journal of Economics* 106 (August), 669–682

Krugman, P. and M. Miller (eds.) (1992). *Exchange Rate Targets and Currency Bands*, Cambridge: Cambridge University Press

Krugman, P. and J. Rotemberg (1992). "Speculative Attacks on Target Zones," chapter 8 in P. Krugman and M. Miller (eds.), *Exchange Rate Targets and Currency Bands*, Cambridge: Cambridge University Press

Michael, P., A. R. Nobay and D. A. Peel (1994). "Exchange Rates, Transaction Bands and Cassel's Doctrine of PPP," *Research Papers in Economics and Finance* 9403, University of Liverpool

Miller, M. and A. Sutherland (1992). "Britain's Return to Gold and Entry into the EMS: Joining Conditions and Credibility," in P. Krugman and M. Miller (eds.), *Exchange Rate Targets and Currency Bands*, Cambridge: Cambridge University Press

(1994). "Speculative Anticipations of Sterling's Return to Gold: Was Keynes Wrong?," *Economic Journal* 104, 804–812

Miller, M. and P. Weller (1989). "Exchange Rate Bands and Realignments in a Stationary Stochastic Setting," in M. Miller, B. Eichengreen and R. Portes (eds.), *Blueprints for Exchange Rate Management*, New York: Academic Press

Moggridge, D. E. (1972). *British Monetary Policy 1924–1931, The Norman Conquest of $4.86*, Cambridge: Cambridge University Press

Perron, P. (1988). "Trends and Random Walks in Macroeconomic Time Series: Further Evidence from a New Approach," *Journal of Economic Dynamics and Control* 12, 297–332

Sargent, T. (1986). "The Ends of some Big Inflations" chapter 3 in T. Sargent, *Rational Expectations*, vols. 1 and 2, New York: Harper & Row, 40–107

Skidelsky, R. (1988). "Some Aspects of Keynes the Man," in O. F. Hamouda and S. N. Smithin (eds.), *Keynes and Public Policy after 50 years*, vol. 1, *Economics and Policy*, New York: New York University Press, 157–161

Smith, G. W. (1989). "Solutions to a Problem of Stochastic Process Switching," Queen's University, mimeo

(1992). "Discussion of Miller and Sutherland (1992)," in P. Krugman and M. Miller (eds.), *Exchange Rate Targets and Currency Bands*, Cambridge: Cambridge University Press

Smith, G. W. and R. T. Smith (1990). "Stochastic Process Switching and the Return to Gold, 1925," *Economic Journal* 100 (March), 164–175

Smith, G. W. and M. Spencer (1992). "Estimation and Testing of Models of Exchange Rate Target Zones and Process Switching," chapter 11 in P. Krugman and M. Miller (eds.), *Exchange Rate Targets and Currency Bands*, Cambridge: Cambridge University Press

Svenson, B. O. (1991). "The Simplest Test of Target Zone Credibility", *IMF Staff Papers* 38 (September), 635–665.

Taylor, M. P. and P. C. McMahon (1988). "Long-Run Purchasing Power Parity in the 1920s," *European Economic Review* 32, 179–197

VI

Conclusions

13 Déjà vu all over again: lessons from the gold standard for European monetary unification

Barry Eichengreen

Historians cannot help but regard the debate over European monetary unification with a sense of déjà vu. The goal is firmly fixed exchange rates between national currencies, the creation of a European Central Bank (ECB) to assume responsibility for the monetary policies of the participating countries, and a single currency for the member states of the European Union.[1] This brave new world resembles nothing so much as the classical gold standard of the 19th century. Under the gold standard the currencies of the leading industrial countries were pegged to one another at stable rates of exchange. Statutory barriers to international flows of financial capital were essentially absent. For this combination of reasons, the monetary autonomy enjoyed by national governments was severely limited. The same will be true over much of Europe assuming the successful completion of European Monetary Union (EMU).

Indeed, the parallels between the two systems extend beyond these technical arrangements. Like today's European Monetary System (EMS), the 19th-century gold standard revolved around the leading European financial power of its time, Great Britain, and its central bank, the Bank of England (for present purposes, the German Bundesbank of its day). Like the prospective EMU, the 19th-century gold standard achieved a high degree of financial and monetary intergration without a matching degree of political centralization.

At the same time, there are limits to the analogy between the gold standard and EMU. Whereas the gold standard always featured distinct national central banks and currencies, EMU will be characterized by a single central bank and, ultimately, a single currency. Whereas EMU, established by an international treaty, will represent a virtually irrevocable commitment, the gold standard was a contingent rule that governments could suspend in response to exceptional circumstances. Whereas the gold standard was characterized by extensive labor flows between participating countries, migration on a comparable scale is not contemplated – indeed, it would not be tolerated – under EMU. And whereas present-day policy-makers foresee a need for statutory restraints on the fiscal policies of participating countries, no such restrictions were imposed in conjunction with the operation of the gold standard.

Even if the analogy is valid, it is not clear whether parallels are better drawn with the smoothly functioning gold standard of the 19th century or the fragile, unstable gold standard of the 1920s.[2] In the second half of the 1920s, weak currency countries, the United Kingdom prominent among them, complained that structural imbalances afflicting the gold standard world were aggravating their competitive difficulties. They suffered persistent balance of payments problems and chronic budgetary strains. Gold standard constraints on adjusting their overvalued exchange rates forced them to restrict the provision of domestic credit, and the stability of their banking systems was undermined as a result. Ultimately, their position proved untenable, and balance of payments crises ensued. There are obvious parallels with the economic and foreign exchange market difficulties of Italy, Spain, the United Kingdom and Sweden in the summer of 1992 and of France and Denmark in the summer of 1993. If the interwar gold standard and not its 19th-century predecessor is the relevant precedent for EMU, then the lessons of history are less heartening.

This chapter explores the parallels between the gold standard and EMU. It asks whether the conditions that rendered viable the fixed exchange rates of the gold standard are present in Europe today. It starts by considering six aspects of gold standard experience in the light of EMU: the symmetry and magnitude of disturbances, labor market flexibility, cohesion, capital mobility, fiscal rules, and central bank independence. It then turns to the contrast with the much less satisfactory interwar gold standard and implications for EMU.

Incidence of disturbances

Following Mundell's (1961) seminal contribution to the theory of optimum currency areas, economists have regarded fixed exchange rates as easy to defend and desirable to maintain when disturbances are small and symmetrically distributed across countries and when labor is allowed to flow freely between them. When shocks are small, there is little need for the active use of monetary and fiscal policies, and the constraints on policy imposed by a commitment to fixed rates are of little consequence. When shocks are large but impinge symmetrically on countries, a common policy response may suffice; hence, the constraints of fixed exchange rates or monetary union will not bind. Similarly, when shocks are asymmetrically distributed but labor flows freely from depressed to booming countries, unemployment differentials will be minimized and the policy constraints associated with fixed exchange rates will be easy to bear.

How does the magnitude of disturbances in the gold standard years compare with recent decades? In Eichengreen (1994) I computed the standard deviation of detrended real national income for nine high-income countries. That standard deviation was 50 percent larger under the classical gold standard than in the post-World War II years.[3] The result continues to hold when the comparison with the post-World War II era is limited to the 1970s and 1980s. Bayoumi and Eichengreen (1994) compute the standard deviation of detrended national income for EU member states since 1960, arriving at the same conclusion. Thus, if the magnitude of output movements is used as a criterion for the viability of fixed exchange rates and monetary union, and gold standard experience is taken as a lower-bound estimate of what is viable, then conditions in Europe today are consistent with the maintenance of such arrangements.

Output movements are not the same as disturbances, of course, since the former incorporate both shocks and responses. Bayoumi and I therefore follow Blanchard and Quah (1989) in using time series econometrics to distinguish disturbances from responses and temporary from permanent shocks (and interpret the latter as aggregate supply and aggregate demand disturbances, respectively). We find that the large output fluctuations of the gold standard years were attributable to large disturbances, not to slow responses. Aggregate supply shocks were two and a half times as large under the classical gold standard as in the post-World War II years. Aggregate demand disturbances were twice as large. This last finding is surprising: whereas the gold standard is commonly credited with having disciplined erratic policymakers, our results suggest that relatively large demand disturbances emanating from other sources dominated these effects.

Not only were output fluctuations larger under the gold standard than after World War II, but they were less correlated across countries (Eichengreen, 1994).[4] This is plausible insofar as some countries like the United States, Canada, and Australia specialized in the production and export of agricultural goods and primary products, while others such as the United Kingdom exported manufactures in return for foodstuffs and raw materials. It follows that aggregate supply and demand disturbances (which were presumably associated with income fluctuations that shifted demand between foodstuffs and other goods) were also less correlated across countries under the gold standard than after World War II. Bayoumi and I show that the variation of output-weighted standard deviations of both aggregate supply and aggregate demand disturbances around the sample mean was about twice as large in the classical gold standard years as after World War II (when the sectoral specialization of high-income countries appears to have diminished compared to the late 19th century). This suggests that a significant portion of the disturbances experienced during the gold standard years was country-specific. But the fact that these disturbances were readily accommodated in the presence of fixed exchange rates suggests that the same could in principle be true in Europe in the 1990s.

The validity of this inference hinges, of course, on whether the adjustment mechanisms that operated so powerfully under the gold standard would be effective in Europe today. It is to this question that I now turn.

Labor market flexibility

One of the findings of Bayoumi and Eichengreen (1994) is exceptionally fast adjustment to aggregate supply and aggregate demand shocks during the classical gold standard years. Although shocks were noticeably larger before 1913 than after 1945, output fluctuations were only slightly greater owing to rapid adjustment. An obvious explanation for the contrast is different degrees of labor market flexibility.

Assume a country-specific shock giving rise to unemployment. If the government is precluded from devaluing the currency in order to enhance the competitiveness of exports, how can the economy respond? An obvious possibility is a decline in domestic currency wages and costs to price exports back into international markets and workers back into employment. Although economists and historians harbor the suspicion that real wages were more flexible in the 19th century than in the 20th, and especially than in Europe today, evidence on this question is far from conclusive. Hatton's (1988) comparisons of wage flexibility for pre-World War I and interwar Britain do not indicate a secular decline in labor market flexibility. Nor does Thomas' (1994) study of labor market flows. For the United States, Gordon's (1982) time series analysis reveals a decline after World War I in the responsiveness of wages to output fluctuations, supporting earlier work of Cagan (1956) and Sachs (1980), but even here recent research by Carter and Sutch (1990) and Allen (1992) casts doubt on the generalization. The judicious conclusion would appear to be that while there exists firm evidence of a decline in the economy's speed of adjustment to shocks, the jury remains out on whether growing wage rigidities lie at its root.

The other channel for labor market adjustment under the gold standard was international migration. Panic (1992) and Goodhart (1992) emphasize the role of trans-Atlantic migration in venting country-specific shocks. When conditions worsened in Europe, workers migrated to North America, South America, Australia and New Zealand, reducing domestic labor supply and unemployment. Remittances boosted spending and strengthened balances of payments in the migrants' countries of origin, helping to stabilize macroeconomic conditions there.

Fenoaltea (1988) shows for Italy that the volume of immigration was responsive to disturbances to the balance of payments. When British lending to Italy fell off, Italy's balance of payments weakened and local labor market conditions deteriorated. Italians migrated across the Atlantic, moderating the unemployment problem and through their remittances strengthening the balance of payments.

Fenoaltea estimates that net emigration as a percentage of Italy's population averaged 0.13 percent annually in 1872–1881, 0.37 percent in 1882–1891, and 0.38 percent in 1892–1901. To get net emigration of labor force participants as a percentage of the labor force, these numbers have to be adjusted upward, since labor force participants migrated in disproportionate numbers. It seems reasonable to double the percentages just reported to place them on a labor force basis. Moreover, net emigration did not proceed evenly over these decades; return migration was large and volatile, meaning that net emigration might turn negative in prosperous years. If we double these figures again to get net emigration as a share of the labor force in depressed years, the mechanism could have reduced the labor force in a slump by more than 1 percent per annum, denting unemployment significantly. While data for other countries account even less adequately for return migration, those for Sweden, Britain and Ireland in the 1880s and Spain in the 1890s suggest flows as substantial as those for Italy (Green and Urquhart, 1976).

Revealingly, the literature on 19th-century migration is couched in terms of "long swings" or "Kuznets cycles." Workers hesitated to migrate in response to short-lived increases in unemployment; a persistent deterioration in local economic conditions was required before the present discounted value of the gains from migration offset the front-end costs. Hence, migration was probably less important as a response to fluctuations at standard business cycle frequencies than as a correlate of long swings. Even at business cycle frequencies, however, there is evidence that migration responded to wage and unemployment differentials between sending and receiving countries.[5]

By the standards of the gold standard era, there is less scope today for migration among the European nations contemplating the formation of a monetary union. The destinations of the 19th-century immigrants were characterized by abundant land and scarce labor; their governments welcomed new arrivals. Destination countries today are less welcoming of Europe's unemployed; they are likely to respond to increased immigration by erecting barriers to the integration of foreign workers into local labor markets.

It might be objected that market forces in the Europe of the future will be impossible to contain – that governmental efforts to stem adjustment through migration are bound to fail, and that this adjustment mechanism will operate despite the authorities' efforts to suppress it. Workers will have powerful incentives to move from high- to low-unemployment regions; employers will have strong incentives to hire them. The EU's Single Market Program entails the removal of barriers to labor flows. Measures to insure the portability of pensions will stimulate intra-EU labor mobility. Such observations notwithstanding, it remains unlikely that labor mobility between EU countries will approach the levels that characterized the Atlantic economy of the 19th century or continental monetary unions like the United States today.[6] Trade unions, apprenticeship programs and credential requirements will continue to place subtle barriers in the way of labor mobility, the efforts of the European Union to overcome them with policies of mutual recognition notwithstanding. Cultural and linguistic barriers to migration will remain. It is unlikely that Europe's monetary union will be able to match the classical gold standard in the latter's reliance on labor mobility as a means of adjusting to asymmetric shocks.

Cohesion

The campaign for monetary union has been bound up with the problem of "cohesion," EU jargon for eliminating national income disparities. Monetary union, not to mention other aspects of the Single Market Program, is viewed as viable only if incomes and productivity in the poorer member states of the European Union are brought closer to EU averages. One indication of the prevalence of this view is that the low-income countries of Southern Europe obtained a significant increase in the Structural Funds (EU programs for transfers of investable funds from high- to low-income members) as a condition for agreeing to the Maastricht Treaty.

The economic as opposed to the political logic for this preoccupation is far from clear. Areas sharing a common currency like the states of the USA, the provinces of Canada or the north and south of Italy, are characterized by significant interregional income disparities. Nothwithstanding the tendency, documented by Barro and Sala-i-Martin (1991), for poorer US states to close the gap *vis-à-vis* their richer counterparts, substantial differentials remain. In 1988, for example, US GDP *per capita*, in dollars, averaged $16,900, but its standard deviation across states was $3,700. *Per capita* GDP averaged $10,800 in the European Union, with a standard deviation of $4,100 across member nations (Eichengreen, 1990). *Per capita* incomes varied only slightly more across the members of the European Union, in other words, than across the states of the USA.

In the United States and Canada, these disparities have called forth institutions of fiscal federalism to, among other things, transfer resources from richer to poorer regions. Bayoumi and Masson (1991) find that the Canadian tax and transfer system offsets 35 cents of each dollar by which incomes of Candian regions differ from one another. An analogous effect of about half the same magnitude operates in the United States. An obvious explanation for these arrangements is that they attenuate the need for exchange rate changes and interregional migration within the monetary union. Fiscal transfers that moderate regional income gaps reduce the incentive to migrate. If the income gap between regions of origin and destination must surpass some critical threshold before migration takes place, then ongoing transfers reduce the likelihood that an asymmetric shock of given size will push the differential beyond that point. If the migration that would otherwise substitute for exchange rate adjustments is perceived as a source of social and political problems, then the sort of measures to promote "cohesion" pursued in Canada and the United States might be a necessary corollary of a common currency. This is one explanation for the extensive fiscal transfers to eastern Germany that accompanied that country's economic and monetary union.

So long as the budget of the European Union remains little more than 1 percent of EU GNP, intra-European transfers will necessarily play only a modest role, despite the fact that a quarter of that budget is devoted to the Structural Funds. This, in turn, will give rise to tensions within the monetary union.

Yet *per capita* income differentials across European countries were as large in the classical gold standard years as they are today, and they were not offset by fiscal federalism. The coefficient of variation of the average *per capita* incomes of the main gold standard countries was 28 percent in 1880 and 1913, compared to 28 percent for EU member states in 1980 and 30 percent in 1988.[7] No international transfers comparable to those which take place between the provinces of Canada and the states of the USA were undertaken by the members of the gold standard club. For the latter, lack of "cohesion" did not prove debilitating.

The explanation for the contrast lies, of course, in the immigration described in the previous section. Immigration was welcomed by labor scarce, land abundant countries, emigration by the more densely settled countries of origin. It was not necessary to construct a system of interregional fiscal transfers to attenuate the incentive to migrate that arose in the absence of exchange rate changes. Unless larger migratory flows or national unemployment differentials prove acceptable to the member states of the European Union, more will have to be done to address the cohesion problem.

Capital mobility

Along with labor mobility, capital mobility is the obvious explanation for rapid adjustment under the gold standard. National capital markets were highly integrated, and governments rarely attempted to restrict the flow of finance. In consequence, international capital movements were sizeable. Bayoumi (1990) shows that savings/investment correlations were weaker under the gold standard than in the post-World War II period in general and in postwar Europe in particular, reflecting the extent of international capital mobility under the gold standard and governments' policies of benign neglect.[8]

Capital flowed freely to finance temporary shocks to the balance of payments. Since governments' commitments to their gold standard parities were credible, especially at the system's European core, when the balance of payments deteriorated and the exchange rate weakened, capital flowed in to finance the payments deficit in anticipation of the capital gains that would follow once the government took corrective action and the exchange rate recovered.[9] Since short-term capital flowed in stabilizing directions, the need for corrective action was minimized. As in models of exchange rate target zones (e.g. Krugman, 1991), the credibility of governments' commitments to their gold standard parities cushioned them from external shocks.

The same was not true of internal disturbances. When the world prices of a country's export staple weakened or domestic economic conditions otherwise deteriorated, there was little tendency for foreign capital to finance the spending shortfall. Capital did not flow in to take advantage of unemployed factors of production; although resources were idle, they were not cheap barring downward adjustments in wages and other production costs sufficient to offset the negative shock that had given rise to the unemployment in the first place. Fenoaltea (1988) shows for Italy, for example, that there was only a weak tendency for induced capital inflows to counteract shocks to domestic production.[10]

Although international capital movements were impressively large under the gold standard, today they are larger still if one includes in one's measure short- as well as long-term flows. In the late 19th century the cost of transferring funds from London to Paris amounted to perhaps one half of 1 percent of the value of the transaction. Present-day currency traders can complete an analogous transaction for a fraction of the cost. Even more than under the gold standard, present-day capital flows can easily finance balance of payments deficits, so long as those deficits are regarded as temporary and sustainable, and risk premia are of secondary importance.

Once Europe's monetary union comes into operation, Belgium will no more be able to run an unsustainable balance-of-payments deficit *vis-à-vis* other European countries than can New York State *vis-à-vis* the rest of the United States. But capital mobility will not relieve Belgium of the need to adjust to an internal disturbance, any more than it exempts New York State. Capital will not flow in if Belgian production costs rise, for example, any more than it flows into New York when the state's competitiveness declines relative to the rest of the United States.[11] Admittedly, risk premia will be smaller and capital will be even more mobile than it was during the 19th century, since it will be harder for participating countries to withdraw from EMU (their participation being governed by a multilateral agreement and codified by an international treaty) than it was for them to unilaterally abandon gold convertibility. But this will still do little to facilitate adjustment to domestic shocks.

Fiscal rules

A prominent feature of the Maastricht Treaty is the provisions designed to limit the autonomy of fiscal policymakers. The treaty's framers worried that monetary and financial integration together with budgetary autonomy would bias policy in expansionary directions. When national financial markets are segmented and capital is immobile internationally, no such bias exists, since the consequences for interest rates and future taxes of a country's deficit spending fall entirely on itself. Increased public spending drives up interest rates and requires additional distortionary taxes to finance the resulting debt service costs only in the initiating country. But as capital mobility rises and financial markets grow increasingly integrated, the higher interest rates available on domestic debt attract foreign investors. They substitute higher-yielding foreign assets for their domestic government's obligations, driving up interest rates overseas as well as at home. Once the completion of monetary union eliminates devaluation risk, the strength of this linkage will grow. Governments other than the one responsible for the initial increase in public spending will then be forced to levy additional distortionary taxes to cover their increased debt service costs. While the benefits of fiscal expansion will still accrue at home, some of the costs will be borne abroad. In the absence of mechanisms to coordinate and restrain public spending, fiscal policies will be too expansionary.

This problem provides a rationale for the fiscal rules incorporated into the Maastricht Treaty. In the two final stages of the three-stage transition to monetary union specified in the treaty, governments will be subject to fiscal rules. In Stage II (when policies are supposed to converge and responsibility for harmonizing them is transferred to the European Monetary Institute (EMI), the predecessor to the ECB, starting on January 1, 1994) and Stage III (when monetary union has commenced), governments will be required to limit their budget deficits to 3 percent of GDP and to reduce their debts to 60 percent of GDP.[12] Article 103 of the Treaty instructs member states to "coordinate [their policies] within the Council." The Council, acting by a qualified majority on a recommendation from the European Commission, may adopt guidelines for the economic policies of member countries. It will then monitor developments and make recommendations to national governments. If a country is officially determined to possess an excessive budget deficit, as provided for under the terms of Article 104c of the Treaty, and it fails to correct it, the Council may recommend that the European Investment Bank (EIB) halt lending to the country, require it to make noninterest bearing deposits with the European Union, or impose unspecified fines.

Although the 19th-century gold standard was also characterized by a high degree of financial integration, there was no perceived need for statutory restraints on national fiscal policies. There was no provision for budgetary coordination nor significant complaint of beggar-thy-neighbor fiscal policies. One reason was the more modest place of government budgets in the economy. Under the gold standard, as Goodhart (1992) observes, "governments played a very much smaller role in the economies of their respective countries." Since the level of public spending was low, any tendency for excessive deficits in one country to drive up interest rates in others could be neglected. Since there was no properly articulated theory of the role of fiscal policy in macroeconomic stabilization, the temptation to manipulate fiscal policy in beggar-thy-neighbor fashion hardly existed. In the countries at the center of the gold standard system, governments effectively imposed fiscal rules upon themselves. They "generally abided by a balanced budget objective, which could be regarded, in effect, as representing the required fiscal constraint on national policies."[13]

Had governments made more active use of discretionary fiscal policies, as they came to do in the 1920s, the situation under the gold standard still would have differed from that in Europe's prospective monetary union. A government which lost control of its fiscal policy or of its capacity to service its domestic debt could abandon gold convertibility and turn to the central bank for money finance. The central bank effectively backstopped the bond market, purchasing debt that the private sector sold and preventing a collapse of bond prices from undermining financial stability. Thus, in countries like Argentina at the periphery of the gold standard system, repeated failure to adhere to balanced budget rules led to monetization of the public debt, suspension of gold convertibility and depreciation of the exchange rate.

In EMU the participating countries, no longer possessing a national currency or a national central bank, will lack this option. The consequences for monetary and financial stability will depend on how the ECB responds. The Maastricht Treaty prohibits it from monetizing government budget deficits. A "no bail-out" rule ostensibly prevents it from backstopping government bond markets. While this minimizes any inflationary bias, McKinnon (1993) suggests that such provisions threaten to undermine the stability of financial markets in heavily indebted countries, with negative repercussions that will be felt throughout the monetary union.

Others (e.g. Bishop, 1993) question whether the "no bail-out" rule will be effectively enforced. They point to lax regulation of bank investments in public debt as creating a danger that fiscal problems will destabilize national banking systems. Notwithstanding its statute, the ECB will come under pressure to bail out the banks by supporting the bond market, even if doing so risks inflation. The knowledge that the ECB possesses this incentive will encourage fiscal profligacy. In this view, the ECB will be damned if it does (bail out the banks) and damned if it doesn't.

One response to this problem would be to apply fiscal restraints to the constituent jurisdictions in order to prevent the conditions conducive to debt runs from arising in the first place. The existence of statutory and constitutional restraints on the debts and deficits of state governments in the United States are often cited in this connection, although they arose for rather different reasons from those under discussion here.[14] The experience of US states suggests, however, that fiscal restraints, even at their strongest, can sometimes be evaded through the use of off-budget financial instruments and other such devices.[15]

Another response is to strengthen the restraints on the central bank. The problem then is what will guarantee time consistent enforcement of such restrictions. Even central bankers operating under a relatively rigid statutes retain significant discretion. They may affirm their commitment to the "no bail-out" rule *ex ante* but still retain the incentive to bail out governments experiencing a debt run *ex post*. Aware of the central bank's incentives, profligate governments may have no incentive to restrain themselves.

A third possibility is to strengthen the rules governing commercial bank investments in public debt (by, for example, requiring that banks continuously value their public debt holdings at market prices), and to require that states promptly divulge information on their fiscal condition so as to strengthen the operation of market discipline.[16] Historical experience suggests, however, that market discipline is less than wholly effective. Fishlow (1985) shows that 19th-century investors were slow to ration governments out of the market when they ran into solvency problems. Default on foreign currency-denominated debts, the service on which could not be guaranteed by printing domestic currency, was a recurrent problem.

The implication of these time inconsistency and information problems is that neither a "no bail-out" rule, nor restraints on government debts and deficits, nor provisions for prompt disclosure of information on the public finances will necessarily suffice to contain the negative repercussions of inappropriate national fiscal policies. That such measures were not required under the 19th-century gold standard reflects the fact that the public sector and its budget deficits were small, so that the international repercussions of fiscal mismanagement at the national level could be safely neglected.

Central bank independence

The Maastricht Treaty and the draft statutes of the ECB lay great stress on monetary independence. Representatives of the European Council are prohibited from serving on the ECB's Governing Council (comprising the president, the vice president and four members at large, plus the head of each national central bank). Governing Council members are prohibited from receiving instructions from their national governments. No approval by national governments or other EU bodies of monetary policy decisions is required. Members of the Executive Board of the Governing Council (which excludes the national central bankers) will serve long terms in office and cannot be reappointed or dismissed arbitrarily. Even national central bank governors on the Council must serve for at least five years, which will require some of the participating countries to revise their national central bank laws.

At first blush, experience under the gold standard appears to support the priority attached by the Maastricht negotiators to central bank independence. Most 19th-century central banks were privately owned and operated. The conduct of monetary policy was less politicized than it was to become subsequently. The balanced budget rule described above relieved central banks of pressure to monetize budget deficits. Moreover, there was little perception that monetary policies might be inconsistent with domestic prosperity. There was only limited awareness that defense of the gold standard and the reduction of unemployment might be at odds. Unemployment emerged as a coherent social and economic problem only around the turn of the century. Those observers who connected unemployment to the state of trade rarely related aggregate fluctuations to interest rates or monetary conditions. They possessed only limited appreciation of how central bank policy affected the economy. There was no well articulated theory of how supplies of money and credit could be manipulated to stabilize production or reduce joblessness. The working classes, possessing limited political power, were unable to challenge this state of affairs. In many countries, the extent of the franchise was limited. Labor parties rarely exercised significant influence. Those who might have objected that restrictive monetary policy created unemployment were in no position to influence it. Domestic political presssures thus did little to undermine the autonomy of monetary policymakers.

The United States was the exception that proved the rule. There, as Sylla (1988) emphasizes, monetary policy was relatively politicized. Although the controversies surrounding the First and Second Banks of the United States left the country without a central bank, the Department of the Treasury assumed limited central banking functions. As part of the Excutive Branch, the Treasury was subject to intense political pressure. Universal male suffrage allowed farmers and urban wage earners to pressure it to pursue cheap money policies consistent with reducing the real value of mortgage debts and enhancing employment opportunities. They allied with silver mining interests seeking the coinage of silver to support the metal's market price in the face of burgeoning supplies.[17] In the 1890s at the height of the Populist Movement, the Sherman Silver Purchase Act compelled the Treasury to inject additional currency into circulation. Interest differentials opened up between London and New York, and the viability of the American gold standard was threatened (Garber and Grilli, 1986). Only William Jennings Bryan's defeat in the 1896 presidential election ensured the survival of the dollar's gold parity. In Europe, where the franchise was more limited, silver mining interests were less powerful and the conduct of monetary policy was sometimes delegated to non- or quasi-governmental entities, no such problems arose.

On closer scrutiny, the extent of central bank independence under the gold standard becomes more difficult to characterize. Consider for example the positions of the German Reichsbank and the Bank of France. While the Bank of France was a private company, its governor was a civil servant appointed by the Minister of Finance, as were three of the twelve members of the Council of Regents. Though policy was made by majority rule within the Council, the governor could veto its decisions. The government's leverage over the Bank rose each time the latter's exclusive right to issue notes came up for renewal (in 1840, 1857, and 1897). The State's demands for central bank financing of its expenditures were considerable: in 1862, for example, fully half the bank notes in circulation were loaned to the government (Bouvier, 1988).

Plessis (1982) shows that the state was rather successful in influencing the policies of the Bank of France. It repeatedly compelled the Bank to reduce the discount rate. In 1867 the Bank of France capitulated to pressure to bail out the *Crédit Mobilier*. In 1897 it agreed under duress to establish a system of permanent advances to the semi-public *Crédit Agricole*.

The German Reichsbank, which began operations in 1876, was not even a private stock company like the Bank of France but a "juridical person" operating under government control. The Reich retained the right to terminate the activities of the Reichsbank or to nationalize it; the latter option was debated in 1889, 1899, and 1909. Central bank employees were civil servants. The Chancellor was the central bank's head official. Although the Bank Directorate, whose members were nominated by the Bundesrat (the federal legislature) and served life terms, decided matters of policy by majority vote, in the event of a conflict with the government it was required to follow the Chancellor's instructions.

Holtfrerich (1988) cites several occasions when Bismarck intervened to influence the conduct of monetary policy. In December 1880 he ordered the Reichsbank to raise the discount rate and restrict Lombard credit. In 1887 he instructed it to stop discounting Russian bonds.

The question is how central bank independence of this limited sort proved consistent with the maintenance of the gold standard in countries like France and Germany. The answer is that support for the gold standard transcended the central bank and pervaded the government and the polity. In 1856, for example, when the Regents of the Bank of France were split over whether to maintain gold payments, it was the government that ultimately compelled them to take steps to maintain convertibility (Bouvier, 1988). In Germany the government pressured the Reichsbank to defend the gold standard more often than it influenced it to direct policy toward other ends.

The history of the gold standard thus suggests that central bank independence is a will-o'-the-wisp. Central banks then, like even the most independent central banks now, were far from free of government pressure to adapt their policies to other ends. Today, German Chancellors who come into conflict with the Bundesbank can, with a sympathetic parliamentary majority, simply change the relevant central bank statute. Accounts of Bundesbank history (Kennedy, 1991) portray German's central bank as not unresponsive to outside pressure. Statutory changes are more difficult to engineer in congressional systems like that of the United States, where the President, the Senate, and the House of Representatives must agree. But even there, the White House appears to have significant influence, via moral suasion, over the conduct of monetary policy. The Fed, it is argued, is reluctant to oppose the chief executive elected by the nation (Maisel, 1980). When a conflict arises between the Fed and the Congress, Reserve System officials are called up to Capitol Hill to testify beneath the hot lights of Congessional hearing rooms. That these procedures matter is supported by evidence (e.g. Grier, 1984) that shifts in the growth rate of the money supply are affected by shifts in the membership of the Senate Banking Committee.

It would be naive to assume that the ECB will somehow enjoy significantly greater insulation than the most independent central banks possess today or than they possessed in the 19th century. For the ECB to pursue policies designed to achieve price stability, statutory independence will not suffice. Support for those policies must also extend throughout the government and, by implication, the polity.

Is there an interwar analogy?

In contrast with late-19th century experience, the performance of the interwar gold standard was unsatisfactory in important respects. Reconstructed in the mid-1920s, the system collapsed in 1931, having failed to restore anything resembling balance of payments equilibrium. In the interim, it guaranteed neither price nor output stability, as the disaster that was the Great Depression illustrated so vividly.

The unsatisfactory performance of the interwar gold standard can be understood in terms of the erosion of the institutional bases for the operation of the prewar system.[18] The extension of the franchise, the spread of unionism and the rise of political parties dominated by the working classes eroded what insulation monetary policymakers had enjoyed. Growing awareness of the links running from monetary policy to employment transformed the former into a contentious issue. This undermined both the limited independence which prewar central banks had enjoyed and the priority attached to the maintenance of the gold standard.

As the credibility of central bankers' commitments to their gold standard parities was called into question, capital no longer flowed in stabilizing directions in response to disturbances to the balance of payments. Frequently it did the opposite, testing the resolve of the authorities.[19]

Finally, the temporary suspensions of convertibility to which prewar governments had been able to resort were no longer feasible in the 1920s. The escape-clause feature of the prewar system was predicated on the credibility of governments' commitment to gold convertibility under normal circumstances and the conviction that the disturbances in response to which suspensions took place were not of the authorities' own making. Neither precondition was present after World War I. The war overturned prewar fiscal conventions, increasing public spending, stimulating the creation of new social programs, and redistributing tax burdens. It was no longer clear that governments would take whatever fiscal steps were required for the maintenance of exchange rate stability. In many countries, failure to agree on the composition of spending cuts allowed deficits, inflation and exchange rate depreciation to persist. Although deficits had been reduced by the mid-1920s, fiscal gaps remained. If the lending which made possible their financing dried up, it might become necessary to rely on monetization, even if the latter threatened currency stability. The politicization of monetary policy and compromises of central bank independence that had occurred during and after the war made this danger all the more pressing.

This was precisely the sort of policy induced exchange rate instability that could undermine the viability of the escape clause. Rightly concerned that any compromise of legal provisions regarding the statutory gold cover might be regarded as evidence of inadequate fiscal and monetary discipline rather than unfavorable exogenous shocks, the authorities hestitated to violate those provisions even temporarily. They remained wedded to defense of their gold standards until banking and balance of payments crises forced them to cave in.

The events leading up to the 1931 financial crisis, which brought down the interwar gold standard, bear an eerie resemblance to the exchange market crisis that punctuated Stage I of the Maastricht process in September 1992. The interwar gold standard was disrupted by the destabilizing policies of the center countries, the United States and France, which between them possessed nearly two-thirds of global monetary gold.[20] Starting in 1928, both countries ran increasingly restrictive monetary policies, drawing financial capital and reserves from the rest of the world and forcing other countries to raise interest rates in order to defend their increasingly overvalued exchange rates. Those other countries, led by Britain, were unwilling to adjust their exchange rates despite being hit by an external disturbance not of their own making, citing the devastating impact on "confidence" of altering the rate. The immediate spark for the 1931 crisis was banking problems in Central Europe. When Germany and Austria were forced to restrict the convertibility of their currencies and the confidence crisis shifted to London, the Bank of England, slow to recognize the gravity of the situation and fearing the impact on the domestic economy, delayed raising interest rates. When the Bank finally responded, its actions were too little, too late.

In 1992 the names and places were different but the pattern of events was similar. In 1992 it was Germany rather than the United States and France that was at the center of the system. In 1992 it was Germany that imparted a destabilizing impulse to other countries, in the form of the restrictive credit policies of the Bundesbank. In 1992, as in 1931, one of the sparks that ignited the crisis was banking problems, this time in Scandinavia rather than Central Europe. In 1992 it was countries like Italy, Britain and Spain – citing the impact on confidence or, to use the currently fashionable term, "credibility" – that refused to realign their currencies so as to insulate their economies from the depressing effect of restrictive credit policies in the center country. And in 1992, as in 1931, it was the Bank of England that waited too long to initiate its defense of the sterling parity.

What lessons can be drawn from this episode for the transition to EMU? I focus on three. First, until policy is formulated collectively by the Council of the ECB, a center country, in the present instance Germany, is bound to exercise a disproportionate influence over its stance.[21] If that country, like the United States and France between the wars, pursues policies that fail to take into account the implications for other countries, strains will arise with the capacity to fatally undermine the convergence process.

Second, in a setting where monetary policy is politicized and impediments to capital mobility have been removed, it is unrealistic to hope that governments will be able to accommodate disturbances by resorting to the escape-clause feature of pegged rate systems. That they could do so in the 19th century reflected their commitment to the maintenance of convertibility under all but the most exceptional circumstances. By the 1920s, in contrast, one of the conditions that had allowed the authorities to temporarily suspend convertibility in response to exceptional circumstances without damaging the credibility of their commitment to defend it in normal times – that the contingencies in response to which suspensions took place were not of the authorities' own making – was harder to satisfy.[22] Policies to reduce unemployment had become paramount, politicizing the conduct of monetary policy. With the authorities' commitment to gold convertibility rendered an open question, resort to the escape clause could seriously damage the authorities' credibility. Governments therefore hesitated to realign their currencies in the period leading up to the 1931 financial crisis. The same was true of the 1992 EMS crisis, of course.

Third and finally, interwar experience makes clear that once monetary policy becomes politicized, the maintenance of fixed exchange rates in the presence of high capital mobility is problematic. Unfettered capital markets will apply intense pressure to official reserves in order to test policymakers' resolve. Even a policy of stabilizing exchange rates which is rational and desirable in the absence of a speculative attack may be rendered irrational and undesirable by adverse speculation itself. If defending the currency by raising interest rates threatens to do sufficient damage to the economy, it may be rational for policymakers who had willingly pursued policies of stabilizing exchange rates prior to the speculative attack to abandon those policies in response.[23] In environments of free capital mobility like the 1920s and 1990s, the terms of this tradeoff between internal and external stability tend to be tilted against policymakers seeking to maintain stable exchange rates. Interwar policymakers learned from their experience: when pegged rates were restored after World War II, those responsible for maintaining them demanded and obtained the extra protection provided by capital controls. It remained for their successors in the early 1990s to repeat earlier mistakes.

Conclusions

The history of the gold standard provides important caveats for aspiring architects of Europe's monetary union. Although gold standard experience suggests that a currency area can successfully encompass countries characterized by very different macroeconomic conditions and that it can do so even in the absence of fiscal federalism, the essential factors that lent the gold standard this capacity are not present in Europe today. One such factor was tolerance of labor mobility. The participants in Europe's prospective monetary union would be unwilling to contemplate migration on a 19th-century scale. Although wage flexibility can substitute for migration, it seems unlikely that eliminating the exchange rate as an instrument of adjustment would force workers to accept a significantly greater degree of wage flexibility; even in the late 19th century, the heyday of fixed exchange rates and labor market flexibility, wages were far from perfectly fluid. In this sense, the experience of the gold standard supports those who insist on the need in Europe's monetary union for alternative shock absorbers such as fiscal federalism.

The contrast between the 19th-century gold standard and Europe's prospective monetary union provides some support for measures to limit fiscal autonomy. The commitment to the gold standard was contingent; governments with debt problems could abandon convertibility and rely on the national central bank to backstop the market for domestic government debt, limiting the scope for financial instability. In contrast, the commitment to EMU will be all but irrevocable, and national central banks will become powerless. Any bail-out will have to come from the ECB, which, despite statutes designed to preclude intervention, may have an *ex post* incentive to intervene. The knowledge that the costs of the bail-out may be borne by the European Union as a whole will encourage national governments to pursue policies heightening the likelihood that intervention will be necessary. Hence the argument for EU oversight of national fiscal policies, for prompt disclosure of public financial information to strengthen market discipline, and for commercial banks to be required to mark their bond portfolios to market.

Gold standard experience also pours cold water on enthusiasts of central bank independence. Central banks have never been as independent as envisaged by the framers of the Maastricht Treaty. They always have and always will be subject to political pressure. If the ECB pursues policies consistent with price stability, this will not be because it is insulated by statute from pressures emanating from the political sphere. Rather, it will reflect the abiding support that policies of price stability have garnered throughout the European polity.

Finally, the contrast between the classical and interwar gold standards raises questions about the Maastricht blueprint for completing the transition to EMU. Once monetary policy becomes politicized, as it inevitably does in democracies with universal suffrage, the authorities no longer enjoy insulation from political pressure or the credibility of an unquestioned exchange rate commitment. In a system of pegged exchange rates, the markets have an irresistible temptation to test policymakers' resolve by running on the central bank's reserves, and in the absence of capital controls their doing so is costless. From this perspective, the strong resemblance between the 1931 and 1992 crises is no coincidence. Exchange rate adjustments – realignments in current European parlance – become difficult to implement because of the questions they raise about the authorities' commitment to the defense of existing parities. Inevitably, the result is a rigid but fragile pegged exchange rate system vulnerable to collapse.

Notes

For helpful comments, I thank Tam Bayoumi and Peter Kenen.

1. The process of European monetary unification (EMU) is divided into three stages. Stage I, characterized the harmonization of national economic policies and measures to buttress the independence of central banks, concluded at the end of 1993. Stage II will feature a hardening of exchange rate commitments and a ban on monetary financing of budget deficits and bail-outs of national treasuries. Stage III, to commence no later than January 1, 1999 (assuming that at least two countries satisfy certain preconditions at that time), will see exchange rates irrevocably fixed and the European Central Bank (ECB) assuming responsibility for monetary policy. Existing national currencies will not automatically be replaced by a single European currency at the outset of Stage III. How and when the substitution of a single currency will take place will be up to the ECB. See Kenen (1992).
2. On this analogy, see for example Hale (1992).
3. Readers should be aware of the possibility that the manner in which retrospective national income statistics are constructed may introduce spurious volatility into the historical data. Substituting estimates like those of Romer (1989) for the United States does not overturn the conclusion, however.
4. In Bayoumi and Eichengreen (1994), we compute the GNP-weighted standard deviation of disturbances around the corresponding mean disturbance for the same year as a measure of this correlation.
5. For a review of the literature and evidence, see Hatton and Williamson (1992).
6. Eichengreen (1992c) shows that labor flows between French *départements* and German *Länder* are only a half to a third the rate for US states.

7. See Panic (1992). Note that different data are used than in the figures from Eichengreen (1990) cited above.
8. McKinnon (1988) and Eichengreen (1994) similarly show that long-term interest rates were more stable and moved together more closely under the gold standard than under subsequent international monetary regimes.
9. Credibility was significantly less extensive at the periphery of the international system.
10. This is precisely the conclusion reached by Blanchard and Katz (1992) for the regions of the United States today.
11. Evidence on the absence of stabilizing capital inflows into depressed US states is provided by Blanchard and Katz (1992).
12. The actual provisions are more complicated than this. Excessive deficits will only be said to exist if the deficit ratio exceeds 3 percent and if in addition either the deficit ratio has not declined "substantially and continuously" to "close to" that level, or that ratio cannot be regarded as "exceptional and temporary and . . . close to" the 3 percent threshold. The debt ratio will be said to be excessive only if it exceeds 60 percent and if in addition it is not "sufficiently diminishing and approaching the 60 percent level at a satisfactory pace."
13. Goodhart (1992).
14. For details, see Eichengreen and Bayoumi (1994).
15. This is not to imply that such restraints are without any effect, only that they are less than completely effective. For discussion, see von Hagen (1992) and Eichengreen and Bayoumi (1994).
16. These are the recommendations of Bishop (1993).
17. Cross-section evidence on the correlation between constituencies' economic characteristics and their support for political candidates espousing cheap-money policies is provided in Eichengreen (1995).
18. Since I have explored this contrast at length in Eichengreen (1992b), I consider it only briefly here.
19. One is reminded of the debate that preceded the French referendum on the Maastricht Treaty, when President Mitterrand reassured the French public that the ECB would be responsive to political imperatives, while Chancellor Kohl insisted that it would be independent of both domestic and international politics.
20. The remainder of this analysis of the interwar situation is drawn from Eichengreen (1992b).
21. Stage II makes allowance for a predecessor to the ECB, called the European Monetary Institute (EMI), one of whose responsibilities will be to arrange economic policy coordination among EMS countries. How much leverage it will actually possess remains to be seen. See Eichengreen (1992c).
22. The importance for credibility of this precondition is emphasized by Obstfeld (1991).
23. Models of such self-fulfilling speculative attacks which formalize the underlying logic are provided by Flood and Garber (1984) and Obstfeld (1986).

References

Allen, S. (1992). "Changes in the Cyclical Sensitivity of Wages in the United States, 1891–1987," *American Economic Review* 82, 122–140

Barro, R. and X. Sala-i-Martin (1991). "Convergence Across States and Regions," *Brookings Papers on Economic Activity* 1, 107–182

Bayoumi, T. (1990). "Saving–Investment Correlations: Immobile Capital, Government Policy, or Endogenous Behavior?," *IMF Staff Papers* 37, 360–387

Bayoumi, T. and B. Eichengreen (1992). "Shocking Aspects of European Monetary Unification," in F. Torres and F. Giavazzi (eds.), *The Transition to Economic and Monetary Union in Europe*, Cambridge: Cambridge University Press, 193–229

(1994). "Economic Performance Under Alternative Exchange Rate Regimes: Some Historical Evidence," in P. B. Kenen, F. Papadia and F. Saccomanni (eds.), *The International Monetary System*, Cambridge: Cambridge University Press, 257–297

(1995). "Restraining Yourself: The Implications of Fiscal Rules for Stabilization," *IMF Staff Papers* 42, 32–48

Bayoumi, T. and P. Masson (1991). "Fiscal Flows in the United States and Canada: Lessons for Monetary Union in Europe," International Monetary Fund, unpublished manuscript

Bishop, G. (1993). "Fiscal Constraints in EMU," *European Investment Research Economic and Market Analysis*, London: Solomon Brothers, September 27

Blanchard, O. and L. Katz (1992). "Regional Evolutions," *Brookings Papers on Economic Activity* 1, 1–61

Blanchard, O. and D. Quah (1989). "The Dynamic Effects of Aggregate Demand and Supply Disturbances," *American Economic Review* 79, 665–673

Bouvier, J. (1988). "The Banque de France and the State from 1850 to the Present Day," in G. Toniolo (ed.), *Central Banks' Independence in Historical Perspective*, Berlin: Walter de Gruyter, 73–104

Cagan, P. (1956). "The Monetary Dynamics of Hyperinflation," in M. Friedman (ed.), *Studies in the Quantity Theory of Money*, Chicago: University of Chicago Press, 25–117

(1975). "Changes in the Recession Behavior of Wholesale Prices in the 1920s and Post-World War II," *Explorations in Economic Research* 2, 54–104

Carter, S. and R. Sutch (1990). "Labour Market in the 1890s: Evidence from Connecticut Manufacturing," in E. Aerts and B. Eichengreen (eds.), *Unemployment and Underemployment in Historical Perspective*, Leuven: Leuven University Press, 15–24

Eichengreen, B. (1990), "One Money for Europe? Lessons from the US Currency Union," *Economic Policy* 10, 118–187

(1992a). 'Is Europe an Optimum Currency Area?," in S. Borner and H. Grubel (eds.), *The European Community After 1992: Perspectives from the Outside*, London: Macmillan, 138–160

(1992b). *Golden Fetters: The Gold Standard and the Great Depression, 1919–1939*, New York: Oxford University Press

(1992c). "Should the Maastricht Treaty Be Saved?," *Princeton Essays in International Finance* 74

(1994). "History of the International Monetary System: Implications for Research in International Macroeconomics and Finance," in F. van der Ploeg (ed.), *Handbook of International Macroeconomics*, Oxford: Basil Blackwell, 153–191

(1995). "The Endogeneity of Exchange Rate Regimes," in Peter Kenen (ed.), *Understanding Interdependence*, Princeton: Princeton University Press, 3–44

Eichengreen, B. and T. Bayoumi (1994). "The Political Economy of Fiscal Restrictions: Implications for Europe from the United States," *European Economic Review* 38, 783–791

Fenoaltea, S. (1988). "International Resource Flows and Construction Movements in the Atlantic Economy: The Kuznets Cycle in Italy, 1861–1913," *Journal of Economic History* 38, 605–638

Fishlow, A. (1985). "Lessons from the Past: Capital Markets in the 19th Century and the Interwar Period," *International Organization* 39, 383–439

Flood, R. and P. Garber (1984). "Gold Monetization and Gold Discipline," *Journal of Political Economy* 92, 90–107

Garber, P. and V. Grilli (1986). "The Belmont–Morgan Syndicate as an Optimal Investment Banking Contract," *European Economic Review* 30, 641–677

Goodhart, C. A. E. (1992). "Economic and Monetary Union (EMU) in Europe: A UK Perspective," in E. Baltensperger and H.-W. Sinn (eds.), *Exchange-Rate Regimes and Currency Unions*, New York: St. Martin's Press, 183–199

Gordon, R. J. (1982). "Why US Wage and Employment Behavior Differs from that in Britain and Japan," *Economic Journal* 92, 13–44

Green, A. and M. C. Urquhart (1976). "Factor and Commodity Flows in the International Economy of 1870–1914: A Multi-Country View," *Journal of Economic History* 36 (March), 217–252

Grier, K. (1984). "The Political Economy of Monetary Policy," University of Washington, unpublished dissertation

Hale, D. (1992). "France to the Rescue," *Financial Times* (September 1), 12

Hatton, T. J. (1988). "Institutional Change and Wage Rigidity in the UK, 1880–1985," *Oxford Review of Economic Policy* 4, 74–86

Hatton, T. J. and J. G. Williamson (1992). "International Migration and World Development: A Historical Perspective," Harvard Institute of Economic Research, *Discussion Paper* 1606

Holtfrerich, C.-L. (1988). "Relations Between Monetary Authorities and Governmental Institutions: The Case of Germany from the 19th Century to the Present," in G. Toniolo (ed.), *Central Banks' Independence in Historical Perspective*, Berlin: Walter de Gruyter, 105–159

Kenen, P. B. (1992). *EMU After Maastricht*, New York: Group of Thirty

Kennedy, E. (1991). *The Bundesbank: Germany's Central Bank in the International Monetary System*, London: Royal Institute of International Affairs

Krugman, P. (1991). "Target Zones and Exchange Rate Dynamics," *Quarterly Journal of Economics* 56, 669–682

Maisel, S. (1980). *Managing the Dollar: An Insider's View of the Federal Reserve Board*, New York; W. W. Norton

McKinnon, Ronald I. (1988). "An International Gold Standard without Gold," Stanford University, unpublished manuscript

  (1993). "One Money for How Many? The Fiscal Constraints," Stanford University, unpublished manuscript

Mundell, R. (1961). "A Theory of Optimum Currency Areas," *American Economic Review* 51, 657–665

Obstfeld, M. (1986). "Rational and Self-Fulfilling Balance-of-Payments Crises," *American Economic Review* 46, 72–81

  (1991). "Destabilizing Effects of Exchange Rate Escape Clauses," NBER, *Working Paper* 3606 (January)

Panic, M. (1992). *European Monetary Union: Lessons from the Classical Gold Standard*, London: Macmillan

Plessis, A. (1982). *La Banque de France et ses deux cents actionaires sous le Second Empire*, Geneva: Droz

Romer, C. (1989). "The Prewar Business Cycle Reconsidered: New Estimates of Gross National Product, 1869–1908," *Journal of Political Economy* 97, 1–37

Sachs, J. (1980). "The Changing Cyclical Behavior of Wages and Prices, 1890–1976," *American Economic Review* 70, 78–90

Sylla, R. (1988). "The Autonomy of Monetary Authorities: The Case of the US Federal Reserve System," in G. Toniolo (ed.), *Central Banks' Independence in Historical Perspective*, Berlin: Walter de Gruyter, 17–38

Thomas, M. (1994). "Wage Behavior in Interwar Britain: A Skeptical Inquiry," in G. Grantham and M. MacKinnon (eds.), *Labour Market Evolution: The Economic History of Market Integration, Wage Flexibility and the Employment Relation*, London: Routledge, 245–269

Von Hagen, J. (1992). "Fiscal Arrangements in a Monetary Union: Evidence from the US," in D. E. Fair and C. de Boissieu (eds.), *Fiscal Policy, Taxation and the Financial System in an Increasingly Integrated Europe*, Dordrecht: Kluwer Academic

Index